THE PORK STORY

LEGEND AND LEGACY

Co-Authored by

Rolland "Pig" Paul   **J. Marvin Garner**   **Orville K. Sweet**

PROLOGUE

*We stand on the shoulders of the past
and view the dawn of a new era.
Lying in clear view is the most important decade
in the history of man. We see a period of amazing new
technology, economic opportunity, innovation,
and world political reform.
The wave of change provides unlimited opportunity
to those who seize upon the time.*

Orville K. Sweet

First Edition
Copyright © 1991 by National Pork Producers Council

ISBN 0-932845-49-5

Printed in the United States of America
by The Lowell Press, Inc. of Kansas City, Missouri

TABLE OF CONTENTS

Union Stockyards, Chicago, Illinois
Through these arches passed more than 1 billion hogs in the 100 year life span of the Union Stockyards.

FOREWORD

The Pork Story

"Hogs are beautiful." The modern pig is the result of the collective efforts of generations of people. From the primitive Sus Scrofa to the European wild boar that led to modern hogs of the 21st Century they were all beautiful to those who nurtured them and whose livelihood depended on them.

Dale Miller reports in the July 1976 National Hog Farmer: "The noble pig, much maligned in prose and verse, may well be the foundation on which this nation was built. Authors have disdained him in favor of lovable lambs, cute calves and bouncy colts, and many have called him filthy, gluttonous, ill-tempered and obstinate. An exception is the book 'Pigs From Cave to Corn Belt', in which Charles Wayland Towne and Edward Norris Wentworth praised the gallant pig."

Long maligned as the lowest of beasts we approach the 21st Century and find pork the symbol of fine dining as well as a staple item in fast food restaurants and home meals.

The hog is unequaled in its contribution to man's health and standard of living. The pharmaceutical products derived from the hog combined with the low fat, nutritionally balanced food products earns for it the champion role as man's benefactor. A little known fact in America is that worldwide pork excels all other sources of meat in per capita consumption.

It raises an interesting question. Why has a product so tasty and nutritious from an animal that for centuries has had the worst of all images continued to thrive as an enterprise and now emerges as a symbol of prestige and the center of fine dining?

E. A. Sothern, the great 19th Century actor, was observing a small boy who wanted to go outdoors and join his older playmates but feared they would not accept him. When the children started to run to the house, Sothern said playfully, "Let's hide behind the curtain and they won't know where we are!" The boy looked at him dejectedly and said, "Suppose they don't care?"

The same could be said for the pork industry in times past. "Suppose they don't care?" No one took it seriously. Ignored by producers of competing species the repugnant pig was taken for granted by most of society and loathed by the rest.

To tell the history of species, the development of breeds, and human organizations is to tell the story of man.

Joyce Kilmer said, "Only God can make a tree." However, it is up to man's collective efforts and his ability to manipulate nature for a breed to be born that ultimately yields a designed product.

A minister was visiting a farmer and admiring the state of development of his beautiful farm. He observed the lush pastures, attractive fields and bountiful crops. He said, "Isn't it wonderful what you and the Lord have accomplished in your partnership together here." The farmer said, "It sure is, but you should have seen it when the Lord had it by himself."

The centuries of development of pork are credited mainly to farmers but it must be shared with many others.

Because of the love and understanding of the pig and the people who nurture them the authors take on the challenge of characterizing and telling their story.

"The most powerful force in the world is the leverage resulting from organization."

That power becomes even more potent if it is participatory democracy. The Pork Story is one of success through progressive leadership and a belief in producer directed controlled organization.

NPPC President Mike Wehler extols the merits of pork to President George Bush and Iowa Governor Terry Branstad, on the occasion of President Bush's visit with the NPPC in Des Moines, 1990.

"True glory consists in doing what deserves to be written; in writing what deserves to be read; and in so living as to make the world happier and better for our living in it."

Pliny (23-79 AD)

PREFACE

In the long list of those in agriculture deserving to be recognized pork producers are at the top for none have contributed more generously to the cause of the human race.

These unsung heroes have excelled over all others in the advancement of animal husbandry and sustenance of human life.

While the world was charmed by the color and allure of the cowboy the hog man was taken for granted. In livestock history no one can compare with the sustained influence of the one who tended the hog herds of America.

Hog herds were driven 700 miles to market more than 20 years before the celebrated cattle drives. It was hogs that sniffed out the trails in the 1840's that became the railroad tracks of the 1860's.

History records that in the mid-1850's, the movement of hogs was no small undertaking. A Kentuckian living on a drover's highway counted 69,187 hogs passing his door in a year's time. He valued the total at $1,037,802. Forty to 70 thousand head were reportedly driven from Ohio to the eastern markets in a year and over 150,000 were said to have made the trek over the national road.

There is no intent to tarnish the image of the cowboy. The cattle industry has a colorful dramatic past and everyone knows it. The pork industry has an equally colorful past and only a few know it. The hope is shared by the authors that this book will inform many more of the epic of the pig.

There is a surprising development in the process as we approach the 21st Century. After 5000 years of evolutionary change pork is beginning to receive deserved recognition. The perception and image of pork in the eyes of the consumer and health professionals have improved markedly in the past decade.

As I was preparing to join the National Pork Producers Council in the spring of 1979 a personal friend and health professional inquired why I would even consider becoming a part of an industry that produced so much fat and was infested with trichinae. Ten years later she said, "We are recommending pork to our heart patients. It is leaner now, you know?"

It is a privilege to be a part of a team effort to record the story of pork. It deserves to be written and read. The world is a better place for pork producers having lived in it.

NPPC President Ray Hankes and Pork Board President Virgil Rosendale sign the Pork in 1986 to unite the industry.

ACKNOWLEDGMENTS

A cast of talented people made this work possible.

Special thanks to: Co-authors, Rolland (Pig) Paul and J. Marvin Garner and Russ Sanders who provided us with a vision of the future and to contributing writers, David Meeker, W.E. Rempel, Kathryn Louden and Marj Ocheltree who provided excellent materials in their special fields.

Larry Heidebrecht and Doyle Talkington for their determined effort and attention to detail in the passage of the Pork Act and the success of the referendum that boosted the Pork Council's revenue from $10 million to $30 million per year.

Mike Simpson, for his masterful job in guiding the transition of the checkoff from voluntary to legislative and his diplomacy in the development of the new Pork Board. Chris Werhman, for exemplary performance over a decade and instant recall, order and organization.

Charlie Harness for his guidance and bridging the communication gap with 200,000 producers, allied industry and consumers.

Nancy Olsen, Linda Riehm, and Jackie Collingwood, my inner circle for 10 years, who struggled to make me look good.

Dick Knowlton and his staff at George A. Hormel and Company for their cooperation in researching the National Barrow Show history and funding assistance.

National Hog Farmer's Bill Fleming and Dale Miller for use of their archives.

Bob Eberle for editing and design and Payson Lowell for counsel and publication.

Breed association secretaries for their assistance in researching the breed histories and we are in debt to all pork leaders and producers who shared the dream and pulled themselves up by their bootstraps to make it a reality.

The staffs of the American Meat Insitute, Animal Health Institute, and The American Feed Industry Association for valuable assistance in researching their respective histories.

Barry Kenney for his graphic arts expertise. And Ernie Barnes for his marketing assistance.

And finally, a special thanks to Lew Sweet for taking on a monstrous challenge of learning computer science for this purpose and devoting more than 500 hours of typing and editing assistance.

Peggy Fleming, pork spokesperson, gets pork preparation tips from the chef at the 21 Club in New York City, as part of the 1987 kick-off for the Pork The Other White Meat campaign.

Polish leader Lech Walesa and NPPC President Don Gingerich discuss international pork markets on the occasion of Walesa's visit to the United States in 1990.

Section I

By Orville K. Sweet
NPPC Executive Vice President 1979-1989.

Part 1

PIGS IN SEARCH OF ROOTS

"Among the ancients the hog was held in high esteem" – Pliny.

Youatt in his valuable work on the pig wrote in the 1700's:

"As far back as history enables us to go the hog appears to have been known and his flesh made use of as food."

Man's alliance with the pig 9000 years ago has been one of worldwide success. Today the pig and man are the two most populous of large mammals inhabiting the earth.

James A. Reasor in 1870 wrote in his "Treatise on the Hog," "The Romans gave much attention to swine and drenched them to repletion with honeyed wine in order to produce a diseased and monstrous sized liver. The 'Porcus Trojanus,' so called in allusion to the Trojan horse was a celebrated dish, and one that became so extravagantly expensive that a sumptuary law was passed respecting it." (Pliny)

Thus, it will be seen that among the ancients the hog was held in high esteem.

In the Isle of Crete the hog was regarded as sacred. It was sacrificed in Ceres at the beginning of harvest and to Bacchus at the commencement of the vintage by the Greeks.

"From the earliest times in our island (England) the hog has been regarded as a very important animal and vast herds were tended by swine herdsmen who watched over their safety in the woods and collected them at night under shelter. Its flesh was the staple item of consumption in every household and much of the wealth of the rich free portions of the community consisted on those animals." (Youatt)

"In an earlier time that the Gauls produced the finest swine's flesh that was brought into Italy; and, according to Strabo, in the reign of Augustus they supplied Rome and nearly all of Italy with gammons, hog puddings, hams, and sausages. This nation and the Spaniards appear to have kept immense droves of swine, but scarcely any other kind of livestock." (Varro)

In all nations, with few exceptions, the hog has received attention, either for food or for profit.

MILLIONS OF YEARS B.P.		
	PLEISTOCENE	
10	**PLIOCENE**	• Sus scrofa
20	**MIOCENE**	• Hiptherium
30	**OLIGOCENE**	• Paleochoerus-Tusked Hog
40	**EOCENE**	• Entelodonts: Europe, Asia, Western U.S.
50		
60	**PALEOCENE**	

ANCESTORS TO SUS SCROFA RACES

THE ROOTS OF THE TRUE PIG
(Sus Scrofa)

As we search for the pig's ancestral roots and speculate in terms of millions of years it is impractical to establish time in terms of specifics. I am reminded of the tourist visiting an archaeological site in New Mexico. While gazing at a dinosaur's bones he met an old Indian that was acting as an unofficial guide. "How old are these bones?" asked a tourist. "Exactly one hundred million and three years old," was the Indian's serious reply. "How can you be so definite?" inquired the tourist. "Oh, the geologist told me they were 100 million years old," replied the guide, "and that was exactly three years ago."

Swine have evolved gradually over a period of 10 million years with a few minor variations. The term Entelodent is appropriately applied to swine because of their ability to adapt to their ecological niche and prosper.

The Entelodent is the traceable ancestor to the true swine types, many of which are in existence today. The Entelodent, or giant pig fortunately is extinct, however, along with its counterparts of the Eocene and Oligocene epochs of some forty million years ago. (Wells, 1920)

There existed a wide variety of mammalian fauna to fill the void at the close of the reptilian empire. Mammals proceeded to fill these ecological niches at a break-neck pace (in geological time), thus yielding a range from insignificant little shrews to sea mammals to gargantuan, terrestrial behemoths. Many of the Cocene and Oligocene mammals were evolutionary dead-ends, but several were predecessors of today's mammalian representatives.

This it was with the Entelodent, mother nature's prototype pig, standing better than six feet high at the shoulder, with an elongated wedge-shaped head, lacking a modern pig's snout, and a body shape closely resembling that of the European boar. The Entelodent might have been omnivorous, as are today's pigs, and an even-toed quadruped with a simple digestive system (non-ruminant). Entelodents ranged from Europe to Asia and parts of the Western U. S.

The Entelodent was somewhat short-lived, but appearing on the scene was Palaeochoerus, or the tusked hog, which thrived until early in the Miocene epoch 19 million years ago. By that time Palaeochoerus had evolved to such a state as to be reclassified as Hyotherium. The evolutionary modification of Hyotherium continued until it became the precursor of *Sus Scrofa*, today a wild boar (Hedgepeth, 1978). (See Fig. 1)

The pig is a member of the order Artiodactyla, the even-toed ungulate mammals, and belongs to the family Suidae, or non-ruminant, even-toed, hoofed mammals. It is interesting to note that the pig was included in the order of Pachydermata in the mid-19th Century with the elephant, rhinoceros, and hippopotamus, since they were considered thick-skinned, short-necked, and "obtuse in most of their faculties." (Youatt, 1956) The typical genus of swine is *Sus*, which includes domestic pigs, the European wild boar, and its allies. The species of true pigs is *Scrofa*.

Most, if not all, of our modern breeds descended from the European wild boar. As we search for the ancestral roots of the pig we discover they are obscured by superstition and mythology. Towne and Wentworth in an intensive study entitled, "Pigs From Cave to Cornbelt," wrote: "Thus the pig has been essential to man's mythology, his religion, and his miracle-making. In reverence man has sacrificed it, drunk its blood, and eaten its flesh. In disgust he has cursed it and raised taboos against it. Its body has been the habitation of the benign corn spirit and the souls of his ancestors. And it has housed devils which have made its very name a hissing and a by-

The European Wild Boar as shown by Youatt (1847). From: A History of the British Pig; *Wiseman.*

word. Man has condemned its milk as a cause of leprosy and explored its liver for omens of good or evil. In the whole gamut of human superstitions there is hardly a spot where the pig has failed to intrude on his calloused snout and strike a resounding note, either sweet or sour. Through the maze of hoary legends, he has thrust his bristled mane and etched his cloven imprint on the telltale sands of time. And all without honor, save the dubious one of being the Dr. Jekyll-and-Mr. Hyde of all four footed beasts."

To determine the remote origins of swine in an objective manner and to discover with any degree of accuracy the evolution that has taken place one must turn to the geologist and the paleontologist, scientist skilled in reading rocks evaluating fossilized bones and fragments.

Their skills enable them to reconstruct entire skeletons from a few bone fragments and fossil formations in the rocks.

Geological sources report that from the beginning the hog has undergone evolutionary structural change and they report that it is the most primitive form of domestic mammal in existence today.

The greatest change that has taken place is in the digestive systems resulting from a change in the kind of feed available. The hogs innate trait of adapting to its environment had made it one of man's most important benefactors of all domesticated animals.

James A. Reasor of Jefferson County, Kentucky wrote "A Treatise on the Hog", published in 1870. This monograph is written in such colorful style that I quote it precisely rather than paraphrase and risk losing its unique flavorful meaning.

"It may not be out of place here to allude to some of the traits and peculiarities of the hog. The author acknowledges himself indebted to Youatt, Martin, and others for much of interest on these points. 'Too low an estimate is placed upon the sagacity of the hog,' says Youatt. 'It is supposed to be a sluggish, stupid, filthy animal; on the contrary, he has repeatedly shown himself to be exceedingly sagacious, and often quite intelligent. Many anecdotes illustrative of this could be related. But it is true that his chief business is to eat, sleep, drink, and grow fat. All his wants in this respect, in his domesticated state, are cared for (or ought to be), and his world is limited to the precincts of his sty or the farm-yard; yet, in this state of luxurious ease, individuals have shown extraordinary intelligence.'

"As to his filthiness, it will be interesting to those who have given but little attention to the habits of the hog, to quote the words of one or two of the best writers and observers on this point. Youatt says: 'It may appear absurd to claim cleanliness as a swinish virtue; but, in point of actual fact, the pig is a much more cleanly animal than most of his calumniators give him credit for being. He is fond of a good, clean bed, and often, when this is not provided for him, it is curious to see the degree of sagacity with which he will forage for himself.' 'A hog is the cleanest of all creatures, and will never dung or stale in his sty if he can get forth,' says a quaint old writer of the sixteenth century; and we are very much of his opinion. But it is so much the habit to believe that this animal may be kept in any state of filth and neglect, that 'pig' and 'pig-sty' are terms usually regarded as synonymous with all that is dirty and disgusting. His rolling in the mud is alleged against him as proof of his filthy habits; if so, the same accusation applies to the elephant, the rhinoceros, and all other of the Pachydermata. May it not rather be for the cooling of themselves and keeping off flies, as we admit it to be in the case of the animals above mentioned? Savages cover themselves with grease in hot climates in

Indigenous hogs of Europe.

order to protect their skins; may not instinct teach animals to roll themselves in mud for a similar purpose? Pigs are exceedingly fond of comfort and warmth, and will nestle closely together in order to obtain the latter, and often struggle vehemently to secure the warmest berth.

"Every one knows with what sagacity pigs provide for an approaching cold "snap." When storms are overhanging, they collect straw in their mouths, and run about with great activity, as if warning their companions to prepare for the approaching storm. Hence has arisen the common Wilshire saying, "Pigs see the wind." Virgil, in enumerating the signs of settled weather, notices this peculiarity in swine—

"Now sows unclean are mindful to provide
Their nestling beds of mouth-collected straw."

"In their domesticated state," says Youatt, "swine certainly are very greedy animals. Eating is the business of their lives; nor do they appear to be delicate as to the kind or quality of the food which is set before them. Although naturally herbivorous animals, they have been known to devour carrion with all the avidity of beasts of prey, to eat and mangle infants, and even gorge their appetites with their own young."

All this is accounted for by another writer, whose views commend themselves to the common sense and justice of all.

Low, an able writer, says: "Instances have occurred in which a sow has been known to devour her young; but rarely, if ever, does this happen in a state of nature. It is not unreasonable to believe that when an act so revolting does occur, it arises more from the pain and irritation produced by the state of confinement and often filth in which she is kept, and the disturbances to which she is subject, than from any actual ferocity" for it is well known that a sow is always unusually irritable at this period, snapping at all animals that approach her. If she is gently treated, properly supplied with sustenance, and sequestered from all annoyance, there is little danger of this ever happening. Roots and fruits are the natural food of the hog, in a wild as well as in a domesticated state, and it is evident that, however omnivorous this animal may occasionally appear, its palate is by no means insensible to the difference of eatables; for whenever it finds variety it will be found to select the best with as much cleverness as other quadrupeds."

"In the peach-tree orchards of North America," says Peunaut, "where hogs have plenty of delicious food, they have been observed to neglect the fruit that has lain a few hours upon the ground, and patiently wait for a considerable time for a fresh windfall."

According to Linnaeus, "the hog is more nice in the selection of his vegetable diet than any of our other domesticate herbivorous animals." This great naturalist states that the hog is more choice in his selection, than either the cow, goat, sheep, or horse. This is shown in the following table:

The cow eats 276 plants and rejects 218.
The goat eats 449 plants and rejects 126.
The sheep eats 387 plants and rejects 141.
The horse eats 262 plants and rejects 212.
The hog eats 72 plants and rejects 171.

"Thus it will be seen that the hog is a much more choice animal than many persons would have been willing to admit.

"These animals have also a very keen sense of smell, and are thus enabled to discover roots, acorns, earth-nuts, etc., buried in the ground; and in Italy are employed in hunting for truffles that grow some inches below the surface of the soil."

"The last charge which we shall attempt to refute," says Youatt, "is that of intractability." All the offenses which swine commit are attributed to an innately bad disposition; whereas they too often arise solely from bad management or total neglect. Would horses or cattle behave one iota better were they treated as pigs too often are? They are legitimate objects for the sport of idle boys, hunted with dogs, pelted with stones, often neglected and obliged to find a meal for themselves, or wander about half starved. Can we wonder that under such circumstances they should be wild, unmanageable brutes? Look at the swine in a well-regulated farm-yard; they are as peaceable and as little disposed to wander or trespass as any of the other animals that it contains. Here, as in many other things, man is but too willing to attribute the faults which are essentially of his own causing to any other than their true source.

Martin says: "It has been usual to condemn the domestic hog in no very measured terms as a filthy, stupid brute, at once gluttonous, obstinate, and destitute of intelligence. Against this sweeping censure we beg leave to enter our protest. With regard to the filthiness of the hog in a state of confinement, every thing will depend on the trouble taken by its keeper. He may allow the sty or the yard to be covered with filth of every description, as disgraceful to himself as it is injurious to the animals. In this case the hog is the sufferer, for naturally it delights in clean straw, luxuriating in it with evident pleasure; its twinkling little eyes and low grunt expressing its feelings of contentment. In fact, the hog, so far from being the filthiest, is one of the cleanest of our domestic quadrupeds, and is unwilling to soil the straw-bed of his domicile if anything like liberty be allowed him."

The above quotations will commend themselves as simple statements of facts. It is with the hog, as with other domestic animals, "like master like stock."

Early American hogs ranging for feed.

Orville K. Sweet

Part 2

IMMIGRANT PIGS TO NORTH AMERICA

"PORK WAS INDISPENSABLE TO COLONIZING"

Immigrant pigs from Europe quickly made themselves at home in the western hemisphere in the fifteenth and sixteenth centuries.

Climatic conditions, terrain and available feed stuffs paralleled similar conditions in Europe and Africa. With exceptions of the arid areas it mattered little whether pigs were confined, ranged the woods and open land, or escaped to lead a feral existence. They faced conditions of existence similar to that they already adopted.

Our earliest account of hogs in the new world was an importation of eight head by Columbus on his second voyage in 1493. These few became the progenitors of all the hogs to later populate the Spanish Indies according to Towne and Wentworth "Pigs: From Cave to Cornbelt."

"The sheep, goats, cattle and horses introduced by the explorers soon became an established part of the communities. The porkers, however, soon ran wild through the jungles and cane brakes. Stories began to emminate about the attacks by wild pigs on soldiers hunting rebellious Indians and escaped Negro slaves. Pigs would attack, especially when cornered."

Cortes was the first to bring swine to the mainland about 25 years later. Since his journeys were through the Gulf of Mexico his first release of hogs was in the land area of Honduras and Mexico.

According to Towne and Wentworth, swine reached the mainland with Cortes - not with his first, 1519 expedition, but after the country had been pacified. It was customary for the invaders to carry their meat with them, on the hoof. For example, there was the excursion into Honduras which Cortes made in 1514, a journey which not only involved meat supplies, but touched the fringe of romance through the fair lady who accompanied him.

It was a colorful cavalcade which set out for Mexico City. At its head rode Cortes, mounted on his famous charger Morzillo. By his side rode Dona Marina, whose beauty did not exclude feelings of naive piety. "God has been very gracious to me," said she, "in letting me bear a son to my lord and master Cortes, and in marrying me to such a gentleman as Juan Jaramillo." Behind the happy couple rode a group of courtiers, tricked out in the latest fashions

from the Court of Madrid: and musketeers and crossbowmen, wearing half-armor and steel helmets. Nor does the historian fail to record that, in the rear, swarmed the ever present drove of swine. If the Spanish chronicler's story seems to stress the erotic at the expense of the dietetic, it neverless concedes the fact that even the lovers had to eat, and that their preferred ration was pork.

Swine flesh was also indispensable in every attempt at colonization. The good Viceroy of new Spain, Antonio de Mendoza - the first to hold this office - was definitely interested in promoting pork production in the settlements. Pigs moved northward with the colonizers and reached present-day New Mexico with the relief expedition to Onate in the summer of 1600.

As the exploration of Mexico progressed northward hogs accompanied them and by the late 1600's they had reached as far north as the Rio Grande and migrated into Texas and California.

More than a century ago, Alexander Forbes wrote of the Spanish settlements in California. He reported that pigs are reared and fed chiefly for their lard and are of a very good kind derived from the Chinese breed. They are fed in a manner to produce as much fat and as little flesh as possible. They are allowed to grow to a certain age in a lean state, subsisting chiefly on such roots and herbs as they can procure at large in the woods and fields, and when they arrive at the proper age and size for killing, they are then shut up, or at least kept at home, and as much maize given them as they can eat; this being administered to them in moderate quantities at a time, so as not to surfeit them. By this means they soon get enormously fat, and when slaughtered they are found to be almost all lard to the very bones. This lard they peel off as blubber is peeled off from a whale, the whole being entirely separated from every part of the flesh and entrails, leaving an astonishingly small proportion of flesh. They are often so highly fed as to be unable to move. I have seen some unable to get farther up than on their haunches, just far enough to reach their food and when satiated tumble down again and grunt themselves to sleep. In the sale and purchase of these animals their weight of flesh is never taken into account; the calculation is how many pounds of lard they will produce. Although they (Californians) delight in seeing every dish swimming in their favorite fat, the butter in any dish, or used in any way as a sauce, is abhorred.

FIRST LANDING IN THE U.S.

The first hog to land on the east coast of the U.S. came with Hernando deSoto, May 25, 1539. They dropped anchor at the mouth of Charlotte Harbor on a point near Boco Grande, Florida.

Nine months later DeSoto began his trek north with Indian slaves, infantry and cavalry as burden bearers. Rations and supplies were running low in the middle of April. "The Gentleman of Elva's", a narrative of the expedition of DeSoto records that the Indians were expert in the skill of hunting. In DeSoto's band there were 600 soldiers besides twenty officers and 24 priests.

We learn from this writing that DeSoto brought 13 sows to Florida and they increased to three hundred swine.

"The maize having failed for three or four days, he ordered to be killed daily, for each man a half pound of pork on which small allowance and boiled herbs the people with much difficulty lived."

First American imports were probably of European wild boar origin.

INDIANS RELISH THE TASTE OF PORK

Following the journey of DeSoto into Mississippi there is the story of an interesting festivity that turns into tragedy because of the relishing taste the Indians had developed for roast pork.

Although at first the Indians were friendly, the Spaniards afterwards had much trouble with them. The first misadventure occurred in October at Mauilla, a place east of the Tombigbee River, in Greene County, Alabama. Here the cacique came out of the town to meet the vanguard with many Indians singing and playing on flutes. After tendering his services, the cacique presented DeSoto with three cloaks of marten skins. This gift apparently convinced the leader that his host was friendly, for in spite of a companion's warnings of possible treachery, DeSoto entered the town with seven or eight followers, where he lodged for the night. When the Indians tried to kill him, and soldiers and natives fought for hours, the Christians finally burned the town and gained the upper hand. As the diarist reported it, "They who perished were in all two thousand five hundred, a few more or less. Of the Christians there fell eighteen. ...Of the living, one hundred and fifty Christians had received seven hundred wounds from the arrow. ...Twelve horses died and seventy were hurt. There was also a loss of four hundred swine." From "Gentleman of Elva's."

In mid-December, DeSoto served his first al-fresco banquet to the natives, featuring roast pork. His company had then reached the Indian town of Chicaca (Chickasaw) in Pontotoc County, Mississippi. After having been taken captive, the local chief sent for two other caciques, Nicalasa and Alimamu, imploring them to fetch along gifts for the noble visitor. This they did, presenting DeSoto with 150 rabbits and some clothing of the country, such as shawls and skins. After a few days, the Governor, evidently seeking to cement a friendship of which he was not altogether convinced, served the Indians a ceremonial dinner, at which the roast pork was so eagerly and joyfully wolfed by the savages that the taste eventually led them to thievery.

SWINE DEVELOPMENT IN THE COLONIES

There were a number of attempts to introduce swine to the northern settlements but the offspring were eaten or failed to survive.

The main swine reinforcement came in 1611 when Thomase Dale, the new governor of Virginia brought them. Thereafter, because of the hog's hardiness and independence, Virginia was never without hogs.

Because of the Indians, it became necessary to confine the first pigs to Hog Island; and Governor Dale ordered that no one should "dare to kill or destroy any bull, cow, calfe, male horse, colt, goat, swine, cocke, henne, chicken, dogge, turkie, any tame Cattel or Poultry of condition whatsoever; whether his own or appertaining to another man, without leave." Under this regulation hogs multiplied prodigiously. However, feeding became a problem and it was so necessary for the colonists to turn their hogs loose in the woods to forage for themselves. Despite wolves, bears, and Indians, the hogs flourished, and were soon spreading through the woods, far beyond the settled frontier. By 1627, it was possible to estimate the number of cattle but swine were innumerable.

Within three years the Indians had been driven away from the lower James River, and the plantations began to spread. But wild hogs and cattle, the progeny of stock running loose were soon ravaging the planted fields. It was difficult to confine them, so the colonists devised the zigzag rail fence — and thus prove the time-honored political qualification of having been a "rail splitter" in order to win election to office. While such a fence restrained domestic livestock, it was not perfect protection against the razor back. He could squeeze through the unevenness of almost any rail fence ever built.

Edward Winslow brought swine to the Plymouth Colony on his second voyage after settlers who landed in 1620 found livestock in the area.

Soon the Indians grew to be such hog thieves that they were required by law to mark their animals, so that they could be recognized in the woodland and identified when sold in the carcass. Yet little attempt was made at enforcement. Hogs adapted themselves so well to wild life that about all the care they ever received was shelter at farrowing time in the tobacco or cotton warehouses. The financial interests founding North and South Carolina pushed the growing of rice and indigo, and restricted the raising of swine, to which those regions were especially well adapted. The proprietors limited the colonists to barely enough domestic animals to meet family needs, without surplus meats for export. Later they imposed laws that would prevent emigration from tidewater country in the uplands.

In the north, lack of livestock was not anticipated by the Pilgrims who landed on Plymouth Rock in 1620. After reporting that corn "did prove well" and the barley "indifferent good" the first season, Edward Winslow suggested that with livestock present, "I make no question but men might live as contented here as in any part of the world." On his second voyage, Winslow brought a small shipment of animals, which were allowed to reproduce for four years. The animals were carefully apportioned at the rate of one cow to six persons or shares, and "two goats the same," although they were first "equalized for age and goodness and the lotted for." Swine,

"though more in number," were distributed according to the same principle.

ANIMAL HUSBANDRY AT THE MASSACHUSETTS BAY COLONY

The Massachusetts Bay Colony, a 1623 venture of the Puritans, did better, bringing thirty cows, twelve mares, and a number of pigs and goats. Seven years later, the passage of the people in the Eagle and nine other vessels to New England came to 9,000 pounds (sterling). The swine, goats, sheep, neat (cattle), and horses cost to transport 12,000 pounds, besides the price they cost. Forthwith a pack of wolves killed and ate some of the swine at Saugus, which prompted the colonists to fence off peninsulas, such as "the neck" at Nahant, to put young cattle in, and wethergoats, and swine to secure them from the wolves. But the feed problem became so acute that the settlers began moving farther out in the country, seeking grassland for the cattle and cornland for the hogs. In the latter case, they could raise barely enough grain to meet subsistence needs, yet hogs were used more efficiently by these farmers than by the farmers of Virginia. All through New England, most of the swine in the early settlements ranged the woods, although a few were kept close at hand, in sties and pens, to convert farm and home wastes. Ten years after the establishment of the Massachusetts Bay Colony, swine were well distributed, and William Wood wrote: "Can they be very poor, where for four thousand souls there are fifteen hundred head of cattle, besides four thousand goats, and swine innumerable?"

THE BEGINNING OF IDENTIFICATION

The Massachusetts rules with regard to Indians' pigs were the reverse of those farther south. In Concord, and later in other settlements, a law required all Englishmen to mark the ears of their hogs, while Indians were forbidden to do so. When the latter brought pork to town to peddle it, they were required to display the unblemished ears of the slaughtered pig, to prove they bore no Englishman's register.

Another problem was the ravaging of grain fields by roving herds of swine. Marking of ears meant little in this event, since few trespassers were in a position to make either financial restitution or repayment in kind. The only safeguard was to prevent the hogs from rooting. Therefore, most of the towns passed regulations requiring the owners to ring the noses of their pigs. The town of Hadley voted to choose hog-ringers annually, and they were to ring all swine fourteen inches high, found unringed on commons or fields from March 1 to December 1. In a few towns hogs were required to be yoked as well as ringed.

To supply the rest of New England, hogs spread from Massachusetts southward into Connecticut and Rhode Island, and northward into New Hampshire. The Piscataqua Plantations, on the border of Maine, had sixty-four pigs in 1635, while Trelawney's Plantation, near Portland had fifty-two head.

WALL STREET IS BORN

Hogs reached the Middle Atlantic colonies about the same time as those of New England. To New Amsterdam, with Peter Evertsen Hulft, a director of the Dutch West India Company, came 103 animals, including swine, sheep, cows and bulls, and stallions and mares. Incidentally, the pigs were shipped in pens floored with sand, preventing any casualties. Since New Amsterdam was intended primarily to be a trading post and not an agricultural colony, a stout palisade was set up on the north side of the settlement for protection—this structure affording Wall Street its name. Outside the wall lay the farms, or "bouweries,"—antecedent of the Bowery of today.

PENNSYLVANIA BECOMES THE GREAT HOG COLONY

The great hog colony was Pennsylvania, thanks to the early Swedish settlements on the Delaware, the English in the "Jerseys," Penn's Quakers, and the Germans or "Pennsylvania Dutch." The Swedes reached the capes of "South" River in 1638, but because of bad weather and miscarriage of plans in supplying the expedition in the Caribbean islands, they had to purchase their animals from New Amsterdam. Yet a few pigs apparently came with the expedition, and increased famously, running wild. In the fall they were shot, and the pork salted, smoked, and preserved for winter food. By the early sixteen sixties the colony had several thousand head of swine.

William Penn, who received his grant in 1681, refused to leave the matter to chance, and required that his Quakers provide feed supplies and shelter for their animals. He was determined to make Pennsylvania self-supporting, and exhorted them to buy livestock, but not to sell it. Thus within a decade the colony was able to export pork products, and even live hogs, to Barbados and other Caribbean islands. Penn also started markets in Philadelphia, Newcastle, and Chester, as well as two annual fairs, one specializing in hogs, the other in cattle.

All hogs, as well as other animals, had to be marked before they were six months old, as proof of ownership, and the mark had to registered with the county clerk. The Pennsylvania rangers were more vigilant and efficient than those of Maryland, and were particularly active in picking up stray animals. Fences in Pennsylvania were of stone, and more durable and effective than those in any other colony. Yet they were not always high enough to bar pigs from cultivated fields; so Pennsylvania adopted the Massachusetts plan of requiring owners to ring their hogs, and in extreme cases also to yoke them. The thrifty Quakers made rapid progress in exterminating wolves and bobcats, and within a half-century following settlement, young litters of pigs were as safe as on English farms.

The Germans were outstanding in their use of corn for fattening livestock, and their grain and dairy by-products produced high-quality hogs and firm pork. Both Germans and Quakers preferred fewer and better livestock than did the farmers in other colonies. Pennsylvania farmers emphasized the need of dry farrowing quarters and sties.

As the seventeenth century closed, the typical farmer owned four or five hogs, which not only supplied salt pork for the family, but helped initiate the barreled-pork trade of the next century. The practice of finishing on Indian corn, first attempted commercially in Pennsylvania, had been adopted in all the Middle Atlantic and New England colonies by 1700. Most important of all, during the ninety years of settlement along the Atlantic Coast, where no domestic meat animals had previously existed, there developed adequate livestock supplies on each farm, in addition to a surplus, on which our first commerce, other than fisheries and lumber, was based.

The introduction of the European hog to American Indian corn launched an industry.

Orville K. Sweet

9

Part 3

HOGS ON U.S. FARMS

Hogs have undergone more changes in conformation, composition and appearance than any other class of livestock. The rapid rate of generation turnover has made it possible to make frequent changes in genetic makeup and to respond readily to changes in market demand.

Until the 19th Century hogs were required to be foragers and very little grain was available for fattening purposes.

In early America hogs were a part of most small farming operations. Four out of 5 farms in the U. S. reported hogs as a part of the farming operation until the mid-twentieth century. Only in the last 40 years have hog operations increased in size and the number of operations reduced significantly.

The development of breeds over the past two hundred years had made it possible to mix and match relatively unrelated parents to produce new types.

Combining the attributes of one or more established breeds provides a quick way to meet market demands and exploit the use of hybrid vigor.

Number of hogs on U. S. farms remained relatively constant for nearly 100 years. From 1880 to 1977 numbers varied from a low of 35 million in 1910 to a high of 61 million in 1940. However, the average number marketed from 1980 to 1990 was about 85 million.

Per capita consumption has remained about the same at 55 to 65 pounds per person throughout the last 100 years.

The gross on the farm value has not varied much over the past 10 years.

It is interesting to note that the gross market value of live hogs for the past 10 years hasn't varied much from $10 billion dollars regardless of the number of hogs raised. 1990 saw a dramatic increase in value per head due to the significant increase in demand for pork.

Large increases in market hogs follow increases in breeding hogs by about one year and will continue to build until the cycle is complete.

The introduction of new technology in improved breeding, feeding and management has affected many aspects of the pork chain including the cycles. Hogs are younger by about 2 months when they are marketed than they were 40 years ago.

New technology has resulted in a younger pork animal that is more efficient and improved in composition yielding less fat.

Confinement operations have resulted in larger operations with higher initial investment but in many instances lower input costs have resulted from the economics of scale. The modern hog operation now readies hogs for market 2 months younger. The most profound influence confinement operations have had is in reducing the impact of the traditional hog cycles.

The large investment required to establish modern confinement facilities does not allow the flexibility to adjust numbers based on market prices. Once a producer is committed to the large investment he cannot afford to let a unit stand idle while the market adjusts.

Modern hog production requires strategic long range planning and production and marketing skills not required by the small operator.

Swine are the most exacting of all our domestic livestock. Commercial producers buy some or all of their feeds that are used. Swine rations cost more per pound than beef rations. Fortunately the feed conversion ratio is much better on hogs. There have been reports of gain on hogs of one pound of body weight to each 2 pounds of feed consumed, however, this is rare. The average ratio of feed to gain is about 3-4 pounds while beef cattle is about 7-10 pounds in the feedlot.

HOG DISEASES

Disease has been a serious problem for pork producers. Confinement operation has been a factor in reducing exposure to diseases, however, once an infection is located in a confinement operation it is difficult to control.

Hog cholera once the scourge of the swine industry has been brought under control. A national program co-sponsored by the USDA and pork producers was successful in eradication of this plague.

A number of other diseases have successfully been controlled. Currently pseudo rabies is the major disease that has defied control. A major national effort is underway as a result of NPPC's strong appeal to the federal agencies to provide adequate funding to fight the disease. A 10 year program is underway with a stated objective to eradicate the disease by the mid-1990's.

The introduction of antibiotics has not only reduced the incidence of loses from disease but has improved performance and enhanced feed efficiency.

Advanced technology in nutrition and formula feeds has likewise made a major contribution to improved pork production. Research in engineering and design of buildings, confinement units and waste disposal has resulted in better sanitation, ventilation and animal comfort.

New and useful technologies advanced by allied industry in cooperation with land grant colleges and private research has revolutionized the pork industry on U. S. farms.

These advances have not only contributed to making pork production a more profitable enterprise but have improved the life style and living standard of the pig. A conscientious study by those concerned about animal welfare will convince even the most skeptical that hogs are more comfortable today than in earlier years when there was no escape from the raw elements.

The following article by Dr. David Meeker, Vice President of Research and Education for the National Pork Producers Council, describes the structure of the pork industry in the U.S. in 1990.

"The structure of the pork industry can be best described by a pyramid with elite breeding stock firms at the top supplying grandparent genetics to multipliers. Multipliers expand the numbers of breeding stock available and sell parent stock to commercial producers. These farmers and corporations use the parent breeding stock to produce hogs for slaughter. The packing industry slaughters hogs and cuts the carcasses into wholesale primal cuts which are sold as fresh meat or go to processors for final preparation and packaging. The retail, or consumer end, consists mainly of grocery chains, food service, institutional food services and export. As various enterprises engage in more than one segment and various attempts are made at vertical integration, some of the lines between structural segments become blurred. In addition, within the segments, there is sometimes very specialized enterprises with a narrow focus such as farmers who only breed sows and produce feeder pigs which are sold to finishers who only feed hogs."

BREEDING STOCK

"The breeding stock segments are divided between the corporate side producing hybrids or synthetic breeds, and the purebred industry consisting of eight major pure breeds. The size of the breeding stock industry—elite and multipliers combined—is $400 to $500 million. The U.S. pork industry possesses a sow herd of 6 to 8 million head serviced by

300,000 to 500,000 boars to produce about 80-90 million hogs per year."

"Most of the firms engaged in elite genetic activities (making genetic change) are also engaged in multiplication—either on farms they own, or contracting with other producers."

"The corporate breeding stock entities are dominated by three major companies—PIC, Farmers Hybrid and DeKalb. There are another 10-15 small firms with annual sales of $1-to-$5 million each. All if these firms started at some point with purebred foundation stock."

"Pig Improvement Company (PIC) was started in England about 25 years ago by farmers and geneticists. PIC entered the U.S. market about 12 years ago and now has a significant share of the U.S. breeding stock market. U.S. corporate headquarters are in Franklin, KY with research and elite herds at Franklin and at Spring Green, WI and an office for Pigtales (record keeping) in Ames, IA. There are PIC operations in many countries, most owned (some licensed) by the Dalgetty Corporation of London. PIC bought the fourth largest seedstock company, Kleen Leen, once owned by Purina Mills in 1985."

"Farmers Hybrid (FH) Company was started in Iowa about 30 years ago by geneticists and farmers. FH was purchased by Monsanto about 15 years ago, then sold to Olin Andrews, a Monsanto employee, about 8 years ago and is based in Des Moines, IA."

"DeKalb Swine Genetics, formerly Lubbock Swine Breeders, was begun in Lubbock, TX about 30 years ago by Roy Poague and his father-in-law, Euel Liner, purebred breeders. The firm was purchased by DeKalb-Pfizer Genetics about 15 years ago, moved to DeKalb, IL. Research is important to DeKalb with an interesting effort using imported semen from Chinese pigs."

"The smaller 10-15 breeding companies are, for the most part, large independent purebred breeders who have incorporated their family business to mimic the successful marketing and service activities of the three large corporations already described."

"This leaves about 70% market share divided among 4,000 to 5,000 small independent purebred breeders and multipliers ranging in size from just less than a $1 million annual breeding stock sales down to practically no sales at all."

PORK PRODUCTION

"There are between 130,000 and 200,000 farmers in the U.S. that raise pigs. Sizes of units range from one sow to 50,000 sows producing from a few pigs to one million head annually. Total production in 1989 was 89,000,000 head."

"Most farms are farrow-to-finish which breed sows and raise pigs all the way to slaughter weight (245 lbs.). Eight percent of farms (usually small farms) specialize in feeder pig production selling to large specialized finishing farms (13% of production). Ten percent of finishing hogs are fed by individuals under contract with firms that own the hogs."

"The top 20,000 farms raise over 70% of the total U.S. production. The largest four producing firms are Murphy Farms, Tyson Foods, Cargill and National Farms."

"Murphy Farms, based in North Carolina, was a small regional feed company 20 years go, engaged in small scale hog finishing to utilize some of their feed products. They grew mainly through contracting to a production level of one million pigs per year in 1990. Substantial growth was achieved in 1986 when Murphy Farms purchased Plainview Pork, an Iowa contract finisher owned by east coast investors."

"Tyson Foods, based in Arkansas, has been in the chicken (broiler) business for more than 25 years, starting with a small family operation. Thus aggressively integrated their poultry operations from feed milling to processing and distribution of retail products. Tyson's started raising pigs about 10 years ago, expanding rapidly to an annual total production rate of one million market pigs in 1990."

"Tyson's has reached a cooperative agreement with a packer—Smithfield in N.C.—to vertically integrate their production operations with packing and processing operations. To date, only a fraction of their production is marketed through the integrated portion of their business and they sell most of their production through normal marketing channels."

"Cargill has been involved in the grain trade and feed manufacturing for many years (at least 50). They have been feeding pigs and contracting with other producers to feed pigs for the past 10-12 years, growing to their present size of 500,000 pigs produced per year. Cargill's main interest in hog production has been as a way to profit more from their feed manufacturing business. Cargill has similar feeding activities with poultry. Cargill has activity in many states, but control of the hog feeding projects are in N.C."

"Hastings Pork started in the hog business in Nebraska about 15 years ago by converting abandoned ammunitions storage bunkers, built by the U.S. government, into farrow-to-finish units. The adapting of these unique facilities has been surprisingly successful."

"National Farms first began operating in Nebraska, then expanded to Colorado. A major packing plant is now being planned in the Colorado area since the production will be available."

"Other large U.S. producers are Carroll, Dreyfus, Goldkist, Hasting Pork and Prestage. Many of these finish only and buy feeder pigs from small feeder pig producers. Very large firms collectively produce about 10% of all U.S. hogs."

"Family-owned pork production farms of a professional nature, numbering abut 20,000 produce about 60% of the nations production. These are large in size ranging from 1,000 to 10,000 hogs produced per year."

A modern pork operation.

Sanitation is the highest priority.

HOG MARKETING

"Most all hogs are sold to a packer when they reach slaughter weights which average 245 pounds. Seventy per cent of these are sold by live weight and 30% are sold on a carcass value basis. The pork industry leadership is pushing for a system in which all hogs will be purchased on a carcass value basis to give producers more incentive for genetic improvement."

"About 90% of U.S. hogs are delivered directly to packing plants or to their collection points. About 10% are sold through dealers, stock yards and auction markets which in turn sell to packers."

HOG SLAUGHTER

"The majority of hog slaughter is done by about 20 companies with the following market shares:

IBP	19%	Excel	6%
ConAgri	11%	Wilson	6%
Hormel	7%	Smithfield	5%
Morrell	6%	Other	40%

"About 9 years ago, Iowa Beef Packers (IBP) diversified into pork processing by buying and remodeling plants from other companies. They now have about 5 plants in the Midwest. In July, 1990, they opened their only newly built plant in Waterloo, Iowa which is the largest hog kill plant in the world. This is a state-of-the-art plant which can kill 16,000 hogs per day."

"IBP sells fresh, boxed pork cuts wholesale, domestically and export. However, much of their meat is sold to other companies for further processing. Con-Agri and Excel are also new entries to the pork slaughtering business, gaining market share through acquisition during the past five years."

"Hormel, Morrell and Wilson are traditional old meat packing companies which also cut and process and have brand name retail products. They are known for quality products."

"Hog slaughtering is a low-margin business that is currently very competitive. There is more kill capacity in the U.S. than is needed for current production levels. All hog slaughtering plants are located in areas of fairly dense hog feeding. States with sparse hog populations have a problem with marketing alternatives, i.e., their plants have closed so they must ship hogs long distances. For example, Texas had one major hog kill plant that closed in 1989, forcing producers to ship hogs 800 miles to Mississippi."

CUTTING AND PROCESSING

"The Hormel, Wilson and Morrell companies cut and process the hogs they slaughter and have their own name brands."

"Oscar Mayer (OM), begun in 1883, was similar to Hormel, but started phasing out of the slaughtering business 10 years ago and no longer kills hogs. However, Oscar Mayer is the largest user of pork for processed meats (bacon, sausage, lunch meats, hot dogs, etc.) in the U.S. O.M. also does more meat processing and new product research than any other company with Hormel being second in that regard. O.M. has 12% of the bacon market and 30% of the lunch meat market. O.M. also raises 6% and processes 10% of all the turkeys in the U.S. under the Louis Rich name. In the last 10 years, O.M. was purchased by General Foods and General Foods was purchased by Philip Morris."

"The Sara Lee Company has about the same market share in processed meats as O.M. after purchasing the Bryan Foods, Hygrade and Kahns slaughtering and processing plants. The various brand names were retained so Sara Lee does not have its own recognizable pork brands."

RETAIL

"Fresh pork consisting of chops, roast, ribs, ground pork and some ham is 40% of the pork market. Processed pork — bacon, sausage, cured ham, wieners, and lunch meats is 60%. Pork is sold in four main ways: grocery chains (44%); food service (24%); institutional (24%); and export (8%)."

"The largest grocery chains are Kroger and Safeway with 1,200 stores each."

"The largest food service user of pork is McDonald's, with 8,600 stores and many breakfast items. Second is Pizza Hut with 6,000 stores."

"Institutional food service consists of cafeterias and hospitals. The U.S. government is a large purchaser of pork for school lunch programs and military food service. Morrell and IBP are the largest exporters of fresh pork to Japan, the largest customer. They buy mainly loins which is the highest priced cut."

"There are hundreds of small operations across the U.S. that slaughter, cut and process from 10-to-200 pigs per week and retail the resulting products on a local basis from meat shops. Some of these have developed strong customer loyalty and brand-name recognition on a local basis."

"There are a few small operations that are vertically integrated from hog production to retail meat sales. There are operations in Arizona, Mississippi, California and Iowa that raise their own pigs and have their own small slaughtering and processing plants, killing several thousand pigs per year."

"Of particular interest is an operation in California owned by Roy Sharp which has 2,500 sows farrow-to-finish and a brand name retail pork operation. He retails only a portion of his hog production. He doesn't have a slaughter plant, but has an arrangement with a medium-sized packer to custom kill his pigs. He takes a load of his pigs to the plant, sells them to the packer, then buys back the cuts he wants for his own cutting and processing operation. This relieves him of the problem of dealing with by-products and less desirable meat cuts."

"The pork industry is trending away from commodity meat and toward brand name retail products. Meat cutters and butchers in grocery stores will give way to case-ready retail product cut and packaged before it gets to the store. There will be considerable opportunity for new approaches which integrate operations and thus control quality from genetics to retail. Many areas of the country don't have available enough quality pork products at retail to meet consumer demand."

The modern supermarket gives pork a wholesome presentation.

Part 4

BIRTH AND GROWTH OF BREEDS IN AMERICA

The hog more than any other mammal has readily adapted to changing environment and economic pressure.

When lean product was in vogue hogs were selected and managed to produce a maximum of lean and a minimum of fat. When fat was in great demand for cooking or during warfare for explosives or for soap in the colonial days hogs readily adapted through selection and management to accommodate the economic trends.

The advances in swine husbandry in the United States has been remarkable since 1840. A great part of the progress in the enhanced value of swine has taken place since 1875 when breeds begin to be recognized.

The original wild hog was rather small and of a slate or gray color. Environment changed his size and color according to climate and available feed.

In tropical climate and lush grazing the hog waxed fatter than in the areas farther north where he was forced to roam widely and venture in more dangerous areas. The tropical hog's color changed toward black to give him more protection from the heat of sun rays.

In the early domesticated environment when there was little or no selection pressure being placed on type structure rapid changes took place. The rather short generation turnover was an asset when change in phenotype was needed.

In response to domestication Professor Thomas Shaw had this to say in his book, "A study of Breeds." "(1) The ears become less movable, the tusks and muscles of the neck diminish in size, the back and sides lengthen, the flank and hindquarters deepen, the body becomes less capacious, the limbs grow shorter, the bristles are partially or wholly removed, and the animal becomes much less active. (2) The stomach and intestines enlarge, they desire more food, and the tendency to obesity increases. (3) The male loses the solitary habit, the female breeds more frequently, has larger litters, and they seek their food in the day."

Most of the breeds now known in America may be traced back to or through those of Great Britain, and the latter were chiefly improved by crossing Chinese or Neapolitan boars upon the native sows. The Chinese were used mostly in the modification of the white stock and the Neapolitans in improving the black sorts. Theses boars were smaller than the native British stock, and had the effect of refining the structure and flesh of their offspring, while enhancing the fattening qualities.

The breed registries recorded 85,236 litters in 1990.

THE AMERICAN LANDRACE

The American Landrace descended from the Danish Landrace that had its origin in 1895. At that time the Large White Hog was brought from England and crossed with the native swine. After that infusion the Landrace was developed and improved by selection and testing. It was mainly through the use of Landrace that Denmark became the chief bacon exporting country.

Denmark today produces approximately 5% of the world's pork and provides about 35% of the world's exported pork. To protect their position, Denmark for many years refused to export purebred Landrace breeding stock.

In the early 1930's the United States Department of Agriculture entered into an agreement with the Ministry of Foreign Affairs in Denmark for the purchase of 24 Danish Landrace. The stock was to be used for swine research studies at agricultural experiment stations, with the stipulation that this breed would not be propagated as a pure breed for commercial use.

During the 15 years following the original importation, Landrace were used in numerous comparisons with American breeds. As a result of this work, four new breeds have been registered by the Inbred Livestock Registry Association.

In May of 1949, the USDA petitioned the Ministry of Foreign Affairs of Denmark to release its restrictions on the propagation of purebred Landrace in the United States. This request was granted, and the American Landrace Association was formed in 1950 to register and promote the sale of purebred breeding stock.

Following the removal of restrictions on commercial use of Danish Landrace, the importations of Norwegian and Swedish breeding stock provided the outcrosses necessary for the expansion and development of the American Landrace breed of today. More than 700,000 offspring have been recorded from the parent stock.

The Landrace breed is promoted on its ability to cross well with other breeds; length of body; high percentage of carcass weight in the ham and loin; correct amount of finish; and prolific sows that farrow large pigs and which are exceptionally heavy milkers.

The identifiable characteristics of Landrace are its white color, with ears that droop and slant forward with its top edges nearly parallel to the bridge of a straight nose.

There were 4,365 litters registered in 1990.

THE BERKSHIRE

The Berkshire is the only one of the basic American breeds that was an established breed before coming to the U. S. In fact, it traces to the late 1700's in Berkshire, England. The livestock historians, Billingsley and Marshall, both mention the black and white Berkshire hog in 1798 and 1790 respectively. Culley, in 1807, indicated that the breed was red with black spots and the presence of red to a greater degree in fact admitted by most later agricultural writers.

According to Lawrence, writing in 1790, the original Berkshire was:

"Long and crooked in the snout, the muzzle turning upwards, the ears large, heavy and inclined to be pendulous, the body long and thick but not deep, the leg short, the bone large and the size great." This description led some to believe it must have descended from the old English breed.

As one of the oldest breeds of swine, it is widely distributed throughout the world, and returning soldiers report that even such remote spots as the islands of Saipan and Korea have hogs with Berkshire characteristics predominating.

The Berkshire is primarily a black hog. White markings are common on the feet and lower legs, face, and tail. These add much to its attractiveness.

The head and face of the Berk are its most distinguishable features. The nose is upturned, the face slightly dished, and the ears erect but slightly inclined forward. People unfamiliar with breeds of swine, but familiar with dogs, would likely compare the face of a Berkshire with that of a prize bulldog.

The breed is known for its long side, right-angle spread of rib, and trimness throughout. The typical Berkshire has a conservative arch of back. The body is compact and the legs only medium in length. Folks are frequently deceived by its weight. It is heavier than it appears to be. The Berks rank higher in quality than in size. Its show ring and carcass contest record is an enviable one.

Berkshires were first imported to New Jersey by John Brentnall in 1823. The American Berkshire Association was formed in 1875, and was the world's first swine registry.

N. H. Gentry of Sedalia, Missouri is reported to be the most outstanding breeder of Berkshires in America. (Briggs—Modern Breeds of Livestock) He began his breeding operation in 1873. Briggs reports that Gentry's success as a breeder may have been due in part to Snell Brothers of Ontario, Canada who were breeders and importers and consistently brought from England the very best Berkshires they could find in that country.

During a period of about 15 years, Mr. Gentry's annual purchases from the Snells consisted of from 1 to 6 pigs, and in this way he secured some of the very best English breeding that had originated in the Stewart and Swanwick herds.

Since Mr. Gentry had the outstanding herd of Berkshires in the United States and one of the best herds in the world, it would have been most difficult for him to select boars of the type he wanted. Furthermore, he was of the Campbellite religious faith and had noted in the Bible that the Israelites had added new blood to their race from females of other races. He adopted this policy and bred his own herd boars. In order to improve his herd Mr. Gentry resorted to a concentrated line breeding program in which he mated rather closely related individuals to

fix the type he desired. At one time he had seven sons of his most noted boar, Longfellow, in service at the same time. Few breeders of any class of livestock have had a more dominant influence on their chosen breed than Nicholas Hocker Gentry had upon the Berkshire, and his herd became a prominent source for other breeders that wished seed stock.

Mr. Gentry and other American breeders were not altogether satisfied with the English and Canadian Berkshires because they were a bit too much on the bacon order to suit the demand of the American farmer. Consequently, the Berkshire was largely remade to give it a stronger back, fuller forerib, heavier and plumper ham, and shorter and stronger pasterns than those found on the English Berkshire. In later years competition from the other breeds caused the American breeders to look for greater size and more rapid growth in the breed.

Litters registered in 1990 were 2,071.

CHESTER WHITE

In 1896 Joseph Harris wrote in his book, "Harris on the Pig", "The most popular and extensive known breed of pigs in the United States at this time is, unquestionably the Chester County breed. Or as they are generally called 'Chester Whites'."

Harris, the hog historian of his day, heaps high praise on the Chester White breed, far more than any other breed. In his description he refers to them as rugged and hardy, needing refinement by crossing with other breeds.

One wonders if he is referring to the same breed we know as Chester Whites today. Perhaps so, when one recognizes the immense change that has taken place in all breeds.

Harris states, "There are several reasons why the

Chester Whites are more popular than the English breeds. In the first place, they are a large, rather coarse, hardy breed, of good constitution, and well adapted to the system of management ordinarily adopted by the majority of our farmers. They are a capital sort of common swine, and it is certainly fortunate that they have been so extensively introduced into nearly all sections of the country. Wherever Chester Whites have been introduced there will be found sows admirably suited to cross with the refined English breeds. No cross could be better than a Chester White sow and an Essex, Berkshire, or Small Yorkshire thorough-bred boar. We get the form, refinement, early maturity, and fattening qualities of the latter, combined with the strong digestive powers, hardiness, and vigorous growth of the Chester Whites."

Records indicate that there were some white hogs in colonial America, but apparently the white color was not fixed. In 1818 a boar of the Woburn breed was imported into Pennsylvania from England and crossed with some of the families of white hogs that were rather numerous in Chester and Delaware counties. There are records within the breed which go back to that boar. The white hogs began to be seen at county fairs in Pennsylvania, and it was a judge at one of the fairs in 1848 who dubbed them "Chester County Whites," and the name, with "county" later dropped, stuck. The Chester White Swine Record Association was first formed in 1884.

The Chester White Swine Record Association was formed through the combination of several different organizations. In 1893 the first of the many Chester White associations was formed when the National Chester White Record Association was incorporated in Kentucky, with headquarters at West Chester, Pennsylvania. This Association continued active for many years but later combined with the Chester White Record Association. In 1885 the Chester White Record Association was established to record the Todd strain, and in 1894 it became the American Chester White Record Association, with offices at Columbus, Ohio.

Five thousand five hundred forty four litters were recorded in 1990.

DUROC JERSEY

About the Duroc Jersey breed, F. D. Coburn wrote in the late 1800's, "That so little is known by the general farmers of the country that such merits as they have are overlooked and neglected. Information respecting them is quite meager."

The National Swine Breeders Association Annual Convention in Indianapolis, November 20, 1872 reported the following:

"The positive origin of this family of swine is unknown. They have been bred in portions of the State of New Jersey, for upwards of fifty years, and with many farmers are considered to be a valuable variety. They are probably descendants from the old importations of Berkshires, as there is no record of the Tamworth, the red hogs of England, ever having been brought into this country; nor is this likely, as the Tamworth were not considered a valuable breed, and were confined to a limited breeding. The Reds resemble the old Berkshires in many respects, but are not much coarser than the improved swine of this breed."

B. R. Evans in his Story of Durocs, wrote:

"Although the source of red hogs in America might have been a number of world areas, there were several likely ones with a well established manner of entry. One of these was the Guinea Coast of Africa where a breed of red hogs was known to be highly regarded. Trade ships plying between that coast and ours provided an obvious entree. Red Guinea hogs, the forerunner of the Duroc-Jersey breed, were shipped into the Iowa Territory for breeding in 1849. Other sources were Spain and Portugal where there existed a red hog breed considered to be very good. The first opportunity for the entrance of these hogs or their descendants into America was through Columbus' second voyage and the subsequent expeditions of DeSoto and others to the mainland and a shipment from Portugal to Nova Scotia previously mentioned. There is some record of importations from these countries by the Clays of Kentucky, statesmen and farmers who were connected diplomatically in Spain or Portugal, and by Daniel Webster."

In 1877 a group of breeders met, organized an association, and set up the breed's standards. Since the Durocs of New York and the Jersey Reds of New Jersey both had been a basic for the breed, the name Duroc-Jersey was selected. The greatest growth in popularity of the Duroc has been made since the consolidation on 1934 of two competing associations into one strong national organization.

There were 22,179 litters registered in 1990.

HAMPSHIRE

The Hampshire is one of the most attractive of the American breeds of swine. The unique color markings sets it apart from all others. The white strip across the shoulders and covering the forelegs is a breed identification strictly observed by the breed promoters.

William Youatt and W. C. L. Martin report in "The Hog", 1955 that excellent hogs existed in England very similar in type to our modern Hampshire.

The Hampshire Swine Registry reports this about their breed:

"The Hampshire is black with a distinctive white belt at the shoulder. It is recognized as an American breed because its development and improvement has been in the hands of American farmers since 1825 when hogs with this color pattern were brought to America from Hampshire County in England, and thus the name Hampshire. Descendants of these early importations gravitated to Kentucky where the

breed had most of its early development. For some 50 years this belted hog was bred, no doubt, with considerable intermingling of other breeds or types of pigs within the area. Common name for these hogs then was Thin Rind, because of their thin skin and shallow backfat. A record association was first formed in 1893 at Erlanger, Kentucky. The name was changed from Thin Rind to Hampshire in 1904 and the office moved to Illinois.

In a ten-year period following 1910 Hampshires swept across the Corn Belt like a prairie fire. Recent surveys of commercial hog growers in several Corn Belt states have shown that Hampshires are used more by commercial growers, straight or crossbred, than any other breed.

The Hampshire breed has an unequaled record in interbreed competition in market hog shows, carcass contests, and swine certification. It has been a leader in performance testing. In 1964 the breed became the largest swine recording Registry in the United States.

Litters registered in 1990 were 18,925.

POLAND CHINA

According to the Poland China Record Association the Poland China is definitely an American breed, fused and developed from 1816 to 1850 in the early American Corn Belt of the Miami Valley of southwestern Ohio. As early as 1816, the records show, there was great interest in that area among farmers in the development of a hog that would convert corn into pork efficiently and carry it to market.

In 1816, the society of Shakers brought into the area from eastern Pennsylvania one boar and three sows known as Big Chinas. Large, deep bodied, white hogs with heavy ears, they had a beneficial influence on the breed in making. Other breeds were brought in, breeds and kinds of hogs with names that have disappeared—the Irish Grazier, smooth and early maturing; the Bedfords; Woburns; Byfields; and others. In 1830 the Berkshire entered the fusion and made contributions toward color, top and bottom lines, and feet.

L. N. Bonham in his book, "The Origin and Development of the Poland China Hog", the Russian hog made a contribution. He states, "How this so-called Russian hog came to the Miami Valley and Kentucky is not known. But that this hog was highly esteemed as one of the first crosses to improve the common hog of the country there can be no question."

The Russian hogs were of variable colors, with some sandy, some black, and many others white. The hogs were said to have been of fairly large size, but were rather flat in their backs, poorly ribbed, long bodied, long legged, and in general lacked quality. They were said to have been of a desirable disposition.

No single breed exerted a predominating influence. By 1850 the new type of hog was pretty well established. It had taken form. It was a hog that never had existed in the world before, a product of the Corn Belt and the work and breeding genius of the farmers of the area.

One of these farmers, Ascher Ascher by name, selling many boars around 1840, was Polish by birth. The boars proved out well. The farmers called them "Polands." Ascher had brought in no hogs to the locality but had been able to produce his superior hogs from materials at hand.

The first Poland China Record was established in Ohio in 1877. Under the guidance of a number of record associations, the breed has continued the development of the Poland China, retaining the essential characteristics fixed in the long pioneer period.

The Poland China has always been a hog of great size, ruggedness, and prolificacy. Its color is black with white markings, usually confined to legs, head, and tail. A typical Poland China has thick, even flesh, is long in the underline, and free from flabbiness. The ears droop. The face is straight, not dished. Refinement in head, ears, hair, and bone is typical.

One thousand eight hundred forty eight litters were registered in 1990.

THE SPOTTED BREED

The present day Spots descent from the spotted hogs which trace a part of their ancestry to the original Poland China, which consisted of 6 separate breeds and was referred to as the "Warren County Hog" of Ohio. One such breed imported into Ohio in the early 1800's was a breed called "Big China," mostly white in color, but having some black spots. They were good feeders, matured early, were very prolific, and produced these characteristics in their offspring.

Three men from Putnam and Hendricks Counties, Indiana, brought boars and sows back from Ohio to cross with their own good hogs; and thus developed the breed from this background which kept the characteristic color of large black and white spots. They had no name, but it was the opinion of most men in the section that these spotted hogs were not only superior as the most profitable pork producer and all around farmer's hog to any other breed, but to any other Poland as well. Farmers who had moved away without them sent back to get this rugged, easy-feeding spotted hog. At this time two hogs imported from England, known as "Gloucester Old Spots," added a wonderful stimulant to the breed in the form of new bloodlines.

There were a number of well-known breeders in central Indiana who had been breeding these spotted hogs to the exclusion of all others for many years, and due to the general demand for them the need had arisen for an organization to record and push the big-boned, prolific spotted hog as a separate and distinct family. This resulted in the organization of a Record Association which was incorporated under the laws of Indiana in January, 1914, and has grown in the past 50 years to one of the top-ranking purebred breed associations in the United States.

In 1960 it was voted to change the name of the association from the National Spotted Poland China Record to the National Spotted Swine Record, Inc. Further, it was voted to refer to the breed as Spotted Swine, or Spots. Ideal color is 50% white - 50% black. They must be at least 20% white or black on the body (legs not counted) with well-defined spots distributed over the body. The coloring should not be intermingled.

The official organization for the Spotted breed is the National Spotted Swine Record, Inc. For all practical purposes, the organization started in 1912, largely from the encouragement of Fred. L. Obenchain, Secretary of the breed from 1914 through 1955. In January 1914, a meeting was called of all Spotted Poland China enthusiasts for the purpose of incorporating an organization. However, differences arose and instead of forming an organization, two organizations were established. The National Spotted Poland Record Association was incorporated on January 1, 1914, at Indianapolis, Indiana, whereas, on January 1 and 2, of the same year, the American Spotted Poland China Record Association was incorporated under the laws of the same state. It is with considerable credit to breeders that on January 11, 1916, the two organizations combined and the National Spotted Poland China Record Association was established, incorporated under the laws of Indiana. This organization has remained the chief recording association. An American Spotted Poland China Record with headquarters at Moberly, Missouri operated for several years but is no longer active.

There were 6,443 litters recorded in 1990.

YORKSHIRE

The Yorkshire breed had its roots in Yorkshire and the surrounding area of England in the late 18th and early 19th Centuries. References are made to the breeds existence in 1805 and 1812. The genetic makeup of the breed is somewhat in question as references are made by W. Youatt (1847 -"The Pig") and John Lawrence (1805 -"A General Treatise").

It was a number of years before the white hog of Yorkshire was considered a breed although they were referred to as Yorkshires.

The old Yorkshire, as the white pig has frequently been called, has been described as an animal of considerable size.

Samuel Sidney (1871 -"The Pig") said, "Nothing draws a crowd of Yorkshire folk as a monster pig." Huge hogs are a novelty and still attract great crowds even today.

Youatt and Lawrence both state that the Yorkshire probably is the result of combining the genetic input of new Leicester, Berkshire, Chinese Neapolitan, and Essex.

The breed finds its origin in Yorkshire and the surrounding counties of England. At an early date there existed in that region a very large white hog, of heavy bone, of great length and showing dark pigmented spots in the skin. By selection and the infusion of Leicester blood (a white hog developed by Robert Bakewell) the present Large White of England was developed. The unmatched prolificacy, suckling ability and carcass quality of the Yorkshire are the result of these qualities having been emphasized in the early and later development of the breed. From the beginning, these traits were considered important.

In the latter part of the 19th Century these Large White began finding their way to this continent, into Canada and the United States, and in both countries they were called Yorkshires. In 1893 the American

Yorkshire Club was formed in the United States, giving a means of registering these hogs in this country. Later, in 1948, there was a reorganization of registry association into American Yorkshire Club, Inc.

During the period of lard's greatest popularity the Yorkshire met with favor in only scattered parts of this country, and for many years the registry activity was very limited. In 1945 there was a noticeable rise in interest with registries beginning to show a marked increase. In 1947 between 4,400 and 5,000 hogs were recorded and in 1948 about 6,000. This number climbed to nearly 30,000 in 1959 as the American housewife increased her demand for a better quality of pork with less waste.

During this period of rapid breed expansion, a large percentage of Yorkshires were brought in from Canada where the breed had long been the most popular hog, due to its ability to produce the choice carcass in demand in that country. There were also importations from England where the breed is typically one of somewhat greater substance, ruggedness and scale. By selection, and by use of its infusion of English blood, the breed in the United States had been modified in type somewhat to meet the needs of the pork producer and the demands of the market in this country. It is noteworthy that the typical characteristics of great prolificacy, suckling capacity, and ability to produce the superior carcass have been maintained in this modification of type.

There were 23,861 litters recorded in 1990.

Part 5

THE NATIONAL BARROW SHOW

"There is no higher form of art than that which deals with the intelligent manipulation of animal life." Sanders 1915

The pen of noted journalist Alvin Sanders epitomizes the dreams that have inspired stockmen since domestication of livestock.

As we approach the 21st Century, challenged by rapid innovation and confronted with an ever increasing amount of new technology, we struggle to keep pace with change.

In retrospect we look back at what appears to us to have been the golden years a more relaxed generation when Sanders wrote, a time when one had the luxury of reflection, study and planning.

The International Livestock Exposition in Chicago, born in 1900 ended its 75 years and is no more.

As Dr. Richard Willham so colorfully stated in "The Legacy of the Stockman", "The stockyards, the packing houses made notorious by Upton Sinclair's 'The Jungle', and the old Stockyards Inn with its British tradition are gone.

"But the memories of 'the splendors of packing town' remain in the hearts of many stockmen, professors and friends of the livestock industry who braved the Windy City at Thanksgiving time each year for the world's greatest livestock event."

Predating the International Livestock Exposition by exactly one century the Smithfield Club of London introduced the forerunner to our traditional livestock show.

In 1799 at London's Smithfield Market, which still serves as London's central meat market, the club held its first competitive hog show. It was accounted as a complete success.

Harriet Ritro writes in her 1987 edition of "Animal Estates in England", according to one admiring chronicler, it, "Did great credit to the exhibiting graziers and great honour to the largest market in the world." She reports, "He characterized the sponsoring society, with its membership composed of 'a considerable number of noblemen and gentlemen,' as 'That admirable, that practical and truly patriotic institution.'"

The sponsoring Smithfield Club was ostensible dedicated to blazing trails for small farmers to follow, but neither the animals they showed nor the economic philosophy suggested much commonality of purpose with much cultivation. Both in speech and action, the members of the Smithfield Club consistently indicated that the main recompense for judging show animals was intangible.

NATIONAL BARROW SHOW SETS STANDARDS

It is ironic that the show ring with few exceptions has maintained the image of intangibility and lack of objectivity for 190 years to this day.

One exception is the National Barrow Show, held at Austin, Minnesota in September of each year, dating back to 1946. It is co-sponsored by the Breed

Registry Associations and George A. Hormel Company.

In 1927 a number of leading swine producers met with packer buyers. The key objective of the meeting was to establish standards for a "meat-type-hog." The goal was to produce hogs that would meet the desires of consumers who were shying away from the meat counter because of excessive fat in pork.

As a result of this meeting, a market hog show was made a part of the currently existing National Barrow Show. It was hoped that the market hog show would more closely tie together the breeding of swine and the production of superior market hogs. The first National Barrow Show, therefore, was held in 1927, in conjunction with the National Swine Show at Peoria, Illinois. The Barrow Show was repeated at Peoria the following year.

During the next 12 years, however, the National Barrow Show traveled around the country. It was part of the National Swine Show at the Indiana State Fair, Indianapolis, Indiana, in 1929 and 1930. The National Barrow Show was made a feature of the National Swine Show at the Illinois State Fair, Springfield, Illinois, in 1931. This classic swine show remained in Illinois until 1939 when it was taken to the World's Fair in San Francisco, California.

Throughout the early years, the National Swine Growers' Association sponsored and managed both the National Swine Show and the National Barrow Show. A significant part of each Barrow Show was the sale at public auction of the first-prize winners and champions—the remaining hogs sold in one lot to the highest bidder.

There was no National Barrow Show in 1940, but it resulted one year later when the National Association of Swine Records collaborated with the Illinois State Fair Director of Agriculture in reviving the show at the Illinois State Fair.

During World War II (1942-1945) the National Barrow Show, like many other expositions, was forced to discontinue. However, with the end of hostilities, the National Association of Swine Records returned to action once again. Arrangements were made whereby the National Barrow Show would be held in Austin, Minnesota, for a period of 3 years - 1946-48. It was decided that the National Barrow Show, for the first time, would be a show by itself— separate and distinct from any other fair or exposition.

The 1946 show marked the first time that the 10 major breeds of hogs had appeared together at a national swine show. The $21,645 prize money was the largest purse ever awarded and, in addition, the 1946 show had more hogs on exhibit than any other previous swine show in history.

After the original 3 year sponsorship agreement expired, it was decided to continue to stage the National Barrow Show in Austin under the sponsorship of George A. Hormel and Company and the National Association of Swine Records. The National Barrow Show has been an annual event in Austin, Minnesota, with the exception of 1952 when the show was canceled because of an outbreak of vesicular exanthema.

The National Barrow Show, now called the "World Series of Swine Shows," is held at the Mower County Fairgrounds. A new livestock pavilion, costing some $42,000 was erected especially for the National Barrow Show in 1946 and dedicated to R. P. Crane, a one-time director of the Hormel Company, a member of The Hormel Institute Board of Directors, and vice-chairman of The Hormel Foundation. A disastrous fire destroyed the original building on April 20, 1955, necessitating the construction of a new pavilion the following year.

Over the years the National Barrow Show has grown in size, importance and stature. It has not only been a medium of comparison between breeds, but a place for standardization of the improvement of each breed. The championship honors are the most coveted of any awards available to swine breeders today.

Nearly 3,000 animals, accompanied by 400 exhibitors in 22 states, enter the World Series of Swine Shows each year. And, the National Barrow Show, as hog producers from across the country have universally proclaimed, is, indeed, the "granddaddy" of all swine shows.

Attendance at the three day show in 1989 was approximately 10,000.

In the 73 years since the inception of the National Barrow Show it has maintained an image of objectivity. It provided industry leadership in the quest for the "meat-type-hog." It was one of the first to incorporate performance feeding trials to measure efficiency and carcass merit. The National Barrow Show Carcass Contest was one of the first to demonstrate the relationship between visual appraisal and objective measures.

For 73 years the National Barrow Show has served as our laboratory to discover facts and make change. As a result hogs today have 50% less fat than 30 years ago. The challenge is to continually advance in knowledge and develop sharper tools.

In this last decade of the 20th Century we are entering the age of artificial based intelligence.

Through artificial based intelligence we have the capability of finding solutions to enormous problems. By feeding into the computer an adequate amount of correct information we are able to generate fairly accurate predictions of breeding value.

The breeder of today has the luxury of parading into the show ring equipped with several generations of performance records and computerized projections of the breeding value of each animal.

To neglect the use of these new tools of technology in showring placing is as absurd as guessing at the weight of an animal while it stands on a balanced set of scales.

Being a stockman is even more exciting and rewarding today because we are on the leading edge of an explosion of new technology.

The speed of change and the challenge to innovate sets a pace today that would spin the minds of the stockman of 50 years ago.

For a decade now, we have been dealing with technology that the turn of the century hogman could never comprehend.

In keeping with its earned image for being progressive the National Barrow Show sponsored by George A. Hormel Co. will be a participant in a state of the art progeny research test in 1991.

Aiming toward the 21st Century the sophisticated project will make detailed evaluations of pork quality including performance, efficiency and quality traits.

Computers and artificial based intelligence has revolutionized our lives and we are only getting started.

Change in our society has been accelerating at astounding speed and is predicted to increase by 500 times in the next 20 years. The dizzying pace of the 21st Century will require a new set of tools and a temperament in tune with the times.

Champion Hampshire boar, early 1920's.

1946 National Barrow Show Grand Champion Barrow. Man Cry Co Farm, Manning, Iowa.

1956 National Barrow Show Grand Champion Barrow. Richard K. Bruene, Gladbrook, Iowa.

Typical show ring scene, National Barrow Show, Austin, Minnesota.

Orville K. Sweet

Part 6

NEW BREEDS FROM CROSSBRED FOUNDATIONS

W.E. Rempel

New breeds are needed in order to combine the desirable traits of existing breeds. The needs arise for a variety of reasons. Shifting demands in the kind of product calls for seed stock to meet the new demands. The increased demand for leaner pig meat is proceeding all over the pork-consuming parts of the world. Changes in the systems of production also require breeding stock that will accommodate to different situations of rearing and feeding in different parts of the world.

The genetics of breeding better animals has two important components. One is the matter of producing seed stock, and the other is the production of commercial animals. In cases where the final product is produced by purebreds, the distinction between purebred and commercial producer is not so great as where the final product is the result of a cross. In the first case, the methods of selection and the traits under selection are similar for commercial and purebred producers as well as from breed to breed. In swine, the bulk of the market product comes from some sort of cross, and this calls for the development of specialized breeds, that in combination will provide the optimum of desired products for the least amount of input in labor, feed and other costs.

In the USA, the purebred philosophy of animal breeding reigned supreme from the time of the importation of the first registered animals in the 1800's until about the 1950's. This philosophy developed from the assumption that "purebred" is automatically superior to any other type of breeding, and that producers should raise the pure breed of their choice, or to grade up to the breed of their choice. This philosophy was widely supported by State and Federal livestock specialists and the most professors of animal science. It essentially denied the existence of heterosis from the crosses of pure breeds, and led to nonsensical cliches such as "there are greater differences within breeds than between breeds," and "there are good ones in every breed."

This philosophy, although far from dead, received a severe jolt from the events that occurred in the corn-breeding arena. Formulation of explanations for the occurrence of heterosis in maize led to the development of the hybrid corn industry and resul-

tant increases in yield. Essentially, the system consisted of the development of inbred lines of corn, choosing the lines that crossed to best advantage and selling the F-1 seed to producers for commercial production. This system keeps the seed stock safely in the hands of the seed producer, as the hybrid cannot be produced without the inbred parents. The seed stock producer, therefore, has a product for repeated sales. The only competition comes from other seed stock producers. Some livestock breeders (notably among these was L.M. Winters, University of Minnesota), themselves a new breed, took heart from these studies and initiated crossbreeding experiments with pigs. Winters' 1935 bulletin showed that crosses of conventional purebreds exhibited heterosis in performance. He also recommended a new way to produce market swine by a continuous two-breed rotation which he termed "criss-crossing".

The Regional Swine Breeding Laboratory was formed in order to research swine breeding in a cooperative approach among the swine-producing states. This organization, under the leadership of Dr. W.A. Craft as coordinator, initiated swine breeding projects that followed the corn breeding example very closely. Most stations embarked on the formation of inbred lines within the existing purebred breeds. At several locations, inbred lines were also formed from crossbred foundations. The impetus for this development came about because Henry Wallace, as Secretary of Agriculture, was able to break through the red tape of the U.S. Animal and Plant Health Inspection Division, and import Landrace pigs. Wallace was a strong advocate of crossbreeding for commercial production, and the utilization of exotic germ plasm. This came about because of his direct association with a hybrid corn seed company.

The introduction of the Danish Landrace (a bacon breed) permitted Winters to develop the Minnesota No. 1 (from a cross of Danish Landrace and Canadian Tamworth), and the USDA to develop a number of lines from crossbred foundations at Beltsville and one line (Montana No. 1) at Miles City, Montana.

Industry interest in utilizing these lines from crossbred foundations or new breeds for commercial production in crossing systems led Winters and a group of producers in 1946 to form the Inbred Live-

24   THE PORK STORY

stock Breeders Registry Association. Notable features incorporated into this registry association were:

1. Provision for the formulation and maintenance of suitable standards based on performance for the certification of animals so entitled.
2. Provision for the establishment of a herd (or herds) of livestock which will serve as a source (or sources) of highly purified and selected breeding animals.
3. Provision for improvement of accepted inbred lines through the introduction of outside germ plasm.

The essential elements for the maintenance and continual improvement of seed stock were all in place. The specifications called for selection of seed stock on the basis of performance with suitable registration certificates to indicate the degree of merit. The establishment of nucleus herds would provide the elite stock for the improvement of the rest of the line (or lines). Improvement of existing lines could be accomplished through pre-planned introduction and testing of outside germ plasm. The various lines would be used in appropriate crossing systems for commercial production.

The guiding rules for improvement of swine performance as set out by Dr. L.M. Winters were as follows:

1. Selection must be based on performance tests rather than show-ring standards.
2. Crossbred foundations will provide more opportunity to select new genetic combinations with higher levels of performance than single-breed foundations.
3. Some level of inbreeding is necessary to stabilize the new breeds genetically ("fixing the breed label," he called it), and perhaps increase the degree of heterosis.
4. Heterosis is greater in crosses of breeds that are less related (Genetic Diversity).
5. Breed improvement is a continuous process, and breeds must be continually improved or replaced.

The impact of this organization and its breeders has not been trivial. Although the stated goals were never attained, considerable influence was exerted on the swine industry of the USA and indirectly to swine production the world over. Swine breeds were influenced to put more emphasis on performance testing, and crossbreeding for commercial production became accepted as a sound practice by all breed associations. Although the breed associations have not officially accepted the introduction of outside genes as a means of improving their breeds, this sort of migration has been proceeding without official sanction.

METHODS - NEW BREEDS FROM CROSSBRED FOUNDATIONS

The collective results of the Regional Swine Breeding Laboratory (Craft, 1958) established that reproductive traits responded least to direct selection, suffered the greatest depression from inbreeding, and yielded the highest heterotic response upon crossing. The reproductive performance of the lines from crossbred foundations was generally higher than that of line crosses within breeds and of the non-inbred purebreds.

New breeds from crossbred foundations that were recognized by the Inbred Livestock Registry Association and fairly widely used in the USA in the 1950's are listed in the Table 1.

TABLE 1. NEW BREEDS RECORDED IN THE INBRED LIVESTOCK REGISTRY ASSOCIATION

Minnesota No. 1	Danish Landrace and Canadian Tamworth	University of Minnesota
Minnesota No. 2	Inbred Poland China and Canadian Yorkshire	University of Minnesota
Minnesota No. 3	Gloucester, Old Spot Welsh, Large White, Beltsville No. 2, and other new breeds	University of Minnesota
Montana No. 1	Danish Landrace and Non-belted Hampshire	USDA, Miles City, MO
Maryland No. 1	Berkshire and Danish Landrace	USDA & University of Maryland
Beltsville No. 1	Danish Landrace and Poland China	USDA, Beltsville
Beltsville No. 2	Danish Yorkshire, Landrace and Hampshire	USDA, Beltsville

Although these breeds performed well in crossbred combinations, their use began to decline in the late 1950's to the point that they are all now extinct, or exist only in small research herds, or as a source of germ plasm for hybrid boar producers.

The decline of the new breeds may be partly attributed to the advent of, and use of, swine testing stations and the live backfat probe. These two developments resulted in the availability of performance-tested boars with lower backfat, from the older, conventional breeds.

In addition, the members of the Inbred Livestock Registry Association chose to go their individual ways and develop their own hybrid boar businesses, rather than work collectively within the Association. This is a natural consequence of a hybrid program, and follows what has happened in the corn and poul-

Orville K. Sweet

25

try industry. Where the final market product is from a cross, it is imperative that the seed stock producer has control of the parent seed stock. In this way, seed stock producers can afford to spend time and effort in improving the seed stock in the hope of gaining the rewards of success in the sale of breeding animals.

The breeding companies in the U.S. and in Western European countries are taking over an increasing share of the seed stock products in the swine industry. These companies develop their own parent lines, do their own performance testing and selection, and develop appropriate crossing systems for commercial production. The parent lines may be of purebred or crossbred origin. Generally, the maternal lines come from breeds that are high in reproductive performance, while the specialized male lines are developed from combinations of breeds that can contribute to improved feed efficiency, lean growth and other attributes of production. The overall breeding systems will be designed so as to maximize heterosis and complementarity and to minimize improvement lag from seed stock to commercial producer. At the same time, they attempt to maximize the use of the elite parent seed stock.

FUTURE DEVELOPMENT

The comments on future development are predicated on the assumptions that market pigs will be crossbreds. The two circumstances that make this almost certain to be true are: a) the beneficial effect of heterosis in crosses, and, b) a hybrid system allowing breeders of elite stock to keep control of the germ plasm, which is not possible in the case of purebred systems.

Specialized lines and specific fixed crosses are almost certain to be used in areas with intensive production systems and a demanding market. The specialized lines for production traits (growth, feed and body composition) will be developed from crossbred foundations, and with intra-population selection within these gene pools. The relative weights of the traits will vary for different target markets. These will be the sire lines, with no emphasis on litter size, and probably will take advantage of single gene effects such as the halothane susceptibility gene.

Dr. Rempel received his B.S. and M.S. degrees in Animal Science from the University of Manitoba, Alberta, Canada. He received his Ph.D. in Animal Breeding from the University of Minnesota. He has spent his professional career in the study of swine breeding.

Part 7

PACKERS AS PARTNERS

"HOG BUTCHER FOR THE WORLD

TOOL MAKER, STACKER OF WHEAT

PLAYING WITH RAILROADS AND THE NATIONS FREIGHT HANDLER

STORMY, HUSKY, BRAWLING CITY OF BIG SHOULDERS"

With these poetic phrases Carl Sandburg not only described Chicago but he characterized the meat packing industry.

If ever there was an industry that grew up with the new world and tested the meaning of free enterprise surely it was the meat packing industry. Outside of farming there has never been an industry that demanded more sweat, required greater risk or was more competitive.

Neither has there been a segment of agriculture subjected to more public criticism and media abuse.

In John Bunyan's "Pilgrims Progress", the word "muckracker" was coined to describe the journalists who were busy making a living exposing corruption in our cities and businesses. No industry was exempt.

The chief muckracker for the packing industry was Upton Sinclair whose best selling novel, "The Jungle", successfully framed public opinion of the packing industry by charging the industry with bribery, collusion and riotous human abuse. In one instance he inferred that people frequently injured, fall into vats and are rendered into lard. A full investigation by the U.S.D.A. found these allegation to be false.

However, the damage was complete and effective, public perception of packing plants was firmly fixed in the consumers minds and lives until this day. The meat industry has entered another era of muckraking the past decade, a time when media and consumer activists are gaining momentum in their efforts to discredit meat as a wholesome nutritious food.

The American packing industry has been performing miracles for so long and under adverse conditions that they have become ordinary happenings and public scrutiny and criticism has become common place and expected.

No other country in the world slaughters and processes annually 45 million cattle, 85 million hogs and 10 million sheep. The growth and development of the packing and processing industry is truly a product of free enterprise and typifies the spirit of a young expanding nation energized by hard working people with healthy appetites.

Owing to the creative genius of the packing, processing industry the hog provided society with a wider range of products than any other animal.

From the widest and most varied range of food products available from any animal to a host of pharmaceutical products, quality leather goods, beauty aids, brush bristles - the list goes on and on. Hogs stand uniquely highest among the animals in their extraordinary benefits to society.

The amazing utility of the hog motivated one packer to place a sign over the loading ramp, "We use everything but the squeal."

History indicates that hogs have been raised in large numbers for food and other products in virtually all parts of the world since earliest times.

America is today the largest commercial producer of hogs in the world. China produces nearly twice the number annually processed in the U.S.A., however, the majority of hogs raised in China are for family slaughter and use.

Today, the hog is at the highest state of quality and utility in history, through modern technology in breeding, management and packer processing.

History of pork production is a story of the unique adaptability of this extraordinary creature, the creativity of producers and processors, and the truly remarkable benefits of the hog to our human society.

In early America rapidly growing cities and developing consumer demands gave rise to larger local butchers capable of processing 25 to 30 hogs per day and delivering to the local grocery stores.

Pork adapted readily to the traditional methods of curing and preserving and became a staple item in the cupboard, smoke houses and storage places, on farms all over America.

Numerous small packers serving larger metropolitan areas delivered their products to central markets and they were redistributed to wholesalers and retailers.

Scalding hogs preparatory to scraping them at the Swift and Company Packing House, Chicago. 1905. USDA Photo archives.

Government inspection of hogs for tuberculosis. Swift and Company, Bennington, Vermont. 1906. USDA Photo archives.

Orville K. Sweet

The famous Smithfield Market of London, dating to the 17th Century, served this vast metropolis and does to this day. In many aspects little has changed since the primeval days. Carcasses are hauled over the shoulders of brawny men and marketing stalls are open from 4 a.m. to early afternoon.

Not so in the eager, impatient new world where innovation and change is a vital part of the dynamic environment. Although tradition prevails in some areas of the packing industry the eternal struggle is to produce faster and more efficiency and better quality control.

Pork production developed into a major economic activity in the early 1600's when farmers raised and butchered their hogs for their own use. Neighbors would gather on the first frost days in the fall of the year to share labor in the handling of the 3 to 5 hundred pound hogs.

Slaughter time on the farm, 1930's. A neighborly chore.

Hog butchering season was an exciting time for all of the farming neighborhood. For kids it was an excuse to miss a day of school. For wives a get-together to exchange neighborhood gossip and cook a meal from fresh organ meats for the men. The men killed, scalded, scraped and eviscerated the hogs and hung them up to cool in the crisp autumn air.

The local butcher rapidly found a place in the community in later years when transportation was more convenient. However, slaughtering only a few head per day accommodated only a few who would sell their surplus pork to city dwellers.

Traditional methods of processing and curing made it possible for pork to be enjoyed in homes or farms and for travelers throughout the world. Before the advent of refrigeration beef must be eaten fresh and cooked or dried which wasn't the most palatable or appetizing.

PORK AND THE MILITARY

Pork became the staple meat item in the soldiers diet during war. When cured it was safe and provided the enormous energy required for the exertion of fighting and long marches of foot soldiers.

From the salt pork and bacon provided to George Washington's Colonial Army, to "sow belly and beans" for the Blue and the Grey Forces of the Civil War, hogs have traditionally provided food products for the military.

During World War II, American forces in the field pried open cans of "C" and "K" rations containing several varieties of pork products, and ate tons of Hormel Spam in the mess halls.

And surely pork has gone into space in the 20th Century.

COLONIAL PORK PRODUCTION AND PROCESSING

Pork processing developed into a major economic activity in the Atlantic Colonies during the middle to late 1600's. John Pynchon of Springfield, Massachusetts slaughtered, cured, and barreled many shiploads of pork for export in the West Indies trade routes from 1660 to 1680. He is generally considered to be the first pork packer in the country.

While colonial Massachusetts grew in importance as pork producers, Pennsylvania in the late 1600's became the leading hog raising colony. Following guidelines set down by William Penn in 1681 for the feeding and shelter of livestock, the Pennsylvania colony was processing and exporting pork products and live hogs to the West Indies trade within a decade.

Early Armour slaughter plant.

At the close of the 17th Century, the typical colonial farmer owned several hogs to supply salt pork, smoked ham, sausage, bacon, and lard for the family, with enough surplus to aid in the supply of barreled pork exported from the country. Of major importance, the practice of finishing hogs on Indian corn had gained acceptance, following its adoption as common practice in Pennsylvania.

The development of the packing industry was beginning to take on shape and character in the 18th and 19th Centuries. By 1700 a sizable livestock and meat industry had grown up in Worcester and Springfield, Massachusetts. Hogs and other livestock were driven to markets in Lynn, Salem, Dorchester, and Charlestown, and to Boston in 1742, with the opening of Faneuil Hall Market. The farmers of the time generally dealt directly with the processors.

Uncle Sam was a pork packer.

UNCLE SAM

In 1812, the United States government acquired a unique personality with the help of the swine industry and a humble pork packer from New Hampshire.

Young Sam Wilson had traveled on foot to Troy, N.Y., where he prospered and became a pork packer. A congenial gentleman, he became known as "Uncle Sam" by his friends on the Hudson riverfront. The remainder of the story goes like this:

One day a vessel tied up at the dock where there were several barrels of pork destined for shipment to the American forces fighting England in the War of 1812. Each barrel was marked "U.S." When a riverboat passenger asked what the letters meant, he was told "Uncle Sam." "Uncle Sam who?", asked a stranger. "Uncle Sam Wilson, of course - he's feeding the Army!" was the reply.

The story of Uncle Sam feeding the army spread, and shortly thereafter the United States government became known as "Uncle Sam." From then on, the image was in the hands of the newspaper cartoonists, then someone added whiskers to a likeness of Sam Wilson, and Uncle Sam was born.

During World War I (1917) Uncle Sam emerged bearded with a top hat and patriotic striped trousers and cloak to beckon young men to join the armed forces. He repeated his recruiting appearance in World War II.

The growing East Coast population centers of Philadelphia, Baltimore and New York provided a ready market for hogs. Livestock were initially driven to market across the Alleghenies in the early 1800's. Hogs were brought on foot in "droves", or larger herds, over routes which later became the New York Central, Pennsylvania, and Baltimore & Ohio railroads.

TRANSPORTATION VIA RIVERS AND CANALS

The Louisiana Purchase in 1803 brought New Orleans into the Union and opened up a large area of the country for agricultural development. Considerable river traffic in livestock and cured pork products ensued along the Mississippi River. By 1818, livestock were being transported in sizable number to New Orleans via the Ohio and Mississippi Rivers.

The opening of the Erie Canal in 1825 allowed livestock and processed pork products to be taken east by water transport. The importance of this canal, the world's second longest, to the early economic development and expansion of the United States can hardly be overemphasized.

Transportation played a major role in the development of the industry. As the population grew and the number of hogs reached 10 million head in 1840, driving large herds on foot overland had become impractical. The river and canal water routes, and later the railroads, were instrumental in establishing the pattern of the growing pork industry that determined the location of processing plants.

CINCINNATI TO CHICAGO

The problem of transporting live animals to processing centers became more acute as the volume of business grew, and Cincinnati, Ohio, located in the center of the largest swine-raising area of the time and a major Ohio River port and later rail hub, became the leading pork packing center of the country from the early 1800's to the Civil War.

Hogs were first processed in Cincinnati in 1810, and by 1863 over 608,000 head were being processed annually. Cincinnati earned the title "Porkopolis", but the Civil War of 1861-65 interfered with access to the city.

Hog drive, 1868.

Chicago, because of its central geographic location on the Great Lakes and proximity to the largest hog raising areas of the country, and with its new railroad connections to the East, grew rapidly as the country's, and the world's, largest pork packing center. Chicago became known as the "hog butcher of the world."

TRANSPORTATION AND TECHNOLOGY

The major problem faced throughout the westward expansion was one of food transportation, particularly meat. The economic development of the west depended in large part on the ability to ship agricultural products to the large population centers of the east.

Since fresh meat could not be sent any great distance without spoiling, livestock had to be transported alive by rail to the eastern markets for slaughtering and dressing. The exception was pork, which could be salted or smoked in Chicago or Cincinnati and shipped east.

The invention of the refrigerated rail car in 1870 enabled the west to supply the best with fresh meat at much less expense. The invention of the refrigerator car allowed fresh pork to be shipped over considerable distances for the first time in history without spoilage, thus greatly expanding the marketing options for pork products.

TURN OF THE CENTURY 1899 - 1900

The closing years of the 19th Century saw large quantities of pork products being processed by major national packing companies, from hogs raised principally in the Midwest corn belt, shipped via railroad for consumption in the large population centers of the east, and to other areas of the rapidly developing American nation.

The United States Department of Agriculture was established by Congress in 1862, and achieved Cabinet status in 1889. Since that time, the USDA has worked with the pork producers and packers at all levels to provide top quality products to the consumer.

The first federal meat inspection law was passed in 1890, followed by the Federal Meat Inspection Act of 1906, which established the present system of inspection for all meat shipped across state lines or sold to the government.

The stage was set for the dramatic developments of the American Pork Industry in the 20th Century.

FROM LARD TO MEAT

Swine have undergone many changes since their introduction to America in the early 1500's.

The major development in the pork production industry in the 20th Century has been the shift from the lard-type hog to the meat-type animal.

Fat, lard-type hogs were in demand in World War I. Photo shows a Grand Champion Duroc Barrow, 1913, owned by Thomas Johnson, Columbus, Ohio.

As World Wars I and II came and passed, the need for fat, from which nitroglycerin is made, greatly diminished. The demand for fat has also decreased dramatically in the 20th Century owing to the use of vegetable shortenings as fat substitutes, the use of chemical detergents in place of soaps made from fat, and changes in dietary habits.

The meat packing industry has been in the forefront of changes necessary to satisfy the needs of an ever changing consumer demand.

With the aid of packers, university researchers, geneticists, and nutritionists, pork producers began to modify the lard-type hog, or "cob roller", in search of the "meat-type" hog, a term first used in the 1920's.

The packing industry grew and expanded as number of hogs increased. In the formative years before the 20th Century records were few and unreliable.

The USDA reported the Chicago Stock Yards receipts of hogs at 392,864. By 1900 receipts had grown to 8,109,064 but by 1939 4,263,810, a 50% reduction. Receipts at the top 38 markets, however were 18,396,684. A good number of hogs were still being slaughtered on farms and in non-inspected plants.

The rapid growth of other central buying stations reflected in the reduced number being shipped to Chicago that never reached the total number received in 1900 again. USDA records indicate the number of hogs received at the 13 largest hog markets in 1937-38-39. Hog numbers had increased from 27 million in 1890 to 62 million in 1920. In 1921, 80% of all farms raising hogs slaughtered them for their own use. Only 40% sold hogs.

RECEIPTS OF HOGS AT LEADING MARKETS
IN THREE YEARS

Market	1939	1938	1937
1. Chicago	4,263,8104	4,188,0554	3,968,398
2. St. Louis	2,625,9514	2,419,4974	9,965,978
3. St. Paul	2,204,9154	2,026,7204	1,590,607
4. Indianapolis	1,913,2544	1,776,8094	1,582,582
5. Omaha	1,629,2764	1,214,3714	1,109,682
6. Sioux City	1,203,4374	1,036,9434	827,170
7. Cincinnati	985,3194	887,002	802,045
8. St. Joseph	822,3774	675,1444	569,197
9. Peoria	602,1284	582,303	489,510
10. Pittsburgh	594,4024	487,385	472,150
11. Kansas City	519,2984	375,8284	371,599
12. Oklahoma City	516,8064	357,899	292,310
13. Salt Lake City	515,7204	365,406	319,147
TOTALS	18,396,684	16,376,292	14,659,669

Sixty-seven markets received 27,974,450 hogs in 1939. The 13 markets listed in the foregoing table received about 66% of this total.

The Big 4, Wilson, Swift, Armour and Cudahay would account for more than half of the pork slaughtered in the early part of the 20th Century while smaller independents and farm slaughter accounted for the balance. While in 1989 four packers accounted for approximately 35% of the slaughter, concentration of the packing industry in fewer hands has been of some concern. There has not been the rapid rate of concentration in pork as there has been in beef processing where four packers process more than 70% of all fed beef.

The trend toward fewer and larger slaughterers has been the result of increased labor costs and the efficiencies gained in the economic of scale.

Competition for the packing industry has forced packers to reduce costs of inputs the same as for producers. The last 30 years, however, has seen the proliferation of many specialized processors of pork and name brands of cured pork products.

The pork industry owes much of its success to the ingenuity and creativity of a highly specialized processing industry. Promoting private labeled pork products has given impetus to pork's desirability.

The meat industry generally and demand for beef specifically has been severely damaged in the decades of the 70's and 80's. During this period of diet/health concerns pork has escaped almost without harm. The pork industry's development of new processed products and offering a variety of options to the consumer has been its strongest selling points.

Innovation, creativity and an industry working together to satisfy a whimsical consumer has been pork's key to success.

THE AMERICAN MEAT INSTITUTE

A major contributing factor to the advancement of the packing industry has been its trade association. The American Meat Institute (AMI) formerly called the American Meat Packers Association (AMPA) had its beginning in 1909. The packing industry had its share of problems in 1906.

According the AMI's 75th anniversary report by Herbert B. Bains, Upton Sinclair's book, "The Jungle" viciously pilloried the meat packers. The muckraking exercise in part was responsible for the poor public image of the packing industry. The damaging publicity from this book, in addition to the threatened federal regulations, gave impetus to the creation of AMI.

AMI has contributed substantially to improved business practices, new technology and improved public image through educational programs.

The packing industry has become an effective force influencing public policy through its cooperative lobbying activities.

At its annual meeting held at Chicago's McCormick Place AMI hosts the nation's packers and allied industry in the meat complex. The convention and trade show attracts visitors from throughout the world and provides a forum for discussion of the issues facing the meat industry.

Part 8

THE ADVANCEMENT
OF SWINE HEALTH

THE EARLY DAYS

America's first veterinarian was William Carter who lived in Virginia in 1625. He was known as an "expert cow doctor."

The successful growth of the livestock industry can be attributed in part to the development of professional health care.

THE ERADICATION OF CHOLERA

The Bureau of Animal Industry (BAI) was established by an act of Congress May 29, 1884 under the commissioner of agriculture.

One of its early tasks was to come to grips with the increasing problems of the spread of disease among livestock.

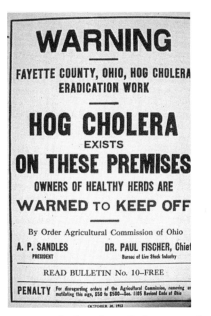

Property was posted when hog cholera was diagnosed.

Hog cholera was the first major epidemic that the BAI had to deal with. In the USDA report, "1000 Years of Animal Health" the following was recorded:

In 1897, the disease was very bad everywhere but especially in southwest Iowa. In response to urgent calls for help, the BAI dispatched a young researcher to test the latest antiserum on herds of Iowa swine. Marion Dorset was a small, gentle man with a limp and an M.D. degree (earned during night classes while employed by the BAI). He knew laboratory work but was completely ignorant of pigs. Dorset was only 23 years old when he arrived at night in

Sydney, Iowa, armed with bottles of serum made in horses. He looked out of his hotel window, then he went downstairs and asked the clerk, "What's the glare of all those fires out over the hills?"

The hotel keeper said, "Them's the fires of dead hogs that farmers can't do nothin' but burn." The next morning, Dr. Dorset set out with his bottles of serum to save the Sydney swine herd. The farmers promptly held up their pigs for free shots of the serum to the "Hog cholera bacillus." Several days later, Dorset returned to check on the results. They had all died, in spite of the shots, on all the farms.

The controversy was finally resolved in BAI laboratories by Emil de Schweinitz, a chemist, and Dorset when they secured a new filter from Pasteur's laboratory capable of retaining bacteria. They found that the hog cholera agent passed through the filter! In 1903, they reported that none of the bacteria championed by earlier investigators was the cause of hog cholera because they had transferred the disease from hog to hog by subcutaneous inoculations of fluids free of all bacteria. Although they could not know it at the time, they had demonstrated one of the first members of a new class of animal pathogens, now called viruses. This was reported the next year in "The Report of the BAI" for 1904; Salmon's name was not included.

Dorset returned to Iowa in 1905 and began working in a small laboratory on the banks of the Skunk River near Ames. Two veterinarians, W. B. Niles and C. M. McBride, assisted him. They had learned that the disease was caused by a filterable agent. By 1906, the BAI knew how to immunize pigs using the serum from recovered pigs and a little of the blood of an acutely ill pig (the virus). The serum was collected from the tail; after the tip was washed and treated with a germicide, it was severed and the blood was collected in a clean dish. When the blood cells were removed, the serum was ready for administration with a syringe.

Vaccination—The next year, over 2,000 pigs in 47 Iowa herds were vaccinated by the serum-virus method. That fall, all of the pigs that were vaccinated before the cholera came, survived the epidemic; but 89 of every 100 nonvaccinated, control pigs died. The results were so exciting that a demonstration of the method was promptly arranged for representatives of all the States of the Union. The method was patented and dedicated to the public; it saved the swine industry at the turn of the century and permitted its growth and technical progress.

The story of the ravages of hog cholera and its control and eventual eradication in 1970 is one of the most dramatic in the history of livestock.

Dr. Frank Mulhern, instrumental in the eradication of hog cholera.

Dr. Frank Mulhern, currently consultant to NPPC in Washington, D.C., played a significant role in the eradication process while employed by the USDA. He is the nation's most experienced animal health official in the area of disease eradication. Dr. Mulhern was responsible for developing the strategy that led to eradicating African Swine Fever in the Dominican Republic and Haiti. Through this process the dreaded disease was prevented from entering the U.S.

The first commercial animal health enterprise was the manufacture of hog cholera vaccine in 1907. Modern technology in animal health was born in an effort to bring this dreaded disease under control.

The discoveries of Louis Pasteur in the 19th Century were the basis of modern medical technology. As the result of his work availability of vaccines helped bring disease under control. The 1920's saw the licensing of clostridium chauvoci bacterin to control black leg in sheep and cattle.

In time the development and licensing of other biologicals followed making it possible to reduce losses by preventative measures.

Before the development of modern veterinary biologicals and pharmaceuticals disease was a natural inhibitor to growth of U.S. livestock and poultry production. The transporting of livestock to feeding areas to gain the efficiencies needed was next to impossible due to the risks of contracting infectious diseases to which they were not immune.

Even up until the 1930's many of the methods of treatment and disease control were crude and bordered on quackery. In the case of cattle to rid a cow of worms called for a dose of chloroform to stun the worms, followed by turpentine to poison them and creosote to force the animal to expel the dead worms. Turpentine was used to treat bloat. Castor oil and opium in alcohol was used for dysentery.

A new era of disease control and the introduction of modern chemical compounds began with the use of sulfonamides in 1939.

Penicillin and its effects on disease causing organisms were being discovered at this time.

Sir Alexander Flemming of England was observing that the growth of bacteria was being inhibited in the presence of molds.

World War II in the early and mid-1940's provided a laboratory for the testing on populations. Bacterial infections in previous wars had take a greater toll than bullets and bombs. Sulfa and penicillin proved to be miracle drugs during this time to control both primary and secondary infections in the wounded.

In a report by Dr. Hilmer Jones, Chairman of the Board of the Animal Health Institute in a keynote speech given at the 1980 annual meeting he said, "The final payoff in the area of antibiotics use for growth stimulants was when the first of the antibiotic feed additives was placed on the market."

The 50's also saw the introduction of the first growth promoting hormones. More than 12,000 feed mills held FDA permits to add it to feed.

The origin of the AHI traces to a meeting in Kansas City in 1941.

Orville K. Sweet

ANIMAL HEALTH INSTITUTE IS BORN

The origin of the Animal Health Institute (AHI) traces to January 1941 when the heads of nine firms met in Kansas City, Missouri to form a cooperative group.

As is the case of most organizations that result from the minds of men of vision they held no limitations in their view of the organization's growth.

They called their first organization "The Animal Serums and Vaccine Association." It actually began as an activist organization at an event in the lobby of the old Muehlbach Hotel in Kansas City.

The motivating factor was an "Amendment 15" passed by Congress to be implemented by the Secretary of USDA. The intent of the rule was to require all manufacturers of biologicals to report to the USDA. The report would include the names and addresses of everyone who bought biologicals. The companies felt this was an infringement on their right to maintain confidentiality with their customers.

They suspected the government officials would use their list of customers for their own personal gain.

As the result of the cooperative effort of the companies involved the Secretary of Agriculture refused to implement the rule.

AHI became one of the first trade associations to focus on regulatory activities and concerns about pending legislation that was harmful to the livestock groups and to their own industry.

Besides the contribution made by member firms in research and development of biologics AHI has been equally effective in influencing reasonable regulations concerning the use of new technology.

Judiciously dealing with federal regulators and influencing change in the agencies themselves has been a key factor in allowing the use of new technology.

In 1965 AHI moved to Washington, D.C. to be in closer contact with federal regulators and legislators who were responsible for creating and regulating any new legislation regarding the use of biologics.

In the 1960's consumer groups became more vocal and a crescendo of activists voices began to rise criticizing the meat industry from the presence of chemical residues in the meat supply to excessive fat and cholesterol. There was an abundance of challenges to hold the organization together and seek the counsel and cooperation of the production segment.

AHI's program initiated in 1968 to promote the proper use of biologics by animal producers was timely. The progress was marked by the "Eye clock" symbol and accompanied by the slogan "take time - read the label."

This program is in part responsible for the USDA's drug monitoring program still in effect today.

PORK PRODUCERS, FIRST TO PROVIDE QUALITY ASSURANCE

The NPPC "Quality Assurance" program endorsed by USDA and popularly acclaimed by allied industry is a proactive program designed to involve producers at the grass roots level.

The Pork Quality Assurance program is a program designed by NPPC to help all producers avoid illegal drug residues, improve management skills, and reduce production costs. The program, when put into practice by the majority of U.S. pork producers, will help the industry protect or even expand its market for pork. This will be accomplished by reducing the risk of incidents that could destroy consumer confidence in pork. Over the next few years, additional materials and programs will be made available to producers utilizing a cooperative system which includes veterinarians, extension, packers, allied industry and youth programs. The educational materials include the following topics: Feed Safety and the Pork Industry; Producer Attitudes; Products Used Today; Routes of Administration; On-Farm Feed Preparation; Minimum Withdrawal Times; Current Regulatory System; On-Farm Testing; Producer Self-Certification.

The program consists now of three levels:

Level I consists of reading a 14 page booklet and enrolling in the program. The booklet puts together residue avoidance management tips from many sources. It leads the reader through the logic of benefits from having an attitude of a food producer rather than just a hog feeder. The Level I booklets are widely distributed. Enrollment consists of sending a postcard to NPPC.

Level II booklet is sent to people who have enrolled. It is a self-test manual designed to stimulate thought and to teach the basics of residue avoidance.

Level III is additional educational materials but also directs producers to take action. Three activities are outlined: A facilities and management checklist, testing of pigs to check for residues, and a written exam for producers. These are to be discussed by the producer and an ag-professional such as a veterinarian, to formulate any corrective strategies.

The Pork Quality Assurance Program is a classic case of a producer funded program whose benefits will be enjoyed by consumers and producers.

BIOTECHNOLOGY – A NEW GENERATION OF PHARMACEUTICALS

"This buzz word of the '90's has drawn the curtain on the 21st Century and exposed a new field of science that will provide the consumer with higher quality food at lower cost."

Until recently the development of new pharmaceutical products was the result of trial and error. The wonder drugs of the World War II era were the fortunate results of chance discovery. The family of sulfa drugs and penicillin were all accidental discoveries.

Fifty years ago scientists laboriously screened thousands of compounds hoping to discover the next generation of wonder drugs.

There has been considerable interrelationship between animal and human research. Because research is costly most research funds have been used to search for solutions to human health problems.

According to the Animal Health Institute "All this is changing in large part because of biotechnology. Scientists now have remarkable new tools for understanding disease and developing rational new approaches to treatment."

Animal scientists now have a much better understanding of the physiology of various species.

Obviously animal drugs will be better designed to meet specific needs of different species tomorrow. The quality of technology of animal health today is a far cry from the quackery of 60 years ago.

The challenge for the future is to utilize biotechnology to augment the immense system and reduce losses from a number of reoccurring and chronic diseases. Shipping fever in cattle, intestinal infection in calves and pigs and swine pseudo rabies, just to mention a few that cause hundreds of millions of dollars in animal losses. These may be reduced through the application of biotechnology.

Diagnostic techniques have been greatly enhanced through the application of biotechnology. Veterinarians will be able to diagnose disease more accurately and quickly.

The most exciting development in biotechnology and the most controversial is the use of recombinant DNA to enhance growth.

According to the Animal Health Institute "Porcine Somatotropin (PST) improves feed efficiency by 15 to 20%. It also reduces fat deposition. Reports that PST has increased the lean content of pork carcasses by 35% are not uncommon.

It is unfortunate that consumer activists have targeted growth enhancers as a threat to human health. The introduction of bovine somatotropin in the mid-1980's as a stimulant to milk production has created a serious image problem for the use of new technology in general.

Although the Food and Drug Administration has approved the use of somatotrophin the activists have struggled to create a socioeconomic problem from the issue.

It is only a matter of time, however, when the use of these technologies will be accepted. Recorded history verifies many instances when new and useful technologies were delayed in acceptance due to resistance to change. When proven effective and economically feasible in almost every instance new technology has been adopted as a matter of course.

Part 9

FEED MANUFACTURERS

Feed for livestock is the single most critical factor in profitability to pork producers.

Profitability not only depends on the cost per unit but the quality, nutritional value, and balance of nutrients.

During the first half of the 20th Century more was learned about nutrient value of various feeds than in all previous history combined.

Today our knowledge of feeding and nutrition has reached a state of art and skill never dreamed of in the past.

Nutrition researchers in academia and private sector have teamed up with allied industry to answer questions that have been on the minds of livestock producers for centuries.

A great deal of credit is given to the feed manufacturer. He combines new technology with his capability to benefit from economies of scale to producer a balanced nutritional product conveniently packaged or handled in bulk form at a reasonable cost.

The American Feed Manufacturers Association, (now American Feed Industry Institute) was formed

75 years ago. Like other trade associations it was a threat of government regulations that was the catalyst bringing the feed companies together in Chicago March 26, 1909.

The federal government was considering passing a national feed law. Feed laws were already on the books in about 30 states.

According to a report by Oakley Ray, AFMA President, entitled "First Seventy-five Years", the critical issue which provided the incentive for establishing the organization 80 years ago still exists. The struggle to maintain uniform state and federal standards. The need for labeling uniformity and acceptance of comparative values across state lines is crucial.

Some of the earliest feed manufacturers*:

1875-Blatchfords of Waukegan, Illinois may have been the first feed manufacturing firm in the United States.

1885-The Tom Moorman family of Big Spring, Kentucky began manufacturing a simple hog product which was the beginning of the Moorman Manufacturing Company. Ingredients were ground in a coffee grinder and mixed with shovels.

1885-The National Food Company of Fond du Lac, Wisconsin.

1891-The American Cereal Company, forerunner of the Quaker Oats Company.

1892-Valley City Milling Company, Portland, Michigan

1894-Ralston Purina Company was founded as the Robinson-Danforth Commission Company. The Checkerboard trademark was copy-righted in 1900.

1895-Albers Milling Company, founded by Bernard Albers at Seattle, Washington.

1898-The American Milling Company was formed through consolidation with another firm. Allied Mills, Inc. was formed in 1929.

1898-Uncle Johnny Mills got its start as South Texas Grain Co.

1898-Aubrey and Company of Louisville, Kentucky.

The feed industry came into existence as a source of utilizing by-products.

New assaying methods soon determined the by-products of corn and wheat to be an excellent source of protein, minerals and vitamins. While different animals varied in their protein requirements depending on their function. Protein was discovered as

a limiting factor in the production of meat, milk, and eggs. This knowledge enhanced the value of these protein rich by-products.

The need to process and mix these by-products with other feed ingredients provided a reason and motive to establish the feed firms and a new industry.

The earliest feed manufacturers ground and mixed feed for the livery stables that boarded the thousands of horses and mules. Very little scientific formulation of feeds was done at this early stage.

According to Oakley Ray's report, "The pioneers in animal science and nutrition laid the real foundation for feed manufacturing when they began their momentous work of developing feed standards."

From 1920 to 1940 a great deal was learned about nutrition and much progress occurred in care and feeding of farm animals.

Trained animal nutritionists were entering the feed manufacturing industry. The practical application of research as well as improved methods were being applied on research farms.

There was a continuous increase in the knowledge level of essential nutrients and their source and application in rations.

New equipment was created and improved. Hammer mills, mixers, rollers and flakers all became a part of a modern feed industry. The contrast between the equipment to condition feed was a far cry from the tools available to Mr. Danforth's scoop shovel used to mix his first batch of feed that gave birth to the giant Purina Mills in 1894.

Kansas State University has been the beneficiary of generous endowments from the feed industry. More that a million dollars has been contributed to fund the purchase of equipment to teach students the techniques of feed manufacturing. In return, Kansas State has trained and provided the feed industry with a number of quality leaders in the research and application of new technology.

FEED ADDITIVES

Adding medication to feeds has opened up a whole new dimension for the feed industry. It has also created a number of problems.

The first of the antibiotics to be added was sulfaquinoxaline to poultry rations to control coccidiosis. The control of coccidiosis that had long been a plague on the poultry industry made it possible to place birds in more highly confined areas.

The addition of synthetic vitamin B12 was recognized as a major break through. Here was a non-animal source of B12 that promoted growth even better

---

*Primary Source: Feed Production Handbook, Chapter 1, by Dr. Robert Schoeff, Kansas State University, 1961.

than the original sources. Scientists discovered the process also developed antibiotics that promoted growth.

Shortly a whole new vocabulary was needed in the feed industry to cope with the new antibiotics to be added to formulated feeds.

Computerized feed formulation was just around the corner and when it arrived it made the greatest contribution in efficient feed manufacturing.

The feed industry has been confronted with every imaginable issue that threatened to hamper its progress. Most of the issues were created by government. Fluctuating feed supplies, embargoes on imported feed sources, heavy handed regulations related to feed ingredients, shifting regulations, banning antibiotics and other additives all are issues that can have a disastrous effect of the profitability and viability of the modern feed manufacturers.

The trend since World War II has been to decentralize production facilities building smaller, highly automated, more efficient plants located in the area where the feed will be consumed. For 25 years prior to this time the trend was toward larger and larger plants, usually located on a railroad, using in-transit milling privileges, and frequently shipping the finished feed a long distance. Improved major and secondary roads, along with better trucks, contributed much to the switch from rail transportation of formula feed. Today most formula feed is shipped from the feed mill by truck. Much of the large volume feed ingredients such as corn and soybean meal continues to be shipped by rail.

Many changes have been made to improve the production capabilities of animals and poultry. Advances in genetics and management practices have helped improve production. Without the industry's aid, these advances could not have been made.

The feed industry has helped livestock and poultry farmers hold down unit costs by improving management and feed conversion rations. In the end, although the feed industry and farmers have gained the greatest benefit has been to the consumer with lower food costs and higher quality meat, milk and eggs.

One must give the American Feed Industry Institute high marks for its performance over the years as a trade association and for the professional contribution its members have made to the pork industry.

Part 10

THE ROLE OF ASSOCIATIONS AND THEIR IMPACT ON THE PORK INDUSTRY

AGRICULTURAL TRADE ASSOCIATIONS

L. Hand, in his book "The use of History," wrote: "Each generation must decide itself how far it will seek refuge in eternal and immutable verities rather than grope its way through the tangle of human passions and human credulity." The history of associations is an interesting scenario of the human struggle to seek truth and create opportunity by combining the resources of individuals who have a common cause.

Organizations and/or associations are formed when two or more people decide collectively they can achieve goals that would be more difficult or unachievable individually.

The desired goals may be social, spiritual, economic, military or simply survival under stress.

Man's desire to organize and form associations can be traced to his earliest recorded history. The family is the first response by man to the need for association. Guilds of medieval times followed a few centuries later bringing together makers of specific products.

The earliest agricultural organizations not only provided a means to exchange information but filled a critical social need in rural areas before the development of towns, cities, and the urban sprawl. Transportation was difficult and opportunities for social interaction was non-existent.

The rapid increase in numbers of agricultural organizations in the 20th Century is in response to the accelerated rate of change in the environment of production agriculture. The increasing influence of public policy on production, processing and marketing of farm products has provoked a collective response from the farm sector.

General farm organizations appeared to be adequate through the first half of the 20th Century. The rush of new technology, however, brought on specialization and unique problems to each commodity. Thus the origin and growth of special commodity groups like the NPPC.

Although not frequently recognized today the need for social and interpersonal activity is still a driving force especially in the motivation of leadership.

THE ORIGIN OF ASSOCIATIONS

Guilds of medieval times have some of the characteristics of business associations and thus can be considered the genesis of today's business association. George Webster, in his book, "The Laws of Associations," states:

> The guild system, particularly strong in England during the period 1100-1500, had a number of functional structures. Two of these were the merchant guild, which consisted of buyers and sellers of goods; and the craft guild, which consisted of producers.

Merchant Guilds were of many types, depending on the product bought or sold. Eventually, they became the ruling bodies of the town that they represented.

Craft Guilds were also of different types, such as fletchers (makers of arrows) and white towners (leather workers). Each craft guild consisted of master, journeymen and apprentices. Craft guilds restricted the activities of their members. Shoemakers could not tan hides, barbers could not be surgeons, and weavers could not do any dying. The early guilds exhibit many attributes of the 20th Century workers unions.

Although there has been an almost continuous line of guild-type associations since that early period, we should keep in mind that business and professional associations as we know them are essentially a product of recent years. According to George Webster, their activity since World War II is substantially different and expanded from that of early dates. In addition, their relevance and significance to our economy is constantly increasing.

THE CHANGING ROLE OF ASSOCIATIONS

The changing role of the association has as interesting a history as does their rise and growth in numbers. Early guilds not only defined and specified the functions of worker classes, but also assumed other duties such as aiding their sick and the families of imprisoned members. However, their main objective was to standardize the quality of products and establish a fair price.

Today, we observe an increasing role for associations to protect their members from adverse public policy and the progressive encroachment of federal regulatory agencies.

Agriculture is more frequently being challenged by consumer groups and confronted with consumer legislation. Its enforcement by various agencies and departments of government can best be met through coordinated efforts of the industry through its trade association.

The modern trade association is industry's response to the changing environment.

THE GROWTH OF ASSOCIATIONS

In the United States alone, there are now more than a half million associations of various types and sizes. They range from local and county associations serving a few members to national organizations boasting hundreds of thousands of members.

Some business associations were formed in the 18th Century. The oldest society of businessmen in the U.S. is the New York Stock Exchange established in 1792; the National Association of Cotton Manufacturers was established in 1854.

THE LIFE CYCLE OF ASSOCIATIONS

An association decays when leaders lose sight of their dream and its individuals lose their vitality.

Recently, a government official describing an old line government agency said, "It doesn't get much public attention and it has gone quietly to sleep. When there is a change of administration, it stirs fitfully, but doesn't wake up."

John Gardner, Author of "Common Cause", writes:

"Every businessman knows of some firms that are 'on their toes' and others that are 'in a rut.' Every university president recognizes that some academic departments are enjoying exceptional vitality while others have gone to seed.

"What are the factors that account for such differences? It is a question that has never been examined systematically. Closer study will reveal that in all examples given, the same processes are at work. They are processes involved in the rise and fall of human institutions. Rome falling to the barbarians, an old family firm going into bankruptcy, and a government agency quietly strangling in its own red tape have more in common than one might suppose." (John

Gardner, Secretary of Health, Education and Welfare; 1960-1964, Founder of Common Cause.)

We rarely think of associations as having a traceable life cycle. They do, however, have a beginning or a birth which is brought about by a specific need to solve a particular problem.

It requires a number of elements to create a successful organization, not the least of which is emotion, enthusiasm and commitment.

The developmental stages of associations may vary in intensity and length of time but they are, for the most part, very similar in their genesis and growth pattern.

All associations have their origin in the dream stage, when one person or a few persons theorize that getting organized is the feasible approach to meeting a need or solving a problem. Beliefs must then be agreed upon and become solidified.

The early believers recruit others who recruit still others in a chain reaction, all of which serves to strengthen the resolve of the early converts. Organization gradually begins to take place in the form of goals and plans.

Structure develops and takes on a traditional form. The organization now has funds and provides services to its members. The functions are expanded and, in time, grow beyond the original intent. The charter members have long since lost control, and may have been forgotten, along with the cause to which the originators were committed.

At some point in the service stage, the organization progresses to its farthest point from the original dream. At this stage there is a loss of the pioneer spirit, the original dream forgotten, and nostalgia may set in. The members may begin to dwell on the "good ole days" of the past. Their attention is diverted from the challenges of the future. The typical characteristics of old age are now obvious. There may be a period of questioning; a questioning of leadership, questioning the effectiveness of the association, and even questioning the need for the organization itself.

Next, a time of polarization may occur, with members taking sides on various issues, thus creating discord, disagreement and apathy. In the final state, a number of dropouts will occur.

An association may drift indefinitely in any particular stage, but continue for lengthy period because leaders may be reluctant to relinquish their position and turn leadership over to others.

There is no average life span for associations. In a special study, a religious group found that for its particular type of organization, the average life of a church was 70 years from dream to drop out. It may be surprising to find that several types of organizations may have a similar life span. There are many centennials celebrated, but a careful study will indicate that a great number of associations are in the dream loss to drop out stages, and are reluctant to accept that fact.

The life cycles of organizations can be altered at any stage by implementing certain "life renewing" activities.

In the ever renewing society, what matures is a system or framework within which continuous innovation, renewal and rebirth occur.

Leadership is the key to developing renewable capabilities of the association. Creative leaders with the talent and ability to innovate in the face of rapid change can insure the long productive life span of an association.

Trade associations likewise have their more specialized services designed to enhance the competitive position of the commodity or service produced by its membership.

The technology that has brought the blessings of abundant food to mankind in a large part can be attributed to the existence of associations.

The super market is a modern marvel. It displays more than 20,000 food items, produced all over the world, processed in every foreign country, and brought together in one location. Even more amazing is that it is fresh, wholesome, and in most cases reasonably priced.

Clearly voluntary organizations are an important part of what makes America run.

STRUCTURE AND FUNCTION OF NPPC

The value of cooperative effort was realized by pork producers while our country was still young. Breed associations had their origin in the mid-1800's and were responsible for the changes in hog types as economic need changed.

During periods of war demand for fat increased to produce explosives thus type changes from lean type to lard type hogs. This happened during the Civil War, World War I and World War II. In World War II housewives were encouraged to accumulate fat drippings in containers and turn it into the government. After the war demand for bacon encouraged the production of leaner hogs. This shift in demand not only attested to the genetic flexibility of the hog but the innovation of the pork producers to change when demand shifted.

The broad general purpose of all associations is to create a system for communication and a means of putting together resources for collective action.

The pork industry showed little signs of organizing itself into a viable association until the late 1930's when the Iowa pork producers developed the first state association.

The motivation to organize at that time was to provide a forum to discuss production technology and to influence public policy.

Other states followed Iowa. By the early 1950's there were associations in Illinois, Minnesota, Nebraska, Missouri and North Carolina. In most other states pork producers were involved in state livestock associations but few were specialized pork groups.

Pork production was and still is predominantly located in the Midwest. The 10 leading states in terms of annual production are located in the Midwest with exception of North Carolina that ranks in the first seven.

The leading states are as follows:

**TEN LEADING STATES
DECEMBER 1987**

RANK	STATE	HEAD (000)
1	Iowa	13,800
2	Illinois	5,300
3	Indiana	4,600
4	Minnesota	4,350
5	Nebraska	4,000
6	Missouri	2,950
7	North Carolina	2,500
8	Ohio	2,150
9	South Dakota	1,520
10	Kansas	1,450

A number of the early leaders of the pork industry were members and leaders of the American Farm Bureau Federation (AFBF). Their experience with the AFBF had a strong influence on the leaders who laid the foundation for the National Pork Organization and that basic structure still stands.

Great care was exercised to provide a strong grass roots orientation for pork producers. A delegate system of representation was established to allow for the voices of producers at the local level to be heard and to have influence on association policy.

Although it is never referred to as such NPPC is actually a federation of state associations and its producer members are members of the state organizations. This is NPPC's most basic similarity to the AFBF. It departs from the AFBF, however, in the manner of representation.

NPPC MISSION
"To enhance the producer's opportunity for profit."

Representation in a delegate body is dependent upon the states market share. Market share is determined by the amount of revenue the state generates from sale of hogs in the form of checkoff.

Each $1,000 checkoff collected within a 12 month period earns a state member one share. Shares are translated into delegates as follows: 1-300 shares, two delegates; 301-600 shares, four delegates. Over 1,000 shares, one delegate for every 300 additional shares. There is a minimum of two delegates per state and the total number of delegates shall not exceed 150.

Each state is eligible to elect one member to the National Board of Directors. The function of the board is to advise and consult with the executive committee and provide a communication line to the state officers and the membership from the national office.

The Board of Directors also provides the body from which the delegates elect the 12-man executive committee.

The executive committee is the managing body between annual delegate meetings. It has full au-

NPPC delegates meet in formal session annually to represent home constituents.

thority to make policy decisions between annual meetings, however, the delegates may rescind executive committee action by resolution and following due process as outlined in the by-laws.

The Executive Committee is the fiduciary body for the NPPC and is responsible for all accounting systems.

The Executive Committee in its organizational meeting after the delegate session at which they are elected proceeds to elect its new officers consisting of a president, president elect, and a vice president, each to serve one year terms.

The system allows for a leader training process at the local and state level. After a few years those with leader capability and who receive recognition in their performance may be elected to a national responsibility. Outstanding leaders are developed through this process.

In the development of the Pork Act in 1985 a provision was made for similar representation. The Pork Act development is covered later in the Story of Pork. To mention it here, however, is appropriate because of its impact and placement in the pork organizational structure.

Orville K. Sweet

Section II

PORK ORGANIZATIONS—1940-1970

By Pig Paul

Foreword

This is the work of Rolland Paul, executive vice-president of National Pork Producers Council from 1966 to 1969, who is known throughout the pork industry as Pig Paul. He acquired the nickname in the hospital where he was born. While many babies wouldn't nurse, he took right off nursing and the country doctor said he nursed like a little pig. When the doctor returned to his mother's room he asked how the little pig was doing. The nickname stuck—he was pig from then on. A story written about him after he became involved in pork association work noted: "A man who carries the nickname 'Pig' all his life and does it with pride, can't be all bad."

Pig was raised on a farm near Dallas Center, IA, and graduated from Iowa State University where he lived and worked in the hog barn for several years. He joined the Iowa Swine Producers Association as fieldman in 1957 and while holding that position, served as secretary-treasurer for the National Swine Growers Council. He left the Iowa group to become the first full-time executive of the Council. During his term as executive vice-president, the Council grew into the largest dues-paying commodity group in the country and the Nickels for Profit voluntary checkoff program, which was started during his tenure as executive vice-president, became the largest voluntary market deduction program by a commodity group.

After leaving the Council, Pig and his wife, Donna, and their family moved to Willow Springs, MO, to raise purebred hogs. He is currently in partnership with his son-in-law, Howard McNew, in a purebred hog farm called Pork Plantation.

Acknowledgment

It's been an honor to record the history of the National Swine Growers (Pork Producers) Council. Those were very interesting years, sometimes fast-moving, facing one crisis after another. At other times the organization was almost dormant, while re-grouping for the next challenge.

The group of industry leaders who held this organization together in the days before checkoff funding will never be excelled for their determination and dedication to the cause. They served with very little recognition, paying their own expenses, but always finding the time and money to fight the next battle. I dedicate this section to those people, many of whom have gone on to their reward.

I have recognized many leaders for their contributions and I have missed recognizing many, for which I apologize, but you know who they were and that's what is important.

In the early years, with no full-time staff and no permanent home, some of the records were either misplaced, or just plain lost. The leaders of that period were often too busy fighting the battles to keep very good records. So this is the most complete record ever assembled of those early years.

Many people helped me with information, but I wish to give special thanks and recognition to the following for their help, tolerance and patience:

Keith Myers for sharing his records and those of Gene Smith, and for the many hours he spent reminiscing and advising me.

NPPC and Iowa Pork Producers for researching files and minutes to find documents and verify dates.

National Hog Farmer for allowing me to go through back issues and then supplying copies of important information.

I am the author and researcher, but Neal Black has been the writer. Neal has taken my scribbled notes, tapes and telephone conversations and organized them so they make sense. Without his knowledge of the industry and writing ability, this would not have been possible.

Chapter 1

Moline Meeting

"We've been going to meetings for years, talking about problems and what we should do, and for years the story has been the same. When we go home, nothing happens … Let's make this meeting count. All of us are busy on our farms and there are many things we can't do from our homes. If we do the same thing again—go home and hope someone else will do the work, this will have been just another meeting."

That was Roy Keppy, a Davenport, IA, pork producer who was well known in the industry as an exhibitor of champion barrows and later as a leader in producer organizations at the state and national level, speaking to a meeting of pork producers May 25, 1966, at the Holiday Inn near the airport at Moline, IL, a meeting which has come to be widely known simply as "The Moline Meeting."

Roy went on to say, "It's time to stand up and be counted if we want to make this meeting count for something. We all took time out of the busiest time of the year to come here. Let's build a Get-Ready Fund, put a full-time executive secretary to work helping keep our efforts going this summer and fall. Let's get organized and keep moving. We've proven for more than 10 years that we can't do this job without hiring the help we need."

Enthusiasm was generated for calling that Moline meeting by a number of events: the first legislative checkoffs in North Carolina and Virginia; a Wisconsin checkoff proposal that was stymied before it got into action; revision of the P&S Act in '63 that made a voluntary checkoff possible, removing a long-standing roadblock to that avenue to funding. Also, Iowa had made several attempts at passage of a red meat checkoff bill, including a proposal in '65 of a 5-cent checkoff to finance a disease research facility. This also ran into complications. In January of '66 Iowa pork producers decided to raise $80,000 in donations to prove that there was a need for additional swine disease research at Iowa State University and to demonstrate that if producers had an opportunity, they were willing to donate to such an effort. They raised more than $80,000. That successful effort built confidence that funds could be raised from producers on a voluntary basis.

In March of '66 a series called "Blueprint for Decision" began in National Hog Farmer magazine. More details on the series are contained in the chapter on that subject. The climax of the series was to be a poll of pork producers on their views on promotion—what was needed, who should do it and who should control it. The Moline meeting was called to develop the questionnaire for that poll, but it turned out to be much more than that.

About 90 people attended the Moline meeting. There was a bus load from Nebraska, a small plane load from Kansas, many from Illinois and Iowa. In the years since, hundreds of people have recalled they attended, but there were only 90 in attendance and there is no official record of who was there. Things moved so fast no one thought to pass around a sign-up sheet.

The first part of the meeting concerned what needed to be done, what was going on and discussion of the first two articles of the Blueprint series. A major topic was how to encourage participation in the poll, how to distribute the poll so, for the first time, there would be a real canvas of producers to learn what they really wanted to do, what their priorities on programs were and how to fund a national program.

At the noon luncheon break the National Swine Growers Council (NSGC) executive committee met, unanimously endorsed the effort and agreed to sponsor the poll and help distribute it through member organizations. The plan was to contact at least 50,000 producers across the country during September, October and November.

Those attending the meeting—10 states were represented—started making commitments of funds. They knew it would take money to get the project off the ground. There were several great off-the-cuff speeches including the one by Keppy. Within half an hour, after two or three other speeches, 16 producers had written checks for $100, other $100 pledges had been made, five breed secretaries in attendance had contributed $1,000 from a dormant fund within their group; the total came to almost $3,000.

To people who worried aloud how anything could be done, Jiggs Sandidge, Missouri producer, made what I call his famous "Let's put on our walking shoes and start walking" speech. "If we want to get somewhere and don't have any other way of getting there, just put on our old walking shoes and start walking. That's the only way we're going to get there."

It's been a common misconception in later years that the Moline meeting was the start of formal pork producer organization at the national level. It very well may be considered the start of an adequately funded national pork producer organization, but that misconception does a disservice to the diligence, hard work and dedication of early leaders, who built the framework for the later well-funded national organization, while creating early organizations which had an impact and influence far behind their financial and personnel resources.

Chapter 2

Early Years

The first national pork producer organization for which any records can be found was American Pork Producers Associated, which existed in the early 1940's. Reference to this organization can be found in the minutes of the Iowa Swine Producers Association for April 27, 1940. When the matter of affiliating the Iowa group with the national organization came up, I. J. Conrad offered the opinion that if the hog men were ever to have a national pork producers association it should be set up by the various state associations. This view prevailed for many years in the industry. Conrad went on to state: "This proposed organization has been built from the top down, when it should have been started from the bottom. It is not a true representation of pork producers." He suggested that if the Iowa Swine Producers Association joined American Pork Producers Associated, the swine producers would not be represented on a fair basis. He also noted that Iowa would probably not have representation in the proposed national group proportional to its share of national hog production.

How was this organization to be financed? The records aren't very clear but it appears the purebred associations put in some original money and the rest was to come from a checkoff, the first recorded mention of a financing device which was to be the subject of discussion for decades in the industry. The Iowa minutes indicate: "President Morrissey (president of the Iowa Swine Producers) read a letter he received from the secretary of the Hampshire association, that they were going to collect 5 cents per head on all hogs for advertising purposes in regard to pork and pork products and the name of this organization would be American Pork Producers Associated." One of the Iowans commented at that meeting that it was his impression the deduction was to be made by the packers and he doubted they would do it.

The Iowa president did not want to join and support the organization. He was acquainted with the fact that a big advertising agency furnished most of the money to start it. There was a great deal of discussion in these early Iowa minutes. One man said it was only a skeleton of an organization. He did not think it was an organization that the pork people should join and the association should be set up right if it was going to attract pork producers.

The first time I ran across American Pork Producers Associated was in the income account in 1954 of the new National Swine Growers Council. The funds, a total of $254.79, left over from that organization, were transferred to NSGC. I was informed that the records of the American Pork Producers—it appeared to have lasted about a year and a half or two years—were stored in the basement of the Duroc Association in Peoria, IL, where Bing Evans, former Duroc secretary, had left them.

Organizers of the group were E. M. Harsh, secretary of the Hampshire Registry Association; B. R. Evans, secretary of the United Duroc Record Association; George W. Davies, secretary of the American Poland China Record Association and F. G. Ketner, C. W. Mitchell and R. C. Henry, who were listed as representing the National Swine Growers' Association (no information on that organization). C. W. Mitchell was later a purebred breed secretary.

It was noted at the Iowa meeting that the American Meat Institute, the packer trade association, was "not too friendly" toward the new group.

It's interesting that the fieldman for the Iowa Swine Producers in 1940 was Rollie Pemberton, and a producer named Wilbur Plager served on the board of directors. These two had a great impact on the meat-type hog effort later and Wilbur was first president of National Swine Growers Council.

The minutes for '40 and '41 of the Iowa association indicate that lard was quite a problem. Most promotion efforts involved lard. One of the big challenges for packers was to produce a uniform standard for lard. Most of the packers had signed up to do that. Competition was coming from the vegetable oils. They were talking about cottonseed oil, which was cheap and off color. Lard was being shoved aside and there was page after page of minutes devoted to reports on surveys of high school home economics classes that found they were using vegetable oil instead of lard, causing quite a commotion. The vegetable oil people were giving the high schools product to use—this was in the early 40's remember—and they were shoving lard out.

There was a note in the Iowa minutes that the soybean industry was definitely an up-and-coming industry and it was thought the vegetable oil people would have to increase prices because soy oil was gradually taking the place of cottonseed oil. As a matter of caution, it was suggested that it would be a good idea to blend soybean oil with lard. This wasn't very well accepted by the swine producers; they didn't want anything added to lard to help it move.

At that time the home economics department at Iowa State was part of the College of Agriculture. The swine producers suggested to Dean Kildee, head of the college of agriculture, that the college develop and send to all home economics teachers in Iowa schools a brochure on the benefits of lard over vegetable oil. Several home economics professors at ISU were called on the carpet for pointing out that vegetable oil might be superior to lard for some uses.

Even with the emphasis on lard before World War II, there was interest in the meat-type hog. The Iowa Swine Producers Association, under the leadership of Rollie Pemberton, who was later to become one of the leaders of the meat hog certification program as secretary of the Hampshire Association, was holding carcass demonstrations around the state during 1940-41. But World War II came along, demand for lard increased and the fat pig was saved for another 10 years.

After that abortive attempt at a national organization, it wasn't until 1954 that the idea surfaced again.

Keith Myers, who was involved in formation of the new group and was later to serve in a number of leadership rolls, recalls that Wilbur Plager led the charge to create the new national group because he was dissatisfied with activities of the National Live Stock and Meat Board. "A strong-headed German by the name of Wilbur Plager wanted a national organization so he could get on the Meat Board and 'straighten out those SOB's,' and also to serve as a platform to 'straighten out' the president of the American Farm Bureau." Wilbur thought Charley Shuman, then president of AFBF, needed help and Wilbur was never bashful about offering advice to anyone he thought needed it.

The first meeting "to discuss the possibility and feasibility of organizing the state swine associations into a national organizations" was held in Chicago,

July 1-3, 1954. The meeting was called by Bob Parkison, president of the Indiana Association and Wilbur L. Plager, field secretary of the Iowa Swine Producers' Association.

In attendance were Harry Russell of U. of Illinois, L. A. (Dutch) Johnson, president of Illinois Swine Improvement Association; Charles Maas, president of the Wisconsin Swine Breeders Association; Harold Marquardt of the U. of Wisconsin; J. A. Hoefer of Michigan State; E. C. Miller of Purdue; Richard F. Wilson of Ohio State; Robert Shannon of the Ohio Producers Livestock Cooperative; Willard D. Brittin and C. W. Mitchell of the National Association of Swine Records; Fred Beard of USDA, and from the Iowa Swine Producers' Association: Marion Steddom, president, Bernard Collins, vice president, Tom Manley, secretary, Keith Myers, treasurer and Wilbur Plager. Approved was the concept that the national association be composed of state associations and that only one state association representative have the right to vote. The name National Swine Council was proposed. A committee was named to develop suggested constitution and by-laws and a second meeting was planned during the International Livestock Exposition in Chicago.

The committee to develop a preliminary constitution and by-laws met during the National Barrow Show in Austin, MN, Sept. 16, 1954, with Maas as chairman. It was agreed that each state have two delegates to the organizational meeting later in the year and that one of them should be a commercial swine producer, plus two delegates from the National Association of Swine Records. Steddom moved that the name be National Swine Growers Council and the committee approved. Bob Parkison served as secretary of that session. Myers moved a fund of $1,000 be raised to start the organization the first year.

The minutes of the organizational meeting Dec. 1, 1954, have been lost. Elected to head the fledgling organization were Plager, president; Mass, vice president, and Parkison, secretary-treasurer.

The first meeting of the executive committee was April 28-29, 1955, in Chicago. Members present were Plager, Maas, Johnson and Parkison. Albert Koller of Parker, SD, was unable to be present.

The treasurer reported that $832 had been received, including $171.50 from individual producers, the rest from assessments to state organizations. The committee agreed that the Council would not solicit individual memberships from producers. Organization down to county level was suggested and it was noted that Iowa county associations had been providing lard for home economics departments in local schools "so tomorrow's cooks will have the opportunity to know how good lard is."

Carl Neumann, secretary of the National Live Stock and Meat Board, reviewed pork promotion efforts by that group. The executive committee praised the efforts of that group.

The following committees were appointed:

Swine Disease Control—Dr. Maynard Spear, Iowa State University; Dr. L. M. Hutchings, Purdue; Dr. Sam McNutt, U. of Wisconsin; Ralph Waltz, Hagerston, IN; Stuart Miller, Forrest, IL; E. C. Miller, Michigan State University.

Meat-Type Hog Education—Herb Barnes, Ohio State; Willard Brittin, purebred secretary; Dick Cummins, marketing from Indianapolis; Dean Snyder, Good Hope, IL; Harry Russell, U. of Illinois; Bob Grummer, U. of Wisconsin; Bernard Ebbing, Rath Packing Co., Waterloo, IA; Jim Hillier, Oklahoma State U.

Pork Promotion—Dutch Johnson; Marion Steddom; Harold Hart, Columbus, OH; Bill Rothenberger, Frankfort, IN; Robert Thayer, U. of Wisconsin; Bill Palmer, Parma, MI; C. W. Myers, Blue Earth, MN; Guy McReynolds, Ashland, NE; Jack Kroeck, Jefferson City, MO; Laverne Kortan, S. Dakota State; C. W. Mitchell, breed secretary, Galesburg, IL.

Among those committee members were many of the future leaders of the industry, in terms of organizational activity, the meat-type hog effort, disease control and eradication.

The executive committee members were guests for luncheon of the American Meat Institute, the packer trade association. Dues assigned for 1955-56 ranged from Iowa's $283 to a minimum of $20, with 26 states listed.

The first annual meeting of NSGC was Nov. 27, 1955 in Chicago. Barnes reported for the meat type hog committee that Ebbing and Carroll Plager of Geo. A. Hormel, Austin, MN, were ready to move ahead on a set of educational slides. Iowa pork lifts were reported, an attempt to reduce burdensome supplies of pork which had resulted in the low hog prices of the period.

The first mention of Dr. Ralph Durham of Iowa State University, the developer and promoter of the backfat probe, could be found in the minutes.

NSGC issued recommendations for promotion projects which emphasized activities by local groups and Plager, in his annual report as president, suggested a 5 cent per hog checkoff for use in promoting pork.

The executive committee elected at the annual meeting in '55 included Plager, president; Parkison, secretary-treasurer; Maas, vice president; Albert Koller, Richard Wilson of Ohio State, Dutch Johnson and Ed Miller of Michigan State.

That was an outstanding group of committees, Keith Myers recalls. "They had no funds, no expense accounts, yet they met and prepared some very good material that achieved widespread distribution. The meat-type hog committee prepared a monthly report that was published for a number of years in National Hog Farmer. As early as the annual meeting in 1955, they were giving quite lengthy reports at the annual meeting.

The budget of $1,000 was raised by Oct. 31 of that first year. Those were not industry funds, all came from individual producers or state producer organizations.

Myers is quoted in the 1955 minutes: "Hog producers appreciate the roles of other segments of the livestock economy." He urged a study of the possibility of a checkoff and that the executive committee undertake this study. These are the first official mentions of a checkoff in NSGC minutes.

At a meeting of the executive committee a program of work for 1956-57 was developed, based on the assumption that a national checkoff was a certainty in the near future. Parkison pointed out at that meeting that some critics of the Council suggested that some of the leaders were thinking of "big-paying" jobs and suggested a declaration by all the executive committee that none of them would except such a post. The minutes don't show approval of that suggestion, but none of those executive committee members ever got rich from any national checkoff.

At the close of that meeting Rex Coleman was appointed to pass the hat to obtain donations for the purchase of a pig to be sent to President Eisenhower. There was no report of how much was collected. NSGC bought the 4-H champion at the International Livestock Exposition and Myers recalls that the Yorkshire association came up with whatever additional funds were needed.

Press reports on the '55 annual meeting showed 14 state associations had joined the Council and contributed to the '54-55 budget. A mailing list of leaders contained 1,000 names. The Council was represented at a Swine Industry Conference planning session by Wilbur Plager (see separate chapter on that institution).

The Council named its first representative to the board of directors of the National Live Stock and Meat Board, Wilbur Plager, so he accomplished one of his objectives in starting the organization. He was also named to the board of Livestock Conservation Incorporated (LCI).

In March '56 a plan for a national pork promotion campaign was starting to take shape. This program had a couple of different names over the next few years, but it was the first of many promotion efforts by the national and state organizations.

Also in early 1956, NSGC met with the provisions (pork) committee of the American Meat Institute and asked for a closer trim on pork products, which was approved by the executive committee of the AMI. Both the National Live Stock and Meat Board and the AMI were conducting in-store pork promotions during that period.

The NSGC during these years was making an impact on the meat industry far beyond its numbers and financial strength. This was due to the dedication of a handfull of industry leaders, spending their own money and furnishing their time to lay the groundwork for the organized industry of today. It is unbelievable how little producer financial support NSGC received. The total annual revenues wouldn't even finance a meeting of the board of directors in later years. One of the main thrusts of NSGC continued to be toward a national meat promotion program with strong emphasis that the producer "and not the packer" or market people were to pay the bills.

At the annual meeting in 1956 James B. Nance of Alamo, TN, was introduced as chairman of the legislative committee of the National Livestock Promotion Committee. He discussed the possibility of a checkoff on red meat animals and stressed that the checkoff efforts would facilitate the work of the National Live Stock and Meat Board. Nance made such an impression on those attending the meeting that when Wilbur Plager announced he was stepping down as president, Nance was elected to replace him. Nance had served as president of the Hampshire Swine Registry.

Dr. Sam McNutt, chairman of the disease committee, moved adoption of a report dealing mainly with the outlawing of the use of virulent virus in the control of hog cholera, one of the first steps in the hog cholera eradication campaign still to come.

At that 1956 annual meeting a decision was made to create a national office with a full-time executive secretary. C. R. Mitchell, editor of National Hog Farmer, suggested that if the Council decided to locate an executive secretary at Grundy Center, IA, Keith Myers might be available for that post.

Grundy Center, IA, plays a unique role in the history of pork organizations. Not only was it the birth-place of the Plager brothers—Wilbur, Carroll and Russell, who were to play major roles in the industry—but it was the home of Keith Myers and of the National Hog Farmer. We digress from our narrative of NSGC to chronicle the beginning of National Hog Farmer, another major player in the development of pork organizations. Myers recalls it was felt there was a need for some sort of house organ or newsletter for the Council, replacing a mimeographed newsletter. "I visited with Ralph Anderson several times about the need for some sort of a hog publication. Anderson was owner and publisher of the Farm Bureau Spokesman at Grundy Center. In those days I was subscribing to the Pig Farming magazine published in England. I took copies to Ralph and said: 'There's no magazine like this in the U.S. and I think there's a need for it.' We never beyond discussing the subject. When it was decided that there was a need for a NSGC publication of some sort, I visited with Wilbur Plager and Ralph and made arrangements to take Ralph to Des Moines to meet Wilbur. We decided there would be a publication of some sort, a continuation of the newsletter. Ralph envisioned that it might grow into a house organ for swine producers, similar to the Farm Bureau Spokesman, house organ of Iowa Farm Bureau Federation, which Anderson printed as an independent contractor. In those days a sum from each Farm Bureau membership helped finance the Spokesman. C. R. (Mitch) Mitchell had a similar publication called Farm Bureau World covering about 16 counties in southwest Iowa, comparable to the Spokesman for the rest of Iowa. In the early '50s Ralph and Mitch had combined the two publications under the banner of the Spokesman. Mitch moved to Grundy Center and worked on editorial for the Spokesman. Anderson tapped Mitch to put information together for what become the National Hog Farmer Newsletter. The masthead listed the executive council of NSGC. It was purely a house organ, Mitch was not listed as editor. As time went on, a relatively short period of time, it became evident it was a good idea. They recognized they were on the verge of something with this publication, but were a little impatient with it. I wrote Jim Nance (then president of NSGC) in 56 or 57 that Ralph was about ready to toss in the towel. It wasn't moving as fast as he would like and he had given three alternatives to the NSGC—to sell it, discontinue it or improve it. They were quite disappointed.

"This was at the beginning of the effort of the livestock industry to get a checkoff. In those days the American Farm Bureau Federation was really opposed to any kind of checkoff for livestock producers. The law prevented such a checkoff. We (pork producers) were trying to get the law changed and had gone to Washington seeking a change. The most vocal opposition came from American Farm Bureau, to a somewhat lesser extent the National Live Stock Feeders Association. Because Farm Bureau was so vocal in opposing the checkoff, Ralph decided he didn't want to show the Hog Farmer as published or mailed in Grundy Center. So it was mailed from the statehouse in Des Moines. I hauled the first two issues in 1956 to Des Moines in my station wagon."

In August of 1956 the masthead of National Hog Farmer read "serving the commercial producers and breeders of 48 states through the NSGC." In 1957 the newsletter became the National Hog Farmer, a trade magazine as we know it today.

Returning to NSGC, Myers recalls that an ambitious program for the next year (1957) was approved, involving a number of areas including organization at the state level and active committees in disease control, meat-type education, editorial (advisory to National Hog Farmer), pork exports and live hog marketing.

In January of 1957 the first headquarters for a national pork organization was established in Grundy Center, in the offices of the National Hog Farmer, with NHF providing part-time secretarial assistance. Myers was named the first executive secretary on a part-time basis (three-quarters time) effective Feb. 1. He had served on many Iowa Swine Producers committees and on the executive board and was a commercial swine producer. His duties were to enlist financial aid from producers and segments of allied industry, as well as emphasis on organizing state and county organizations. Things were simpler in those days. His phone number was 50. His annual salary was $5,800 "payable contingent on funds being available." If funds failed to materialize to meet the salary, the executive board could terminate the employment without prior notice. States were asked to double their 1957 dues to finance the office.

Myers recalls: "We didn't have the money. We adopted an ambitious budget that year with no idea where the money was to come from. There wasn't that kind of money available and later on we arrived at an agreement that I would be paid $200 a month. National Hog Farmer didn't have room in their building so they rented an office in the Farm Bureau building which was next door. The rent was $35 a month and for that I used their office equipment."

Among the major activities of NSGC during those years was the meat-type hog education committee, which was a factor, along with numerous carcass shows and the meat hog certification program, in the move to change from the fat hog of World War II to a producer of meat for the consumer. Leaders in that effort were Carroll Plager and Bernard Ebbing. One of the early efforts of the committee, in which those two were instrumental, was the development of a set of slides on the meat-type hog. The minutes of the executive committee meeting of September, 1957, indicate the slides and a lecture plan would be made available by NSGC for $5 per set.

In minutes of NSGC during those years hog cholera eradication started popping up. In '58, after the second defeat of a checkoff bill (see separate chapter on checkoff attempts) there were a couple of rallying points in the industry. One was the National Swine Industry Conference (also covered in a separate chapter). The other was hog cholera eradication.

Again turning to Myers: "My first knowledge of the possibility of hog cholera eradication came at a meeting in Chicago, seems to me it had to do with brucellosis. After the meeting, or during the noon hour, Dr. Frank Mulhern, who was then administrator of the division of USDA involved in disease eradication efforts, said he wanted to visit with me. He was enthusiastic about the possibility of hog cholera eradication. When I became Council executive secretary I found there was a lot of interest on the part of many different groups and people in identifying a voice for swine producers. Frank sold me on the idea that cholera could be eradicated. Perhaps the first approach to hog cholera eradication came through the cholera eradication committee of the American Veterinary Medical Association, so it was not necessarily a new idea. There were people in Washington, like Mulhern, looking for a way to get producer involvement. It didn't take too long for Frank and I to get together. I relied heavily on him, had a great deal of confidence in him. One of the first things he suggested was that we get the industry together two-by-two, so to speak, two producers, two purebred people, two marketing people, for a meeting. We decided to call a meeting in Omaha, which I chaired. Frank was looking for a vehicle. He knew an eradication effort wasn't going to work without producer support. In preparation for that Omaha meeting I asked Frank to list the steps needed to eradicate cholera. He prepared a list of about nine steps. It was from that meeting that other meetings developed leading up to the time of the Congressional action supporting eradication.

"Producers had incentives to eradicate cholera—restrictions from foreign markets, plus the fact that there wasn't anything that put more fear in the minds of producers than cholera, particularly if they hadn't vaccinated and discovered their neighbor was losing hogs from cholera. It was a fearsome disease. Hogs didn't get hog cholera and get well, they got hog cholera and died.

"We used virulent live virus along with serum to protect. Then modified vaccines were developed, using serum with them at first, less than with the live virus. It was recognized that there was some chance of contracting cholera even from the modified vaccine. Dr. McNutt warned the industry there was a danger from the modified vaccines and we weren't going to be able to successfully eradicate the disease until we did away with modified vaccines, would have to go to killed vaccine."

Myers chaired the preliminary committee of LCI which investigated the possibility of cholera eradication and then the cholera committee that succeeded it. He was instrumental in mounting the campaign to secure producer support for eradication. When he stepped down as chairman of the LCI committee, Dutch Johnson, another NSGC leader, succeeded him. Bernard Collins and Marion Steddom of Iowa were two others of the many producer leaders in the effort. So it was NSGC leadership which made the cholera eradication campaign possible and cholera eradication was a major thrust of the Council during the '60s. The success of that effort is a major accomplishment for which NSGC can take a great deal of credit.

The philosophy of the Council organization structure during those years continued to be one of an association of state associations. Meetings were called to discuss the checkoff with state governors for example, and there was very little reference to hog producers attending these meetings. I attribute this to Bob Parkison as much as anyone. His feeling, and it was reflected in the opinions of others on the board, was that this should be an organization of state associations—thus the name Council. There was not much emphasis placed on individual producer members. The states were supposed to develop state and county organizations made up of producers. Emphasis can be found in the minutes that the council would not solicit individual memberships.

It wasn't until '60 that there was an indication in the minutes of a change in that philosophy. In developing the by-laws and constitution there is a reference in the minutes that for the first time the Council would solicit individual memberships.

NSGC and several state groups ventured into the public policy area during that period. Myers recalls the hog business was quite depressed in the mid-'50s. "Hogs got down to 10 cents, about as bad as you could get. Other agricultural income was not too good. It was a rather critical time; lots of unrest and agitation. NFO was born, started as a protest organization. Politicians were no different in those days than they are today. There were all kinds of proposals by politicians, farm organizations and others to solve the plight of the hog man. One of proposals—not of Iowa Farm Bureau officially but they did indirectly toss out the idea—was to pay a premium of $20 or $25 from federal funds for bred sows and gilts to go to slaughter. Wilbur (Plager) and I figured farmers were smart enough to know that if they were going to pay a premium they could breed sows and gilts for that market. So we got in touch with Sen. Hickenlooper of Iowa and convinced him this wasn't the way to go. That idea was dropped, but there were many other proposals on how to solve the problem of low-priced hogs, such as marketing boards and allotments—if you raised 200 head of hogs last year, this year your share would be 180."

The Iowa Swine Producers Association adopted a policy statement early in '56 as follows: "The advantages of direct supports on livestock are outweighed by the problems of production controls and maintenance of quality that would accompany subsidized production."

A meeting worth noting during those early years was the Minnesota-Iowa Swine Producers Institute. Ezra Taft Benson, the U.S. Secretary of Agriculture, speaking at that meeting in 1956 at Austin, MN, noted that for the past 19 years it had been the outstanding forum in America on hog raising. He said the Institute was known for two issues, multiple farrowing (farrowing sows throughout the year rather than only in the spring as had long been the custom) and the meat-type hog. Benson advised that those two issues were more important to producers and to the future progress of the swine industry than anything that could be done in Washington. The Council worked on those two issues through it
s meat-type hog committee and through the National Swine Industry Conference, which had as one of its goals the stimulation of multiple farrowing.

Perhaps part of the reason for the strong feeling during this period that the Council should be an association of state associations was that Iowa had a state association with state financial support. Other state groups were swine health associations or associations of purebred groups—far from the pork producer organizations of a few decades later.

Myers notes many extension/university personnel held early leadership positions; they were about the only contact the Council had with many states. Some states had very little organization, perhaps just a short course. When debates concerned whether the dues of state organizations should be $20 or $25 a year, it gives an indication about the strength of the state groups. "In Iowa, had it not been what Wilbur Plager called his left hand pocket, there were no funds from producers. Iowa Pork Producers operated on state appropriations and receipts from sales of advertising in a directory. Absence of bona fide producers attending these meetings, unless they happened to be a state officer, was intentional. When we really got involved in changing the law to allow a checkoff, the college people didn't want to be a part of it, weren't supposed to get into lobbying activities. Producers were recruited to go to Washington to work on the checkoff. The extension people stayed behind the scenes."

The first annual meeting outside of Chicago was in Davenport, IA, in December of 1957. It was moved to Davenport, away from the International Livestock Exposition, in an attempt to get more producer involvement. Myers points out that Scott County, IA, where Davenport was located, was getting nicely organized and there was a fairly good organization across the river in Henry County, IL. "So we selected Davenport as a place to meet and planned a combination educational/business meeting, starting with a trade show, forerunner of the American Pork Congress. About 400 registered for that meeting. There was a feeling that was too ambitious a program and perhaps in conflict with what the organization should be about, so it was decided that the educational sessions and the trade show should be dropped. For about the next three years, the annual meeting was a business session held in connection with the Swine Industry Conference." The minutes of the Dec. 1, 1957 executive committee meeting indicated that the committee felt there was insufficient time for discussion of Council business at the Davenport meeting and there was general agreement that the education program was not needed.

A story in NHF reporting on the annual meeting indicated that Council officials were disappointed in the attendance of producers from the area. Myers, in his address to the convention, called the lack of enthusiasm on the part of producers "hog pessimism disease," which "inflicts people rather than hogs." He said symptoms of the disease are speakers at hog meetings who talk only about what's wrong with the business, producers who feel sorry for the business, apologize for it and describe themselves as "only a hog man."

The minutes of the 1957 annual meeting include the name of W. E. (Gene) Smith of Missouri, who was to play a major role in NSGC activities in years to come.

Also at that meeting, Dutch Johnson of Illinois discussed the voluntary self-help or checkoff program of the Illinois Swine Herd Improvement Association. The plan was endorsed by NSGC. By-laws of the organization were finally adopted at that meeting. A resolution supported legislation outlawing the use of live virus in vaccinating against hog cholera.

In May of 1957 the Farmers Elevator Service Company (Felco) contributed $500 to the Iowa Swine Producers Association to help with Iowa's share of the NSGC budget. Contributions from other feed companies and other allied industry companies, as well as individual producers were being sought to finance the organization.

A financial summary as of Nov. 12, 1957, showed a balance of $393.72, with unpaid obligations of $1,454.67, including just over $1,000 owed Myers. Receipts for the year totaled $6,621.65 and expenditures totaled $6,492.37, including $750.00 paid the executive secretary.

Keith was working on the come and there was nothing coming.

As a result of that financial experience and a deficit of $1,500 to $2,000, the executive committee voted in December to close the national office and that the executive secretary carry on restricted activities from his home. The assessment of member states for 1958 was set at $5,128.

Contributions were being sought from packers to become associate members with a donation of $1,000 each and the purebred associations were asked to consider remitting one cent per pedigree to help finance NSGC.

Chapter 3

The Checkoff

We interrupt this narrative to explore the subject of checkoffs. The history of NSGC-NPPC is bound up with the idea of a checkoff to finance pork promotion. It kept the organization going for many years. While finances were tight there was always the dream of a checkoff that would solve all the financial problems. Enthusiasm waxed and waned through the years as the prospects of a checkoff brightened and dimmed through frequent trips to Washington. This dream finally became a reality in the late-'60s with the voluntary checkoff stimulated by the Moline meeting.

The checkoff idea which spread throughout the livestock industry during the dark days of the mid-'50s, when the hog market plummeted, began to flourish in early 1956 with a governors' conference in Omaha in March, followed by a meeting in Des Moines the next month. But opposition was apparently rising in the form of editorials in "big city newspapers."

A National Livestock Promotion Board was created at the Des Moines meeting. NSGC appointed Charles Maas, Bob Parkison, Dutch Johnson, Marion Steddom and Jim Nance to the Board, which was composed of representatives of a number of livestock organizations. The Board's efforts were based on the concept of a meat promotion plan that would be producer-financed and producer-controlled through representatives proportional to money invested in the program. Part of the money would be spent on state programs; the plan would maintain the prestige of the National Live Stock and Meat Board (NLS&MB) and be fair to all marketing agencies.

In June of that year NSGC announced its recommendations on how swine funds should be distributed—40% to NLS&MB, 40% to NSGC and 20% to state associations.

In April of 1957, 68 swine, beef and sheep producers appeared at Senate and House hearings to testify in favor of an amendment to the federal Packers and Stockyards Act permitting market agencies under the jurisdiction of the act to make deductions at the rate of 5 cents a head on hogs and sheep and 10 cents on cattle. The checkoff would be voluntary on the part of both the marketing agency and producer. Twenty-five of the witnesses represented the NSGC.

In August the House defeated the measure on a vote of 175 to 216. The vote was on a rule to permit debate on the proposal. The votes of midwestern and northeastern congressmen defeated the proposal; however, generally congressmen from rural districts in the midwest voted in favor.

The minutes of the executive committee of September, 1957, put NSGC on record in favor of pursuing legislation to permit a uniform, voluntary checkoff at the point of sale on livestock sold at posted markets. Another motion supported (1) making this checkoff through NLS&MB if possible, but if that was not feasible, (2) a single national collection agency (The National Meat Promotion Board was obviously the intended agency). A joint meeting with beef and sheep interests was urged prior to Nov. 14, 1957, to coordinate efforts along these lines.

As a result of the failure to achieve success in the Congress, Executive Secretary Keith Myers proposed to the NSGC executive committee at a meeting in December of 1957 a plan to start a checkoff without waiting for such legislation. Since the Meat Board is permitted to make a deduction, a county could start a checkoff by assuming consent, he reasoned. The Meat Boad for many years had been financed through a voluntary checkoff made by packers, with packers matching the funds collected from producers through the checkoff. This system had never been challenged and had wide support through out the livestock industry. Myers was simply proposing that swine producers use the same system. He suggested sending a letter to all producers in a two-county pilot area, telling them there was going to be a checkoff and if they objected to make that known. He was given permission to try the plan in one or two pilot counties. Myers recalls: "The idea never got anywhere. We didn't have the interest or the manpower to make up a list of all the producers in a county." This is an example of how projects failed, primarily because of lack of funds, a scenario which was repeated time and again over the years.

NSGC was not deterred by that defeat in Congress. At the same meeting Myers was authorized to run a pilot test of a voluntary checkoff, the executive committee discussed another attempt at leg islation and authorized President Nance to meet with cattle industry leaders to determine their interest in another try.

By March of 1958, when the executive committee met, the checkoff effort had again gained steam.

Nance reported that a committee composed of himself and Bob Snyder from NSGC and seven representatives of the American National Cattlemen's Association had been to Washington supporting legislation to change the Packers and Stockyards Act to permit a checkoff. He said seven congressmen had introduced identical bills and committee hearings had been scheduled. The NSGC executive committee approved a preliminary policy statement regarding how the funds would be handled—through a single agency or organization which would make any refunds and dispense funds to the species organizations.

So producers trooped off to Washington again, to testify before Congress in support of a checkoff.

They failed again and after this defeat they turned their energies to other efforts, although at the '58 annual meeting the delegates approved a motion suggesting the Council study the possibility of going back to Washington with a checkoff program on pork alone.

They had been defeated twice. They had been to Washington at their own expense. There were no expense accounts. They were defeated, but they didn't give up.

About that time pork, beef and lamb people in Iowa decided to attempt a state legislative checkoff, called the red meat checkoff. Twice this was defeated, but it was obvious that a meeting called on a red meat checkoff in Iowa would attract 200 or 300 producers. The interest was there. They lobbied. They worked hard, but never were successful. Gail Danilson was secretary of the Iowa Beef Producers at that time and I was fieldman for the Iowa Pork Producers Association. We were not always completely legal or ethical, since we spent a lot of time lobbying the Iowa legislature and our organizations were being funded by state appropriations. History will show that about 20 years later this type of legislation passed the Iowa House and Senate with overwhelming support, hardly a dissent.

In those early days serving as a lobbyist, we had a checkoff bill in a 9-man committee which was meeting after the session one night. We knew we had 6 of the 9 votes and the chairman was a personal friend. We waited in the Capitol for the committee to approve the bill and move it to the floor. The chairman came out and I asked him how we did. He replied: "You got beat." I said we can't have lost, we had 6 of the 9 votes when the meeting began. He looking me in the eye and said, "Pig, several people lied to you." I've thought of that on numerous occasions when I think I have everything set and going my way—

maybe someone has lied to me.

The next attempt at the Iowa red meat checkoff got as far as the floor in the final days of the session, but was defeated. The support among producers was there; this was the route they wanted to go—a checkoff to promote their industry.

The first voluntary checkoff, to my knowledge, was put together by the Iowa Purebred Swine Council, a group that represented the purebred segment only. They voted (this was about the time of the Moline meeting) a checkoff of 2% of the selling price on every boar sold through the test stations in Iowa, to prove to legislators and others that the majority of producers, when they had an opportunity, supported a checkoff. Midland Coop., operator of a test station at New Hampton; Farmland Industries, with stations at Ida Grove and Eagle Grove, and the station at Ames owned by the Iowa Swine Breeders Council, all cooperated. These funds were earmarked for promotion and improvement of the purebred industry. About 98% of the breeders participated and didn't ask for a refund. That checkoff is still being made.

There was growing interest. I know I'm only writing about Iowa, but at that time Iowa was the only state with a full-time, paid employee, so there was a little more activity there.

Returning to attempts at a national checkoff, another twist in the checkoff saga involved opposition on the part of NSGC to a checkoff proposal by USDA in 1962. The proposal would have required a written document from each producer authorizing the deduction. Not only would that have eliminated the automatic Meat Board checkoff, but it would have made the checkoff that pork producers wanted difficult, if not impossible.

One of the alternatives considering in 1963 by the Iowa association for financing the state's share of the cholera eradication program was a checkoff. That didn't materialize and the legislature appropriated the funds. Also that year, the Wisconsin Swine Breeders group was studying a state checkoff for promotion and research. One cent per head was being proposed, but it never was approved.

In 1963, Nance, now president of the Meat Board, was back in Washington lobbying for legislation to forestall the USDA regulation which would have required prior written authorization from livestock producers before deductions could be made on livestock. The legislation in effect banned the secretary of agriculture from regulating deductions from sales proceeds of livestock for the purpose of financing promotion and research, including educational activities. With passage of this legislation, by a back-door route the industry finally had at least part of the goal it sought—the right to make a voluntary checkoff by market agencies. This legislation made possible the concept of "implied consent," which meant that a market agency could decide to make the checkoff from all producers, assuming their consent; however, the producers would have the right to obtain a refund. This made the later voluntary checkoff of NPPC possible.

The Meat Board had been operating on this basis with its check off for more than 40 years, but without legal sanction, and efforts in Washington until then had been devoted to making that system legal, as well as authorizing a legislated checkoff in which all producers and marketing agencies would be required to take part. This ruling became very important in the future development of the NPPC Nickels for Profit voluntary 5-cent checkoff program. With-

out the ruling the program would not have been possible. This legislation was very important to future NPPC activities, even though it was passed to save the Meat Board and wasn't used by NPPC until '66.

Following passage of that legislation, USDA declared it had no authority to approve or disapprove checkoff programs by livestock producers which met guidelines set out in federal law. The announcement was in reply to a query by Iowa Swine Producers on the legality of a proposed one-month checkoff on Iowa hogs to finance remodeling of a swine disease research building at Iowa State University. The USDA response called attention to the amendment of the P&S Act approved in 1963. Iowa never got that checkoff off the ground and later raising the money through donations, but the USDA ruling clarified the situation for the Nickels for Profit program to come.

Chapter 4

1958 to Moline

At a meeting of the executive committee in March of 1958 it was obvious that the treasury wasn't growing very fast. Unpaid bills exceeded the amount in the treasury and executive committee members were owed about $800 for travel expenses. It didn't pay to serve on that executive committee.

Myers reported that the Yorkshire, Poland China and Berkshire breed associations had approved a one-cent deduction per pedigree to help finance the Council. Myers comments: "They sent in their money. I think others took part in that program as well."

He also told the committee that at the Omaha hog cholera meeting it was felt that farmers weren't ready for a complete eradication program and an effort should be made to increase the amount of vaccination with modified vaccines before an all-out eradication program was begun. That had a lot of support from people such as Dr. McNutt. That was one of the first steps in the eradication program, to achieve enough vaccination to prevent epidemics. It was about this time that the companies producing cholera vaccines contributed a rather large sum for those days, about $10,000, to be used for encouraging increased vaccination. The ultimate goal was to put those companies out of the cholera vaccine business, a goal which was achieved in near-record time for a U.S. livestock disease eradication program, but either those companies didn't believe that goal would be achieved, or the short term benefits were

greater than the long-term result.

The executive committee met jointly with the board of NLS&MB to ask for the right to name the three swine directors on the Meat Board. Charles Shuman, who was then president of the American Farm Bureau Federation and a Meat Board director, questioned whether NSGC really represented swine producers and asked how many swine producers each executive committee member represented. When Shuman asked for cooperation of the Council, representatives of the NSGC pointed out that cooperation was a two-way street and he had twice ignored invitations from the National Livestock Promotion Board for a meeting to discuss a checkoff. Shuman replied that the invitation had not been received in time for him to be present now or in the future.

After yet another defeat in Washington on the checkoff, at the 1958 annual meeting the delegates turned to a number of other issues, including hog cholera eradication, the spread of leptospirosis, opposition to federal price supports on hogs and the meat-type hog. Robert Snyder of Wilmington, OH, was elected vice president, replacing Maas who had served in that capacity since formation of NSGC. Nance was re-elected president.

At the 1959 annual meeting it was reported that, for the first time, NSGC was in the black. All bills were paid, Myer's salary had finally been brought up to date. It appeared this was possible through the efforts of Myers and Nance in obtaining financial support from other industry segments. State organizations still weren't doing their share. For the first time NSGC had a realistic budget and had finances to back up what the organization said it was going to do.

A special pork promotion campaign was planned for the fall and winter to move the large quantities of pork on hand. During these years promotion efforts were pretty much stimulated by the hog cycle—in years of surplus pork production, promotion efforts were geared up.

The first National Pork Queen Contest was conducted in 1959 during the International Livestock Exposition in Chicago.

A charter membership campaign was conducted in 1960. For the first time the NSGC moved from a Council with state members to seek ing individual producer members. The campaign was approved in late '59-early '60, about the time Myers left the post of executive secretary.

An example of the concentration on other issues by NSGC during this period is the early '59 report of the Illinois Swine Herd Improvement Association on the growth of local interest in organizing and improving the quality of hogs at the producer level. Harry Russell of University of Illinois, one of the early leaders in the test station movement, reported on test station data. Testing stations were built during the 60's under the sponsorship of state producer associations in Iowa, Minnesota, Wisconsin, Ohio, Illinois and other states. Fredric B. Hoppin, executive secretary of the Illinois group, reported 35 local organizations were affiliated with the state group. The state's attempt at a voluntary 3-cent checkoff "was not accepted as well as hoped," raising only $364.91 during 1958.

Merle Lesage, a hog buyer on the Chicago market who was to become one of the leaders in the meat-type hog effort, told that meeting only 10% of the hogs going to market were meat type and "we are way off base if we think it's just a matter of backfat and length; we need meat in them."

There were carcass shows everywhere. Every regional or state market hog show was sending hogs to slaughter and entering them in a carcass show. The breed certification program was in full bloom. Every type conference had a certification class and breed magazines were full of cutout data.

Testing stations were reporting not only on meatiness of the hogs, but how fast they grew and how efficient they were. Central test stations probably did more to bring producers of all breeds together with

a common goal than any other program. Nothing makes a producer more humble than being asked to compete head-to-head with his neighbor of another breed. For the first time breeders were forced to socialize with breeders of other breeds.

NSGC, through its meat-type hog education committee, played a major role through the 60's in all these developments. Committee members contributed to a monthly article on various aspects of production of the meat-type hog.

A major discussion topic during these years was the champion carcass at a major show such as the National Barrow Show, even more than who produced the champion boar.

NSGC and the industry encouraged USDA to change its market hog grade standards. The hog was being changed so rapidly the grades had not kept up.

State association interest in disease control and the meat-type hog was apparent in resolutions passed by the Iowa Swine Producers at its '59 annual meeting. They supported cholera eradication, vaccination for cholera of all hogs being moved, except to slaughter; brucellosis testing before movement of breeding stock; promotion of red meats and creation of a marketing division in the state department of agriculture. There was renewed interest at the state level in supporting legislation providing for a state checkoff to fund a state promotion council.

In 1959 the politicians wanted to get into the act and threatened legislation if the industry didn't solve the fat hog problem. This put fire in the eyes and mouths of NSGC and other industry leaders, since the politicians didn't mention or recognize the meat certification program, test stations, carcass shows, or the meat-type hog education committee. The major effort mentioned was new breeds being developed by USDA and state experiment stations. Many leaders in the meat hog movement felt the only impact the new breeds had was negative.

After all kinds of hell-raising by the industry, the effort was dropped by the politicians. The lowly hog was once again left to fix its own problems, thankfully.

The 1960 annual meeting of NSGC was scheduled away from any other meeting in an attempt, once again, to involve commercial producers in the program. This was also the first meeting to use a new voting delegates system. The voting delegates were based on the amount of state dues paid to the Council and the number of individual producer members in each state. The membership campaign was to be conducted by the Council and all funds from charter members, up to a goal set for each state, was to be retained by the Council. After the state goal was reached 25% of each membership would be sent back to the state. The goals for states ranged down from 400 for Iowa and totalled 1,823 for the country. The effort didn't succeed.

Nance, president for the past three years, stepped down and was replaced by L. A. "Dutch" Johnson of Illinois. He became the first full-time commercial swine producer to serve in that capacity. He had been on the executive committee since the start and for several years was the only full-time swine producer on that group. W. E. (Gene) Smith was elected vice president. The resignation of Myers as executive secretary under the press of personal business was announced at the meeting. J. W. Ralph Bishop of Indiana was appointed executive secretary to replace him in February of 1961. He served for the next two years.

At the annual meeting in 1962, Jim Nance, who was then serving as chairman of the National Live Stock and Meat Board, reported for that organization. A hint of friction between NSGC and the Meat Board, which was to continue off and on for years, was contained in a resolution of NSGC commending the Meat Board on its reorganization program, including creation of species committees and "the progress made in settling the differences which have existed between the Meat Board and various livestock organizations."

Resolutions continued support of hog cholera and swine brucellosis eradication and adoption of the new term "validated" for free herds and states. The Council assumed responsibility for assisting in the organization of state cholera eradication committees.

In 1961 the Iowa Swine Producers Association had called for formation of a state-wide committee to promote cholera eradication. Those state advisory committees proved to be a major factor in the success of the eradication campaign.

Bernard Collins replaced Marion Steddom as president of the Iowa association. Collins was recognized as a leader several years before he became president of the Iowa group, had served on several national committees and had been honored with the National Hog Farmer award for outstanding service. He's the one who called the meeting that resulted in the Moline meeting and sent a personal check for three market hogs to prove his sincerity. It doesn't take a very good employee to look good under this kind of leadership—I'm proof of that.

One of the future leaders of NSGC came to the attention of producers at that 1961 Iowa meeting. Jim Peterson, a leader in the Benton county, IA, as-

sociation, described activities of that group, including a runt-roundup, a ham barbeque at the county fair, a meat display cooler trailer built by county farmers, spring and fall county barrow shows and a pie-baking contest. This is evidence of a new trend—hog farmers rising through the ranks of county and state associations, proving their mettle at the local level. Peterson was a former lumberyard operator who had natural instincts for promotional work and believed that anything worth doing could be done. He served on the Iowa board, spoke at several NSGC meetings on promoting our product and produced the Iowa Farm Fair in Chicago in 1962, one of the greatest pork promotions up to that time. He later served as president of NSGC and presided over the change in name to National Pork Producers Council (NPPC).

At the 1962 annual meeting, a system of dividing dues income among local, state and national organizations was approved. Previously producer membership dues had been collected by the Council and a portion remitted to the states. The state associations had been assessed a small amount as state dues, as well.

The Council reaffirmed its support of the hog cholera eradication program. That effort, under the leadership of Myers and Johnson and with Bernard Collins playing a major role at regional meetings at which interest of producers was stimulated, was reaching the stage of formal implementation. Early in 1963 producers obtained passage by Congress of legislation authorizing the eradication program and it was officially under way.

Another producer who was destined to gain prominence in the industry, Russ Jeckel of Illinois, was one of the speakers at the '62 annual meeting banquet.

At the 1963 annual meeting, Jim Peterson was elected president and Bill Rothenberger of Indiana was elected vice-president. Rolland (Pig) Paul, field secretary of the Iowa Swine Producers Association, was elected to replace Myers as secretary-treasurer of the Council. Myers had resigned earlier in the day. Gene Smith was named executive secretary. He served in almost every capacity, the board of directors, the executive committee, vice president and executive secretary, a position in which he served from 1963 through 1966 and then he served as secretary-treasurer until 1969. He also served as president of the Missouri Pork Producers, executive secretary of that organization and president of the National Spotted Swine Association. What a trooper.

At the meeting of the board of directors of NSGC in early 1964 Smith outlined a comprehensive membership program. Receipts were to be shared with member state and county organizations. Carroll Plager was named to head the meat-type hog education committee and George Brauer of Illinois, another producer who was to achieve prominence in the industry, was named chairman of the swine disease committee.

The name of the Council was changed to National Pork Producers Council at the 1964 annual meeting, Dec. 10 and 11 in St. Louis. Peterson was re-elected president and thus became the first president of NPPC. Rothenberger was re-elected vice-president. One of the new board members was Albert Gehlbach of Illinois, who was to succeed to the presidency later. The meeting was geared to strengthen county and state organizations and their membership and the first award for the best state program for the year was presented to the Iowa Pork Producers, with honorable mention to Illinois and North Carolina. The council was urged to make a study of the possibility of financing the council through a market deduction on hogs.

A new women's auxiliary was formed by the wives of the producers, named the Porkettes. Mrs. Bernard (Dorothy) Collins was elected chairman and Mrs. J. R. Beatty of Illinois was elected vice-chairman. Mrs. R. C. Coddington of Illinois was elected secretary-treasurer.

At the annual meeting in December of 1965, Rothenberger was elected president, setting the stage for his role at the Moline meeting. The report of the health and research committee recommended the organization go on record in support of trichinosis eradication, which was somewhat controversial and has never been implemented. The committee recommended promotion of a uniform, practical, nationwide system for identification to farm of origin of all slaughter hogs. That sounds familiar. The committee noted that a committee of United States Livestock Sanitary Association, now United States Animal Health Association, had recommended consideration of methods to control spread of disease through sale of boars from testing stations. A study of this subject by NPPC was recommended.

Chapter 5

Blueprint for Decision

In 1966 a six-part series "Blueprint for Decision" was published in National Hog Farmer starting in March. It was written by Dan Murphy of Des Moines, who had quite an impact in later years on NPPC and the voluntary checkoff program. He had broad experience in farm organizations working with the Farm Bureau, the American Dairy Association, to name just a couple, and was an excellent farm writer. The articles in March and April discussed the need for a checkoff and a program. At this time the Council was still trying to secure a national checkoff on hogs. Several states had checkoffs or were asking for them. The Iowa Department of Agriculture invited all commodity groups in to discuss a mandatory checkoff bill. There was a great deal of activity, but up to this time no one had ever put together all the elements and walked through the steps with the producer as the Blueprint series did.

The first article outlined the situation and it didn't sound so much different than it does today. It said 20 years ago (1946) consumers spent 3% of aftertax income on pork and the family at that time (1966) spent about half that much. The consumer image of pork was bad. Retailers disliked handling it because of the lack of uniformity. Some of these things still sound familiar. The packer and retailer also experienced wild extremes in supply. One of the sections was entitled "Where to Start." It discussed a number of road blocks that had stifled attempts to put together a pork industry promotion and growth program. Wishful thinking won't make these hurdles vanish and each one must be studied and some way found to get over them, Murphy wrote: "Let's look at some of these factors that have kept us right where we've been after 10 or 15 years of attempting to do something."

The plan was to publish a ballot, after numerous experts had offered views on solutions. Later articles quoted university people, packers, farm organizations, producers and others on how they thought the necessary decisions should be made. Then would come the nationwide poll. No one dreamed how extensive and how important the poll was to be.

C. R. Mitchell was editor of National Hog Farmer and conceived the idea for the Blueprint series. As an illustration of how much he was dedicated to the success of a pork organization, one day he called me from St. Paul (National Hog Farmer had been purchased by a St. Paul company and moved there). Mitch asked what I was doing that evening. I told him I didn't have anything scheduled. He said he'd be in Des Moines in time for supper. I was always glad to see Mitch and figured he had some new idea or program up his sleeve. That night we had a very interesting conversation. Even though he was very much a supporter and believer that something was going to happen with the National Council he kept quizzing me on how sure I was. He wanted assurance that this program was going to get off the ground. This was about a month or so before the pilot area checkoff in 6 counties started. I couldn't understand what Mitch was driving at. Finally he said he had been informed by his boss that if this thing did not go that it was his job, since the National Hog Farmer had stuck its neck out so far, and that if Mitch felt it would not succeed he had better back off now and save face for the magazine. Mitch jumped in the plane that day and flew to Des Moines to make sure his dream and his efforts were not in vain. This shows how far some people, other than just producers, had their necks stuck out in the great dream that there would be, some day, a strong and vital National Pork Producers Council.

One of the Blueprint articles suggested producers could send money for a Blueprint Plans Fund. Bernard Collins, an Iowa pork producer and leader, took the bait. He sent a check and this letter:

"Congratulations. In your ten years of publication, the Hog Farmer has done a tremendous service to the producer as well as to the industry, but your past service is small compared to the potential of the Blueprint series started by Dan Murphy.

"A nationwide consumer education and promotion program backed by producers is a must for those of us whose 'bread and butter' is pork production.

"In five years as president of the Iowa Pork Producers, it was my privilege to talk to producers and producer groups in many of our states. Believe it or not, I've yet to talk to one producer who wasn't in favor of a self-help program.

"The interest IS there. All that is needed is the catalyst to start action and I sincerely believe you at the Hog Farmer can provide that.

"Dan Murphy has outlined the need and how other groups have met this challenge. Isn't it unfortunate how most agricultural groups delay until outside forces dictate survival measures to continue in competition?

"Several states, including Iowa, have unsuccessfully attempted to promote state set-aside programs, but—let's face facts—we in the corn-hog belt must sell our product in the population centers far from home. We need a national promotion and education arm financed by the producers of many states.

"You at the Hog Farmer, with your national circu-

lation into the homes of the producers, can best provide the leadership for initiating such a program. Granted that there will be stumbling blocks and problems. I'm sure that there are none that are insurmountable if producers are as interested as they have indicated to me.

"Producer attitude has changed remarkably in a few short years. In Iowa this winter, we exceeded our $80,000 goal for swine health research funds through hog donations in less than three months— and at every meeting I attended, the comment was: 'This is fine, but it's only a one-shot deal. Why not a market deduction for other projects?'

"This Blueprint that Murphy has so ably initiated will take money to get off the ground, and I'm so sure that it is a necessity that I instructed my hog buyer to send the sale receipts from three head of butchers hogs marketed today (March 30, 1966) to Blueprint Plans Fund in care of your publication. This will be the equivalent of 3 cents a head checkoff on my production.

"'Strike while the iron is hot' is an old axiom. You fellows have done a good job of heating the iron. I'm convinced that it's time to stand up and be counted before time runs out, and I hope other producers will put their money where their mouth is, or forever hold their peace.

"Lip service doesn't make near the noise that cash does."

That check caused consternation in the offices of National Hog Farmer. The magazine didn't want to become a collecting agency for producer funds, or set up an organization to do so. So the question was what to do with this check and any others from producers accepting Bernard's challenge.

To discuss those questions, Editor Mitchell, Author Murphy, Collins, the instigator of the situation, and I, along with our wives, met one Sunday afternoon in May at the Starlight Motel in Ames. The purpose was to decide where to go from here. A poll was to be taken, but if funds were going to start coming in, who was going to handle them? Who was capable of handling them? I was instructed, as fieldman for the Iowa association and also secretary-treasurer of the Council, to call a national meeting.

I had no authority to call a national meeting, but that's the way things often got done in those days. If it advanced the cause and contributed to progress we didn't worry much about the niceties of who had what authority. The meeting notice was on Iowa association stationery. Bernard was past president of the Iowa group and he called the meeting, even though he didn't have the authority to do so either.

Since he wasn't real sure the National Council wanted to get involved in another try for a self-help program, Bernard called Bill Rothenberger, president of NPPC, from the motel that Sunday afternoon. He told Rothenberger he was calling a meeting and he hoped the Council would endorse the movement toward a poll and an all-out effort by pork producers to reorganize under the name of NPPC, but if the executive board chose not to do so, he would put his time and effort into organizing a new group. No way was this to be construed as criticism of NPPC, but Bernard was so enthusiastic and so ready to go, if the existing organization wasn't going to do it, he would help fund and organize a new national group that would. Rothenberger called an emergency meeting of the NPPC executive committee to coincide with the Moline meeting.

Notices were mailed May 12, 1966, calling a meeting for May 25, at 10 a.m. at the Holiday Inn near the airport at Moline, IL. The letter was sent to as many of the state officers of the various states as I had on hand, to breed association leaders across the U.S. and to the swine specialists at 12 midwest universities. The letter said those in attendance would be asked to develop a questionnaire. This would be the poll that would culminate the Blueprint series. The poll would be used to canvas the states to determine what kind of program producers wanted, what needs to be done, how it should be done, who should do it and how it should be financed.

Chapter 6

Get Ready Fund/Producer Poll

At the close of the Moline meeting the Get Ready Fund was established, with a goal of raising $40,000 as soon as possible. Also it was recommended unanimously that the Council executive committee hire Rolland (Pig) Paul on a full-time basis. For years the Council had been operating on a budget of $15,000 to $18,000 and in the early years much less than that. At that meeting it was decided to conduct a poll of 50,000 producers, hire a full-time executive secretary and raise a fund of $40,000. In a few minutes $3,000 was raised. That's why in the old files that meeting was referred to as the Great Moline Meeting.

Things were on the move. People were asked to mail their contributions to Gene Smith, who replaced me as secretary-treasurer. In June a meeting was held in St. Louis that was never given much publicity, but a couple of events are noteworthy. The executive committee members signed a note for $10,000 personally. They felt so strongly about this effort they were willing to put their own credit on the line. At this meeting the organization structure was changed, Gene Smith and I officially switched positions and Dan Murphy was employed on a part-time basis.

Soon after that meeting, an office was opened on Ingersoll Street in Des Moines, IA. We had no funds except those coming into the Get Ready Fund, so we sub-leased an office with another agricultural unit to open up and get started. Mrs. Leone Turner, who was the long-time secretary of the Iowa Pork Producers, had to be very tolerant—she had worked for Wilbur Plager, Kenny Fulk and me. When I came home from that June meeting she asked what was going on and I said: "Well I'm going to go with the National Council." "When are we leaving?" she asked. "We don't have any money," I replied. "I didn't ask you about money, when are we going to leave?" There were many dedicated people in addition to producers.

The Get Ready funds started rolling in June; by July we were up to about $14,000. Then in August and September funds came from purebred breeders who met at the state fairs. Perhaps I was too enthusiastic and thought everyone else was, but I don't ever remember the industry being caught up in such a campaign to see something happen. By September 1st, we'd reached half the $40,000 goal. It was now time to run the poll. The poll has never taken as important a place in the history of NPPC as it really deserves—it was always overshadowed by the Moline meeting. It was intended to find out what producers really wanted done with their money. It's the first time I know of in any such organization when producers were polled first. Often a group is put together, a program is developed and attempts are made to sell it to producers. This was done the other way around.

Not only did producers decide on the program, how it would be financed and how they wanted to see it operate, but the poll had an organizational impact as well. In states and counties that weren't organized, it gave producers a reason to organize, to get the polls filled out. FFA chapters in some states took as a project to see how many polls they could get filled out in their area. Remember our goal was

50,000 completed polls. The majority of these were the result of door-to-door contacts by producers. In those early days my primary purpose was to organize county and state groups and one of the things I was doing was making sure the polls were filled out. I went to many field days that were not really hog field days and encouraged people to fill out the polls. I can't overemphasize the importance of the poll in getting the voluntary checkoff off the ground.

The early emphasis was on forming state and county organizations. Then we geared up for the December annual meeting. We hoped it was going to be the largest meeting yet, with the main drawing card being the results of the poll. For the first time pork producers were going to build a program and direct the way it should go.

Material mailed out in 1966 had two primary goals: The first was the Get Ready Fund of $40,000 and the states were making their quotas fairly easily. Each state had a quota based on percentage of hogs produced. Iowa's quota was $8,648, Illinois $5,600, Missouri $2,800, South Dakota $1,200, the states with around 2% of the hogs had quotas of $800 to $900 and so on, with a large group with small hog numbers with $200 quotas. The states that made quota early were the ones that exceeded their quotas by quite a bit. Iowa came in with over $10,000 way early in the game. The $40,000 goal was met by December.

The other major thrust was to get the polls filled out. About 180,000 copies were printed and we were sending them out at the rate of about 10,000 a week. Several national breed secretaries helped get them filled out. The Porkettes rolled up their sleeves and pitched in. Mrs. Dorothy Collins and Mrs. Myrtle Keppy contacted more than 200 wives and asked them to serve as poll captains, with each lady to mail copies to 8 to 10 other producers or have them in for coffee to fill out the polls. The message promoting poll participation was: "We can't have a wait and see attitude."

The poll climax came at the annual meeting in Springfield, IL, in December of 1966. A quick summary of the poll: To a general question "Should producers develop a program to strengthen pork's position?" of course 98% of the respondents said yes. In the areas of projects, the one that attracted 49% yes votes was improving hog quality and leanness. The second was improving the hog marketing system and the third was research on disease. Those same three would probably come up again.

In the consumer area, at the top was consumer education, followed very closely by paid advertising

to consumers. In third place was public relations for pork with the consumer.

One question asked what kind of organization should develop, carry out and control these programs. You must remember these polls were handed out across the country to anyone interested, not to a selected group. Forty-seven percent said the National Pork Producers Council and 35% voted for a cooperative program between the Meat Board and NPPC. The third general question was how much they wished to invest. The overwhelming response was 5 cents per hog, 43.5%. Surprisingly, in second place at 23.6% was 10 cents per hog and 3 cents was in third place. There were more people interested at that time in investing 10 cents in a program than three cents.

How do you prefer this funds to be gathered? Automatic checkoff garnered 51.5%, compulsory (legislative) checkoff got 16.6% and those two were far ahead of anything else. In third place was membership dues with 6.2%.

Completed polls came from 41 states but 79% of them came from the 10 north central states, which is almost right on the mark with the percentage of hogs produced.

So at that meeting a nickel per hog was decided on as the amount to be collected in a voluntary, implied-consent checkoff. Remember that this was in December; just the previous May a group got together to discuss a national program and by December it was already out in the country, local organizations were being formed and producers were being asked for their opinions, quite a contrast to the American Pork Producers Associated—this was being built from the bottom up.

There were about 1,000 producers in Springfield, representing 21 states. Producers came from as far away as Virginia, North Carolina, South Dakota, Nebraska and Oklahoma. Many came in groups by bus or plane. They came not because of an exhibit of products, as they did later for the American Pork Congress, or for educational seminars. They came to hear the results of the poll and to decide on the future of their organization. They were divided into three separate workshops to analyze the poll and vote on various aspects of the checkoff program. The check-off session was co-chaired by Bernard Collins and Jiggs Sandidge. The vote was 139 to 6 against state legislation for a checkoff if funds were to be controlled by government. They also voted to carry on the activities of NPPC, until a checkoff came about, through a voluntary 5 cent per head checkoff without going through the markets. Russ Jeckel of

Illinois and John Morris of Iowa chaired the production session. The preferences for projects at that session involved uniformity at testing stations and disease. Quality improvement and disease kept coming back with marketing coming in third place.

The pork consumption session was chaired by Lindell Loveless, one of the vocal producers in the Illinois group, and Jasper DeVore from Kansas. Jasper was one of the real stem-winders from Kansas at that time and quite a while later.

The week before the meeting, the goal of $40,000 had been exceeded. The big push came from Iowa and Illinois, as it should have, with both exceeding their goals, Iowa donating $10,547, 22% over its goal and Illinois with a smashing 80% over its goal with $10,107, almost matching Iowa, the No. 1 hog state.

Immediately following the December meeting the board met. It was a meeting of some frustration—the first time the board had met with some direct goals. Producers had told them where their money should be spent, how much per head they wanted to spend, how they wanted it collected and then they went home and the following morning at breakfast this challenge was left with the producers on the board. It was decided that for membership in the Council a state would need 5% of the producers and/or 35% of its hog production in its membership, with a deadline of Jan. 1, 1968. At that time a nationwide checkoff would be started. So there was a heck of a lot of work to be done during the next 12 months.

Another important action regarding financial success before the checkoff started was to encourage states to change their dues from $1, or $10, or whatever their state dues might be, to 5 cents per head voluntary membership. Dues for the coming year would be a nickel for every hog produced in a year. These were the funds that carried the Council from the Get Ready Fund until the checkoff started in January of '68. Of the dues collected on the state level, 40% was to be retained by the state organization, 60% would go to the Council for the continuation of the Get Ready Fund until the checkoff started. That voluntary membership checkoff had another purpose. As producers were asking their colleagues for this financial support, they were really running another poll asking producers if they were willing to voluntarily contribute 5 cents per hog. At that time the funds were going purely for organizational work, not for promotion or research. A continuation of the Get Ready Fund; it was called interim financing.

Quite a bit was done by states sending in their share of the 5 cents divided on the 40-60 basis. Several states just sent straight donations. Illinois sent $6,000, Iowa $6,500, Kansas and Michigan $1,000; Minnesota $2,500, Missouri $1,200; Nebraska $1,500. That's where the interim funds came from. The $40,000 took us into '67 but by the second or third month of '67 there was interim financing from states that were organized. In '67, when money was scarce as hen's teeth; very little industry money was solicited. Some companies helped with the Get Ready Fund. As we went into the interim funding stage, to the best of my knowledge, no industry or company funds were collected, not that they weren't offered. It was policy that we did not accept them, because if this was really going to be a producer program, if the producers really wanted this, then producers were going to have to pay for it and not rely on industry funds as we had in the past.

Chapter 7

Nickels for Profit

The first 6 months of '67 were spent working with state and county organizations, knowing full well that if this voluntary checkoff program was going to work, it was going to have to be done on a local level. At that time our goal was to have a minimum of 8 or 10 producers go to every market in a state to ask for the voluntary implied-consent deduction to be made by that market. There were many state organizations in the old Swine Council days and the early NPPC days that were purebred breeder or extension organizations. Those were being converted to include commercial producers and broaden their base of membership. This happened in state after state. Iowa and Illinois were about the only two that really had what could be called a producer organization at that time.

Also in those first 6 months many hours were spent putting together the Council program. Many questions had to be answered: What is the real purpose of NPPC and its program of work in a broad sense? How will it affect the Meat Board? How will it affect general farm organizations? I recall many meetings in the Meat Board office, including Albert Gehlbach, Roy Keppy, Jim Nance, Dan Murphy, and me, meeting with the Meat Board and Farm Bureau people explaining the division of work. The feeling was strong that it was all the same producer's money and the last thing in the world producers wanted to have happen was duplication of effort. This may sound very simple, but it was a very basic philosophy that had to be carried through.

In June, 1967, there was finally a memorandum of understanding between the Pork Council and the Meat Board. The Council would be financed through voluntary support in cooperation with the marketing agencies, and the division of work was basically spelled out, that we would stay out of pork research, because the Meat Board was recognized as the agency in that area. The Meat Board was not in the advertising or promotion areas, the Council would be. Also, the Meat Board was not interested in any way in on-the-farm production problems, such as meat hog quality or disease or housing. That was the Council's area.

It was agreed that one cent of the nickel off the top would go directly to the Meat Board. Not every marketing agency in the country was cooperating with the Meat Board checkoff, so this provided a potential of increasing Meat Board funding. The Council had four cents to be divided with state groups. The memo also provided that if the total nickel checkoff was made and sent to the Meat Board they would send the Council four cents.

It was also understood that on the state and local level NPPC would continue a membership program, so producers actually belonged and we knew who the Council represented. This was one point the Farm Bureau was interested in.

NPPC was not to do any legislative work. If the Council went to USDA or another agency in Washington after money had been appropriated and asked for a larger share of that budget, that was fair game, but we would stay away from the Congress. This did not affect what our state membership organizations could do. It was always difficult for people to understand that NPPC, under our organizational structure, represented states only and did not represent individual producers. Consequently NPPC did not influence one vote in Washington. Our state and producer members were the ones who influenced the votes. This was quite a big step and was never accomplished completely. But this step had to be taken before we could secure any kind of support from some of the farm organizations and the Meat Board.

The other important task in those first months of '67 was defining the work program—the blueprint for operations for a total pork program through the state member organization and down to the local county organizations. The program that was decided

on was that production problems and quality improvement must be handled close to the farm, NPPC could not handle these issues. Therefore funds must be available so state and local organizations could work on those production problems. The states' primary responsibility was to organize local organizations and obtain memberships, because that was what it was going to take to make the voluntary checkoff successful. The national and state organizations would share some in the disease work, because many of those issues were nationwide. The responsibility on merchandising and promotion was assigned to the National Council. It was as simple as this: where the hogs were produced the people weren't and where the people were, there were no hogs and no promotion funds. So to move Iowa or Illinois pork out of Iowa and Illinois, funds were going to have to be used on a national level. These two major policy decisions, the memorandum of understanding and the definition of responsibilities of the national, state and local organizations, became the framework under which NPPC operated.

In general terms the percentage of that nickel for the nation as a whole, not on an individual state basis, broke down 20% to the Meat Board, about 42% to the national Council and 38% would go back to the state groups. At that time there was also a voluntary 2 cent checkoff on feeder pigs. That was a state program and all the funds stayed in the states because not every state had an active feeder pig industry. Since they were unique in that respect they needed funds in the state to work on feeder pig problems. Also, the funds from voluntary seedstock checkoffs stayed in the state, so states could end up with a little more than the 38% with the feeder pig and purebred checkoffs.

The return to individual states was based on a somewhat complicated, but really simple formula. It was in proportion to the number of hogs produced. At one extreme, Iowa, with 20% of the hogs, kept 20% of the four cents. At the other extreme were states with under 1% of the hogs; they kept 90% and sent 10% to NPPC. It was based on the concept that states with most of the hogs needed to send more money, along with the hogs, to sell the pork. States in the middle rank, 5 to 7% of the nation's production, split the funds 50-50.

The term Nickels for Profit was developed at a lunch between Dan Murphy and I. We were asking each other questions about why a producer should be interested in this kind of program. We realized that there is only one reason why a producer would want to become involved and continue that involvement—if he was going to make a profit from his investment; thus Nickels for Profit.

The emphasis was on building individual memberships to contact local markets to sell them on the checkoff program. This had to be done neighbor to neighbor, producer to producer, door to door. The membership dues collected on the local level were staying at the local level to work on local projects.

We were geared to go nationally with the checkoff on Jan. 1, 1968. Then along came a trial balloon. The directors decided we'd start in September in a pilot area. This would give 4 months in a pilot area to learn if there were problems and if the material we'd prepared would work, or if a great deal of revamping was needed before the kickoff on a national level. While the board was confident that it would work, we needed an example so we could say this is how it worked in the pilot area. The local organizations selected to be the pilot test areas were in Illinois—Knox, Henry and Whiteside counties—and Iowa—Scott, Muscatine and Clinton counties. That's a heavy hog population area in both states around the Davenport, IA/Moline, IL area.

This was our first attempt to make a direct contact with the buying stations and packers. There were two major packers in that area, as well as company buying stations, independent order buyers and auction markets. It was a nice mixture of the kind of markets we'd be working with nationally. In August, '67, a meeting was held in Moline at the site of the famous Moline meeting, with representatives of producers from those six counties and as many of the marketing people as we could get to attend; I think almost all did. The purpose was to explain that this was the pilot area for the checkoff, that it was legal, the memorandums of understanding that had been worked out with farm organizations and the Meat Board, the program of work and the division of funds with the state organizations, also the long-range promotion program NPPC had in mind. We weren't selling blue sky. These things had been developed.

By that time the number of state fieldmen had increased to five. In late May of '66 one state had a full-time fieldman and here it is July or August of '67 and five states had some staffing and were really on a roll. Not long after that a couple more states added staff. These things had been worked out, the poll had been run, producers had spoken and we were ready to give birth to this child.

An interesting aspect of that pilot area meeting was that Dubuque Pack and Oscar Mayer had packing plants in the area. Dubuque Pack had never co-operated with the Meat Board checkoff and at that meeting representatives said they would go on a four cent checkoff. The national Council board had said we'd have only one program, a five-cent program; cooperate with that one as we don't have any other program. If that policy had not been established when the pilot area meeting was held, we would have had all kinds of problems down the road. Groups kept coming along saying they'd contribute to the Meat Board or the Council share or they just wanted to contribute to the state share. Many wanted pieces of the project, but not all of it. One of the most important decisions made by the Council was that there was only one program.

Both states involved in the pilot project had full-time fieldmen, Chuck Bloomberg in Illinois and Mike Ford in Iowa. After the first week only three of the 69 daily hog buying points weren't cooperating to some degree in the program. The 66 cooperators asked the seller if they approved the checkoff before the nickel deduction was approved. Several asked for a written consent form the first time and then didn't ask that producer after that. Some would ask orally and then not ask again. Our goal was implied consent: an assumption that the producer was willing to cooperate with the program unless he said no. That took quite a while to get around to. About 20% of the producers did not cooperate, but a survey of the non-cooperators revealed about a third had not gone to the buying point with their hogs, so there was no way they could have been asked. Maybe the percentage of non-cooperators was not that large.

In the initial pilot area we were getting 80 to 85% cooperation from producers and 66 of the 69 marketing points were cooperating. Two of the buying stations that were not cooperating were out of business in that area within six months.

I can't over-emphasize the importance of the local organization. A news story on the pilot area quoted 17 producers who delivered hogs the first day of the checkoff; 15 approved of the deduction and the comment was made by most farmers that they liked the work done by the local organization in presenting the information on the checkoff and the use of the funds.

Membership was also on the move. These don't sound like big figures today, but they certainly were in those days. Illinois had climbed from 950 members the first of April, the month after the Moline meeting, to over 3,000 by July. There was sure something brewing out in the country.

The role of the state staff, as well as the national staff—myself with the able assistance of Dan Murphy—was that we were to prepare the material. Every buying point was supplied with wall posters and pocket folders. General information was put out to local newspapers. That was our job. The program was sold by producers. Local producers sold their neighbors. Paid fieldmen were in the area only briefly on a few occasions and more to learn what worked and what failed than to do the selling. The six counties only had theories to guide them and it was a trail-blazing effort. All the credit of the successful start of the checkoff should go to the leaders and members of the six county producer groups who got the experiment rolling at such a high percentage of the buying points.

An important day for pork producers, promotion and pork organizations, was Sept. 2, 1967, when a check arrived at the NPPC office written on Sept. 1 for $4.90. This happened to be a Heinhold buying station in the pilot area. That buyer started turning in the funds every day, but after a week or so he switched to a monthly payment schedule. A bronze reproduction of that check hangs in the Council library.

One of the first major presentations I was asked to make on a national level was at the Pork Industry Conference in Nebraska in 1967, when I was the luncheon speaker. I was about as nervous as you could get. I told the conference audience: "When you see an industry attempt to pull itself up by its bootstraps you can expect we will miss some steps and will fumble occasionally. We sure have no road map to go by. I have just one request to make: come to us to help us fly right, rather than broadcast your doubts. Your counsel and advice will help us succeed." I went on to say that the pork industry had been on defense for years. Now the industry is putting two teams on the field, one on offense as well as one on defense. They are determined to do the work, knowing that problems will decrease and opportunities will increase, so our defensive team will be able to take a break.

The battle cry heading into December was best presented by Ohio Pork Producer president and executive committee member, Marvin Beam. He listed for his workers 12 big steps, each seemingly impossible, already accomplished, and added: "We're now within 30 days, 3,000 leaders and 30,000 producers of the first self-help program in agriculture on a voluntary basis."

Johnny Halstead, executive secretary of the Indiana group: "We need 15 producers to work as area finance chairmen, we need 66 producers to work as county finance chairmen in the major hog producing counties, we need 100 teams of four to five producers to work each and every one of the markets as contact teams."

In Iowa, Willis Keeker sounded the keynote for producer work on the local level. "On the national and state level we have hired some help," he said, "but here on the local level these two jobs—membership and market contacts—must be completed by local producers. This is where we producers carry the ball or the ball stops."

The Nebraska group had set a goal of teams contacting every market in the state in the last two weeks of November and the first five days of December, getting ready for the national checkoff on Jan. 1. The momentum was growing, no matter which state you were in.

Dan Murphy's sermon to state fieldmen and leaders was: "We have no time for hurt feelings or long-winded debates. We have no intent to blame anyone. We only want to list mistakes for the sake of saving others from making the same ones. Let's start with the don'ts. Don't broadcast family trouble. Don't assume your producers or buying points are different. Don't apologize—our progress is without parallel in agriculture. Don't duck responsibility by blaming others; the stockpile of excuses has already been used up. Don't assume anyone else can or will do your job in your state. Don't wait for miracles."

While all this pilot checkoff activity was under way, the Porkettes were getting ready to conduct a consumer survey to find out what people thought about our product. In August the Iowa Porkettes ran a quickie consumer acceptance survey in three supermarkets in Des Moines, IA, to test the survey questions and learn how to conduct the survey. The Porkettes were planning three-day surveys in five major market areas—Pittsburgh, St. Louis, Chicago, Minneapolis and Dallas, the first major consumer project conducted by the Porkettes.

State staff members at that time were Don Paulson in Minnesota, Mike Ford in Iowa, Doyce Friedow in South Dakota, Terry Shrick in Nebraska, Chuck Bloomberg in Illinois and John Halstead in Indiana. The national office staff was still made up of yours truly, Dan Murphy and one secretary Leone Turner. You can see the emphasis continued out on the local and the county level.

Without much question something was going to happen, but we didn't know how big it was going to be. The annual meeting in Kentucky in December, 1967, was probably the low point in the meetings of those years. We only had about 400 people in attendance. I think people were getting tired of going to meetings. I could sure see why they might be, because there had been many county, state and national meetings held in the past year. We had a pilot project story to tell; we had many things going, but the enthusiasm seemed to be dwindling. It might have been because this was the first time a meeting was held outside the traditional corn/hog belt. There was poor attendance from the south and it was a long way from the major hog country. I felt people were sitting back and saying: "Now let's see what's going to happen." It was the first time I felt that way and I didn't again.

The Porkette survey in five major cities was reported at that Louisville meeting. In those metropolitan areas, according to the report by Porkette President Myrtle Keppy, consumers said pork has a reputation as the one meat to avoid in a diet. Ham did not rank very high as a meal to serve if you were having company. Roast beef was the highest. Steak was second with ham in third. Pre-cooked ham didn't rank as a convenience food. Hamburger was called a convenience food, as were steak, chicken and hot dogs, but not pre-cooked, ready-to-eat ham. Mrs. Keppy pointed out that few people served hamburger, they served ground beef. The poor image of pork came out time after time. People would rather say they were serving beef, although at the checkout counter it didn't represent nearly as high a percentage of their meat purchases. Nothing new, the same old story, the image of the pig was poor.

At the Louisville meeting many positive things happened. It was estimated that in the pilot area a quarter of a million head of hogs would be checked off. About 55 to 60% of the checkoff funds were turned in to the Meat Board rather than NPPC, an indication of the confidence the markets had in the Meat Board; they weren't so sure about NPPC. Of course the Meat Board kept its penny and sent the other four cents along to NPPC. Before the pilot area started, NPPC had suggested, to make bookkeeping simpler and have only one set of books, the collections should all go to the Meat Board. That is not the way it happened, because many packers were not cooperating with the Meat Board; several wanted to make two checks. There was also a packer matching amount involved. Packers cooperating with the Meat Board checkoff added their own matching funds to the penny Meat Board checkoff. If they didn't cooperate with the Meat Board in that matching program, then they preferred to remit the entire nickel to NPPC and NPPC sent a penny to the Meat Board. So checkoff funds went two ways, but they all

ended in the right place.

Also at that meeting, Albert Gehlbach of Illinois became president, Roy Keppy moved up to vice president and Gene Smith stayed as secretary-treasurer. Combining of the annual meeting of NPPC and the Pork Industry Conference was approved. Both would hold one more separate session. The NPPC annual meeting was moved from December to March so the next annual meeting of NPPC was in March of 1969; there was no annual meeting in calendar year 1968. The last National Pork Industry Conference was in the spring of 1968.

By mid-1968 eight states had full or part-time fieldmen. The national office was still composed of a full-time secretary, Murphy on a part-time basis and me. We had numerous states that had an executive secretary on a full or part-time basis, but didn't have the funds to really get their state show off the ground. A policy was adopted by the NPPC board that some of the funds from the national organization would be allocated back to the state, in addition to their revenue share of the hogs that were checked off in the state, for a temporary period to help supplement their state executive secretaries. A contract was drawn up between the national and state organizations allocating limited funds to the state for the purpose of organizing that state and also so the Council had some control over the activities of the state executive secretary. Supposedly they were also to be available to assist the national organization in organizing a neighboring state. The national Council had the authority to ask them to come to a training meeting so everyone across the nation was telling the same story. This was not accepted everywhere. The majority of states accepted it, but several thought we were trying to control their state exec and they were losing authority over him. This was worked out later on. This was all quite a radical change from past operations, but the majority of the field staff was in the states—employees of pork producers—and there had to be some way to tie them together, keep them motivated and encourage states to put this kind of people to work.

In January of 1968, when the checkoff began nationwide, support wasn't uniform by any means across the country. Most of the activity was in the hog belt. The majority of major packers agreed to cooperate, not all of them on implied consent, but in one form or another. A large percentage of the country hog buyers were supporting the program, a real strength at that time. On the other hand, producers were finding the biggest gap in the program at the terminal markets and at some auction markets; they were opposed to cooperating.

By February the checkoff had been made on more than 600,000 hogs; the first four months 2.5 million head, the first nine months, over 6 million and at the end of the first year about 8 million hogs had been included in the checkoff. This still represented only about 10% of the hogs marketed that year. Some states were a little slow in getting the voluntary checkoff started; some were just finishing their organizational work and weren't completely ready during the first three months of the year, but half a million head of hogs a month or so would provide more revenue than we'd ever seen before.

I personally knew the program was really going to fly when a car backed up to the office entrance off the parking lot one afternoon in February and into the office came Clayton Kingston, who was the head hog buyer for Geo. A. Hormel and Co., and Carroll Plager, the livestock service man. They were starting a tour of meetings of Hormel buying stations. As only Carroll could do, he asked if we happened to have any surplus material available about the Nickels for Profit program they could distribute to their buyers. We loaded the trunk of that car with checkoff signs and promotion material. As that car drove away I knew the program was going to be a success.

Up to this time most of the effort, except for consumer surveys done with volunteer help by the Porkettes, had been on the checkoff. There had been very little work done on the long-range goal of merchandising and promoting pork on a national basis. It appeared that we were going to have some funds to actually do what we had set out to do, so in September of that first year of the checkoff Creighton Knau from South Dakota radio station WNAX became the second full-time employee of the Council. He was to serve as program director, supervising national projects and working with states on the cooperative projects on promotion.

There had been a lot of work done on paid-up producer membership. At the end of '68 our membership had grown to 25,500, a phenomenal growth in two years. The goal for the end of '69 was 40,000 producer members, which was achieved. At that time we were the largest dues-paying commodity group in the U.S. and as far as I know in the world. Some general farm organizations had many more members but no commodity group was bigger on the basis of paid membership.

In '69, we were finally getting around to really starting a full-fledged advertising campaign. During '68, as the checkoff was building up, we told producers we really weren't sure that advertising paid, so

before a lot of money was put into paid advertising, we would run a test market and find out what impact full scale promotion actually had. In 1969, starting in February, a test market program was put together, with $75,000 appropriated. The plan was to test a newly adopted cooperative promotion technique. The Meat Board supplied store promotion material and recipes worth about $30,000 in the first true cooperative project between NPPC and the Meat Board. This was the first major commitment of funds applied to consumer direct sales. It had two objectives. It was another pilot project for NPPC, involving a nine-month pork promotion blitz in two cities, Eugene, OR, and Roanoke, VA. Results in those cities were to be measured against sales in two control cities, Spokane, WA, and Charleston, WV. The reason for picking these four cities was that they were basically isolated, were self-contained as far as the newspapers, TV and radio stations that served them, so there would be no outside influence of other meat promotions. The second purpose was that we had promised producers we would run a pilot project and report back on the value of promotion. While $75,000, plus $30,000 coming from the Meat Board, doesn't sound like a lot of money today, in those days it was. A detailed study was conducted on pork sales figures as a base. Every 3 months at least 200 ladies in each city would be interviewed to learn if our promotion was having any impact. This program was put together as though we had 2 million dollars for a promotional budget, to learn what impact it might have nationwide over a 9-month period.

We promised producers a detailed report on the results of advertising, the return per dollar invested, and if we didn't get a sizeable increase in pork sales we would look at alternatives. Unfortunately when the project was completed there was never a final analysis. Preliminary data at three months showed a definite increase in sales, but I don't think the return per dollar invested was ever determined. The view seemed to be that the funds needed for that part of the study would be better spent somewhere else. That decision didn't go over very well in some areas, but it was soon forgotten. I personally felt the money would have been well spent.

The 1969 annual meeting of NPPC, the last annual meeting before the American Pork Congress began, was in Omaha, NE, March 5 and 6. An excellent crowd was on hand, there were many interesting reports. I've failed to stress the work of the production committee. That group by this time had reviewed all the research completed and underway

HOGS ARE BEAUTIFUL!

with a goal of preventing duplication of production research. The committee developed a swine research Bible that was announced at that meeting. Also there was the unveiling of a pork advertising campaign with the slogan: "Pork, always tastes good, always in good taste," which later won national awards. Through many of the earlier, amateur surveys, one of the positive things that came out regarding pork was the homemaker loved the aroma and taste of fresh pork; thus the slogan.

Jimmy Dean, who was getting ready to open a processing plant in Plainview, TX—Jimmy Dean Sausage—was to be our banquet speaker. About 48 hours before the annual meeting we learned that he would be unable to attend because of illness. His herdsman proved to be an able substitute. There was such a large demand for tickets to the banquet that closed circuit TV carried the program to all parts of the hotel—the rooms, the lobby and even the bars. Albert Gehlbach was re-elected president and Roy Keppy vice president. This was also the meeting that I turned in my resignation, effective July 1, 1969.

The "Hogs are Beautiful" button burst onto the scene at that Omaha meeting. The first one I saw was worn by Mr. Phillips from Alabama at the Pork Industry Conference earlier in the year. One of the staff members of the National Live Stock and Meat Board, Bob Nelson, who was working with the pork people at that time, found one in a box of buttons with crazy legends in a Chicago novelty shop. We

had several hundred made for the Omaha meeting and planned to give them to everyone who registered, but then I got cold feet about them and we kept them hidden and handed out just a few. All of a sudden everyone at the meeting wanted a Hogs Are Beautiful button. We ordered more from a button maker on the east coast, probably from a guy who didn't even eat pork or didn't know what a hog looks like, but we started receiving requests from state organizations, from button collectors, and from many others.

At about that same time the picture of the two loving pigs was published in a farm magazine which is now out of business, called Farm Quarterly. That picture has become one of most popular swine pictures ever published. It was taken on the Iowa farm of Ralph Howe, who later became a great leader of NPPC and the Meat Board, not because of the picture, but because he was an exceptional leader. The photographers had taken numerous pictures trying to find one for the cover. If you look at the pig on the right, he has his eyes closed and looks kind of relieved. I understand he should have been because that's exactly what he was doing, down the pants leg of the person holding him. Since I've heard that story I've appreciated the picture more.

The story of how those two, the picture and the button, combined into a major promotion for pork's image illustrates that all good things aren't planned, some just happen. Nothing will move an organization like a good, bad break. The Keep America Beautiful people at that time were doing quite an extensive public service advertising campaign. One of those TV spots pictured a pig wallowing in a gutter, degrading the pig. Stimulated by that negative view of the pig, on April 27, 1969, Iowa Congressman Fred Schwengle (Roy Keppy's congressman) scheduled a day in the House to hail the virtues of the pig and what the pig meant to the country. Several of us went in for that day and took the first framed pictures of those two pigs. We'd obtained reprints from Farm Quarterly to present to the Secretary of Agriculture, the Speaker of the House, and the chairman of the ag committees.

That was an amazing day; almost every Congressman was wearing a Hogs Are Beautiful button, a couple gold plated. The farm editors were meeting in Washington that day, that wasn't planned, it just happened. So the farm press was invited to a luncheon held in the House. The president of the farm editor's association at that time was Don Muhm of the Des Moines Register and he was also presented with a gold-plated version of the button. Because of the farm editors meeting in Washington at that time, because of the day in Congress, the picture and the buttons, none planned, they just happened, the pork industry got quite a boost nationwide. Ten pages in the Congressional Record were devoted to pigs. The National Provisioner, which is the magazine for the packing industry, in '67 had made a negative statement about what was going on in the pork industry to the effect that the lowly hog man could never get himself out of the rut, in fact asked if a $6 billion pork industry could muster enough zeal to get out of the rut. An issue in May of 1969 confessed the magazine was wrong and said: "Everyone seems to want one of those yellow and green Hogs Are Beautiful lapel buttons." The editorial asked: "What's the pay-off on this?" and probably the best answer was the head on the editorial: "Pig Pride."

There were stories about the buttons in the National Observer, the Wall Street Journal, Des Moines Register, Chicago Tribune and several other newspapers. A New York based news syndicate sent out an article nationwide. That article referred to the $75,000 producers had invested in a campaign to determine whether fresh pork promotion was profitable and pointed out all the nickels they could gather for years wouldn't pay for the free publicity the Hogs Are Beautiful button and the Congressional pork show created. The article said everyone was probably a winner—producers, processors and consumers, because of the end result: pride in a better product.

As the picture of the two pigs was reproduced, someone came up with the idea of adding the slogan Hogs Are Beautiful to the bottom.

That button kicked off quite a craze in the pork industry and for several years commercial exhibitors at hog meetings had buttons to give away that said Go Whole Hog or Pigs Is Pretty or Hogs Are Beautiful or something like that. I managed to collect several of them but didn't get them all.

Enthusiasm was on a roll. Many editorial voices noted the pork producer had a checkoff, but probably more important, the program had the support of the producers out on the farm actually raising the hogs.

One of the things I'm proudest of during this period was that producers were doing some things on their own. They were showing they had pork power. They had pig pride. This was contagious. We started receiving industry help. Many of the early promotion committees were not hired people. Elanco and some of the major packers offered some of their top talent to participate on these promotion committees to help come up with ideas, because they were also very interested in the future of the pork industry.

A year or so before this, Elanco had quite an advertising campaign on a dysentery product. They had a big red splotch on bill boards across the country and said it could be cured with the Elanco product. We told Ed Fehnel of Elanco that was the most negative pork campaign that could be put together. In early '69, Elanco announced at the annual meeting that they were putting up 1,200 billboards across the country with a beautiful picture of a pork roast with the message: "We help farmers produce delicious pork." At the same time help was coming from other sources. For each nickel the Council was spending on films, brochures, etc., two more nickels were being provided by the Meat Board and the American Meat Institute. The same multiplication of effort occurred in advertising of fresh pork in a six-city test area.

Chapter 8

Pork Industry Conference

Keith Myers, one of the founders of the National Swine (later Pork) Industry Conference, who was then executive secretary of National Swine Growers Council, tells about formation of the Conference.

"Russ Ives and Paul Zillman of American Meat Institute and I met in the office of AMI in Chicago in '56 or '57 and from that conversation came the idea that we needed some sort of meeting to focus attention on the direction the swine industry was going. NSGC didn't really have a heck of a lot going for us. We had an organization made up of state organizations. Our dues structure called for $20 minimum

dues from the states and we had a hard time getting that much from some of the state organizations. Money didn't come easy; so we looked outside NSGC to get some help, figuring there was a big enough job we could invite in some other people to help. We lined up 27 sponsors for the first conference. At one time we had over 30 sponsors—farm organizations, packers, marketing organizations, etc.

"We had no real organization. We got people together from the sponsoring organizations and planned a program. The sponsors were never asked for money, their contribution was helping to plan the program and supporting it by encouraging attendance. The goal never was for a large attendance, but rather attendance of the leaders, the movers and shakers of the industry."

The AMI was interested in promoting progress on the meat-type hog and on multiple farrowing—farrowing pigs throughout the year to even out the supply of finished hogs. NSGC was interested in a forum for those issues as well as other industry issues, including disease, highlighted by cholera eradication.

Purpose of the conference was to bring all segments of industry together—anyone who had some input—to develop a direction for the industry. The conference was not a policy setting conference, more of a goal setting meeting.

The first conference was at Purdue in 1958 with Myers serving as chairman and Ives as secretary. They continued in those roles through the meetings at Iowa State in 1959 and Lexington, KY in 1960. In 1961 Zillman replaced Ives as secretary for the meeting in St. Louis. In 1962, Zillman become chairman and Neal Black, who was managing editor of National Hog Farmer, served as secretary for the meeting at Columbus, OH. They continued in those roles through the 11th conference in Raleigh in 1968. To indicate the kind of budget the meetings were operated on, when funds were gathered to give Paul and Neal a thank you gift for their service to the conference, they were encouraged to contribute to the fund, but weren't told what it was for. They contributed to their own retirement gifts. Speakers at the conference were asked not only to pay their own expenses, but to pay a registration fee as well.

After 1968 the conference was merged with the annual meeting of NPPC to become the American Pork Congress. Zillman and Black continued to arrange the programs for the educational sessions of the Pork Congress through 1975.

The conference proved to be quite popular, as well as influential—400 attended the first one. In 1958 the NSGC annual meeting was held immediately following the Swine Industry Conference, also at Purdue. So the Conference served as the educational aspect of the annual meeting, with the business sessions following.

Myers comments that the conference "was criticized for not having enough producers involved, but when you looked at the list of sponsors, there were more than producers involved in the sponsorship. In the early days of the NSGC, we welcomed, indeed sought, help from other segments of the industry. We were pretty weak and we looked for any help we

could get. With respect to hog cholera, we went out and deliberately tried to get anyone we could find to help with the program. We didn't confine our efforts to NSGC. Swine producers were directly involved, but we sought help from marketing, extension, regulatory, research, farm organizations. We weren't proud. We'd take help from anyone."

During those early years from the late 50's to the early 70's there were three places where people from the industry gathered—hog cholera meetings, the National Barrow Show and the Swine Industry Conference. Those were the three events at which information was exchanged at the national level.

Myers recalls that the NSGC was weak, as far as funds were concerned, but it most certainly wasn't weak as far as dedication and talent were concerned. A look at the budget would lead to the conclusion that the organization amounted to little, if anything, but look at the backgrounds of the people on those committees and their leadership and it was as good as anyone could ever put together.

Myers recalls: "An example was Dr. Sam McNutt. He didn't have an expense account. The University of Wisconsin wasn't going to pay his expenses to attend NSGC committee meetings or the conference. Sam used to travel across the country on a bus or a train at his own expense to get to the meetings of our group, as well as LCI and the Pork Conference. Several college people who were part of the NSGC couldn't get funds to attend a NSGC meeting, but they finagled around and did it on their own."

During the two years Jim Peterson was president, we'd meet in the Meat Board office in Chicago because we could get it at no charge. People came by train. Arleigh Rankin of Ohio came by bus because that was cheapest. Most of these people were spending their own money for an industry cause. I wonder if we have that kind of dedication today.

The registration for the second conference was 560 and 355 attended the third meeting in 1960 in Kentucky. In summing up the conference Myers said at the first meeting the problems of the industry were defined and at the second conference the industry began to move toward solutions to some of the problems. He said big steps forward were taken at the 1960 meeting.

Recommendations came from a number of the workshop groups, in two cases they resulted from preliminary work done by committees appointed as a result of recommendations at previous conferences. One involved marketing and the production of a brochure designed to increase the amount of information which a farmer receives on his hogs from his marketing agency. The other committee, on swine diseases, developed a series of recommendations.

A highlight of that meeting was a prediction by Jim Hillier of Oklahoma State University on what the hog would look like 30 years from then. His goals included:

1. A hog that does not have to be defatted—an average backfat thickness of .3 of an inch or thereabouts. With so little backfat, there is likelihood of having a thin, skippy belly, Hiller said. This would have to be watched closely and some effort made to shift fat from the back to the belly; "however, most bacon today is too fat and would be improved by some reduction in the percentage of fat."

2. Eight-square-inch loin eyes and a yield of lean cuts above 45% of live weight. "Some will say that the cuts from such a pig at a slaughter weight of 200 pounds will be too large for the consumer. That is fine. Lighter weight hogs are more economical to produce."

The pork stress syndrome (PSE), farrowing problems, labor costs at the packing house, all played a part in stalling the movement to meatier hogs and we threw the baby out with the bath water in some cases, as the move to continue to produce meatier hogs was put on hold. In recent years the packer-stimulated trend to heavier slaughter weights has reversed the trend to reduced backfat on market hogs. And we sure don't have a problem with bellies that are two thin and too lean from those 250-pound market hogs.

The name of the annual conference was changed to National Pork Industry Conference following the meeting in November of 1961.

At the fifth conference in 1962 a contest was conducted on new ideas for pork cuts. The winner was Boston bacon made from the butt, cured and sliced as bacon. The workshop on pork quality urged establishing minimum standards for pork quality to be included in the certification program, signaling a change in emphasis at the conference from production problems to promotion and pork quality.

A feeling had been growing in the industry for several years that two meetings each year, the National Pork Industry Conference and the annual meeting of National Pork Producer Council, were one too many and they should be combined into one large event. At the Raleigh Pork Industry Conference in November of 1968 the sponsors voted to effect such a combination, confirming a decision made the previous December at the annual meeting of NPPC.

At the next NPPC annual meeting in March of 1970 in Omaha we had some commercial exhibits and Neal Black suggested that we include a commercial trade show in the new combined meeting. I said it was a good idea, but asked who we'd get to run it; remember NPPC still had a minimal national staff. Black asked Leon Olsen of Hawkeye Steel Products Co., Waterloo, IA, if he thought a trade show at a big, combined meeting was a good idea. He said, "Yes, but who are you going to get to run it?"

"You," Black replied. So Olsen signed on to manage the trade show for the first Congress and continued in that role for many years, a significant contribution, again by a non-producer, to a producer effort. Much of the financial success of the American Pork Congress over the years is a result of his efforts.

I was stepping out as executive secretary of NPPC that summer, but before I left we met to discuss the new meeting, which was to be in Des Moines in March of 1970. We didn't yet have a name for the meeting. C. R. Mitchell and Neal Black of National Hog Farmer suggested American Pork Congress and that was approved. Murphy, Black, Zillman and Marv Garner, who was to replace me as executive secretary of NPPC, met in Des Moines to decide on a location, among other details. Murphy and Black pushed for holding the meeting in Veterans Auditorium. I was hesitant, in fact I was very concerned, because we didn't have any funds and if we didn't sell enough booth space or get enough other revenue, we could lose a bundle. I wondered if we could afford to take the gamble. I wanted to schedule the meeting in a Des Moines hotel, where the cost would have been much less and the gamble smaller. Also, the Nickels for Profit checkoff was just getting into high gear and I felt a financial failure of this meeting would reflect badly on that program. Murphy and Black kept walking me up to the Auditorium and I kept talking about the hotel. Finally they harassed me into accepting the Auditorium as the site. But only after I proposed that if NPPC took the financial risk, NPPC should receive any profits. Black agreed for the Pork Conference and the deal was made. Neal and I laughed about this after the Pork Congress became such a financial success; he says it's the worst deal he ever made.

We planned on an attendance of over 1,000 for that first Congress, surpassing any previous attendance at a hog meeting. Pork producers kept streaming in until more than 5,000 were registered. Black handled the registration and about mid-way through the three-day meeting, he ran out of registration forms. For a while you had to bring you own paper if you wanted to register for the meeting and pay your $1 registration fee. That fee was the subject of much discussion: whether producers would pay $1 to regis-

ter for such an event. Later, of course, the Pork Congress grew into one of the largest commodity meetings in the country.

Chapter 9

People/Reflections

Wilbur Plager, the first president of National Swine Growers Council, was a hog man's hog man. He was a motivating force behind many things that happened in the pork industry. He and his brother, Carroll, and Bernard Ebbing, decided to change the image of pork and the kind of hog we were raising. Wilbur and Jim Nance, the second president, had different styles but you never had to worry about where they were coming from on issues involving attempts to make the pork industry prosper. While Wilbur was a great motivator he was not great on details. As president, he often left NSGC meetings mid-way through the business session with an excuse of another commitment. He just wasn't much interested in the nuts and bolts. After he got the Swine Council started and achieved a major goal of appointment to the Meat Board, he turned the presidency over to Nance to pick up the loose ends.

Wilbur later became executive secretary of the American Yorkshire Club, but his advice was sought by breeders of many other breeds. Wilbur judged many hog shows in the early days and was often referred to as the "One Armed Bandit" because during his farming days he lost an arm in a corn picker accident. He often said that was one of the best things that happened to him, for if that accident hadn't occurred he probably wouldn't have become so instrumental in leading the growth of the hog industry. He was a great story-teller. While his primary goal was the meat-type hog, I'm not so sure that down deep he may have been even more interested in attacking something he didn't approve of—like the fellow who imported Wessex Saddleback hogs and promoted them as the answer to the meat-type hog movement—or playing a practical joke on someone and then telling about it again and again before a crowd of people at a hog show. If you attended a hog show during the 60's or '70's and saw a group of people, laughing and paying little attention to the show, it was likely that Wilbur was the center of the group. If he could get two or three people around, which wasn't difficult for him, he'd tell a story, starting: "Uh, uh, uh, let me tell you . . ." There were two expressions everyone knew him by: He'd tell about somewhere he had spoken and hadn't gone over very

well and add he was "about as popular as a bastard at a family reunion, but they found out that your Uncle Wilbur was right." Or he would be discussing someone he didn't like—he seldom left you in doubt about that—"The only way he could be dumber was if he was bigger, or twins." Those remarks and his stories were his trademark through the industry. Everyone knew him and loved him. Most of the time he was chuckling and telling stories his mind was running as fast as could be. Many give him credit as the motivating force in organizing NSGC, but people who knew him well in those early days, say he was not only trying to organize a group to represent pork people in Washington and in other organizations, he wanted more input in those organizations himself. Two of the first appointments after NSGC was formed were Wilbur to both the National Live Stock and Meat Board and the board of LCI. Wherever he was it seemed everyone knew him and had a story to tell about him. He wore an artificial arm and it wasn't unusual, when someone asked him to do something, for him to twist his arm around backwards and say: "Twist my arm and I guess we can go do it." He liked to tell the story about the time a waitress asked him if he'd like another drink. He replied: "If you twist my arm I'll have another." She turned white and about fainted when she thought she'd pulled his arm off.

Wilbur was one of the key players in the meat-type hog. As far back as the 40's, when he was on the board of the Iowa Swine Producers, getting the lard off the hog was one of his primary goals. Later on as secretary of the Iowa Swine Producers and during the early 60's, when the real moves began to trim the fat off the hog through testing stations, carcass shows and the certification program, Wilbur was one of the motivators. I doubt that few people were as dedicated to reducing fat on hogs for the benefit of the consumer. Wilbur often found fault, as he got older, with the idea of selecting breeding stock with a computer. He used to say that any hog man worth his salt walking into a farrowing house could tell a good sow better than "some damned computer." He touched many lives, not only through the NSGC, but through his many other activities and he was active for more than 4 decades.

Jim Nance of Alamo, TN, the second president of the Council, became quite a spokesman for the livestock industry. At one time he was president of the Hampshire Swine Registry, also later was president of the National Live Stock and Meat Board. He probably served on more boards and organizations in agriculture than any one other person in recent years. He was a very interesting individual. He loved to serve on boards. He was brilliant during the days of the memorandum of understanding between the Meat Board and the Pork Council. He led the effort several times in Washington, D.C. to make the Meat Board a legal entity. He could spot a problem five months in advance and pretty well had a solution in mind. He was certainly one of the best negotiators and peacemakers in agriculture at that time. In later years, when he was involved in many of these activities, to the best of my knowledge he didn't own a hog or a cow. Some of his family members did, but Jim himself didn't. His niche in life was to see agriculture promoted. He was active in many marketing organizations, worked some with the sheep people, some with the beef people, but what he did for the Meat Board and the Swine Council was a great contribution. He was a master board member. I've never heard of that term, but he certainly qualified as a negotiator and manipulator of a board. I'd been executive vice president of NPPC for about a month when Jim called me aside after a board meeting and said: "You ought to be smarter than that." I replied that probably I should, but about what? "You brought up something at the board meeting that you felt you were obligated to bring up, but you weren't for." I agreed and asked how I should have handled it. "There are two things an executive vice president should know," he replied: "Bring up something you oppose at the very end of the meeting when everyone is ready to go home; nine times out of ten it will be tabled for later discussion and you can tell people and show them in the minutes that it was brought up. The other thing you've got to learn is you don't bring up anything you want approved unless you have the votes. Count them before the meeting. Don't let it be defeated just because board members aren't aware of how strongly you support it. Get the votes before you bring it up." In about two minutes he gave me a university lecture on how to get things done. He did these things very quickly and very easily, as only a master board member could.

After one of the Iowa checkoff attempts in the '60s failed, it was decided that a legislated checkoff was not feasible at that time, so we'd try to organize state groups and build the NPPC into a membership organization. You can say that this was not successful, or you can say that without this early movement there would be no NPPC today. I would say that both views are correct. The organization put together then became the group we now know as the NPPC. The organization functioned to the best of its ability. It never really had a big budget, but there were a number of men who spent a great deal of time and effort keeping NPPC alive and waiting for something to happen (by waiting I don't mean sitting on their hind end and doing nothing); they weren't going to let it die.

Without those dedicated people, like Marion Steddom from Granger, IA, C. R. Mitchell of National Hog Farmer, Bill Rothenberger, Albert Gehlbach, Gene Smith and Jiggs Sandidge from Missouri, Jasper DeVore from Kansas, and many others, this history of pork organizations would have been very different.

Extension service and swine specialists were a vital group in the formation and continuation of early pork organizations, as well as in furthering programs of the Council, organization of state and county producer groups, the meat-type hog effort and the Nickels for Profit program.

In Illinois Harry Russell and Dick Carlisle were just about as dedicated to seeing the pork industry prosper and reach its potential, as the mortgage-lifter and elite of farm animals, as any two people could every be. They were old-time extension people; they worried about the industry and the people involved in it; they were our friends. In Nebraska there was Leo Lucas. The bus load that came to the Moline meeting from Nebraska was organized by Leo. In the late '60s, as Nebraska was being organized on a district basis, Leo set up many of the meetings and ran them before a paid executive secretary was available. Down in Kansas, Wendell Moyer was the extension swine specialist. I recall Jasper DeVore was the ringleader of the producer effort in that state and we were holding two meetings a day. Wendell was at every one of them. Jasper and I were flying from meeting to meeting, but Wendell was afraid of flying, so he would leave a few minutes before the meeting was over and drive as hard as he could to the next meeting to be there when we arrived. One doesn't forget that kind of dedication.

In Texas, T. D. Tanksley led the parade to see Texas organized. In Indiana, Jim Foster and Hobe Jones at Purdue had a great deal to do with arranging for John Halstead to become the first Indiana executive secretary. I never did quite understand the arrangement. Halstead was getting his masters degree under Jones and working for the Indiana Pork Producers at the same time.

In Ohio, Wilbur Bruner was the dean of performance testing and the test stations which flourished across the country in the '60s. His services to producer organizations continued through several decades. It was his idea that grew into the Pork All American program still recognizing young producers many years later. Rick Wilson and Herb Barnes were two more stalwarts in Ohio on the meat-type education committee.

In Pennsylvania many and many a night Dwight Younkin and I rode together to meetings of producers he had set up. Only someone with the kind of contacts he had could have set up those meetings. I can't talk about characters without mentioning people like Buddy Richmond in Mississippi.

A college man who was active in the formation of the council and stayed active over many years was Ed Miller of Michigan State. He served as secretary-treasurer of the Council for four years and was active in the Michigan pork organization, as well as the national.

The extension swine specialist I was personally closest to was Mac Whiteker, who served in that capacity in Iowa and later in Kentucky. Probably no one spent more hours driving up and down the road in behalf of pork organizations than Whiteker. His boss at that time, the head of the animal science department at ISU, called Mac and I in one day and spelled out the ground rules. "Iowa State will be glad to help in any way it can to see the pork industry organized, but at every meeting, if we're going to have a role in it, there must be an educational aspect." Mac was the educational part of the program, but he also helped cook the meal, entertain the crowd, clean up afterwards and then pack up to be ready to go the next day. What dedication.

Of course there were many other university people who not only helped the pork industry as far as organization was concerned, but served as sort of guardians all along the way. Not all of them were in extension; for example, Jesse Bell, head of the animal science department at Fresno State in California, was one of the leaders in that state in organization work and the meat-type hog. He was one of Wilbur Plager's cronies and the stories about their travels together are classics.

Without the assistance of these university people and others I've failed to mention, the states would not have been able to put together an organization as early as they did.

The day the board decided to move ahead with the voluntary checkoff, there was never any question in the minds of the board members that something was going to happen, something great. They decided to start the pilot area program and their concern that night was the fact that we had better hire an accountant and perhaps get legal opinions before we started. At that time there was very little money in the account. Gene Smith, who has the treasurer and one of the great leaders in the early days, kept track of bills and checks and other records just as if they were his own. At that time we owed a printer $10,000 (Gene didn't know it) for printed material for use in the pilot area and around the country in organizational efforts. There wasn't enough money to pay both Dan Murphy and me, so since I was the boss I got paid. I often wondered if the board really knew this, but If they had, I doubt it would have stopped them; they were still thinking about the things that had to be done—getting a bank account set up, an accountant and a record system that no one could question.

That printer, Joe Freeman, was our most frequent visitor in the office. He laughed at the news releases we put out with million dollar budgets for this and that. The advertising agencies and printing companies would line up at the door to tell me what they'd do for us, and that they weren't planning on making any money, they just wanted to help us get started. I'd tell them if they weren't making any money we didn't want to do business with them; we wanted to do business with someone who would be around for a while. Joe ran the printing operation for the Iowa Farm Bureau and moonlighted to do our printing, borrowing the money to buy the equipment. We had no assets to put up to guarantee payment. He came in my office, looked me in the eye and said: "I apologize for eavesdropping, but I've heard you tell those other people that you didn't want to do business with anyone who wasn't going to make any money off you, because both people had to make money. I'm in here to try to make some money off you." When we got $10,000 into him, he wasn't sure he was going to make any money off us, but almost daily when I was in the office Joe would be drinking coffee and asking how we were doing. He mentioned his banker was asking for a little more than just a stack of brochures and pamphlets as security for his loan and wondered if we were ever going to get his bill paid. At the same time the attitude of producers, particularly the board, was that we were just starting to roll; we had no problems; we had put all our money into a field of corn we were sure we would harvest pretty soon.

Freeman's family and our family became close friends. He had about moved in with us in our office; I think the total bill got up to $17,000 before we started paying him off. Here was another person who stuck his neck out in the early days and helped make things happen whom very few people knew about. Freeman was one of the most interested non-producers in the U.S. in the progress of NPPC at the start of the voluntary checkoff.

During the years I was executive secretary of the Council I had what I called a balance wheel. A personal friend of our family, Jack Moran, and I were partners in farrowing about 35 or 40 litters of hogs a year on a little 160-acre farm in Polk county, Iowa. It's easy to go to meetings and talk about quality improvement, accrediting and validating, or testing, and ask someone else to do it. But when you have your foot in the door a little bit in the actual production end and you open a hog house door some morning and smell TGE, or when you call the rendering truck, or pay the feed bill, it keeps you a lot closer to who you're working for, the pork producers of the country.

In the early days we were invited to numerous meetings to relay the messages we producers were telling across the country. The United States Animal Health Association scheduled a special session on feeding garbage to hogs one year in New Orleans. I was invited to appear to discuss a policy adopted by the board of the Council in favor of outlawing feeding of garbage to hogs. USAHA represents the livestock regulatory people—state veterinarians and federal veterinarians. Preceding the USAHA meeting was a meeting of the secretary of agriculture's hog cholera eradication committee. At that time hog cholera eradication was in full stride; the controversy wasn't over by any means, but definite strides were being made toward eradication. I was not a member of the secretary's committee, but I attended many of the meetings as an observer, to keep informed and to express what I felt was a producer's viewpoint. It was always a very formal meeting with very few disruptions. At the meeting in New Orleans, a group of five or six people came in who weren't familiar to me and by that time I thought I knew every pork producer who attended that kind of meeting on a first name basis. I leaned over and asked Neal Black who those folks were and he said I would know them before the meeting in New Orleans was over. They represented the garbage feeders in New Jersey. I figured if they were pork producers I could sure get along with them, so when the formal part of the meeting

was over I walked over and introduced myself. One of them said: "We know who you are, you SOB." He pulled out a picture of me that had run in a magazine and said "I think I should break your arm." A young spokesman for the group said "No, no, don't do it now. Let's go have a drink with him and find out just where he really stands." I very seldom turned down a beer so I went with them.

The garbage hearing was one that asked speakers to submit a copy of their remarks prior to the meeting. The garbage feeders had a copy of mine and asked me if that was what I was going to say. I replied: "It most certainly is. That's the stand the board of directors of NPPC has taken." The attitude of these people changed somewhat; they seemed to admire the fact that someone had taken a stand and wasn't going to be wishy-washy about it. In fact they took me to supper that night and ordered for me. I thought that was a little unusual, ordering for me, but I wasn't real sure where I stood with those folks.

When the meal came there was ample food, a lot more than any one human being could ever eat. I wondered about that, but figured that's their style. I learned the reason the next morning. As I was walked out of my hotel room headed for the garbage hearing, there in front of my door was the remains of the meal I had not eaten the night before. On it was a sign that said: "This was good enough for you to eat last night, but not good enough to feed our hogs." That made quite an impression on me. It was over 20 some years ago and I still remember it vividly.

At the hearing I presented the position of NPPC and stepped off the platform wondering what the repercussions would be, since those same gentlemen were all sitting in the front row looking right at me. They followed me to the back of the room and shook my hand and said: "We don't agree with you and we'll get you, sooner or later, but we admire someone who doesn't buckle under pressure." They also informed me that at every national NPPC meeting, or any other meeting where I was speaking, they would have a representative present. I doubted that, but in the following months I began to believe them—someone was at every one. They also were very interested in my whereabouts. At that time the farm press listed most of the national or statewide swine events and their programs, so they had a pretty good record of my whereabouts. They called my home about 10 p.m. on several occasions and asked my wife, Donna, where I was; she would tell them in Ohio or Pennsylvania or wherever I was scheduled and they would question that and say they had information I was elsewhere and maybe she'd better check up on where I really was. This was a different tactic than I was used to. After the Omaha meeting, which was when I resigned as executive secretary, Donna and I arrived home about 11 or 11:30 p.m. The phone was ringing, how long it had been ringing I don't know. The only words spoken when I answered were: "We said we'd get you and we did."

An interesting footnote is that several of the garbage feeders and I have become, in later years, good personal friends. We have served on several national committees together, in Washington and elsewhere and I've become a little more familiar with their problems and their stand and that they were being falsely accused of many things. I don't mean to say, in any way, that they were lily-white, but I found myself, in later years, taking a stand on their behalf at swine health committee meetings.

That story illustrates the many fragments of the industry. For example: two meetings I attended a couple of days apart in Texas and Minnesota. In Texas milo was equal to or sometimes exceeded the value of corn and they told me our production research should be geared more to milo. Several nights later in Minnesota I was told that milo was equal to only 85 or 90% of corn, milo research was a waste of funds of any organization, because milo could not compete with corn, so all the research should be done on corn. At that time the Arizona pork producers group was primarily a marketing organization. Cudahy Packing Co. in Phoenix was the only major packing company in the state. The primary purpose of the producer organization was to market their hogs through Cudahy. They booked their hogs through the Arizona Pork Producers and the organization booked them to the packer. We had people in the east coast who were interested in promoting garbage feeding. That was a grain deficit area and one of their main feeds was garbage.

It was almost impossible, or perhaps impractical, for NPPC to get involved in regional or state issues. Eighty percent of the early checkoff funds that came into NPPC were earmarked for promotion. That was the primary thrust and primary purpose. Production problems were left up to the states. The role of county or area organizations was to get membership and to represent producers in the local area. There are pockets of feeder pig producers whose goals and interests in research on management and nutrition were certainly different than those in farrow-to-finish production areas. So it was real important that everyone understood where they fit into this scheme of things. The state's responsibilities, along with stimulating and collecting checkoff funds, involved production.

Legislative activity was left up to state groups. Arizona and New Jersey legislative activities, for example, probably wouldn't be the same. I can't see how any national organization can take a stand in Washington on many, many issues and not alienate a segment of producers in some part of the country. So the legislative work in Washington was done primarily through the state organizations.

NPPC never has or never will own a hog. NPPC never has and never will have a vote in a state legislature or in Washington, DC. The members, the people who own the hogs, are the ones who have the votes.

This philosophy regarding lobbying was also based on the feeling that we would not compete with the producers' own money, primarily in Washington, by lobbying, sometimes in opposition to general farm organizations to which many pork producers also belonged. The comment starting many organizational meetings made it clear that we were a commodity group, that we represented hogs, that we did not represent people. If producers wanted to be represented as people they could join their favorite farm organization, also they had congressmen and senators capable of representing them. Our purpose was to represent hogs.

Hogs were what counted, people didn't. We used to jokingly say that the only reason we put up with people was because the pigs couldn't come to meetings and make policy. The return to states in terms of funds was based on the number of hogs checked off and the number of hogs represented, not how many producer members they had. The board of directors allocated votes on the basis of the number of hogs in the states the directors represented, not the number of members. For a state to join NPPC it had to have at least 10% of the hogs in a state signed up and I recall that I was out in the Washington-Idaho area holding a district meeting and told them they must go out and sign up 10% of the hogs. We didn't say how many members they must have, because that wasn't important, it was the hogs we wanted represented, because that's where the power was when you went to the marketplace. A gentleman from Oregon stood up and said: "We've already got that done." I replied, "That's great, you're way ahead of most states and way ahead of where we hoped you'd be at this time." A veterinarian raising hogs on an old air force base all by himself owned over 10% of the hogs in that county and he had committed to the checkoff, so automatically they had their 10%, but that was an exceptional case.

NPPC was a council and not an organization of producers. The memorandum of understanding with other groups specified that we were only representing hogs and hog issues and not the people that owned or raised the hogs. Disease eradication, product improvement and swine research, promotion and merchandising would be proper subjects of concern for the organization; issues like the gas tax refund, daylight saving time, general farm legislation, were not. We were a commodity group, not a general farm organization.

This philosophy was difficult to maintain, at times, since frequently a producer would come to a meeting with a burning personal problem that he wanted NPPC to take a stand on.

The general farm organizations and pork producers never questioned who was to work on quality, advertising, promotion or disease research—it was NPPC. But producers always wanted to get involved in that great mystery in Washington and not leave lobbying up to their general farm organizations and elected officials. In later years they prevailed.

While we did no lobbying, it certainly was ethical and legal to work with the various departments within USDA, to have them assist us in programs and help direct some of the research money to the pork industry. As I went into various offices to talk with the chief of a department I was surprised to find that no one representing pork producers had ever pounded on those doors. When I told them NPPC had several thousand members, all of a sudden their doors would open and they were more willing to talk. They had numerous contacts from representatives of veterinary organizations, AMI, farm organizations, etc., but this was the first time pork producers had ever been to Washington. We didn't call this lobbying because we didn't go up on the hill. We visited with them after money had already been appropriated.

Some people would rebel once in a while and disagree over the way the funds were distributed, or how policy was established. They sometimes threatened to pull out and start a voluntary checkoff on a state basis. It didn't take them long to discover that very few packers or buyers were willing to have numerous checkoff programs, one for this state, another for that, and one for the national. There has never been, except in states with checkoffs established by legislation, a checkoff for a state program. The checkoff was always for the national program, with funds allocated back to the states on the percentage of hogs involved in the checkoff. Hogs were the criteria that determined not only the amount of money

the states received, but how many votes they had on the national level.

In my younger days I wasn't much of a rabble rouser or womanizer, but I'm one of the few people who has slept with a charter member of both the Iowa Porkettes, the National Porkettes and the Missouri Porkettes. She happens to be the same lady, my wife, Donna, a charter member of all three of those groups. The Porkette purpose at that time was to serve as an auxiliary for the NPPC, do some of the things the Council needed done, not as a separate organization. They were much more capable of putting together in-store demonstrations or pork queen contests, make-it-with-lard contests, or pigskin promotions that were a part of the early days of the Pork Council and they filled a valuable niche in those days.

In those early checkoff days of '66, '67 and '68 there was never, to my knowledge, a closed meeting held by the board of directors of NPPC. I don't know whether the sunshine law was even in effect in those days, but the press, most of the major hog press anyway, was always notified and invited to the board meetings. We certainly didn't have anything to hide. We were in the early planning stages, which was a great asset because we didn't have any long-established programs to reject that would have made bad press for us. Every meeting was basically a new beginning with a new set of ideas and a new set of programs. The whole farm press was more than kind to us. They took the attitude that here is a new child, let's don't criticize, let's help them take their first steps. They did that through our teething and while we made our first mistakes. The editors wrote flattering stories when sometimes it took a little imagination to come up with them. I can remember few, if any, negative stories. Not only would they feature the state officers and boards, but the national boards as well, and never suggested that their readers take a closer look at these leaders to see what they were really up to. Without the support of the press the Council would have never got off the ground.

A major factor in the press support was the NPPC board's philosophy of having everything in the open. In later days, out of necessity, because of personnel problems, there were many closed meetings, but in those early days anyone who wanted to come to a meeting, anyone who showed any interest was more than welcome. Another reason the major farm press was invited was related to the fact that National Hog Farmer was the first one on the bandwagon, one of the first leaders. We didn't want to get labeled as the Hog Farmer program, alienate the other press, make them think they weren't important and did not have input. National Hog Farmer had the early association as the official publication of the National Swine Growers Council and continued close contacts with the Council through the years, reporting on activities and supporting its efforts. Editor C. R. Mitchell attended many of the board meetings for many years and was closely involved in the effort for the voluntary checkoff through the Blueprint series and the events that followed. His ideas were a vital part of the late-night sessions that resulted in many of the developments of the late 60's. In spite of that close association, or perhaps because of it, it was important to us that we not carry a stigma or label as a one farm publication organization.

Many organizational stories could be told; they would take a book in itself. In 1967 we were in the process of reorganizing the state of Texas. The state had about five major pockets of hog production. T. D. Tanksley of Texas A & M was traveling with me to meetings around the state, with the final one in the panhandle at Texas Tech. A prime mover in that area was Euel Liner, a great pork promoter and later president of NPPC. He had set up the meeting at the college. We kept asking him if there were any problems. He replied: "A couple of guys will get up, but don't worry, I'll get up and take them on." An organization called the Pork Chop Club included the panhandle of Texas, parts of Kansas, New Mexico, Oklahoma and Colorado. It was headed by Mrs. Martha Romer. She had said a couple of times there was no need to organize another national group, she already had a national group started with those states. Tanksley and I kept asking Euel about whether there was any conflict between the two. He assured us he had talked with Mrs. Romer and everything was peaceful. When we got to Lubbock, before we went to Texas Tech we asked Euel again. "Don't you worry I've got everything under control." So Roy Poage, Tanksley and I got in the car and went to the college. Sure enough there was Mrs. Romer. She was kind as she could be and was helping register people. They were charging a $10 membership. As Euel had predicted, several hundred people attended—the auditorium was packed. Tanksley and I gave our presentations about the pork industry and NPPC and that we were moving toward a checkoff. Two guys from the crowd became a little critical. As Euel had promised, he shot them down. At the end of the meeting Mrs. Romer asked if she could say something. Euel, being the gentleman he was, said, "You bet." She thanked Euel for organizing the meeting, thanked Tank and I, said it was the largest membership the Pork Chop Club ever had, put the money and the mailing list in her purse and took off. Roy Poage and I didn't heckle Euel much going back to Lubbock, except to ask him repeatedly if he had everything under control. If you've never seen Euel Liner with nothing to say, or a story to tell (I hadn't before), that was the day.

So many funny things happen in organizational work. That one had all the elements, the extension service helping us, as occurred frequently, a key producer in the area setting up the meeting and sometimes things still went wrong. To the best of my knowledge Euel never reclaimed the money or the mailing list.

For those of us who lived in the midwest, there was one outstanding character—Harley Peters. Harley was not a hog producer, never served on any national boards, never was director of any pork organization that I knew of, but as far as promoting the industry and pork there will never be a more dedicated individual. He was a hog buyer for Western Order Buyers at Charles City, IA. I'll never forget how proud he was when he called one day and said: "Hey, hey (he stuttered a little), guess what, a hog buyer is now chairman of the chamber of commerce in Charles City." He felt this was a great event, for a hog buyer to hold that position. It signified pride in the hog business. I could tell stories by the thousands about him and they wouldn't really be stories, they would be true. He was the only person I know of who went to the National Barrow Show for about 15 years and never made it to the show. He'd find a group of people he wanted to influence to do something, or party with, and play golf with them all day. In the evening he'd set up a big hospitality suite and visit with people after the show ended. I happened to be one of his friends and my job every day after the show was to tell him who won and what happened, so Harley could visit with his guests as though he had been at the show all day. I doubt he even knew where the show grounds were.

Harley became interested in the pork industry during the Swine Industry Conference days. He knew that's where the leaders were and where he could find out what was going on in the industry. He always rented the largest suite available in the conference hotel, so he had room to entertain. When it was held at Purdue in the Memorial Union, Harvey arrived to register with several cases of spirits. He was informed that was not allowed. He got back in the car, went downtown and bought a couple of cheap suitcases, packed the bottles in them, went back and checked in. Once, when we were trying to pass some legislation in Iowa, Harley bought every representative and every senator a ham. He bribed his way into the Capitol one evening and when the legislators arrived the next day there was a pile of hams in the rotunda of the Capitol with each of their names on one. He didn't believe something couldn't be done. His boss, Virgil Smith, didn't know how much Harley was spending on these projects. He wrote checks for slaughter sows that didn't exist; the checks for $400 or $500 were cashed and the funds used for Harley's pork promotions. Harley financed many of my promotion efforts that way. He was a showman. One day I walked into his buying station during the NFO strike. Harley was trying to get higher prices from packers, saying there were no hogs coming to market. He had a box of fireworks beside his desk and while he was talking to a packer he'd light a firecracker, throw it out the window and say to the packer buyer: "I think I can get you a load of butchers, but they're shooting at me for buying hogs." Then he'd light another firecracker and throw it out the window.

When Nickels for Profit started, Harley was one of the first to cooperate. He kept hundreds of nickels in his desk drawer and would ask a producer if he wanted to check off for the Nickels for Profit program. If the producer he was buying hogs from said no, he would reply: "I'm going to deduct it from your check anyway and if you're that hard up I'll just pay it myself," as he counted out nickels. As often as not the producer would say: "Harley, just keep the nickels." That's the kind of showman and character he was.

If there was a civic or business event in Charles City—there were several major industries in the city—Harley would buy a bunch of boned pork loins and put on a whale of a barbecue.

Once Mac Whiteker and I were holding a series of field days around Iowa called Pork Appreciation Days and we'd announced there would be a carcass show at every event. We didn't get as many barrows entered in the first two or three as we had hoped, so we called Harley and asked him to bring us 20 or 30 barrows when we held the event in his area. While I was doing the cooking and preparing for that meeting, Mac was judging the hogs. He came to me and said: "What kind of mess do we have here? I have 300-pound hogs, 180-pound hogs, fat ones, thin ones, meaty ones. What did Harley do to us?" I suggested he just judge them as they were. The next morning I called Harley: "Harley, we wanted you to bring 20 or 30 meat-type hogs for this carcass contest." He replied: "Oh, if you wanted quality, why

didn't you say so. I thought you just needed numbers." He couldn't be flustered. Mac and I were holding a meeting with Harley one time trying to encourage hog buyers to pay a premium for meat-type hogs. He listened very patiently as we illustrated our comments with slides and graphs to convince him that meat-type hogs were worth more and Western Order Buyers should change its buying program to pay a premium for meat-type hogs. When we were finished, Harley stuttered a little and asked: "Gentlemen, are all the hogs in Iowa good?" We replied "Of course not." Then he said, "Well, s-s-s-somebody's got to buy the other b-b-bastards." You couldn't get the best of him no matter how you tried.

Among organizations that were helpful and supportive during the early part of the checkoff program, we must mention the pork committee of the American Meat Institute, the packer trade association. Even though those packers weren't sure where we were going, how we were going to get there, or how it might affect them, at least twice a year at their meetings, we were invited to tell them what was going on and ask for help. They never failed to give us a pat on the back and encouragement to keep trying. They could just as easily have opposed us, or at least ignored us in hope we would go away. Clayton Kingston of Hormel was chairman of the committee for a time and his support, along with that of other members of the committee, was appreciated.

The Meat Board was very helpful. In the early days, when we were telling producers about our promotion plans, most of the promotion material we used as examples of what could be done with their nickels was produced by the Meat Board. There have been many reports of friction between the two groups at various times, but while I was at the Council I couldn't have hoped for any more loyalty or assistance than we received. Bob Nelson was the staff man for the pork committee of the Meat Board at that time and whenever I needed help or assistance I could always call and it was forthcoming. Many times I left Chicago with a trunk full of Meat Board pork material. Often it was surplus to their needs or had been replaced by new material, but it was still of great value to us in holding producer meetings, to show what could be done in pork promotion.

A good agenda item at the many meetings when the checkoff was being considered was to have Dave Stroud, the chief staff officer of the Board, and me appear on the program to discuss the checkoff from different perspectives. The Meat Board had its own red meat check off and we were proposing a pork checkoff. Dave and I promoted the appearance of a controversy, made it appear that we were battling over the checkoff. I even suggested that Dave looked a little Jewish and questioned whether we wanted someone with that heritage running a pork promotion effort. Many thought we were opponents. Actually we were good friends, often traveled together and shared a motel room, but we never arrived at the meetings or left together.

Bernard Ebbing of Rath Packing Company at Waterloo, IA, and Carroll Plager of Hormel and Company in Minnesota have been mentioned before, but they merit another mention. Both were dedicated to the industry. The were very different personalities. Carroll was solid, certainly had the Plager sense of humor, but always more or less played the part of the laid-back professor type at meetings. Bernard, on the other hand, was more flamboyant, more boisterous, in supporting the industry and promoting the meat-type hog. Carroll's influence was primarily through the National Barrow Show, which he ran for many years, as well as through his speaking engagements and work on the meat-type hog committee. Bernard was the premier hog judge of the days when barrows were judged alive and then on the rail, a process which put many judges on the other side of the fence after their placings on foot proved to be way off on the rail. Bernard was one of the developers of the meat certification program, which involved recognition of sires based on cutout data of off spring. It took some selling to convince purebred breed organization leaders of the need for the program. One method Bernard used for convincing them was typical of his approach. Every year at the Iowa Spring Barrow Show at Cedar Rapids, the breed secretaries had a poker game in the evening after the judging. Bernard was a frequent judge at the show, as well as a participant in the poker games. When it came Bernard's turn to deal, he gathered up the cards and held them while he lectured the breed secretaries on the necessity of carcass cutout work and the need for the meat certification program. After making his point, he would deal and the game would resume. Bernard could be very persuasive, especially when he was holding all the cards. The breed associations all eventually adopted the certification program.

Dan Murphy and I were often accused of not being very accessible on Friday afternoons. People used to say they could contact Pig Paul any time, 24 hours a day, except on Friday afternoon if he was in Des Moines. Jiggs Sandidge always said if you want to contact Pig do it any time except Friday after-

noon. We were still holding many meetings on Saturday and Sunday, but we'd often be in Des Moines on Friday afternoon. As I've pointed out, there wasn't a lot of money for fancy meetings in those early days. It seemed logical to Dan and I that the place to meet with the attorneys and accountants and consultants was at a little tavern near the Capitol on Friday afternoon. Also included was anyone else we could get to come by. This was about the only time Dan and I had to sit down and bounce ideas off each other and other people. The other feature was free fish and beer at a dollar a pitcher. You can see by the menu and the beverage list that it didn't cost several hundred dollars to hold a staff conference. As you may guess, by about 2 p.m. everyone was very congenial and many great ideas were proposed and written on napkins, while we planned what we were going to do the next week.

I recently came across a Hog Extra article written in 1969 in which I was credited with making the statement that the board of directors of state organizations in the midwest averaged under 40 years of age.

In '68 and '69 we had many young people. I called it a youth movement—young thinkers. Certainly the catalysts were those men with some grey sprinkled in their hair, but they were willing to step aside, at least listen, to the young people coming along. Most of the board members of state producer groups and NPPC in those days were under 40 years old. Several of these people in that age group were also being elected as state officers.

Those young producers weren't sure why something couldn't be done. They thought everything was possible. Many of these good, solid business people were going to make it because they had to make it. They had invested their money, put all their savings and their life into this hog business and were prepared to do whatever it took to make it happen. I was also credited with talking about deserving to make it in the hog business. During that time there was a philosophy that hogs would be raised by whoever can handle them and produce them the cheapest and that was basically the way we thought it should be. When the industry gets sound we're going to encourage some speculators, some people with money to move into the hog business, so there's no room for complacency. But we felt family producers would stick with it and be the major producers as long as they did the best job and they shouldn't be there one minute longer.

I had the privilege of working with some dedicated, sound hog men during my years with the Iowa

Swine Producers. Two of them were Bernard Collins and Marion Steddom. They were farmers, hog men. Both operated about the same way. They had a theory that when the hog market was good, that wasn't the time to attend meetings; that was the time to stay home and take care of business. When the hog market was bad and there was no possibility of making money, they both said, "Now's the time to stop, reorganize and go to meetings, it won't pay to stay home anyway." When it came time to plant or harvest, they were seldom available to counsel with. I could always tell when the harvest was done, the phone would ring at 9 or 10 p.m. and they were ready to go again. Unique characters.

Section III

BUILDING A FOUNDATION

THE NATIONAL PORK PRODUCERS COUNCIL — 1969-1978

By J. Marvin Garner

This is the work of J. Marvin Garner, Executive Vice President of the National Pork Producers Council from June 1969 to 1978.

Garner's tenure as CEO spanned a decade of growth and development of NPPC exceeding that of any other commodity group.

His lifelong association with the pork industry includes serving as the Director of the St. Joseph, Missouri Market Foundation and Executive Secretary of the Chester White Records Association.

He worked a year for Wilson Meat Packing Company and served as a County Extension Agent in Missouri.

He assumed the role as NPPC's second chief executive officer following Rolland (Pig) Paul who served from 1966 to 1969.

Garner, a third generation seed stock pork producer from Mendon, Chariton County, Missouri, was a 1939 State 4-H Club Winner in Pork Production, Graduate of U. of Missouri in Animal Science, following three years in the Armed Forces; and worked first for Wilson Packing Company Provision Dept. in Chicago, Illinois. In 1948 he became County Extension Agent, resigning to become Director of the newly formed St. Joseph Market Foundation on the St. Joseph Livestock Market in 1951. In 1958 he became the Ex. Secretary of the National Chester White Swine Registry in Rochester, Indiana. In 1969 he became the Ex. Vice President of the National Pork Producers Co. He is now retired and living in St. Joseph, Missouri.

The NPPC national office in 1969 was located in three rooms of the basement at 3101¹/₂ Ingersoll in Des Moines, Iowa.

CHAPTER I

Before 1966 it was desire and a birthing of industry pride that fed the spark of life into the National Swine Growers Council. From early 1966 til mid-1969 the structure fed on the emotion of new growth at county, regional and state levels. It was also fed by the emotion of starting a voluntary check-off, something that had been dreamed, debated and attempted over the previous decades. This emotional period of three years was fanned by an equally emotional person, Pig Paul, the first full-time paid executive officer of the now renamed National PORK Producers Council. This period required a young energetic emotional person willing to stay out on the road, that could communicate with pork producers. Pig Paul filled that calling. Paul had stated early that he was not a figures, records and data person, but that he would spend three years in helping to get the organization started. During the '69 Annual NPPC meeting in Omaha a recent rumor surfaced that Pig planned to resign July 1. The NPPC Ex. Board called a quick meeting and discussed trying to find a replacement quickly to follow Pig's resignation. My name was proposed to be that person; but with two daughters in College, and the NPPC still not on the most sound financial ground, I was not ready to commit. I proposed that it would be best for all if immediately after Pig's resignation the President would announce that the Board of Directors would be accepting applications for the position. Then if after I had discussed the job with my wife, and decided to try for it, I would pursue it thru the interview system with all other applicants. With a family background in pork production, and my life's work having been in pork production education, marketing, promotion, breed improvement, on the NPPC Ex. Board since '63, and the Nat. L. S. & Meat Board for the same period, I felt that I knew the ground rules for the position about as well as anyone. With my wife's endorsement I entered the interview process with others in a St. Louis session and was selected for the Ex. Vice President position to begin June 1969. In mid-June Pig pulled anchor with the parting comment, "I'm going to the Ozarks to raise kids and pigs." On that date I found a staff of two; Creighton Knau, a former radio Farm Director; Mrs. Leone Turner, probably the most capable and qualified 75 yr. old secretary I've ever known and Dan Murphy, a part time assistant on the newsletter and State Staff work. There were two four drawer

files, three desks, mimeograph, addressograph, a file of address plates, chairs to accommodate, adding machine and a copy machine, but keep in mind that three years before we had no office equipment. We had an office landlord that was a basketball nut, so we got along well, being one myself. During my first day on the job I had taken part in a meeting with Pig, Neil Black, and Paul Zillman during which I became the holder of the proverbial "bear by the tail." That bear became known as the AMERICAN PORK CONGRESS. For some years the Pork Industry Conference, which included members from all segments of the pork industry, but very light on participation by commercial pork producers, had been decreasing in attendance. Our NPPC annual meetings were on the up-swing and we found many of the same faces at both affairs. There not being any elected structure of the PIC, and Black and Zillman having been the going force behind it, they were able to make the decision to blend it into the NPPC annual meeting. They would also assist the first year in helping to set up the workshops. The name AMERICAN PORK CONGRESS was selected because a trade show, annual meetings of the NPPC, Porkettes, and later other organizations were to be held in conjunction. The NPPC was to assume all arrangement, program and financial responsibilities. No one dreamed it would grow to be the largest commodity sponsored meeting in the nation. Tentative dates of March 3, 4 and 5, 1970, Des Moines, Ia. at the Veterans Auditorium were set; tentative because this was in the middle of girls state basketball and state wrestling, both of which are carved in stone in state calendars. Within a week I was off to fill an engagement that Pig had accepted to attend the Annual Meeting of the Livestock Marketing Assn. and appear on their program. Few, if any, auction markets were checking off nickels at this point and we needed to acquaint them with our program and seek their cooperation. Jim Nance, an NPPC board member and former President was active in the LMA and made my entry into this meeting very comfortable. It was also good to see an auction operator from Missouri in the audience, whom my father had worked with for thirty years. Less than 30 days later, on my first working trip to Washington, D.C., accompanying NPPC Pres. Albert Gehlbach and Prof. Wilbur Bruner, Chairman of our Production Committee, I woke up at 2 A. M. with a burning poker pain in my side. Eight hours later my nearly ruptured appendix was out and I had missed my first meeting in Washington. Albert and Wilbur met with the administrator of the Fed. Ext. Service seeking cooperation and funding for a study of swine research status. Producers had been promised that a portion of their funds would be invested in research in those areas of greatest problem to them. At this point there was no central listing of previous research in these areas and no identification of who was interested in or qualified to conduct such research. Wanting to avoid duplicate research and yet attempt to find qualified researchers in these areas the Research Coordination project was initiated. This proved to be an excellent step in that it not only identified well qualified researchers, it also pointed out the voids in past research efforts. The funding achieved from this trip helped to start up a study of research in four critical production areas: Baby Pig Diseases, Carcass Quality, Reproductive Efficiency and Waste Management. By Spring of 1970 complete texts and over 55,000 of the Fact Sheets prepared from these texts had been printed and distributed to pork producers and colleges across the nation. The Fed. Extension Service funded $2 for every NPPC $1 to make this project possible. While laying in that hospital bed in Washington, it dawned on me that we had no recent report on the status of a Consumer Research project being conducted in cooperation with the Nat. L. S. & Meat Board. In 1968 the NPPC had conducted consumer attitude polls to determine what negatives and positives they had with pork as a main course meal for their families. From this information some tentative ads were prepared and consumer tested in their ability to change or improve the IMAGE of pork. With this information in hand we had kicked off a six city market test project to actually measure our ability to change image thru newspaper ads, radio and promotion. Two comparable cities, Portland, Maine and Eugene, Oregon, one on each coast, were to receive paid newspaper ads, radio spots, in-store promotional materials, Meat Board staff would make TV and personal appearances and the NPPC Pork Cookout King would also put on live demonstrations. Two more cities, Watertown, N. Y. and Boise, Idaho were to receive in-store materials only and two more cities were to be check cities and receive no advertising or promotion efforts. 1800 consumers were surveyed at the beginning and end of this six month project to determine if there was change in image of pork. There were also interviews with Meat Market Managers in all six cities before and after to determine

change in their minds, and to get tonnage movement during the promotional period. The consumer and meat market surveys were conducted and all data summarized by Market Facts Inc. of Chicago. Despite a breakdown in the Meat Board getting the in-store promotional material into the stores as planned we did obtain very valuable information and statistics proving that paid newspaper ads and radio spots were able to change consumer image of pork and to increase the tonnage of pork sold, as compared to cities receiving no promotional efforts. The contacts developed with meat market managers during this project helped to get their cooperation in later promotional efforts. This was the beginning of NPPC promotional efforts to increase pork consumption thru image changing paid media advertising and in-store promotion. It was a small step, but a sound step that built a foundation upon which later programs could develop. From the very first producer meetings, even before any funding started, pork producers wanted to be involved in the promotion of their product. Nickels had been checked off for some months and now producers were wanting to see some action from their investment. It was not long before NPPC staff and leadership came under fire because few pork producers lived in the urban areas where the advertising and promotion was being tested. It took a period of time to convince them that it was a poor investment of their limited funds to place advertising in the less populated rural areas and in farm publications but should be placed in large urban consumer markets. The number of consumer exposures per dollar took on a new meaning to pork producers. This was a total learning stage for the pork industry because no one had been down this road before. Budgeted for a $75,000 project, the Image city project was the first time any voluntary producer funded organization had attempted to change the image of a meat product, using image oriented paid advertising. From the consumer surveys conducted by Market Facts Inc. we were able to identify the most critical objections to pork. It was interesting to find that "fat" was not the only problem. Through the surveys we found that many urban consumers were not aware that ham, bacon, canadian bacon and some other cuts came from the pork carcass too. We learned that some of their objections were as old as history and were actually handed down as fables and often without factual background. We found that if housewives wanted to be sure that their Sunday dinner or dinner for guests would be sure to please, they served ham. They also liked the aroma and taste of pork. Others who knew where all pork cuts came from, liked the versatility of pork. From these positive points we coined the advertising title and slogan "PORK, Always Tastes Good–Always in Good Taste." We also decided that if folks didn't know the true origin of some of the time proven pork cuts, and most of them were cured, processed and often brand name products, then we should invest in the promotion of the other 30% of the carcass that was fresh pork and unbranded. In reviewing our NPPC ads used during this Test Market project it became apparent that our organization needed a "Logo," something that would identify the organization in the ads without taking up a lot of space. It also needed to be something that could be used on our letter heads, promotional materials in the meat counters and could be adapted for all member states to use. This is a more challenging project than it appears at first. After a few weeks of scratching out rather crude figures and designs, I happened to glance at an Ozark Airlines ticket folder and the sweep-like figures that marked their planes. By reversing two of the sweeps, adding a couple of lines and another sweep, putting it on a solid block with the words National above the block and Council under it, the NPPC LOGO was hatched. It seems to have stood the test of time and is still marking the many ads and images that tie a proud group of producers to their efforts to promote their product and image. It hadn't taken long for other segments of the pork industry to notice our efforts and that we were for real. Herb Bain, Promotion Director for the American Meat Institute, had contacted the NPPC to join them and the Meat Board in the production of a film about the "facts" on the new pork. It was a committment of $7,000 but the line-up of known authorities that Herb had collected proved to be a good investment. It was completed in early 1970 and quickly became an outstanding program item for State and National meetings. "NEW FACTS ABOUT PORK" was a 17 Min. full color 16 mm film with a 13 1/2 minute version edited for TV that featured Floyd Kalber interviewing Dr. Philip White, Sec. of the AMA; Dr. Franz Ingelfinger, editor of famed New England Journal of Medicine; Dr. Wm. Darby, Chairman of the AMA Council on Foods and Nutrition and Dr. Dorothy Rowe, Chairperson, American Dietetic Assn. It was an impressive report with well known TV commentator Kalber getting the facts about pork from these leaders. Copies of the film were made available to member states who did an excellent job of getting it shown to many Home Ec. classes in schools and groups of home makers. Some states also paid TV time for it to be shown on some of their local TV stations. Nearly 200 copies of this film were made and became a part of the national effort to correct the consumer image of pork. About two weeks after my trip to the hospital, while in Washington, I returned to Washington, D.C. to meet with representatives of the Shell Chemical Animal Health Div. This meeting was to finalize the guidelines for a recognition program for outstanding young pork producers. After a few waltzes around the table with the promotional agency that worked for Shell, we settled down to the fact that the NPPC would set up the requirements and run the program with member state cooperation; and Shell would furnish $300 per individual and plaques for the honored producers that would be presented in each state's Annual Meeting by a Shell representative, when possible. The $300 was to pay each winner's trip expense to the Annual Meeting of the NPPC. This program was named the Pork All Americans with each state selecting their winner. The winners were to be actual pork producers, under 40 years of age, and active in their home community, while producing quality pork. The Pork All American program was approved by the NPPC Ex. Board September 22, 1969 and activated on that date. This has been an excellent program that has stood the time test. Three of the early honorees now hold Dept. Head positions in the USDA: Virgil Rosendale, Head of Packers and Stockyards Div.; Keith Bjerke, Head of ASCS; and Hilman Schroeder, President of the Pork Board. Many others have become leaders in state and national pork organizations as well as their local, state and national governments since the first class honored at the 1970 American Pork Congress. Farm Quarterly, a Cincinatti based magazine, had a picture of two red pigs with noses crossed for their Spring '69 cover. They had hired photographer Jay Monroe to accompany a writer to the farm of Ralph Howe, Clemons, Iowa. This photo gained world reknown, starting with the publishers offering use of the picture to the NPPC. Contact was made with Fred Swengel, Representative in Congress from Davenport, Iowa, and he carried the ball from there. In the April copy of the Congressional Record there are eleven pages of information introduced by Rep. Swengel. Pig, myself and Harley Peters, a hog market buyer from Iowa, the Nat. Pork Queen, Claudia Arndt and her mother and others attended the affair, presenting copies of the picture to members of the Ag. Committee. From that day on "Hogs Are Beautiful" became the "CHARGE" symbol of the pork industry. The picture of the pigs, buttons, belt buckles and many other images of that picture spread across the nation and to Europe, the far East and to South America. Farm Quarterly gave the NPPC all rights and uses of the picture, but after the picture became so famous the photographer came back on the council for royalties even tho he had been paid for his services by Farm Quarterly and they owned the picture. Needless to say we were like the proverbial turnip and especially so after we found out that Howe had not been compensated for furnishing the photo stars. Ralph Howe, really didn't need the pig picture to become known in the pork industry. He later became President of the Iowa Association and a leader on the Meat Board. Ralph says that he learned while holding those two pigs for the picture that they were not "house-broke" and he later needed a change. No wonder that pig had such a "relieved" look. Framed copies of the picture were also presented to President Jones of the American Meat Institute and Clayton Kingston, Chairman of the Pork Comm. of the Institute, at our annual appearance before that committee. In these meetings we were able to gradually wear down the opposition that some packers had toward the NPPC implied content voluntary checkoff. In later years some of these individuals became Presidents of their company and were able to make those decisions needed to help build the NPPC funding program. Presidents Nixon and Regan received framed copies of this "Pigs" picture in later years. The Production Comm. Project of Research Coordination in the four selected problem areas that had started earlier in the year were completed late in 1969. Considerable credit was due Iowa State's Emmett Stevermer, Illinois' Prof. Art Muehling and Dr. A. D. Leman; and Missouri's Prof. Bill Stringer for heading up the four projects and editing the enormous stacks of collected materials. By this time eight states had staff and there had been temporary arrangements made for some of the checkoff funds to be returned to these states to help pay these staff people and their expenses. Early in 1969 the NPPC Policy Committee, of which I was a member, had been appointed and presented the task of preparing a formula of fund sharing that would help the states with staff costs, but allow the NPPC to continue to develop promotional and research funding programs. Actually when a checkoff program was first dreamed of, there was no thought of states sharing in the checkoff. The original $2 per year token membership that was collected and kept at state level was not sufficient, even in the larger states, to support a staff person. A policy was developed to share with member states with staff men, up to $10,000 per year, based on the same percentage of the funds that was retained by the NPPC from those states. As mentioned earlier, this was the first time any organization had been down this path, and frequent adjustments in policy, and working agreements with states had to be made as stress points appeared. Not the least of these problems was the attempting to accept some states as members of the NPPC that had started their own legislative checkoff programs. A program was finally worked out that if they attained the percent of membership that our regular checkoff states had to attain for membership in NPPC; and if they sent the NPPC that percent of checkoff designated for their size of pork production, they would be accepted as members of the NPPC and have a Director on the NPPC Board. Complicated as it might seem, it worked but needed modifications from time to time. By mid-August of 1969 we found that accounting of checkoff funds by an accounting firm outside our NPPC office lacked the coordination that was needed to keep accurate check on cooperating markets and also in making refunds that were requested. We set up our own in-house accounting system that gave us an accurate breakdown of funds from each market by state of origin and balanced out at the end of each day. Another staff person was hired to handle this growing job and to assist with the secretarial duties needed for an expanding Nat. Porkette program. Organized at a NPPC Board Meeting in Springfield, Ill. in 1963, the National Porkettes had been struggling to gain membership. They needed program and activity to help build that membership. The new film "Facts About Pork" and some newly produced pork information gave them tools with which the program of "Pork goes to School" was started in the fall of 1969. Some of the more active county Pork Producer organizations budgeted their Porkettes funds to be given to the Home Ec. Teachers for the students to learn how to purchase pork in the stores and then prepare it in their classroom training. The National Porkettes developed into a very active pork educational arm of NPPC programs. Some of these ladies were seeking an identity and share in the pork production business due in part to the inference made in this poem that my Mother sent me, expressing her feelings I'm sure. It was written by Leta Fullmer of Amazonia, MO and titled: "The Other Woman In My Life" "Husband's in the barnyard mixing rocks and sand, Working on a hog house—I'll never understand. I've been with him much longer than any sow in sight, But my house can go straight to—well—while theirs is winter tight." Checkoff funds were making a gradual growth but now we had successful program results to help obtain greater market and producer cooperation. On Nov. 12, right in the middle of the football season we organized our first PIGSKIN MARKET PARADE. It was a team design in that pork producers at county levels would go in pairs or small groups to visit their local hog markets. The plan had a three-fold purpose: first, to THANK those markets that were cooperating in the "Implied Content" checkoff, second, to SEEK greater cooperation from those markets on "Request Basis" checkoff, and third, to INVITE those markets not yet cooperating with the NPPC voluntary funding program, to get on the band wagon of a growing program that would no doubt benefit them too in the long run. Over 1,000 markets in our less than twenty member states at that time, were contacted by pork producers. "Nickels For Profit" gained more identification on this one day than we had ever been able to attract. It proved that our organizational strength was firm, that our producer members had quarterback and fullback strength to get the job done, and it proved to market people that pork producers warranted their cooperation in collection of funds. The term "Implied Content" means that a market deducts 5 cents on all animals sold at their market, UNLESS requested by the pork producer not to do so. "Request Basis" means that markets would deduct 5 cents on each animal ONLY when the producer requested it be deducted. If the producer later wanted a refund or was not with his shipment at the time of sale, he could send a copy of his sale receipt to the NPPC and we would refund his money in full. It was amazing, yet gratifying, to see the requests for refund drastically reduce as numbers checked off doubled and our program efforts became more publicized. In the fall of '69 the NPPC entered into contract with the University of Wisconsin to produce a 25 min. film on the Market Grades of live hogs, corresponding carcass grades, and cuts from the carcasses. Start of the film was taken at the '69 Nat. Barrow Show in Austin where footage of live animals of all breeds was shot. Oscar Mayer Co. of Madison, Wis. aided greatly in permitting U. of Wis. Prof. Bob Kauffman and his staff to select animals from their buy, pursue them thru the plant with photo work being done and tests completed on the carcasses. It was my pleasure to work with a really fine German photographer, Fritz Alberts, I believe, in identifying the breeds of animals during the cutting and splicing of the film. I'm sure the knowledge I gained from him in this venture was greater than him learning our breeds of hogs in this country. It was about this time when we began to see something begin to grow and shine at the county, state and national level in the NPPC. It was PRIDE, pride in product, occupation and organization. It has been said that a man's dignity is like his top hat; the more he stands on it, the less impressive it becomes. Pork producers were putting on their caps of pride, their buttons of identity, and waving the banner of "their" organization. "Nature gave man two ends; one to sit on and one to think with." Pork Producers were standing up and using their heads to build their industry. In the midst of final preparation for the first American Pork Congress, the NPPC was asked to participate in a White House Food and Nutrition Conference, called by Pres. Richard Nixon. A committee of representatives of Agriculture had met and prepared a mutual statement for this event. President Nixon had called this affair and put a Dr. Jean Mayer in charge of the event. Dr. Mayer was active in an Eastern College and very close to the negative factions beginning to build negative programs toward the food industry. It was enlightening, to say the least, to take part in this Conference of over 2000 people, 98% of whom were primarily interested in government supported food programs, housing and minimum wages. It was a perfect illustration of futility in action. Due to some sharp exchanges among the dissident groups, we were able to establish the Agricultural group as a rather rational group and in doing so made some pluses with Dr. Mayer that later were cashed in our work with consumer education on pork. The 1970 1st American Pork Congress was a tremendous undertaking, considering the size staff we had at that time. Not in the greatest financial condition at this point we had to plan every event with an eye on its cost, versus what we could expect in attendance and income because it had been established policy from day one that NO NICKELS INCOME would be used for this affair. We had some members of the planning committee that wanted to give free passes and meal tickets, without limits, to all press, media and program participants. That is a fine gesture, IF YOU are not responsible for getting bills paid should there happen to be an attendance failure due to weather conditions. We had NO financial reserve upon which to fall back at this point. The first part of March is always "nervous" time for weather conditions in Iowa, especially Des Moines. Insurance coverage for this event took on new dimensions when we attempted to use bottle gas for the Pork Cookout Contest grills. Liability insurance had taken on a new status also since there had been a food poisoning incident at the auditorium in the not too distant past. With some excellent input from Leon Olsen, Ex. Vice President of Pride of the Farm Co. in helping set up the design and plans for the Trade Show; Harold Minderman, the Pork Cookout Contest; Gene Smith the Registration, Black and Zillman the Seminars, Joe Freeman the printing, excellent input from eight State Staff people, and a dedicated but small NPPC staff it turned out to be a successful event with about 4600 attendance. As we look back and check the pictures of the events thru the years it is amazing and in some ways humorous to see how the quality, size and content of the various company booths has grown. At that first event most booth fixtures were brought in the trunk of a salesman's car or a company pickup. There were many signs lettered by salesman, who wouldn't qualify as artists. It wasn't long before pickups were replaced by straight trucks, then trailers and vans. Signs became professional pieces and molded plastic signs and frames became booth show pieces. By the late '70s some exhibitors were spending over $30,000 to have new booths designed, built for the American Pork Congress and delivered in padded crates in moving vans. Exhibits at this first American Pork Congress filled about 80% of the floor of Veterans Auditorium in Des Moines. The other 20% was used as a large meeting room. Following the banquet that was served in the basement, which was rather bleak and horrible acoustics, a crowd of about 1200 moved to this area for the program. Marlyn Bidner was our first NPPC Pork Queen selected at an American Pork Congress. She represented the Hampshire Swine Assoc. American Cyanimid had come forward to award a $1500 Scholarship to the Queen. Our first class of Pork All Americans were honored, with about 13 states being represented by a young pork producer and his wife in most cases, their expenses paid by Shell Chemical. One of my biggest surprises was the number of USDA divisions that wanted "free" booth space for this event. Not overwhelmed with booth numbers this first year, we used some of their booths for spacing between competing product booths. After all the smoke had cleared, bills paid, and lost items located, the first American Pork Congress was a success beyond the dreams of most. There was more than just a little pride in the Pork Producers that had attended the 1970 event and they helped to spread the good word for future events. No doubt many of the exhibitors reported the attendance to their headquarters, and plans started immediately for their booths for 1971,

because we started getting requests for booth space within days after the 1st American Pork Congress. Thru the tireless efforts of Gene Smith, NPPC Treasurer, and the guidance of our legal council, the NPPC was issued an IRS Certificate of Exemption as a 501-C-5 Non-Profit organization in early 1970. We had come thru a period of no-funds, some-funds, and now increasing funds so it had become imperative that we obtain this classification. Since we had been operating under this system for some period of time, there was no change in our system but we now qualified for recognition as such. Policy recommended by the NPPC Policy Comm. and approved by the Ex. Board in early 1969, pertaining to donations, established an excellent foundation that was used many times in later months and years. We had accepted assistance from previously named companies, but it was understood from the start that these funds were to be used for a definite project and that their acceptance meant no endorsement of their products. With the success of the first American Pork Congress, we were suddenly confronted with industry supplying companies wanting to get our identity tied in with their product lines. As meager as our funds still were at the time, we held firm to the policy that the NPPC would not be a part of a sales promotion of any company or product. It was a bit tempting to not turn down some of the ventures that were proposed, but the NPPC gained in stature and respect that helped in years to come. A new NPPC President of the Board, Roy Keppy of Iowa, took over the reins at the 1970 APC from Albert Gehlbach. Roy was a well known pork producer of prize winning barrows at major national shows for some years. He hit the position running, with a quickly filled date book, many wanting to meet the new President, and no doubt some hoping to get a pointer or two on how to produce top winning barrows. Feed additives and residue in livestock production had been boiling for some years, mostly in Washington, D.C. and activist circles. In 1970 this subject became a real hot potato. Roy Keppy and I made our first trip to Washington to meet with the Bureau of Vet. Medicine head of the FDA, Dr. C. Donald Van Houweling. There had been rumblings for some time that the FDA was going to put the hammer on sulfa products that were widely used in the pork industry to control dysentery problems. Our efforts were to gain some extension of time before any action was taken so that research studies could be completed to determine the true dimension of the sulfa problem and to find alternative products to protect the health of the pork industry if the sulfa products were withdrawn. We also asked that another product be approved for pork producers use, that was approved for use in turkey production in this country and in pork production in Europe. The pork from which was being imported into the U. S. consumer markets, but use of this product was being denied pork producers in this country. Dr. Van Houweling was not aware of the products' use in the poultry industry but was interested when we told him of our concern that with its known use in controlling swine dysentery in Europe, there could be a pork producer or two that might get a few turkeys so they could legally obtain some of the product to control problems in their swine if sulfa use was stopped. About this time a new electron microscope was being developed that was millions of times more powerful than anything previously available to examine minute amounts of any tissue. With this instrument, minute particles of sulfa could be found, for the first time, in pork tissue if the sulfa products had not been withdrawn from feed rations, a specific number of days before marketing & slaughter. The activist quarters pounced upon this new found stage of torment with great gusto, despite the fact that there had not been and has not been to this day any scientifically proven data that any ill effects were caused in consumers by this minute amount of sulfa. Proof and facts are not in the vocabulary of the activist. It was their claim that if consumers consumed meat containing even minute amounts of sulfa or other pharmaceutical products they would develop physical problems immune or resistant to sulfa treatment and thereby ineffective in treatment of commonly known human diseases. This has never been proven to ever have happened. For some years they hung their claim on a story that a pregnant woman, caring for dairy calves that were being treated with antibiotics, passed along a resistance to her new born baby that prevented the use of these antibiotics in her baby. That's a far piece from positive proof, and could never be duplicated again by them or any researcher. The pharmaceutical companies have probably learned by now to get FDA clearance and approval for products specifically for animals or for human use, but not multiple species use. A few weeks after our visit with Dr. Van Houweling, I received a call from him asking if I could send him a set of slides depicting pork production on the farm and showing how and why feed additives were necessary for the profitable production of healthy meat. It seems that the FDA had set up a feed additives review board composed of medical researchers, FDA staff, USDA representative,

and even doctors in human medicine. Getting a set of slides that would show what we wanted to get across to them would still leave a lot of doubt in their minds, so I asked Doc why not get that group out to some hog farms in Pennsylvania or Ohio where I could line up a tour of typical hog farms. He commented, "Well I'm from Iowa, Pella that is, why don't we just come on out to Iowa." About 30 days later we had made arrangements for a tour of several hog farms in the Iowa City and Cedar Rapids area, reserved two large buses, made room reservations for the group and a meeting room in the Cedar Rapids/Marion area. The selected hog farms represented all size production units from 200 up to 5,000 head. Few if any of the tour group had ever been on a hog farm, but they were in position to make some very important recommendations that could seriously affect the pork industry. In fact, one of the committee, a lady representing the USDA, had three degrees, two PHDs and one MD. Sitting in the front of the bus, she asked me to please point out a soybean field if we happened to go by one during the day. I told her to look out either window because there were bean fields on both sides of us. During the two days we fed them pork every meal and got some pretty good points across that pork producers were serious business people and that their veterinarians were not on their farms every day and week of the year. These MD and PHD research people were under the impression that pork producers had a vet visit every week and that they were constantly sticking a needle in the hogs thereby creating a highly resistant strain of infection that could be passed on to those consuming pork from the animals. This was considered a successful event; so much so that Dr. Van Houweling later took the committee to the broiler industry and the cattle feed lots. Our friends in the farm press were somewhat perturbed that we did not announce this tour. However it was the feeling of the planners that the industry did not need a lot of publicity on this affair and if you invited part of the press you had to open it up for all, and right at that point we did not need a lot of negative urban press on the pork industry. During this same period a Nat. Animal Drug Committee was formed in Washington, D.C. including representatives from all species, farm organizations and drug industry. From this committee came a voluntary certification program for all species to follow in proper use of feed additives and proper withdrawal before marketing. This all helped to stave off FDA action at that point. The rumble continued however. A symposium at U. of Kentucky on September 10, 1970 held in cooperation of the Nat. Pork Producers Council, U. of Kentucky, Fed. Ext. Service, and Kentucky Ext. Service brought together some of the foremost authorities on the subject of Swine Feed Additives. Dr. Virgil Hayes became identified as a leader in this field as a result of this meeting and quickly became an outstanding and qualified leader for the pork industry in holding off this challenge and has continued to be so identified in later years. Dr. Mac Whiteker, U. of K. Ext. Specialist, and NPPC Production Committee member, chaired this affair and prepared an excellent summary and fact sheets for later use. 1970 was not a very good year for pork producers with prices squeezed down onto costs to a point that no profit remained and in some cases losses were piling up. With little regard for Producer problems the EPA started building up their fires of torment that had been smoldering for a couple of years. The increased number and size of pork production units were causing a potential problem area with increased concentration of waste from these units. Poor zoning or no zoning laws left many pork producers in a bad position. Some producers started joining the businessmen's clubs and luncheon organizations in their local communities so they could do a better job of public relations for their business to exist in the local community. However some states jumped into the fray with their own EPA structures hoping to acquire Federal funds for another state department. ENVIRONMENT became another watch-word for the activists and it wasn't long until some states were sitting up "sniff boards" that would drive by a certain location that had been reported as "Hi-odor." It was humorous to notice that neighbors and communities had more problems with "hog odors" when hog prices were high than when they were low and the pork producers losing money. Few times have I ever felt so futile as we were in trying to get EPA staff in Washington to realize the unrealistic rules that they were trying to form into a environmental protective program. Their perception of animal units, the effluent produced per animal unit, what was a navigable stream, and their complete disregard of economic feasibility were glaring faults in their approach to the problem. Like too many federal employees, they didn't care. The NPPC again reacted to the "heat of the moment" and quickly structured an Environmental Committee of producers, researchers and extension leaders to help set up guidelines for pursuing this industry problem. From their efforts Environmental Guidelines for Pork Production were developed from a study of all research on the subject by Meyer and Van Fossen of Iowa State. Legal Guidelines for Pork Production followed quickly, prepared by Ext. Lawyer Don Levi, U. of Missouri. Art Muehling, Ext. Ag. Engineer, U. of Illinois had prepared an excellent set of fact sheets from his study of Swine Housing and Waste Management research in cooperation with the NPPC, Fed. Ext. Service and U. of Ill. Ext. Service. Many of these materials became the "bible" for many pork producers and extension people working with them as challenges and problems continued to confront them in relation to environmental problems. The animal cruelty group were not pointing at our pork production system at this point, but there was little doubt that they would be in the near future. Plans were made to initiate some research on the gases produced in swine confinement buildings to determine if there were health factors to the human beings working there. Stan Curtis of Illinois initiated this project and was funded by the NPPC. During this period we had been growing in membership structure, state organizations and in "nickel checkoff." When we first initiated the checkoff program, most efforts were pointed to direct packer points and country buying points because about 70% of the nation's hogs were being marketed there. It was also easier for producers to make personal contact with the market buyers and gain their cooperation in making the checkoff. Having worked on a Central Public Market I was acquainted with a number of those market people and started making contacts with them. With local state staff people and local producers shipping to those markets we contacted Kansas City, St. Joseph, Sioux City, St. Louis, St. Paul and Louisville during this period and gained excellent cooperation from most of the firms on these markets, even tho some did not go on implied consent immediately. Some of our tentative member states were actually members in organization only at this point and had not pursued a strong market development plan. However by late 1970 we had started checking off about 17% of the potential hogs marketed in the nation, or about double the previous year at this point. Back in the Spring of 1970 we had started plans for a State Pork Month to be conducted in Pennsylvania, considered to be an Urban state, and we had an excellent dedicated group of pork producers ready to help with the local promotion distribution. This "Pork Month" project was to include newspaper ads and radio spots using some of the "facts and terminology" that our earlier consumer research had produced. Our staff and the Nat. Pork Queen met with the meat suppliers and supermarket chains of the area telling them of our intention. In-store promotional materials were also going to be furnished to them. By late summer it was evident from current hog prices that extra effort was needed to help build a greater demand for pork and thereby a better market. At this point we moved to "October Pork Lift" a national effort with member states buying radio time and some newspaper ads in their state with the NPPC furnishing the tapes and ad copy. We ended up with radio spots and or newspaper ads on 55 stations in 30 cities across the nation. We took our first ad in the Super Market News, a weekly magazine going to supermarket managers across the nation, telling them our plans, our offers of in-store materials and the support that our producers were going to make in their market. We contacted the packing companies with the same information and asked the cooperation of both groups to join us in the promotion of pork during this fall marketing period. New York, Miami, and Los Angeles were not included in our efforts at this point because our funds could in no way scratch the mass of these population centers nor deter the ethnic eating habits of non-pork consumers in these cities. In our surveys following Pennsylvania Pork Month we found that 47% of the supermarket Meat Managers reported an average of 25% increase in pork sales during this month. We found that they would use in-store promotional materials IF they were supplied to them free of charge. Most NPPC available funds were invested in this fall Pork Promotion because there was a massive amount of pork to be marketed and hog prices were really squeezing all pork producers into loss levels. I'm not sure how much we increased pork consumption, but we certainly made some good contacts with retailers, packing companies and above all our producer members that shared in the effort were pleased with the effort that helped to increase membership in many areas. Allan McGhee, editor of Drovers Journal commented in his editorial "It is a program in which every hog raiser ought to be proud to have a part."

CHAPTER II

SUCCESS AND GROWTH BUMPS

When we review this foundation building period, we find a much stronger organization, a better financed program, growing producer involvement, and greater recognition by related industry leaders. We found that we could conduct a pork promotional program on a larger than state scope. We found that the packing and retail industry that processed and marketed our pork products were aware of our presence, but still somewhat lacking in all out cooperation. They had to be shown yet that we were for real and not a flash in the pan. We had created enough of a stir in the agricultural segment that some other organizational structures were concerned with our possible growth and recognition. During the late '60's and the '70's there was a mushrooming of a number of commodity organizations, each with their own goals and self identifying programs. Each was dead set on serving their farm product producer membership. General farm organizations had found they could not build a shed system that would cover all commodities in a manner that would satisfy the needs of all. The time was ripe for commodity organizations to sprout. The success that was evidenced by the Nat. Pork Producers Council became a pattern for others. Some general farm organizations begin to move their state groups towards a blending process that would attract our state pork council members to form a combination that would still give them a pattern of control. One state group went so far as to start their own pork checkoff program, with all funds staying at the state level, and seeking to block that states pork producers from becoming a part of the National Pork Producers. They succeeded even tho they were not a major pork production state because they were riding on the coat tails of the state general farm organization and operating under the policy of that group. It served its purpose as intended, but the pork producers of that state did not get to share in the pride and identity of the Nat. Pork Producers Council until the mandatory federally legislated checkoff started in later years, that included Alabama. Three other states were on a state checkoff system but adapted their program to become a membership and funding members of the NPPC, including North and South Carolina and Virginia. In our growing contacts with the Washington, D.C. circles we had found that the old adage, "the squeaking wheel gets the grease," was still as true as the day it was concocted. We found that the Pentagon, right in the midst of our burdensome low hog prices of 1970, had decided to buy their pork from European countries, some of which were Iron Curtain at that time. We found that the USDA had to have pressure to get our pork on the PLENTIFUL FOODS LIST that they mailed out to schools, and consumer groups. This gave us the opportunity to set up a network of producer members in all member states to contact their senators and representatives to help get these unfair practices corrected. There is no more effective and sincere lobbyist than an informed pork producer. I sincerely believe that this effort gradually grew into one of the most effective and respected commodity representative groups working the Washington scene, at least that was the report from a number of congressmen. In January 1971 we received our first and largest shot in the arm of our NPPC financing from a related industry firm. Oscar Mayer packing company, represented by Allan Mayer, Vice President; Ex. Vice President Harold Jaeke and Bill Marquardt, Head of Procurement, met in Des Moines and presented Pres. Keppy and Vice President Euel Liner with a check for $50,000 to be invested in the pork promotion and consumer programs of the NPPC. Needless to say that this recognition by a major packing company gave a lot of positive stability to the NPPC at this point. Roy Keppy, being a consistent seller of hogs to the Oscar Mayer plant in Davenport, Iowa, and having started as a young man selling hogs to Mr. Jaeke when he was a hog buyer, could have played a part in attracting this investment. However Pres. P. Goff Beach in a later letter commented, "Our contribution is an indication of our belief in the Council and of our long standing conviction that a good team effort by producers, processors and retailers is the only way to solve industry problems to the best benefit of each member of the team." This $50,000 investment equalled our income from about 2 1/2 million hogs, or just one year early it was equal to 2 1/2 months NPPC income. The Elanco Company, manufacturer of a number of pharmaceutical products used in the pork industry, initiated an annual affair at the American Pork Congress when they hosted a breakfast for the NPPC Board of Directors and presented a $5,000 check to be used in funding the promotion of pork by the NPPC plus they developed billboard ads and purchased space on roadside billboards promoting pork and welcoming pork producers to the APC. This company grew into a major support factor for the NPPC programs and the American Pork Congress function. Among their voluntary efforts was the production of a consumer film on pork, "Surprise Me," copies of which were presented to all member states and to other educational film users across the nation. The NPPC presented Elanco

President Malcolm McVie a plaque at the Indianapolis American Pork Congress, expressing thanks for their industry cooperation. A number of things were looking better at this point with nickel checkoff up 79% over what it was just one year ago in January 1970. Idaho, Mich. and Miss. had joined 19 other states and helped attain almost 25% of the hogs marketed being checked off. By March 1971 we were in the 50,000 member range from 30,000 one year before. We had the 1st and 3rd largest Central Public Markets, 12 large packing companies, their buying points and over 40 Auction Markets on Implied Consent checkoff. We had learned that our efforts with Congressmen had helped to reverse the Pentagon plans to buy their meat supply for overseas troops from foreign suppliers. Our presentation before the Senate and House Agric. Budget Committees must have rung a bell because it resulted in $420,000 being added to the USDA budget on an annual basis to be invested in Swine production and product research. It was ironic but we had to constantly monitor what the USDA was doing with those funds to keep them from swinging over into some other species project. It was also my first awakening to the fact that the USDA takes a rather large percent off the top of any of these appropriated funds for their "overhead costs" and when those funds went out to some Land Grant College research center, the College then also took a percentage of the funds for their "overhead costs." It ends up with the research project getting into action with as little as 50% of the original funds that were appropriated by Congress. From this experience we quickly learned to ask the research project presenters to outline their expendable costs for supplies, materials, animals and feed and etc., separate from staff salaries, lab costs, etc. From this outline we could then identify and select those portions of the project costs that we would fund, thereby avoiding paying "overhead costs" on these items and getting the full reach of our dollar investments in the actual research that was needed. Some College financial department heads bucked and snorted on this arrangement, but when we pointed out that pork producers in their states were paying taxes to their state and thereby already supporting some of the "overhead costs" of their state universities, they became a bit more cooperative. USDA Secretary Clifford Hardin invited the National Pork Producers Council and its member states to attend and participate in Pork Producers Price Seminar in Washington. We were there with 27 representative pork producers, somewhat overshadowing other farm organizations that were invited. Pres. Keppy presented a statement for the NPPC and the member state leaders also had their turn at the podium. Keppys comments "we've created our own problem with over production, but we believe that the USDA can benefit, yet help us in better distribution and use of this surplus pork thru government agencies," was pretty much the tone of the meeting. We also urged the USDA market reporting system to use a previous five year average when comparing livestock forecasts rather than just the previous year. This, coupled with their inaccurate estimates of production, was misleading to pork producers in their production planning. We later found that part of the actual error in USDA pig production forecasts was due to them taking the amount of their error and lumping it into "hogs slaughtered on farm" to keep their former estimated forecasts within reason. They were often reporting one to three million hogs slaughtered on farm when actually farm slaughter was almost nil due to intensive state and national restrictions that had been put on locker plants, the last bastion of farmers using their own animals for family meat. It was a good session and after it was over Sec. Hardin, and one of his assistants Clayton Yeutter (present Sec. of Agric.) were impressed with input from the NPPC and its producer members. It later became known that Bill Rothenberger, a past NPPC President, had visited with Clifford Hardin, a fellow student at Purdue in earlier years, when he had visited the home area recently, and suggested this Pork Price Seminar. Bill represented the NPPC Consumer Development Committee, of which he was chairman, at this meeting. From the common sense input by pork producers at this meeting, a recommendation following within the USDA that they set up a man to keep closer contact with the swine industry and to feed back to them more direct information to help guide them in the future. It ended up that we had three USDA staff people checking regularly with the NPPC on pork industry problems and helping us find the correct doors to knock on for assistance in many areas. Roger Gerritts, USDA Agric. Research Service staff man in animal research areas became a very helpful person and assisted us in improving our methods and information to obtain research funds for the pork industry. His boss Dr. Edminster was one of the sharpest and best administrators we came in contact with. He spoke to our Board of Directors, attended a Pork Congress and became well acquainted with our organization. Unfortunately, cancer shortened the tenure of this fine fellow. The 1971 American Pork Congress, the

second, was larger and better than the first with over 6,000 in attendance. The NPPC Annual Meeting, the Nat. Porkettes, the Iowa Pork Producers Assoc. and their Porkettes Annual Meetings all combined with the activity of the Trade Show and Seminar Meetings to make this the largest commodity event in the nation. The American Society of Swine Practitioners also joined in with their meeting and became a part of this growing affair. Pattie Cline of Illinois was selected the new Pork Queen, Ben McKay of Ness City, Ks., a County Agent won the Pork Cookout Contest, nineteen new Pork All Americans were honored, and plans were announced to have the next American Pork Congress in Kansas City. The feed additive residue in pork problem had continued to be a problem of major importance. We were now being contacted by pork producers who had shipments of hogs detained or refused normal marketing channels due to residue in the carcasses from earlier shipments. A hog ready for market is kind of like a watermelon. You pick it when its ripe. We had developed enough information from these complaints to prove that many pork producers were not aware that they were feeding sulfa products to their hogs thereby causing possible residue problem. Some insisted that they had never fed any antibiotics or feed additive products, yet they were being singled out at the packing plants as producing contaminated pork products. It became apparent that many producers relied completely on their feed company suppliers to change their rations as needed for most efficiency and profit. It was apparent that our residue problems in the pork industry did not center on any one cause. Some producers who carelessly or unknowingly did not remove finishing rations containing sulfa or other additive products the required days before marketing; some feed company advisors were not stressing withdrawal periods; some vets were not checking with the feed suppliers to determine what antibiotic level they were putting in a producers feed supply and thereby often doubling the allowable level that was being fed to hogs; and some tissue samples were not being handled in a proper manner at the packing plants thereby letting some decomposition occur before the sample reached the Fed. Lab. in Peoria, Illinois, and these resulting in false positive tests. Frankly it was an industry problem that had to be corrected post haste. With that in mind I included in my American Pork Congress Annual Report some recommendations that might help the industry start correcting the residue problem. Pork producers had to become more aware of what was in the products they were feeding and follow exactly the instructions for withdrawal for each product. Feed companies were asked to enlarge the WARNING information and withdrawal instructions on their feed tags and to be more alert about informing the producers using their products. To illustrate part of the confusion on the use of feed additives by pork producers was the fact that Arsenicalic Acid, a widely used product to prevent scours in pigs was approved by the FDA in five different names or terms, some of which did not include the term "arsenic" in any manner. Without a degree in chemistry it was extremely difficult for pork producers to determine just what was being used in their feed mix. Those companies doing commercial mixing, formulation of complete rations, and making bulk delivery to pork producers facilities should do a better job of purging their mixing plants and trucks when changing from a medicated ration to a non-medicated one. We asked them to put printed labels on the bulk tanks when their staff delivered medicated feed to the farm, stating the feed additive content and required withdrawal time. We also recommended that swine vets check to see what medication levels were being fed before they either gave shots or prescribed any levels of medication in all hogs, especially those close to marketing weights. The American Feed Manufacturers Association jumped up stiff legged and said they were doing what the law required. The Nat. Hog Farmer editor, whom had not endorsed me for this NPPC job, pounced on this affair as an opening to take a bit of my hide. Of course their publication achieved a rather pleasant income from the advertising of the feed companies, so any action they could ferment to take pressure off the feed companies was also protecting their income. The facts were apparent. The pork industry had a problem. It was being caused by multiple factors. It was time for all-out effort by all parties to get with correcting the problem post haste, because pork producers were being hurt financially every day and the image of our product that we were trying to promote was getting at least a gray eye. We asked the feed companies to enlarge, capitalize and print in red on the front and back of feed tags the WARNINGS and PROPER WITHDRAWAL INSTRUCTIONS. We asked them to include in their sales promotion materials the importance of producers following the approved use of their medicated products. We asked those in the mixing business to checkout the cleaning of their mills between mixing medicated and non-medicated formulas. For too long feed companies, vets, producers, and government inspectors had been blaming each other for the problem. It was time for all to get involved in correcting the problem that was mutually important to all. It was encouraging to work with a Purdue Swine Ext. Specialist who had successful set up a series of meetings in the heavy swine population counties of that state and invited feed companies, elevators and veterinarians to meet and discuss the feed additive residue problems. We were happy to have this kind of cooperation and it was an eye-opening affair for some that couldn't believe that they were actually a part of the problem. State vets, Fed. vets and research vets participated. Several more areas took up this program and it did a lot to start action on the problem. The NPPC voted to endorse a Voluntary Certification of Drug Withdrawal certificate program that asked each producer to sign when he marketed his animals that he had followed all requirements of feed additive withdrawal before shipping the animals. This program was developed by the Animal Health Committee that included the NPPC as a member and all other animal and poultry commodity groups plus general farm organizations and the Animal Health Institute membership in Washington, D.C. As greater effort was made by the industry to correct this residue problem we were amazed to learn some of the possible contamination sources that were unknowingly causing problems. We found that some of the sulfa products were ionized or sticking to the insides of metal bulk feed bins and came loose when bins were pounded on to prevent bridging of the feed. The major suppliers quickly started coating their products to correct this problem. One producer found that a small nail hole in the side of a drop spout from his automated feeding system was dusting out sulfa products that dropped into the feed trough of next pen hogs near market weight and thereby caused a residue in animals marketed from that pen. We found that it was possible for sulfa contamination to be passed on to hogs on SULFA FREE rations, if they were moved into a poorly cleaned pen in market facilities where hogs that had been fed sulfa had been penned. As the problem grew and we learned more about what caused the problem and how to control it, cooperation begin to build. It was a real battle to get the government inspection people to even admit that poor sampling techniques could be contributing to the problem. Finally with some inside cooperation we found that some of the tissue samples being randomly taken from animals in the slaughter plants were being left in an unrefrigerated state for periods of a few hours, until the next break, before they were quick frozen. With the intensive heat on the slaughter floor the tissue was beginning to break down and the results were found to possibly cause a false positive test at the lab. We also found that some of the tissue samples being sent air mail or express were arriving on Friday or Saturday at air terminals or mail rooms and tho they started out packed in dry ice, they were thawed and some break down occurring before they entered the government lab. The big problem was that when a pork producer's shipment of hogs were sampled and the tissue showed up a residue above permitted level, that producer could not ship any more animals until he had brought in a test lot of five animals and their tissue test was negative. This created a monstrous marketing problem for some large producers that marketed hogs every week, because the total testing procedure sometimes took 30 days or more to get a clear report. Some even started hiring private planes to fly tissue to the labs after government vets had taken and sealed the samples. Before long a number of major feed companies and feed additive supply companies began to join us in the educational and information program that was needed to inform the industry of our mutual problem. In later years even the Federal Extension Service joined in with a widespread information program. Those that had been sitting on the sidelines and yelping at my efforts reminded me of the old country store tale of the howling hound. It seems this old hound would sit behind the pot-bellied stove and howl by the hour. One old fellow asked, "Whats wrong with that hound?" The store keeper replied, "He's sitting on a cockle bur." "Why don't he get off it?" The storekeeper replied, "it takes less energy for him to bark and howl than it does to get up off the bur." In May 1971 President Nixon invited the NPPC to participate in a "Salute to American Agriculture" that included all species and commodity people, the NPPC being represented by Pres. Roy and Mrs. Keppy. Exhibits of all types of agriculture products, machinery, livestock, etc. were displayed on the White House Lawn. It would have been a really fine affair for the 100 attending, but rain made things a bit soggy on that beautiful lawn. Also in May we made an attempt to get the pork industry honored by getting the U. S. Post Office to issue a commemorative stamp of the "Hogs are Beautiful" picture. Even with Rep. Paul Finley, Ill. joining Rep. Fred Schwengel, Ia. and Sen. Jack Miller, Ia. for pressure from that side and the farm press also joining in we were not able to pull this one off, but it was and is still a good idea. As stated in the early pages of this book, a News Letter prepared by Wilbur Plager,

President of the NPPC quickly became a printed piece that within short weeks became known as the National Hog Farmer and it carried the NPPC news material. For months and even years many of us promoting membership in the NPPC touted that if they would pay the $2 to join the NPPC they would get a subscription to the National Hog Farmer free. You might say the NPPC and the magazine grew with support from each other during this early period. Actually the Nat. Hog Farmer was owned by a printing company at Grundy Center, Iowa and it grew quickly from its identity with the fast growing NPPC. The editor of the NHF attended all NPPC board meetings, committee and other functions, and from time to time voiced opinions in these sessions. During the early growth period of the NPPC this input caused little problem; we were glad to have the interest in our activity from anybody. However as the NPPC program grew in activity, staff changes were made, and more farm press and media became interested in the workings of the Council, its announcement of new programs and developments as they occurred. It quickly became apparent that if the NPPC was to be a truly National organization, we needed to conduct our business, meetings and program announcements on a business basis and open them up to all interested farm press and news media people on an equal basis. NHF had exclusive access to these affairs in the past and this brought continual complaints from other farm press who wanted an equal shot at any news that might be forth coming from the NPPC meetings. This problem was presented to the Ex. Board of the NPPC and after much discussion it was decided to open up all board meetings and invite in all farm press that wanted to attend. So it was done. During the first board meeting with several farm press people present, an educational film project came up that would need about $15,000 to fund. Despite this project having been proven successful in an earlier short term basis, the board members were hesitant to open up and openly discuss the expenditure of that many scarce dollars in front of the open press. The motion to invest these funds on the film project darn near failed because of the pressure of the occasion. This later became one of the most successful projects in the educational field for use by FFA and 4-H that the NPPC ever financed. At this point it quickly became evident that the directors functioned better, were more open in thoroughly discussing the business affairs, and debated among themselves and staff if the meetings were held without any press people present. So from that period on press sessions were held following the meetings and announcements were made concerning the content of the meeting. The NPPC staff had grown by this time and we had staff to prepare and deliver news releases of the activities of the Council to all media and thru a weekly radio news tape. We quickly built close working relationships with all of the major farm publications, radio farm broadcasters and TV people across the nation. But the National Hog Farmer people were rather caustic with me from that time on. Even tho they had used their relationship with the NPPC to build a very successful magazine that later sold to another publishing company for a considerable amount of money and established the editors with rather long term jobs, they were more negative than positive in their coverage of NPPC programs and activities, especially editorially. It was a growth bump in NPPC development. From all of our consumer research and surveys on consumer attitudes towards pork, we found that image was one of the major negative factors. After a number of weeks of planning we kicked off year round pork promotion efforts in two cities. We called these "Image Cities" and planned a $100,000 budget for this yearly program. St. Louis, Mo. and Milwaukee, Ws. were our first cities in this program. We found that advertising sales people with the Newspapers and other media would help open the door to us getting to the Meat Market Managers of the major chain stores. We held evening dinner meetings in each of these cities and invited the store managers and meat market managers and their wives. We announced our pork promotion program that would soon be started in their city, displayed our materials, newspaper image ads and radio spots. We asked their ideas, suggestions and cooperation. Excellent cooperation was obtained from the major chains that sold more than 80% of the meat in those cities. Later we got some tonnage figures from them that proved our efforts were paying off in greater sales of pork. A few weeks after the kick-off of these promotions we went back to each of the cities and sponsored a "Pork at the Baseball Game" at the Brewers and Cardinals parks. At each of these events we passed out pork recipes to all attending, presented hams to every member of the home club and to the managers of both clubs. We also were assisted by local processors and packers in serving pork dinners and sandwiches to all of the press at both parks. These press people, radio, TV and newspaper, all commented in their media about the good pork they had eaten and actually got more pork promotion to more people than we could afford to spend at this point. Our reason for picking these two cities to start was that we wanted plenty of pork available in the market, we wanted positive media available, we wanted major chain store cooperation and we wanted them close to us so that we could monitor the programs. We also had good state staff people in these states and in St. Louis we had over 500 pork producers in attendance and handing out pork materials. This again was a first for anyone in the meat industry and we were learning with every step. In our St. Louis kickoff dinner we invited Ray Hankes, Ill. Pork Cookout King to prepare the meat for that dinner. Ray became President of the NPPC some years later. Usinger Sausage Co. of Milwaukee was a wonderful cooperator in that market and took the lead and furnished the products for the dinner for the press at the ball park. NPPC staff and state leaders were a part of the game opening ceremonies at each park with the Nat. Pork Queen throwing out the first ball. We continued to open up one or two new Image Cities each year as funds would permit. Boston, San Jose, Oakland, Seattle, Cleveland, Houston, Atlanta, Philadelphia and others were added later. Positive things continued to develop in pork promotion for the NPPC. Gov. Ray of Iowa was the host for the Mid-West Governors Conference to be held in Sioux City and invited the NPPC to prepare and serve Pork Chops to the more than 600 attending. With the state staff Paulsen, Minn.; Ford, Iowa; Schrick, Neb.; Freidow, S. Dak. and Minderman, Ia. Farm Bureau all joining in we hauled the more than 600 one inch chops to an island in the Missouri River, where the Governors, guests and the press landed from boats and enjoyed our pork presentation. It brought forth many favorable comments and gained a lot of press, radio and TV time. President Keppy and I met with Mr. George, a sales representative for Kraft Co. livestock products, who had volunteered the possibility that the Kraft Foods Div. might be a partner with the NPPC in developing and placing colored ads in major consumer magazines, featuring pork and some of their products. From this meeting the two staffs worked together to develop an excellent ad presentation on pork ribs and Kraft Barbeque sauce that went into three or more major womens magazines in four color. This was the first venture of the NPPC promotion program into national consumer magazine advertising. We could not have had a better partner. Kraft is world reknown as a quality firm with excellent ad production and food photography preparation capability right in their own kitchens and studios. In fact it is one of the best in the nation. We learned a lot from this project and it gave us new status in the field of food promotion, but mainly it doubled the effect of our promotional dollars because we paid only one half of the ad costs yet got full display of pork products in a favorable and attractive presentation to the consumer. I did learn however that I needed to be not only a referee, but also a bit hard nosed, when two Home Ec. people, two ad agencies, and two products were to be involved. Positioning of product in the ad, getting positive appearance of both products in the photo, and getting some name recognition for the NPPC in the ad so our producer investors could identify efforts being made in their behalf was always a challenge. The NPPC promotion program later developed co-op ad programs with the Cling Peach Board, Dole Pineapple, Kikkoman Soy Sauce, and other major food products, plus repeats with Kraft, that complimented our pork products, yet helped us stretch our limited funds to reach a greater consumer audience with quality presentations. Most of these product promotions included in-store presentations materials, distribution of premium programs, shelf and dump card development and most of all, we gained experience in how to get our promotional materials into the retail food centers, get them used, and obtain the cooperation of those store managers. We quickly found that if retail chains, and even more the independent store owners, were going to cooperate with our promotion programs, these in-store sales materials had to be furnished to them free of charge. For years the Nat. Livestock and Meat Board had been making promotional materials and selling them to livestock producer groups that were attempting to promote their products. Some store groups made limited use of these materials. However it quickly became apparent to us that if we were to become proficient, capable of following up on delivery and use of in-store promotional materials in our pork promotions we were going to have to develop and print our own materials. It had also been policy of the Meat Board that they not enter into the "paid" advertising field because they believed it might deter the media from using some of their free food information releases that was made available by their staff to the media. With the NPPC growing into a full pork promotion program that included developing our own materials and buying paid advertising time and space, all of which carried our own identity, there began to develop some touchy areas between the two organizations that shared their funding from the same nickel. No doubt personal ego conflict of staff entered into this growing problem, but there was also some producer leader egos of each organization

that fueled the situation. Just previous to the starting of the voluntary "Nickels for Profit" checkoff that was started by the NPPC, the Nat. L. S. & Meat Board had set up a Beef Committee division to help handle the take-over of a defunct beef checkoff program. Serving on the Meat Board as a Director at that time I joined a number of other Directors asking that a Pork Committee also be set-up. We also asked that there be an identification of fund income by species and that pork get its just share for pork programs. For some reason there was doubt as to whether the income could be accurately broken down by species. It was also during this period that NPPC representatives were asking for a meeting with the Meat Board to set up an agreement on a mutual funding program. This meeting was deterred and debated for some time. Being on the Meat Board Directorship at that time, it fell my lot to introduce the proposal into the Annual Board Meeting of the Meat Board, that they appoint a committee to meet with a committee of the NPPC to see if they could agree on a mutual funding system by pork producers. Charlie Schuman, Pres. of American Farm Bureau; John Copeland, Vice President of Swift & Co.; Charlie Jennings of the American Stock Yards Association and a gentleman from Sioux Falls representing the Nat. Livestock Exchange Assoc. jumped up almost in unison to oppose my motion and followed with very vocal opposition. I had happened to sit down next to Glenn Pickett, a past Meat Board President, and representing the Ka. Livestock Assoc. Having been acquainted with him from earlier days on the St. Joseph Market, I had explained to him what I was going to introduce before the meeting started. Jim Nance, who was representing the Pork Industry on the Meat Board, was President at that point and being a very capable political person he nimbly side-stepped getting into the following debate of my motion. After due discussion, Glen Pickett, Ks. Livestock Assoc., got the floor and commented that as he understood the motion, it was not asking for approval of the NPPC, but merely asking for a meeting of representatives from the two groups to determine if a mutual funding program could be worked out and he seconded the motion. The motion passed by one vote, I think, and thereby started the competition for the pork producer funds later known as "nickels for profit." I kid Glen Pickett yet that, even tho he was a died in the wool cattle man, he helped get the NPPC program started. In this early development period of the NPPC, we knew that marketing organizations would not make two checkoffs and send one to the NPPC and one to the Meat Board. It was therefore imperative that we find a point of agreement on division of the nickel, no matter which organization received it from the market. The NPPC had stated a policy early that they would seek only a full nickel or nothing, and that the Meat Board would get one cent of each nickel. The Meat Board had been accepting 3/4 cent from some markets and one cent from others so if the NPPC was successful they would be getting a full penny on all hogs checked off. Our success would mean that they would be assured of increased income because they were collecting on less than 30% of the hogs marketed at the time the NPPC started the Nickel Checkoff. Its now history that the Meat Board did appoint a committee. They met with the NPPC committee and a Memorandum of Agreement was formulated and accepted by both organizations. As stated earlier in this book, a trial checkoff was started in six counties of Iowa and Illinois. Despite the success of the voluntary "Nickels For Profit" program, this memorandum came under fire from time to time, was amended a bit, but prevailed. Later it became a mutual policy that the Ex. Boards of the two organizations would meet at least once each year to jointly review any problems or complaints that had arisen. One joint venture of the Meat Board and NPPC was the Pork and Potatoes promotion that was attempted with a large food firm in Minneapolis. When the ads and materials for the program came out they had no identity on them that the NPPC was an equal funder, nor was our Home Ec. person invited to participate in the planning. When you are being voluntarily funded, investment of those funds is your responsibility, and when those investing their nickels do not see their organization identified in the promotions, it creates some doubt in their mind as to whether their staff has functioned. This experience put a definite strain on the Memorandum.

LOST SWINE RESEARCH FUNDS

When we appeared before the House Agric. Committee in Washington, D.C. back in March of 71, one of the Representatives, Neal Smith of Iowa challenged our request and need for additional funds for swine production research. He commented that they were already funding millions of dollars to the USDA Clay Center, Nebraska Research Station and that twenty-five percent of that was for swine research. He caught us rather flat footed because, even tho we had been pretty involved in researching the research on swine about the nation, we did not know of any being done at Clay Center. A few weeks later we followed up on Rep. Smiths challenge and asked for Roger Gerritts to see if we could not tour the Clay Center facility and determine what, if any, swine research was being conducted there. Upon our arrival we were given a tour of the facilities which included massive cattle research exhibits of thousands of cattle, a few hundred sheep, and NOT ONE HOG NOR HOG BUILDING was seen, because there were none. For more than ten years millions of USDA research funds had been allotted by Congress to this facility, with 25% of it to be in swine research, and not one dollar had been put into swine research. The manager of the facility was gracious enough to roll out some blue prints for a proposed swine research unit. After looking at them a minute or so I asked who designed them. He said an engineer from California had. IT WAS EASY TO TELL THAT A PERSON WITH NO KNOWLEDGE OF HOGS WHATSOEVER HAD HELD THE DRAFTING PEN. There was another good sized fine looking brick structure next to the Research Administration Building and I asked what was conducted in that. The reply, "nothing at present, it is a meat science research unit that is not in operation yet." (It was a few years old and unused.) With mixture of frustration, despair, anger and disgust I returned to Des Moines bent on seeing that the research efforts at Clay Center Research Center would include pork production in the near future, as approved and funded by Congress for many years. There was an advisory committee that supposedly functioned in guiding this research center. But with infrequent meetings and apparent lack of awareness of the original intent of the funding of the facility by Congress, this committee had let this research director ignore the original intent and do his own thing, cattle cross-breeding research. I wrote a letter to each member of this committee, told them what I had found and asked that they find out what had been done with that 25% of the research funds that had been directed to that center for swine research over the past years. I also asked that they start an immediate effort toward the development of the swine research that had been funded and intended. It would have been self-defeating to approach Rep. Smith or other congressmen because if they had become aware of what had been done, they would probably have cancelled the whole darn facilities funding. Another of the farm press got hold of a copy of my letter from one of the committee members and tried to singe my hair a little because I had exposed some lax activity by that committee and facilities management. Things flew back and forth for a bit, but it wasn't many months before they broke ground on some hog facilities at Clay Center and hired a man to activate some research projects on hogs. Here again we did not achieve the type of research that was needed by the pork industry. Some Hi-fat Lo-fat strains of two breeds that had been doved-tailed at the Beltsville Research Station outside of Washington, D.C. were transferred to Clay Center and continued. A year or so later the NPPC board was invited out to see the facility and found the buildings had 12 to 24 inch steel I-beam design and not what most pork producers would consider practical. Hilman Schroeder, Chairman of our NPPC Research Coordination Committee was equally unimpressed with the animal research at that point. It was difficult to get good research people to work at that station partially due to upper management and partially due to few wives and families wanting to live in such a desolate area for a long period. I hope that this facility is now enjoying a more progressive and aggressive swine research program. Some changes in NPPC staff were made during this period. Monte Flett a long time staff person with the Meat Board, who was one of the best meat display preparation people ever in the business joined us and we excused Dan Murphy as our advertising agency because our programs were growing beyond the capabilities of a one-man agency. This brought some discord among the old guard, but our program development quickly showed improvement that proved our move was correct. The Baker, Johnson and Dickinson Agency of Milwaukee had a staff of 35 people including artists, creative staff, media buyers, market research people; had other clients in the retail food and meat processing business, and were still small enough that we would be a major client. We continued to change advertising agencies thru the years as our promotion programs grew and as personnel changes occurred at the various agencies. The dollar volume of our account gave us greater leverage in driving for a better contract with the agency. We had learned that some larger advertising accounts were able to press their agency to handle their accounts for just the 15 and 2 percent of the actual ad costs or time costs, due to the size of their advertising budget. When we started approaching that level we started pressing for this savings and in doing so were able to enlarge our program further. In the earlier days, when our ads were smaller and in less than national magazines, we had to pay for creative, layout and materials costs in addition to the actual ad space costs. When you start buying full page four color ads in Good Housekeeping and three or more like publications, each costing $50,000 and up, yet use the same color separations and art work, I felt that the normal commission of 15% and 2% was just compensation for the agency; and they agreed finally.

CHAPTER III

NEW PORK HORIZONS

In December 1971, the NPPC Ex. Board approved the funding for a pork product research project that proved to be one of the most important and industry valuable ever made. Despite the genetic and management innovations that had been made to improve our hogs and the resulting pork from them, our industry still lacked a product that would meet the portion control, quality control and volume efficiency that would meet the needs of the institutional and FAST FOOD business. Roger Mandigo, Professor of Meat Science at the U. of Nebraska presented a fresh and innovative research project to the Ex. Board that involved taking pork trimmings, boneless cuts and other less saleable pork of known fat to lean ratio, chilling them into uniform blocks of product, then flaking them into bits and pieces that were then hydraulically pressed into logs of product of various shapes and chilled again to just barely frozen status. These logs could then be put into Betcher slicing machines that would produce very uniform pieces of product, ready for meal preparation, uniform and controlled fat content, that would be ideal for fast food, institutional or home use. From day one pork producers that dreamed of building their own organization and pork program had grasped for new pork product development that would meet the changing consumer trends. Mandigo made a very positive and challenging presentation. It struck an equally positive note with the NPPC Board, and even with income at that point at a very variable state, they pledged $85,000 over a three year period to pursue this pork product development research project. During this three year period, we were invited to visit the Nebraska campus in Lincoln and view the progress of the research. It was a most exciting period for the NPPC and Mandigo did little to slow down the emotion that surrounded this project. He had surrounded himself with a number of upper graduate and graduate students that took into this project with a fervor equal to that of the "Big Red" football team. It was not as simple as it might sound to formulate this product. First it was necessary to find the correct fat to lean ratio to make the product moist and tender when prepared. They found that it was necessary to tumble the pork mix in a tumbling machine for a period of time to break down the surface protein cells so that the particles would adhere together when it was put it into a pressure and forming press that would shape it into a uniform product and frozen. They did not want a sausage like product, but chewable like a bite from a pork chop or ham. After finally getting the correct fat to lean ratio, getting the shaped portions desired and finding proper slicing equipment they then turned to various seasonings and how they affected storage capability. Next came the taste tests of the final product. Mandigo's imagination on types of dishes to be prepared from the FLAKED AND FORMED PORK was just as inventive as his original idea. Some cuts were shaped like a pork chop, a Nebraska shaped chop, loaf, thin slices, etc. Seasonings were also varied to meet the various tastes of different folks with different strokes. In April, 1974 Mandigo and the NPPC went public with FLAKED AND FORMED PORK resulting from the research of Mandigo and his staff. We held two meetings, one in Lincoln, Neb. and one in Ohio to which we invited all of the packing and pork processing companies. A wide array of different products were presented and sampled by the company representatives, many of whom were Vice Presidents, and product sales people. They all endorsed the product, made many favorable comments, and then failed to commit their interest in making the product available to their customers in volume. This was disappointing at first, but we had forgotten just how secretive packing company people are about their entering into new product lines. A few days later Mandigo called and he was being flown on packing company planes and other means to a number of company headquarters about the country to further detail the manufacture of the new pork product. Flaked and formed pork products were soon in the development stage with a number of these people, but the big surge in use of pork in this manner came when the young researchers working on the project with Mandigo graduated and left for jobs in the meat industry. Some went to packing companies and some went to meat product processors, one of whom was the

product supplier for McDonalds. After some further research and market development by that firm the now well known "McRib" was test marketed about the country in regions of the McDonald chain. Later they introduced it into their 8,000 restaurants about the nation. During one four to six week period they served an estimated 80 million McRib sandwiches. From the investment of sparce nickels in 1971 came millions of dollars in pork sales in later years from those research results. During this introduction period the NPPC, with Mandigo in tow, presented this new Flaked and Formed pork product to the Nat. Assn. of Food Editors in a special presentation during their annual meeting in New York City. All of the major housewife and food market magazine editors were present and very favorably impressed with the variety of products, later commenting in their columns about the new pork on the market. In addition to the McRib and several other pork products that resulted in fast food presentations about the country, this process has helped in making greater use of pork in the tremendous pizza industry across the nation. It was a real stretch in 1971 for the NPPC Board to approve this meat research investment. But is has been returned to pork producers many fold in successful sale of pork products in this competitive marketing of meat to the consumer. From my early days in the hog marketing and purebred association work with carcass improvement of our hog population I had become acquainted with quite a number of University Meat Science people. With our involvement in the Mandigo research we had found that these people and their graduates going out into the meat industry after graduation were prime agents to assist in research and development of the pork marketing program of the future. As of 1972 the NPPC started sponsoring the Annual Meeting Banquet of the Reciprocal Meat Conference. This group included the meat science staffs of all the Land Grant Universities and meat specialists in the nations meat industry associated with the packing and processing industry. This later proved to be a good investment when the NPPC entered into the nutrition research projects. The association and contacts developed with this group equipped us better to take a positive part in the selection of the proper scientists to carry on this important nutrition research that was over 15 years late in starting. Our work with committees, hearings, EPA, FDA, USDA, and other cooperating commodity groups drastically increased our trips to Washington, D.C. at this point. Pres. Euel Liner, Vice Pres. Gerald Beattie and I appeared before Senate and House Committees ask-

J. Marvin Garner

99

ing that the $420,000 approved the previous year be extended and new research projects were presented for future finance consideration. State groups were growing rapidly and calling for more attention and work with our state staff people. Early in 1972 the NPPC designed, developed and produced a new set of in-store promotional materials titled, "PICK PORK." From our consumer research of earlier programs we had determined that the public thought of pork as a VALUE, a CONVENIENCE, a GOOD TASTE, and GREAT VARIETY for diet, family, and guests. These terms were featured on four color wall posters and meat case strips. In our early promotional materials development we found that other food product people as well as related industry people had good photography featuring pork with their products and they were willing to share these with us. This helped us hold down costs of meat photography, one of the most critical and costly parts of getting promotional materials printed. Our PICK PORK program went extremely well in our image city programs in St. Louis, Milwaukee and the two added in 1972, Boston and San Francisco's bedroom areas of San Jose and Oakland. It also went well with the State Pork groups as they were now really opening up with local pork promotions that not only helped tell the story of pork but gave pork producers a chance to promote their own products and attract more members. The American Pork Congress moved to Kansas City in 1972, taking over the Municipal Auditorium, Muehlebach Hotel, and all other Hotels in the downtown area. The Trade Show had grown to 309 booths, all much developed over past years. We had tremendous assistance from related industry and the Missouri and Kansas state associations, who had their annual meetings on the first day of the event. The Porketts of the National and both states also held their meetings in conjunction with the NPPC. The National Assoc. of Farm Broadcasters and the American Association of Swine Practitioners also held their annual meetings in and around all of the other activities. Meeting rooms were at a premium and scheduling had to follow a rather rigid pattern, sometimes upsetting a few folks. With almost six thousand registered, it had to be considered a success. In preparing for the program I knew we had to get at least one drawing card big named person. With high hopes of getting at least one, I invited Earl Butz, Sec. of Agriculture and Jimmy Dean, entertainer, pork producer and processor with plans to build another plant just over the line in Southern Iowa. In my invitation to Dean I expressed belief that his appearance on our program

would greatly enhance the start-up of his new pork plant when it opened the next year in Osceola, Iowa. Much to my surprise and great appreciation both headliners accepted the invitation to appear on our 1972 American Pork Congress Banquet program. When in this position, which one do you ask to be first on the program; both were nationally known; both were crowd pleasers? Luck prevailed when Mr. Butz asked to go first because he needed to fly back to Washington that night to be on hand for an early meeting with the Nixon cabinet the next morning. When I visited with Jimmy Dean about the program he didn't care when he appeared, but he asked if it would be out of line to take a hack or two at the way the USDA Meat Inspection Div. had caused unneeded problems in his new plant. I told him it was not our place to decide what he could or could not say in his comments. We had no idea as to what his presentation would include so I asked if he would need a piano or anything of that nature. He quickly informed me that no he could not sing or play anything or he would have to make a minimum appearance fee charge of $10,000 to keep the music and entertainment unions happy. His appearance on our banquet program cost only his airplane ticket and hotel bill and Sec. Butz made no charge at all. We did have a suite reserved for his use while in Kansas City and it was surprising to watch the FBI make a floor to ceiling search of that suite and put a 24 hr. guard at the door until his arrival. After more than an hour visit with Dean I found him to be not only a warm personality but also an astute businessman. From his start in the rural Plainview, Texas area, up thru the entertainment world, he now had agriculture and farm investments in Texas, real estate holdings in New Jersey, where he lived when not traveling, a leather goods business, a pork plant and offices in Dallas, Texas and New York City. His Ex. Vice President of Jimmy Dean Enterprises was Willie Bruffy, one of the most unforgettable ladies I've ever met. Dean credited her with much of his success in life and business. I'm also indebted to her for helping me book the "Oak Ridge Boys" for a later Pork Congress, just as they were beginning to rise on the strains of "Elvira" and had not reached the appearance fees they get today. The 1972 American Pork Congress Banquet gave me more "learning experiences" than any I ever had before or since. To comfortably seat and serve almost 2000 for the affair the Muehlebach Hotel people joined both of their large Ballrooms together. Due to a mix-up with Kansas, Missouri and us selling tickets to the affair, we found about one hour before the banquet that we were oversold by more than 300 tickets. Amid considerable verbal heat more tables were set up on the Mezzanine to serve the over-sale and they were quieted with the promise that they would be moved inside the banquet area for the program. I have found that ever so often an old friend will step forward and save your hide in critical moments of life. Dave Nollar, Sigourney, Iowa, a friend from Meat Board Directorship days tapped me on the shoulder and said, "Marvin, I saw something done in this same hotel a while back that could work here." Dave's idea was to have the outside people pick up their chairs and move into the ballroom in between the tables of people after they had eaten. We extended that plan a bit. After a rather heated debate with the banquet manager of the hotel, who said it couldn't be done, we got state and our staff fellows together, moved out two or three rows of tables right in front of the Head Table, asked those people to move their chairs back into rows and then brought in those 300 plus people from the Mezzanine, who then ended up with front row seats and much happier. Again, some verbal heat from those that were moved back, but my mother and dad and family were among those moved back and this helped to smooth things. The program—IT WAS GREAT! Probably the best we had ever had. Butz and Dean had a short visit during a Hors d'oeuvres session just before the banquet and as Dean moved to the banquet he commented, "that old boy ain't so bad, when you get to know him." Butz went first and Dean chided him throughout. Butz stuck around for Dean's presentation and returned the jibs making it a great affair, thoroughly enjoyed by all, especially the two of them. Jimmy's jokes took on a blue tinge once in a while, but as long as I saw my mother laugh, I felt they passed censure. We had asked Jimmy to crown the new Pork Queen during the banquet, but he had declined. However when he saw the group being presented, he changed his mind and stepped up to crown Eunice Schroeder, Charter Oak, Iowa the 1972 Pork Queen. Another young lady that is well known in pork circles today, was crowned Pork Princess, JoAnn McCalla, Ann Arbor, Mich. It was a fun entertaining evening that many people commented to me about years later, including Butz and Dean. Euel Liner, Lubbock, Texas director was elected President of the NPPC to succeed Roy Keppy, president for the past two years. Dennis Atwill, Utica, Ks. won the Nat. Pork Cookout Contest and put on some excellent demonstrations for us during the year. This annual meeting began to show competition in the states to be a director on the

NPPC Board, and also competition between the states to get their director elected to the Ex. Committee of the Board. Some non-pork producer agitation heated up the activity during the election, but had no effect on the outcome of the election. Liner was well known in the Southwest and in recent years had become known in the Midwest from his appearance at hog shows, sales and meetings. He and his son-in-law had developed a rather large successful seed stock production unit near Lubbock. His hat, boots and unusual knot in his tie became an identifying introduction for Euel, our new president. His sage, experience and common sense served him and the NPPC well for the next two years. Ann Norman, home economist and Ken Kohl, former Iowa state staff assistant joined our rather limited staff at this point. Ann was to work with the Nat. Porkettes in their programs and assist with pork promotion and advertising. Ken worked with the state staff people, market development and was staff representative on some NPPC committees. Our first full fledged leader training sessions started at this time with more than 40 attending the two meetings held in Omaha and Indianapolis. It was about this period when beef prices came under attack from some loud consumer activists and some pork producers that were also in the beef business thought we should join in the fight at this point. Since pork was not being mentioned in the "price controls" being politically mentioned by Pres. Nixon at this point, we thought it best to perhaps lay low until we were included. We later were invited into Washington, D.C. to take part in some price control discussions and when they started talking about putting on price controls and rolling meat prices back, we did become very vocal at that point. As the NPPC program grew and more farm press reported our activities thru magazines, newsletters, and radio farm directors we also started getting requests from major hog marketing systems to visit with their hog buying personnel. They suddenly wanted to be identified with our success and were seeking information on all new programs so they could better help in the voluntary collection of nickels. Some of us had wondered if this would ever come to pass. We met with the Nat. Producers Marketing Assn. hog salesmen, St. Joseph Stockyards commission men, the St. Paul Market salesmen, Rath hog buyers, Hormel hog buyers, Oscar Mayer hog buyers and many others. We were pleasantly surprised when Harold Heinold called one day and asked if I would like to make a presentation to all of their hog buyers at their annual meeting in Kouts, Ind. Even tho Harold Heinold had sent in the first check for nickels checkoff at the start of the program, some of their buyers did not have a very good track record in collecting nickels, but Harold had come to believe in our organization and thought with more information they could do a better job. This was the first time in history that anyone outside of their organization had been invited to appear on their annual program and we were quite appreciative. After many months of planing, the 1st National October Porkfest kicked off on Oct. 2, 1972 at the Annual Meeting of the American Meat Institute in New York City. Press, Radio, TV and industry home economists attended the affair that included the Presidents and major officers of the meat packing industry of the nation. President Liner and Pork Queen Schroeder keyed the presentation. The American Meat Institute, the National Independent Meat Packers Assn., Nat. Chainstore Council and the Meat Board helped present this 1st Porkfest program. October was selected for this special promotion because this was the time of year when larger marketings of hogs and price pressure occurred. A Porkfest Logo was designed and this became a trademark in all of our printed materials, store advertising and TV ads as well as many of the Chain Store newspaper ads during the month of October. The NPPC budget for this affair was $250,000, more than 1/4 of our yearly income at this point, but small when compared to other national promotions. More than 16 million households across the nation were exposed to two half page newspaper ads in 44 major key market cities across the nation. Another 110 newspapers carried the same ads in smaller cities and towns, inserted by our member states. Eleven thirty-second spots were carried each week on the entire national CBS and NBC radio networks of 481 stations plus 12 spots per week on 14 additional large independent radio stations. These spots during housewife time exposed over 42 million adults to our new pork information during the month. Wally Just, a Milwaukee advertising person worked with our advertising agency in making a 30 second TV spot featuring Eunice Schroeder our Nat. Pork Queen. This spot appeared on the Dinah Shore NBC-TV program three times during the month. We had page ads in the October issues of Sunset and Southern Living magazines that would reach almost 2 million homes. Through the efforts of American Cyanamid's cosmetic division, we were able to get Queen Schroeder on the popular TV show, What's My Line, giving a little more exposure of the pork industry efforts. Kraft Foods designed and had their sales force distribute over 20,000 in-store promotion displays featuring pork with their products. The Meat Board prepared in-store promotion kits for distribution to chain stores and in addition we distributed pork photos and recipes to several thousand people who had seen or heard our ads on radio and newspaper offering these items. This was the beginning for a very successful yearly event that not only helped sell more pork, but it was a promotional event that our member states and their staffs could join with to feature their product and industry in their own home areas. It attracted more members and more market cooperation. Pork producers could see their nickels working for them at last. During this same period the Dole pineapple people held a recipe contest in Hawaii and the winner featured "Pork and Pineapple." On the way back from New York Pres. Liner and Queen Schroeder, Monte and I stopped in Washington, D.C. and presented Sec. of Agriculture Earl Butz with a display of fresh pork, also featuring the kick-off of October Porkfest. Sec. Butz later wrote us, thanking again for the pork and commenting that 12 to 15 of his office staff people shared in the pork and expressed their thanks too. It was strange, but after that I got in to see Sec. Butz more quickly, with less delay in the outer office.

CHAPTER IV

FINDING THE RIGHT DOORS

By this time we were beginning to find the right doors and to grab the right ropes to attain some of the goals of the pork producers. We had been conducting a producer poll each year that gave us a guide as to their needs in production information, disease control, breeding problems and housing difficulties. We had been using this information to prepare presentations for the Senate and House budget committees in request for funds to carry out research on these industry needs. We had found where some funds had been appropriated but were not being invested as originally intended by the Congress. We also found that too many of the Land Grant College Research Fund seekers were tied so closely to crops, and their personally favored species of crop or animal that they were not requesting any funding for the pork industry problems in their presentations to the Senate and House Budget committees. They were always very quick to come around and thank those making the pork industry requests for research funds each time, but had nothing in their requests for pork. It came to a head one day while having lunch in the basement of the Agriculture Administration Building with a Missouri Dean of Agriculture and another Dean who I didn't know as well. The Missouri Dean asked me why we did not mention the importance of Congress funding the CSRS (Cooperative State Research Service) in our statement to the committees. I answered, "From the lack of any mention of swine research needs in your presentation, I didn't think you were aware that we existed. When you don't request any funding for swine production, the congressmen and their aids cast a doubtful eye at our requests." I learned later that the other Dean at the lunch table was Chairman of the CSRS research fund committee. I did notice in later years that swine production research was included in their request for research funds. It was also interesting to learn that if monies appropriated and assigned to certain departments and divisions of departments within the USDA are not used or spent by a certain date of each governmental year, that they go back into the general USDA fund and the Secretary has the say in where they go. However the Chairman of a department can re-assign uncommitted funds if he is aware of a real need of those funds in his area. As a result we always had a real hot pressing need, with a documented research project proposal to back it up, to present to that Chairman about the 11th month of the fiscal year. As a result the NPPC was able to acquire funding for several projects, one of which kicked off the research on modern day nutritional value of pork. For some years we had noticed some unusual happenings in the periodic USDA hog numbers reports. They didn't follow thru in some areas according to previous forecasts, yet the final year totals always checked out. I was also concerned that the government refused to compare present production numbers with a previous five-year average rather than just the previous year. This would have reduced the drastic percentage changes that often caused drastic movement up or down in hog prices and pork product prices. It seemed that they wanted to have these drastic changes to favor the commodity traders rather than give a more sound trend movement. After several door knockings in that multi-floored monster of the "South Bldg." of the USDA, I finally located a fellow in the second or third level below ground that gave me some true answers. Everyone had always argued that the USDA figures were accurate to within 1% of what they had estimated in the previous report. This young man was originally from a South Dakota farm and seemed pleased that anyone would be concerned with his area of work. When I asked how he could come up with figures so accurate each reporting period, he answered. "After we get all of the figures added up, we ESTIMATE THE NUMBER OF HOGS SLAUGHTERED ON FARMS and DIED ON FARM, in order to bring our numbers within 1% of what was previously estimated in farrowings." Now that figure had been ranging from 1 1/2 to 3 million hogs slaughtered on farm. With all states having initiated restrictive locker plant and small packing plant slaughter rules that had put most of them out of business, and knowing from personal experience that pork producers were not doing any slaughter on their own farms anymore, this figure was totally incorrect and misleading to the entire pork industry. I suggested then, many times after and still that a better estimate on future pig farrowings could be obtained if the Government numbers checkers would get a count on the number of sows marketed and gilts marketed at a representative group of markets on specific days of each week, put into a computer program that would show trends and thereby make estimates on future farrowings that would be much more accurate. Some packers have used this system in their own company for many years but the government folks still must not be aware that if increased numbers of sows and gilts are marketed there just can't be more pigs on feed three months hence. As a result I still cast a cautious eye at any USDA commodity reports. I doubt if they are anymore accurate than a good "windshield" estimate. By this time the NPPC Staff and I had begun to feel like hampsters running constantly on an endless wheel of activity ahead each day. To more correctly balance staff, committees, projects, and watching operational expenses, I asked the Board to approve the combining of about eight committees down to four. These four were to include the Policy and Planning Committee, to be composed of the NPPC Board Vice President as chairman and seven producers active in state or national programs. The Production and Research Committee would include a member of the Ex. Board as Chairman with eight more members to be selected from Ext. Swine Specialists, Animal Science Staff, Extension Vets, and Research Vets. The Environmental Quality Committee would be chaired by a member of the Ex. Board with eight more producers or not more than three

College Ag. Engineers. The Consumer Advisory Comm would include an Ex. Bd. member as chairman with eight more from the fields of Media (food editor), College Meats Specialist, Home Ec. Spec., retail meat person, AMI, etc. These were all accepted at this point with the President making the selections and to be approved by the Ex. Board. Later, with the growth and participation of the Feeder Pig Industry, a Feeder Pig Committee was initiated with an Ex. Bd member and eight feeder pig producers as members. Ron Hanser had joined us at this point and worked the communications and publications for the NPPC. Membership had moved up into the 65,000 range and we were getting about 37% of the potential hogs marketed, checked off. Just as we begin to get these areas moving well the consumer concern over pork prices and the image damage caused by Swine Flu became pressure points of work effort. Pork Producers were sort of enjoying the price of hogs in 1973 after healing up a little from the depressed period in '70 to '72. Beef was also up at a pretty good level at this point, which made a perfect blanket for the poultry industry to make some strong moves into the consumer food basket at this point. Negative headlines like "meatless days," "eat cheese," "switch to fish," and "boycott meat" were in the press daily. However cost of production for pork producers was also at record levels too so it was a nervous time for all. Our weekly taped message that was carried by more than 500 radio stations across the country, mainly in the heavier hog states, was being well received. It was a most effective way to get information out quickly to pork producers on hot topics so they could react with their congressmen. I will be eternally appreciative of the cooperation extended to us by the Radio Farm Directors using our tapes on their stations and networks. Among the "hot topics" during this period was the government exchange of 727 airplanes for pork from Poland; the U. S. financing of pork packing plants in Poland and training of foremen to run them; the German government stopping our shipment of pork offal to their sausage industry; the EPA in Washington proposed restrictions on pork production; and consumer reaction to high pork prices. Our aircraft manufacturing companies were in a slump at this point and suddenly some bone heads in Washington, D.C. decided that in order to help that industry and perhaps open the Red Curtain that surrounded Poland it would be good to exchange 727 airliners for pork to be imported into the U. S. and handled by importing firms on the East Coast. There were two things wrong with this project. One, it

helped to develop a pork importing system that has continued to function even after the end of the exchange, and two it added undue supply pressure to our U. S. pork industry. In addition it was about this time that the World Bank, which is largely financed by the U. S., loaned Poland several million dollars to build four pork packing plants in Poland. One of our major pork packers in the U. S. was having financial problems at this point and they took the contract to train quite a number of people from Poland to be foremen and manage these new packing plants. We also had quite a number of pork plant equipment people that wanted to sell their products for these new plants. So their pressures were felt too. When I asked Sec. Earl Butz why had he allowed such a procedure to develop, his reply, "We hope this will help pull back the Red Curtain that surrounds that nation." And my reply, "What is to keep them from taking all of our giving and then shut the curtain again?" And that is what happened. Within 18 months the largest exporter of pork to the U. S. became Poland, replacing Denmark. Despite no inspection equal to ours in their packing plants these pork products became a major challenge to U. S. pork and Mr. Jacobson and Co. of the activists group in Washington never peeped. A major market for pork offal had been developed through the years with Germany. Now all of a sudden they put an embargo on these products coming from the U. S. Offal products are used to make their specialty old country type sausage products. Pork was again being USED in the trade negotiation wars between nations. We did join the American Meat Institute in making some pointed visits in Washington that could help to work out this problem. You can freeze and store just so much offal product before it becomes more ballast than bologna. It became a football type problem that still exists today, but nobody really has the ball. The Federal EPA came out with a permit program for all pork producers to fill out and apply for approval to produce hogs on their farms. It would have been an impossible task, and would have accomplished nothing but more federal jobs. This was one area that we quickly stopped with quick contact to our member states and they to all of their legislators. After some months of wrangling with people that did not have any agriculture or animal science backgrounds they finally came out with a permit program for all hog units having an inventory of 2500 hogs at any one time of the year. However the Federal EPA then put the hammer on the state EPA Departments to follow up on smaller production systems, thereby passing the smaller unit headache to them. Again overnight pork producers started making their way onto state committees and held this activity within somewhat reasonable lines. A number of law suits were filed however and this brought country zoning into a prominent place. Protecting the right to raise hogs was getting more challenging by the day. Consumers were busy in their Washington based groups trying to discredit meat of all kinds. Some said it was to get prices down, price controls put on by the government, and some took on the nutritional battle. It always puzzled me that several of the upfront leaders of the group ate no pork, so I doubted their sincerity. We did start running some ads in major city papers based on telling the consumers that it took 301 days from the start of reproducing hogs until they became pork in the retail market. This was to get some of the misled folks back into the realm of reality on how quickly pork producers could make drastic changes to increase the number of hogs they produced. In the Spring of '73 we came out with a "Pork For Pop" promotion to head for a share of the Father's Day menus across the country. It centered on a cookout promotion and ham the always pleasing dinner. It gave us a spring promotion project that took off real well with the packers and the retail people. They jumped in and really got behind this project that was actually low cost budget and even tho the beef people beefed a bit, it did move some pork. We added Atlanta to our Image City program with this project featured in the promotion. The Indiana folks put on quite a demonstration and drive to get the 1973 American Pork Congress moved to a totally new facility in Indianapolis. They succeeded in their effort and with tremendous help from the Indiana group, Elanco, our State Staff, Mark Duffy & crew of Manncraft Decorating and my NPPC staff it was another resounding success with 7,000 attending. The 1973 American Pork Congress was the first group to make use of the entire Indiana Convention Center. We had over 350 booths in the trade show and served over 1,800 at the Banquet. Soo Klingaman of Waterloo, Iowa was chosen queen and Pork All Americans from 25 member states were honored. We received many letters complimenting us on the organization and smoothness of program. A little luck always helps to make things like this successful. On Monday before the affair was to open on Thursday, I received a call from the Washington, D.C. office of Vice President Agnew who was scheduled to be our speaker at the Banquet. Panic is a short word for what I felt for a short period. I called Ray Wilkinson, Radio Farm Director of the Tabbaco

Network Raleigh, North Carolina, that carried our NPPC radio tapes, and told him that I was in BIG trouble. He answered by request of him to be our fill in speaker with a request. Could I get his mother a room and a seat at the banquet if he would fill in as our speaker?" Ray grew up just outside of Chicago and this would be an opportunity to visit with his Mom if he flew into Chicago and drove her down for the Banquet. Needless to say, she had a front row center seat. And needless to say, Ray had the audience rolling in the isles with his country humor. It wasn't but a few weeks until V. Pres. Agnew was in hot water and I was sure relieved that he had cancelled out. I'm not all Irish, but I think a little helped. During this period we were having some price problems with hogs and pork, bringing forth some rumblings from our membership. It didn't seem to be the proper time to be picking a fight with the packers who were just beginning to really cooperate in collecting nickels and with the retailers who were giving us good cooperation in our pork promotion efforts. To help relieve this situation, I arranged for Herrel DeGraff, President of the American Meat Institute and Clancy Academy, President of the National Association of Food Chains, both out of Washington, D.C. to be on our Annual Meeting Program. These men I considered to be two of the most intelligent people I knew in the food industry. Their comments and explanation of their segment of the meat chain to the consumer helped to clear up some of the doubts being cast in their direction by our pork producers. The FDA had called for the packing industry to eliminate the use of nitrates in the curing and preserving of pork in the fall of '72 and that part of the industry had been spending large amounts of time and money trying to convince the government to let them continue use of the product until a substitute could be found that would be equally protective to the consumer. Mr. Academy represented 200 chain store systems across the nation that operated over 25,000 supermarkets and he told of their problems with thin or no profits from meat sales at that point. Their comments helped to sooth pork producers somewhat, but the big plus was that our pork producers learned a lot more about the problems in other segments of the food chain that handled their products on the way to the consumer. President Liner was re-elected for another year during the annual meeting, but one of the highlights was South Dakota presenting a check to President Liner for $4800 to replace the same amount that had been invested in swine disease research projects in South Dakota State University and asked that it be used in the pork promotion projects. This was a show of the strength beginning to build in the member states and their willingness to share in the total program. A special Hawaiian Luau promotion with Dole Pineapple and Kikkoman Soy Sauce cooperating helped stretch NPPC promotion dollars during August of 1973. Very colorful and high quality in-store promotion materials, national magazine 4-color ads and an all new pork recipe book featuring all of the products was distributed nationwide. Not only did the three-way split of the costs of this program help, but the distribution system of the Dole people helped get the products into the retail stores. It was about this time that during one of my visits with Sec. Earl Butz in his Washington offices I mentioned that it appeared no effort was being made to have a coordinated drive to increase pork exports to Japan. Canada had been making some contracts with the Japanese that put a base under the Canadian hog market that was already government supported. He suggested that I contact Elmer Hallowell, Ass. Admin. of the Foreign Agriculture Service of the USDA. In that meeting I learned more about how the egg, broiler and some other commodity organizations had moved to increase their export volume. I found that there are USDA funds that can be used for promotion and development work in foreign countries as long as they are spent outside of the U. S. Mr. Hallowell suggested that perhaps a federation of U. S. meat groups would be a way to build a strong export program that the USDA could recognize and assist. Within the next year Dick Lyng, President of the American Meat Institute, John Mohay, President of the Nat. Independent Meat Packers, Bill McMillan, Vice President of the Nat. Cattlemen's Assn. and myself met with a person retired from the U. S. Feed Grains Council an organization that had a very successful export program already underway. This gentleman gave us further information on how to structure ourselves, develop our program, apply for Federal funds and move into a meat export promotion program. The U. S. MEAT EXPORT FEDERATION WAS BORN in that meeting. The four of us were the charter members, and I was elected the Treas. of the group during our organizational state. NPPC members had shown interest in the export of pork earlier, so Board approval for the NPPC to pursue helping structure the organization came quickly. Dick Lyng, myself and a representative of a meat processing company in Chicago met at Ohare Airport and interviewed applicants for the staff position of the newly formed U. S. Meat Export Federation. Bud Middaugh, a farm advisor for a Colorado bank and former employee of Monfort Packing Company was our selection and was later hired by the fledgling organization. I believe he still today heads up the U. S. Meat Export Federation that has grown rapidly so our selection must have been correct. In 1975 I was a member of the first trip to Japan by the MEF to study how more pork sales could be developed in that country. We needed to know the type and kind of promotion materials needed, the type of pork cuts they desired, and how we could break the strangle hold that Agriculture organizations in their country had on shipment of meat products into their country. I quickly found that meat of all types is used more for flavoring than for its protein content in dishes of Japan. Few buy any type of meat in a full cut, such as a ham, roast, or chop. Practically all is boneless and sliced into small thin pieces, and families buy their meat supply daily, mostly from small shops and a limited amount from large supermarkets. It was pleasing to find that next to fish, pork was the next highest consumed meat. The Japanese average consumption of pork is only 4 ounces per day, but that ads up to a potential market of more than 7 million pounds per day. Denmark and Canada were strong in the market, but a fast growing pork production system in Taiwan, that the U. S. Feed Grains Council had force fed, looked to be our major competition in the years ahead. Learning to bow and say "hi" without appearing too awkward to people a foot shorter than yourself took some getting used to. We met with the Department of Agriculture of Japan, the Ham Processors Assn., the Retailers Assn. and the Board of Directors of the largest farm organization in Japan. The people of Japan are represented in their government by a single representative from each perfecture or state, irregardless of population. With most perfectures (states) agriculturally accented, the government action on tariffs and trade agreements are heavily weighted toward protecting their own agriculture. Since the late 50's Japan pork producers had been coming to this country and carefully selecting breeding stock to improve upon the Danish and other bloodlines they had. Breeding stock producers in the U. S. were pleased to have this aggressive buying of their breeding animals and after visiting some pork production units in Japan it was plain to see that they had selected well. Their hogs were very meaty, their production methods very precise, and they had learned, copied and improved on the best that they saw in our country. They know good pork and hogs that produce it, but have very limited feed grain supplies. It was interesting to find that the Japanese government requires a certain percent of offal fish products be mixed in with imported corn before it is sold to the pork producers so that it could not be detoured into human consumption instead. Some of the pork processors and retailers complained that they were having problems with U. S. imported pork being pale, soft and exudive (PSE). This had been a problem in the United States when we went to extremely heavy muscled animals, but efforts by breeders and researchers had reduced the problem to a point that our packers were not complaining. I wondered if this complaint by the Japanese was a bit of a non-tarrif barrier that they hatched up to help maintain their present quota levels on our pork. After seeing some of the pork and beef products that had been shipped by refrigerated boat, I was convinced that the shipments were being allowed to thaw and refreeze a couple of times during shipment and this was causing the PSE problem. Also our pork was being shipped in unwaxed lighter boxes that deteriorated quickly when thawing occurred. We contacted all major packers that were exporting pork at that point and expressed the complaints we heard and our suggestions as to the problem. We found that too often the Japanese were buying boxed frozen loins from storage and shipping them without reboxing or packing for long shipment. We did find that they are very good sausage eaters and we were able to help in arranging contacts for some exporters seeking quality sausage supplies from processors in the U. S. It has been gratifying to see the continued development of greater export of pork to Japan. Swine identification had been urged for some years by the packers and some organizations that represented their wishes, such as Livestock Conservation Inc., who were also heavily funded by APHIS, An. Health Inspection Service of the USDA. Early in this year the NPPC endorsed hog identification IF it was part of an eradication program and IF indemnities were paid. There was a strong feeling that if identification was forced on the pork industry without these requirements that it would merely become a method by which packers could bill back to the producers certain losses that appeared in the carcass, many of which occurred AFTER the animals left the farm. Who would do the identification and keep the records was another stumbling block that slowed the program. There were estimates at that time that over 65% of all market hogs were identified by packers and buyers so that if trace back to farm was necessary it could be done. If disease location was really desired, identification of all boars and sows going to market would

have worked well. Consumer pressure on beef prices and the political threats coming out of Washington for price controls and ceilings gave us a good umbrella under which to continue our promotion of pork for the October Porkfest. In addition to Radio and TV spots that were developed, some featuring the NPPC Pork Queen, new newspaper ads were used, full page four color ads in Good Housekeeping, Woman's Day and Family Circle covered the housewives. Weight Watchers finally approved pork in their recommended diet program, carried our ads in their publication and allowed us to use their name in some special recipe folders. We also hired a famous Chicago Chef, Louis Szathmary, to work with the Hotel Management program of Cornell University to make a new Hotel and Restaurant Food Service information packet of recipes on PORK FOR GRACIOUS DINING. We made this available to all graduates of the various Chef Schools and Colleges about the nation. During years of depressed hog prices the government purchased large amounts of pork products for later distribution in school lunch and other government feeding programs. During one of these periods we started receiving requests from the management people in school lunch programs for recipes for volume preparation of pork because they were using large amounts of pork on their school menus, but the students were getting tired of the limited recipes they used. Again we worked quickly with the folks in Cornell University to prepare a variety of ways to prepare pork for volume serving, and advertised their availability thru Home Ec. and Food Service publications. Watergate was getting a lot of the political attention in Washington during this period, but it didn't stop the EPA, FDA and Consumer activists from continuing their jabbing efforts. It became a rather bitter pill for pork producers to swallow at this point because due to very high corn and meal prices they were loosing $8 to $15 per head during this period, while pork prices were still high in the consumer eyes. Actually during part of this period hogs were selling higher than beef cattle, but costs had chewed away at any margin that should have been available. In addition, with the high hog prices came the trend for pork producers to keep back more gilts to increase production next year and this worked to reduce the amount of pork available. We found NPPC Budget planning based on a voluntary income becomes almost impossible when also based on a quickly changing source. Ken Kohl left the NPPC staff during this period to return to his home farm area and also sell feed. Steve Beckley, a California grown lad joined us and quickly established himself as a capable organization trained person, having worked for the Beef Growers.

'74 A YEAR OF REACTION

Leadership of the Meat Board could see the NPPC was growing quickly and its programs were achieving successful reports from the pork packers and the retail markets. We had become a factor in the promotion and sale of pork products to the consumer. The Meat Board begin to agitate thru some of the pork people on their board in attempt to get more funds directed their way and thereby reduce the program potential of the NPPC. They joined hands with an irritating segment of the pork press to create pressures that consumed considerable NPPC staff time to counter. Perhaps it served a purpose in keeping us on our toes and careful not to make mistakes in our program work. The Meat Board hired a Ag. Econ. Professor Uvacek from Texas to make a study of the entire producer funded programs and organizations hoping to get some backing for a redivision of funds. No surprise to many of us that his report closely resembled one done by Dr. DeGraff fifteen years earlier and stating that the NPPC was a viable and truly producer funded and directed organization carrying out its duties in a businesslike and successful manner. To appease some, it was agreed that the Ex. Boards of both organizations meet at least once per year to discuss questioned areas. Due to government price controls, ceilings, gas rationing and other economic disturbances we spent considerable time trying to get the shortage of di-cal phosphate back into normal production and distribution. It is a very necessary mineral segment of the diet for all animals in confinement, such as hogs and chickens. This was a real political football with no real handle to get hold of. It was a combination of controlled gas supplies for the production of phosphate in Florida, foreign export and import wrangling. Some of the pork producers with large confinement units had been buying large shipments in a co-op program that was cancelled when the mixed feed companies exerted their pressure on the phosphate suppliers. After numerous meetings in Washington that involved the Treasury Dept., Price Control Office, USDA and the Congressional leaders the NPPC joined the Nat. Broilers Council in a mutual effort that finally succeeded in getting production of di-cal back into almost normal production. The activists in Washington, that replenish their funds by stirring up turmoil, started a MEATLESS DAYS PROGRAM to counter the meat prices they considered high. This set the hair on our pork producer members who were loosing money on hogs at this point. Fighting these folks in a nose to nose confrontation is futile because they have no regard for facts or reality, and I doubt if they would change if they did. Nonetheless some of our pork producers wanted us to open up the battle with these folks. We, the NPPC Ex. Board and staff, proceeded to counter their efforts by putting forth cost of production information and cost comparisons with other family living overhead costs. We did not get the urban headlines, but we did achieve some attention from the Washington scene when they later invited the NPPC to participate in meetings where our comments did get into the urban press covering the meetings. It was one of those "Tomcat like fights" in which you feel lucky to only get scratched. Lots of noise and action with little achieved by anyone. The Ex. Board of the NPPC requested and obtained a meeting with USDA Sec. Earl Butz to report on conditions in the farm and pork industry, urge his help to prevent price controls, and to use reason in the limiting of grain exports. They stressed that they did not seek price supports or subsidies in their pork production efforts, but did seek some practical action by the government in programs that affected them. Butz, in a letter, expressed his appreciation and practical advice from the NPPC group. However 24 hours later Pres. Ford vetoed an animal research bill that had passed the House 324 to 23 and by a voice vote in the Senate. There were some high points in '74, such as the largest American Pork Congress ever. Almost 12,000 attended this fifth Congress in Des Moines. Gerald Beattie of Nebraska was elected President; Kim Schoen of Downs, Ks. was selected Pork Queen and Richard Sellard, Medila, Mn. won Cookout King. Twenty-seven more Pork All-Americans were honored and it was becoming more evident that exhibit, meeting room and hotel rooms were at capacity available in Des Moines at that point. Mrs. Julie Heberer, Illinois who had been a hard working President of the National Porkettes for three years turned over the reins to Mrs. Maxine Nash of Indiana. The Porkettes mailed out four separate Medical Mailers to 25,000 doctors and their offices during this year. These mailings keyed on golf sayings and included golf tees and ball markers plus latest information from the "New leaner pork." Our Flaked and Formed Pork was introduced during this year to the press, the urban press, the magazine editors and the pork processors. Our Pork for Pop Father's Day promotion was enlarged and received exceptional cooperation from retailers with 20,000 kits of in-store promotional material distributed. We were invited to a Cabinet Room meeting with Pres. Nixon pertaining to inflation, grain exports, and meat price controls. Following this meeting we got acquainted with Assistant Sec. of the Treasury, Dave Mcdonald. This man later became an excellent contact in working to reduce pork imports to the U. S. and also establish equalizing tariffs. During this period we worked with Dick Lyng who had joined the AMI, to visit legislators pertaining to formation of the U. S. Meat Export Federation and to increase meat exports. On one occasion we got caught in a down-pour of rain with no coats or protection and I discovered Lyng's aggressive nature. We tried to stop cabs repeatedly, but none accepted us. When one stopped for a stop-light and we saw only one person in it, Dick opened a door and we climbed in, much to the surprise of the lady passenger, and driver. Drowned rats would be a correct term, but after we identified ourselves and expressed our willingness to pay her fare, she didn't jump out the other door or call the police. (I probably would today, if in her shoes) Watergate took its toll during this year and in December the NPPC was invited to another White House Cabinet Room meeting with Pres. Ford to discuss feed grain exports and the import-export problems that had been caused when Canada put an embargo on U. S. Beef using stilbestrol feeding as a reason. We urged Pres. Ford to react by putting the same restriction on the shipment of all boars and low-grade animals to the U. S. Sixteen days later Pres. Ford did issue a proclamation doing just that, but including feeder cattle and veal as well. October Porkfest increased in scope with Baltimore, Washington, D.C., Seattle, Tacoma, Los Angeles and San Diego being added to our Full Support Markets, formerly called Image Cities. Our checkoff rate had now increased to 44% of all the hogs marketed in the nation and our membership had passed 75,000 in 35 member states. This allowed us to increase our promotion coverage to the consumer. Readers Digest and Redbook were added to Family Circle and Woman's Day for housewife coverage, each with four color full page ads on pork. These four gave us coverage with 51% of all U. S. adult women. Our ads included coupon offers and product information booklets that gave us a chance to evaluate each publication, based on the requests we received. We had TV spots on Let's Make a Deal, Hollywood Squares and Match Game plus TV Stations in our 11 cities to make a coverage of 151 million consumers reached during October Pork Month. Many in the pork system from processor thru retailer expressed the belief

that this program helped to move 14.6% increase in pork tonnage from August thru October. 31% of our requests for pork recipes and information came from California and New York during this period, indicating that we were getting to the proper people. Another high point of this period was an invitation to speak to the Central Markets River Markets organization at their Annual Meeting in Sioux City, Iowa. These represented most of the major Central Markets of the nation and had been among the slowest markets to cooperate with our nickel checkoff. About half of them were cooperating and it was an excellent chance to get those people to endorse our efforts before the other half. With these markets handling only about 30% of the market hogs at this point, it had become a competitive action for them to participate in order to hold their present customers. This meeting helped open up more individual meetings when pork producers joined staff members in visiting each of these markets and asking their cooperation. The 1975 calendar for the NPPC programs included an awful lot of Washington, D.C. dates. For some time we had been countering and suggesting to the EPA, FDA, and APHIS. Now the U. S. Meat Export Federation, the U. S. Trade Negotiation Comm., Animal Health Institute, Foreign Ag. Service and USDA divisions were all appearing regularly on our work schedules. Ron Jenkins replaced Hanser in our Communications department and added quite a lot of spark to our media releases and to our staff reports. We nudged into the 50% of hogs marketed being checked off with a nickel each investment and this was an 8% increase over the previous year. Hog numbers were down and prices hit a record $60 per cwt, but feed costs were also bumping record levels too. Most packing companies reduced their working hours and some closed down due to narrow margins and low number of hogs to slaughter. One packing company in Western Iowa should have closed down earlier. It was involved in a money float situation that left a group of pork producers really hurting when the float program struck a leak and their checks bounced higher than a TV tower. Between feed additive residue, pollution suits, zoning threats, and chasing bankrupt marketing systems our state and national NPPC staffs were kept very busy. With the increased hog prices came investment in new facilities for hog production. To help get the best information sorted out and available to pork producers, our Research Coordination Committee held a Swine Housing Conference in Lincoln, Neb. in January and a Swine Facilities Symposium in Des Moines in October.

Over 500 producers attended the latter meeting and it keyed a lot on the environmental problems as well as structure and equipment. Fact sheets full printed reports were prepared from these affairs and received wide distribution. These Symposium Meetings and Fact Sheets conducted by our Research Coordination Committee had been conducted for some years with the NPPC paying the bill except for the Fed. Ext. Service helping with extra pay for the Specialists that put the material together and prepared the fact sheets. It was an extremely important program for our membership and it was an excellent tool for our member states to use in attracting new members at the state level. The Extension workers and researchers doing the work on these projects were proud of their identity as authors and their Department Chairman and Deans were pleased to have their institution identified in the information that covered the pork industry. The program was so popular that we designed a loose leaf book of all the fact sheets and information to form the Pork Producers Handbook, probably one of the most useable sources of production information available anywhere. All of a sudden, a department Chairman in Purdue University started a move to get all of our fact sheet and Research Proceeding books, including the Handbook, printing and mailing moved to their campus. He started up quite an irritating situation, not only with we NPPC staff people, who had spent a lot of time and effort getting the program put together, but also with quite a number of the Extension specialists who had worked hard to obtain and write the materials plus their University Staff. Purdue's Chairman must have believed it was a chance for them to get additional Federal funds and publicity. We had enough to do without fusing over the situation, but felt it was unfair. However with one of our NPPC officers endorsing the plan and serving on the committee at that point, it moved. A few years later it was amusing to see Purdue shuffle to excuse themselves from this duty and responsibility. Each year we had conducted a pork producer member poll that was printed in our monthly newsletter. From this poll we got some trend on production trends, needs for answers to production problems, disease controls, regulatory problems and their evaluation of the programs we were conducting for them. For two years we had been getting the poll designed so that it could be summarized on computer. In 1975 we began to get a real computer program design that gave us the information that we sought. From this information we were able to more accurately determine the basic concerns of the producers

so that our requests to Washington Budget people carried more weight. It also helped our Research Coordination Committee make their selections more accurately. In April 1975, USDA Sec. Earl Butz and Ambassador Dent named an Agriculture Trade Negotiations Team including an Advisory Committee, on which NPPC Pres. Gerald Beattie served, and eight Technical Advisory Committees, one of which, Livestock and Livestock Products, I served on. The futility of these sessions was evident when one day in looking thru an eight inch deep computer printout, I found some data that I knew to be very old and determined that they had us pouring over data six years old. The chairman of our group was extremely head strong and pretty much ignored all input from the committee except his own. It didn't surprise me much when the U. S. Trade Negotiator gained little if anything for U. S. agriculture during the negotiations in Geneva. PSEUDORABIES reared its ugly presence in 1974 and really turned up the temperature for many pork producers in 1975. Our American Pork Congress included a special session on this problem disease. Since we had just concluded celebrations over the eradication of Hog Cholera in the U. S., we had some clamoring for an eradication program of this relatively new disease in the U. S. pork industry. Not knowing for sure how it was spread, doubts of some test efforts, no proven vaccines available and just pure lack of knowledge helped common sense prevail at this point. I feel that some of the pressure for an eradication program came out of a Washington USDA office that now had about 200 Federal Veterinarians twiddling their thumbs since the Hog Cholera and New Castle Disease had come under control and they needed something to keep them busy. This disease has been in Central Europe for centuries and continues to be a major problem in this country. The 1975 American Pork Congress went back to Kansas City and even tho not in the center of the major hog state, had over 9,0000 attending. Gerald Beattie, Nebraska was re-elected President of the Board. Gerald was a pioneer in the formation of the Nebraska pork producers organization. He and his two sons operate a large farming and confinement pork production unit near Kearney. He was a very efficient and dedicated officer of our organization. A Kentucky girl, Joyce Clements was elected Pork Queen and Nick Schermer of Minnesota, the Pork Cookout King. For too many years we had been keeping this event within the confines of the Pork Congress where it was mainly viewed by pork producers, who were already heavy pork cookout users. The following year we went to an early Image City, St. Louis, and held the cookout in the midst of a large open mall where thousands could view it. Our Pork All American group had grown to 31 states with representatives. The Alumni of this Pork All American group were active and having mutual interests and they began to have informal get-togethers during Pork Congress. Due to a number of USDA departments being involved in the hot spots of the years hog business we had Frank Mulhern, APHIS; C. Donald Van Houweling, FDA and Marvin McLain, Packers and Stockyards division to present the latest on their areas of work. Sec. Earl Butz was our luncheon speaker, where we presented him with a plaque that included a walnut framed picture of him, mounted on a stand holding an imitation boneless ham and Jasper (a pig statue) with an inscription "To a ham like Johnny Carson you might be Earl The Pearl, but to us you have been a gem." Carson had been riding Butz at this point and it fit well. Later Butz told me that when he got on the plane to return to Washington, he kiddingly handed the trophy to an airline hostess and asked if she could keep it refrigerated during the trip. It was a very realistic appearing ham. Our pork promotion and image improving programs had really begun to move by this time. In the February issue of FORECAST magazine, that goes to 65,000 Home Ec. Teachers, plus 10,000 home economists and nutritionists, we developed and placed a 16 page four color insert titled "All Pork Needs—Is A Little Understanding." It was extremely well received and won the Gold Leaf Certificate Award from the Food Council of America, sponsored in part by Family Circle magazine. Pork For Pop, our Father's Day promotion again rang a bell with concentrated promotion thru newspaper, TV and radio in our 11 Image Cities, plus 30 second radio spots carried on 910 radio stations of the CBS and Mutual radio networks. These spots were estimated to have been heard by more than 40 million listeners, 21 million of whom were housewives. These spots were centered around news programs. Our July and summer promotion was built on a co-op promotion with Dole Pineapple and Kraft Barbeque Sauce. A very colorful ad picture of a side of ribs prepared with barbeque sauce and a couple of rings of pineapple on top made a delightful sight in six major consumer magazines, Woman's Day, Family Circle, McCalls, Good Housekeeping, Better Homes and Gardens and Southern Living, going to 83 million consumers. We, the NPPC, distributed over 15,000 in-store promotion kits, with Dole and Kraft adding thousands more thru their sales force.

An ad with a Free Recipe offer appeared in the ads in the magazines. From these we received thousands of requests for "Budget Feast" recipes. From these requests we were able to determine which magazines had the most impact and ready attention to our ads, thereby helping us decide which magazines were our best investment for future ads. This Co-op promotion effort made it possible for pork producer nickels to buy three times the exposure we could afford if we had done it alone. Also thru consumer surveys that we conducted on a regular basis, we had found that housewives liked the idea of suggesting PORK with OTHER foods because it gave them ideas for meal preparation. Also during this summer period we prepared and had printed large billboard ads showing thick pork chops, candied yams and a salad with the title "Tonight, serve Pork Instead." Banks with large agriculture accounts, feed companies, and other related industry companies bought billboard space and these posters. Member states found these to be excellent image association builders and the billboards could be individually labeled for each sponsor. To fill out our promotional year, October Porkfest was again enlarged with special advertising effort on the term, "INSTEAD." This word was used "Pork 'n Chips, Pork Instead; Southern Fried Pork, Pork Instead; Pork Pot Pie, Pork Instead," etc. Our efforts were pretty effective with numerous comments from the other product people whom we were effectively replacing. Our consumer surveys were showing that they were constantly looking for menu changes and we were suggesting they change to "PORK." New TV spot ads were prepared and space bought on network game show programs with high housewife viewing audience. Family Circle, Good Housekeeping, McCalls and Redbook carried full page four color ads with a free recipe offer. The food markets, packing plants and meat processors were now aware of our annual promotions and began to key their promotions to join with ours, and were more receptive to using our promotional materials. Member states and even county pork organizations within those states began to buy TV time and ad space in their local areas to further stretch pork promotional efforts. We furnished tapes and ad slicks for these efforts. From the delegate session of the '75 Annual Meeting came a request for the NPPC to move from a voluntary deduction of a nickel to a dime per hog marketed. We had now moved to a little better than 50% of the hogs being checked off and some felt we needed to increase that percentage before increasing the amount. Some states were wanting more funds and some other organizations were pushing for more funding also. It was pretty simple for them to make their requests because it was the NPPC that was going to be the identified organization pushing for the increase that all would share in. Representatives of the Meat Board Staff and officers were quite pushy about wanting a larger share of the increased income and pursued same with a rather strong lobbying effort with a number of our pork producer leaders. Their ignoring the NPPC structure and going to individual pork producer leaders did not make for the best of public relations with NPPC officers and staff. The elected pork producer leaders that were going to be the identified party responsible for the final decisions on dispensing and investment of the new dime income took a rather dim view of others wanting to make demands, yet they would not be responsible to pork producers for how their funds were spent. After a number of meetings of NPPC Policy Committee, Ex. Board and Full Board, a distribution breakdown design was prepared for presentation at the '76 Annual Delegate Meeting IF the checkoff was increased to a dime. This gave member states time to study. In the final weeks of 1975 the entire pork industry was under heavy pressure from a buildup of pork in cold storage, due in part to the higher price level of earlier in the year and now due somewhat to the excessive retail profit margin markup that was evident. For many years the entire retail meat marketing system has put a higher markup on all pork products than they did on beef. With the lesser amount of pork available during this year and the record high prices that consumers seemed to accept, the retailers left retail prices high on pork, even after supplies had begun to increase and we normally saw lower prices to the consumer. It was so evident that producers and consumers alike began to cast wary a eye toward the entire retailing industry, even some threats of seeking government intervention were rumored. At this point we contacted our old friend, Clancy Academy of the Nat. Food Chains Assn. and stressed the unrest in the tepees across the nation and asked if he could casually pass the word to his membership. I'm not sure just what move was effective but over a period of a few weeks we began to see a lesser markup on pork. We had been working for years to develop a cooperative spirit among retailers toward giving pork more counter space and to use our pork promotion materials so it was a "walking on eggs period" during this time.

YEAR OF THE DIME

The tempo of staff activity stepped up drastically in 1976. New staff members Dan Hoffman, Warren Pitcher and Lou Lalko joined our National staff. Dan was American Pork Congress coordinator, worked with checkoff markets, the Nat. Feeder Pig Comm. and the Environmental Quality Committee. Warren was our Sec. Treas., in charge of accounting and bookkeeping, budget preparation and recorded Board Meeting actions. Lou Lalko, a delightful little Polish fellow, very experienced in the advertising and promotional field, was our promotional director, supervising all of the pork promotional activities and working with the advertising agency. Annual meetings of member states made the early months schedule heavy with travel, but a real opportunity to keep in touch with the pork producer members, learn their concerns, and to show them new program materials for the coming year. This was another election year so it was easier to get the ear of most politicians, at least until the fall election. With Pseudorabies continuing to spread and become an ever more important loss problem, it was joined by an extra heavy out break of years old problem TGE during the winter farrowing season. The NPPC again pressed for some Federal effort on the pseudo problem, but they continued to dodge it. Our delegate body had requested we strive to get some structure set up to attempt a control program for pseudorabies. We did have a meeting including the state veterinarians, research people, and affected pork producers in those states with the heaviest losses. It did produce information that proved we did not have all of the information needed to start an effective program of control, vaccination, proper testing, and above all this group had no authority outside of each of their states. This is why we had tried so hard to get the USDA APHIS division involved. Another organization or two jumped into the foray of the Pseudo problem and found some of the same stone walls that we had. When you are dealing with many unknowns, people in trouble jump at every straw of hope that presents itself. We had researchers wanting to get involved in order to get research funds; there were pharmaceutical companies wanting to push their products, tho none had vaccine markers at that time to help determine source of outbreaks; regulatory people were chomping at the bit to get involved, but the purebred swine breeders and associations were really emotional because they were on the front lines of the outbreak problems, not only with their own breeder members but also with a few large commercial herds. Some progress has been made at this point, but confusion and the problem still remain today, fifteen years later. Pseudorabies may have first been identified as Aujesky's Disease along the Blue Danube in Hungary a century or more ago, but it has certainly been no waltz for pork producers of this country. With tenacious action we had finally got Weight Watchers to accept our pork promotion advertising in their monthly magazine. It was not easy due to the old outdated nutrition information that was still being used by the USDA nutrition information department. Our wording in the ads had to be exacting and to their approval, but we did get quarter page ads run every other month for a period. "Pork Goes to School" materials had now developed into a complete package with not only recipes, cut selection, history of pork, and cooking methods, but more up to date nutrition information on the new pork was included. Some of the information was in the form of games for the younger students to hold their interest. The National Porkettes took this material and did an exceptional job in getting it placed with schools in their areas. A colored art form insert was placed in a spring issue of Forecast magazine that went to 65,000 home ec. and nutrition oriented people. This wall chart "All Pork Needs Is A Little Understanding," met with great response from these people. Policy Committee, Ex. Board and Full Board meetings were held almost up to the opening day of the '76 Pork Congress trying to get all of the sharp edges honed off the proposal to increase the checkoff up to 10 cents per hog. During this period it was recommended that an NPPC Feeder Pig Committee be added to our program. It was also recommended that a national checkoff of 5 cents per feeder pig be made with 3 cents going to the state of origin and 2 cents to the NPPC for funding of research most important to the feeder pig production industry. During these sessions most of the discussion was over division of the increased funds. I fully believe that the mathematical wizzardry of one Ed Cox, Director from Arkansas, was the salvation that eventually gained unanimous approval. His formula was based on the first echelon of animals checked off from every state would have a major share going back to the state of origin to help finance their state program. Each additional numbers level would have a lessor amount going back to the state. This formula surprisingly pleased most states because as the amount of money retained by the National office increased the number of delegates from that state increased and they in turn had more power in the policy and program decisions at

National level. This worked fine until the two larger states started to counter each other in trying to force their ideas into acceptance by everyone else. Some rather static conditions have emerged during some of the delegate meetings in the years since, but hog sense blended with common sense has continued to reign and the results are about as democratic as you will find anywhere. The pre-planning and hashing over all points must have paid off because in this 1976 Annual Meeting of the NPPC Delegates the increase to 10 cents per market animal and 5 cents per feeder pig passed unanimously after Indiana and Illinois changed from their initial "no" vote. It was pretty evident that they were concerned because Iowa produced 25% of the hogs and thereby would have 25% of the delegates. Their arithmetic must have been a little rusty because 25% isn't a majority and its been proven in several NPPC Delegate sessions since. Virgil Rosendale was elected President of the NPPC at this session, and he proved to be the right man for the troubled times that were to reign. Virgil, a seed stock farm manager, from Augusta, Ill. had a great ability to show little visible emotion when you knew he had to be churning inside. He had gone thru a pretty good seasoning period as Chairman of the Policy Comm. during the planning for the move to the 10 cent checkoff. The NPPC and its staff had to this point an extremely dedicated and well qualified person to be its elected head, and Virgil continued that trend. Over 12,000 registered in for this Indianapolis event that featured the largest Trade Show yet. The Porkettes elected Bonnie Erickson, a long time worker from South Dakota, as their President; Terri Ward of Illinois was elected National Pork Queen and Cole Younger of North Carolina, Nat. Pork Cookout King. Over 2,000 attended the annual banquet with Jerry Clower entertaining. Despite the tension and debate of the business meeting this was another growth year for the American Pork Congress. This being the headquarters city of Elanco's Eli Lilly company, they were quite active and helpful in busing and entertaining pork producers during this affair. It seemed to we NPPC staff that not only did our potential program budget double this year but our program pressure and industry pressures doubled also. The FDA had been getting some negative pressure from an activist segment of the human medical group for some years and this year they decided to react by declaring that they were going to investigate the use of penicillin, tetracycline and streptomycin in the animal industry to determine if there was a possible build up of immunity that could be passed to human beings thru consumption of meat. It is still my feeling that this effort was only a part of the activist effort of the same group that opposed eating of meat, the vegetarian move, and now they were jumping on a new horse. It was humorous to see the government take off on a salmonella control program in the food industry, when these three medical treatments were our best means of controlling the problem in animals. We had known for quite a period that there was an immunity build up within an animal unit, but no one had shown a transition of this immunity thru consumption of meat. Pork producers were using these products to a much lessor degree than the FDA realized, and the medical people just plain assumed. Actually it was the doctors that were probably making repeated use of these products on their human patients to the point that they were building up an immunity in them, rather than getting that immunity from eating meat. Nitrate use in the curing of pork products had been festering for a number of months and continued to be another club used by the activist segment in Washington, D.C. We had the foremost research person in the entire government structure doing research on this problem in Philadelphia, Pa. featured on our Pork Congress program. Nitrate, in various forms, had been used for centuries to cure or prepare meat for storage to prevent botulism when little or no refrigeration was possible. In fact it is believed that even back in the cave man days naturally occurring salt deposits, containing nitrate, were used for short term meat preservation. The meat processing industry had gone into very involved research on the possibility of reducing the level of nitrate being used in bacon and ham curing. At this point Dr. Cassens of U. of Wis. presented an interesting proposal on nitrate use for research funding. It was one of the seventeen industry problems that was funded in the NPPC research budget for the year. At this point pork producer funds and government funds attained thru NPPC efforts totaled over a half million dollars annually. In a number of these projects the NPPC was funding only the expendable supplies portion and thereby avoiding overhead costs normally sliced off by the facility doing the research. For quite a few months we had been battling with the USDA food labeling division over their permission for the poultry industry to use pork meat terms to label and identify, what to us was imitation products made from turkey or chicken parts. In our challenge we presented the facts that the USDA regulations said that the term "ham" must be applied to a cut from the hind leg of the animal. We repeatedly

asked to see the hind leg of a turkey. It was plain to everyone that the poultry processing industry was riding on the popularity of our pork products to gain a larger space in the meat counter, without regard to whether it was mislabeling or not. As is well known today our efforts were not successful, but it was humorous to watch the activists wrestle with this one and how it stretched the term "truth in labeling" that they were always fighting the USDA over. I still fuss when I see the turkey hams in the same meat display as pork hams and spend a few minutes tossing the turkey products to the back of the display or covering them up with the "real" hams. It has been a pleasure to watch the activists, no doubt encouraged by the turkey people, raise a storm about "The Other White Meat" program terminology. They and the consumer both know that it is more accurate labeling than what they use on fowl meat. Shortly after the close of the Pork Congress Hilman Schroeder, Wisconsin Director and Chairman of the Research Committee, and I made a presentation to a joint meeting of the Agriculture and Appropriation Committee of the Senate. We asked for three million dollars to be appropriated thru the USDA and assigned to specific pork industry research that had been identified thru producer polls and research committee investigation. This included a request for $600,000 to conduct research on the present day nutritional content of pork. The USDA's own handbook on pork nutrition information for home ec. and nutritionists was twenty-five years old, but still being used as the reference bible for the industry. We were successful in getting $200,000 assigned, each year for three years to conduct nutrition research on pork. Aides to Wisconsin Senator Proxmire and Missouri Senator Eagleton were the real keys to getting this pork nutrition research project funded. We had found that often times the right hand man or aid to the Congressmen was the key to success in this kind of effort. There are just too many demands for the elected person to cover all subjects and requests, so they have to depend on aides, some of who are sharp and helpful, to sort out the facts on all proposals so they may make proper decisions or votes. Despite it being difficult to obtain the Federal funds for our pork nutrition research, the real battle was just beginning. Trying to keep peace and follow the recommendations of our two Boards of Directors, we asked the Meat Board to assign staff to meet with our staff, Hilman Schroeder and the USDA person to structure the final design of the pork nutrition research project. Our NPPC Home Economist, Ann Norman, had earlier worked for the Meat Board and she joined Hilman and I to work on the project planning committee. From our earlier work with carcass evaluation, PSE stress problems, and suggestions from highly qualified meat scientists in our Land Grant Colleges, Hilman and I wanted as many facets of the genetic and production systems of the industry to be an initial part of the selection of animals for this pork nutrition research. Katz Ono, an Agriculture Research Scientist with the USDA was to be the project coordinator, since the funds were to be handled thru that division. It seemed for the first two or three committee meetings that every point attracted extensive debate. It was also apparent that Meat Board Staff and K. Ono were trying to delay the start of the project. First it was research facilities were too busy in Beltsville, then it was no experienced taste panels were available; both of which were counter to our original intent for the research. It had been our intention that after the project was designed, we would then select two or more colleges with the staff and facilities to conduct the research and then turn them loose to proceed, with quarterly reports to be made to the committee. After much heated debate, limited smoke, and extended dialogue we finally found other sources that gave us information on the foot-dragging delay. It seems that the Meat Board and Katz Ono had a beef nutrition research project that had been started a year or more earlier and it had not gone as well, nor as fast as intended. It was running out of budget. Apparently Katz and his group felt that if they could delay the start of the pork nutrition research, our funds could be used to underwrite the beef project. As far as pork people were concerned, this was just like pouring gasoline on an open fire. The turmoil that surrounded our pork nutrition research project at this point never surfaced to the general public, but Hilman and I kept our NPPC Ex. Board informed. Mr. Ono, was extremely evasive and took on the cloak of federal government cover, and that is like pinning the tail on a donkey while blindfolded. This also did not improve our working relationship with the Meat Board. We finally, after many months, began to get some movement started on our pork nutrition research project. We needed the data from this project day before yesterday, but that seemed to matter to no one except we pork people. The real research work was still not in action when I resigned my position more than a year later. The pork industry can thank Hilman Schroeder for continuing the battle with the Meat Board and ARS to force the pork nutrition research into action and the results that came forth another three or more years later.

This was an excellent training ground for Hilman who, at this writing, is Chairman of the Pork Board that oversees the investment of all checkoff funds. Eye-balling was a technique used to evaluate hogs up until the early 1900s when carcass shows were first held. However it was still an eye-balling of the carcass that determined its worth. Finally in the 40's some weights and measures were started to determine carcass value. Then came loin eye size, fatback, then color of lean and a progression of points to evaluate the value of a hog carcass. Early in this period the Nat. Association of Swine Records, an organization including all major breeds of hogs in the United States, joined with Hormel Co. of Austin, Minn. to start the National Barrow Show. This was to be a terminal barrow show in which all barrows were to be slaughtered and the carcasses evaluated. These efforts were started to help seed stock producers more correctly identify their best animals for improvement of the meat hog industry. With these increased interests came a multitude of different systems of carcass evaluation. Actually hog carcass evaluation efforts were the prime moving force that started most of the Meat Science departments and new meat testing labs in most of our Land Grant Colleges. In 1976 the NPPC introduced a set of procedures TO EVALUATE MARKET HOGS, that had resulted from an in-depth study conducted by Bob Kauffman, Meat Scientist, U. of Wisconsin, his associates and with the input of twenty fellow meat scientists and pork industry people. Contained in this publication was, to my knowledge, the first accurate colored pictures of pork loin cross section showing the true color of lean and degree of fat marbling for the various carcass grades. It quickly became a reference manual in the meat education field, a guide for a number of packing companies to shape their carcass grading systems that based their pricing structure, and for meat judging in pork carcass shows. The teamwork in this project came from Hormel and the Nat. Barrow Show staff, Oscar Mayer Co., hog breeders, students and staff from many colleges. It was this type of teamwork that endowed your belief in the pork industry and firmed up your pride in being a part of it. This spring the popular Pork For Pop for Father's Day program went into 56 major newspapers and included an offer of a free new 32 page pork cookbook. The number of requests from each newspaper area again helped us determine the impact of our ad and the number reading it, as well as finding which publications were most effective pork funds investment. Elanco Company asked us to sit in on the planning and preparing of a 14 minute film on the promotion of pork titled, "Surprise Me." It was TV oriented but made an excellent tool for state pork producer groups to use locally and many bought the TV time for it to be shown in their area. We started a specific Market Newsletter to be sent to all of the markets that were making the voluntary checkoff of nickels. Thru this medium we hoped to keep them informed as to our programs and activities that were made possible with their cooperation and the producer nickels. It gave them, the market people something to show non-member pork producers who were not permitting their nickels to be deducted. The NPPC promotion program gained another co-op product with the joint promotion of Pork and Avocado Board of California. This cooperation made it feasible for the story of pork to be shown to 12.5 million more households thru the Ladies Home Journal, Good Housekeeping and Cosmopolitan, at half the price it would have cost us to go it alone. Dole Pineapple, Kraft Foods, and the NPPC joined up in another mutual promotion of products thru major consumer magazines and in-store promotion materials that offered a brand new cookbook, with recipes using everyones products. The NPPC paid for 1/3 of the costs of this project and gained just as much exposure, plus the sales forces of the retail contacts of the other two partners who placed the in-store promotion materials into the retail centers. After many months of effort the U. S. Meat Export Federation, that NPPC had helped to found, received approval for use of Federal Funds in the promotion of meat outside the United States. It seems that there are funds from sources outside the U. S. that must be invested outside of the U. S. and they therefore could be used in our meat promotion work. They could not be used for any costs within the U. S. but were rather unlimited in their use outside. I've often wondered just who the CPA is that checks on where those funds are invested. In July 1976 USDA Sec. Earl Butz appointed me to be one of nine serving on the USDA Advisory Committee on Regulatory Programs in Washington. The committee included representatives from commodity organizations, consumer groups, and related industry. This was no doubt the most important and most involved activity that I was privileged to take part in Washington. We got to delve into food labeling, impact of OSHA and EPA on agriculture, overlapping of state and federal meat and food inspection, USDA grading programs, excessive government regulations, some of which might not be within their authority, the extent of federal employees control of regulatory powers, and the food pricing regulations, such as milk, that were under fire. I was rather surprised that this committee was permitted to continue their work even after the fall election that changed the administration in power. Corn went to $3.25 per bushel and soybean meal to $220 per ton in mid-year '76, with hog prices taking a drastic drop in the Fall. A severe drought was putting a lot of pressure on profit margins in pork production after several months of pretty good prices. One fellow said he had three six-inch rains in a 30 day period. What he really had was three showers with drops six inches apart. It was about this time that the packing industry started their move to increase the weight of market hogs if you wanted their top dollar. This was brought about in part by the hourly wages that strong union activity had built over recent years. The packers found that their cost per head to slaughter was about the same for a 250 lb. animal as it was for a 200 lb. one. This program wasn't sold overnight because for years we had been told that heavy pork loins produced too large pork chops for per family member serving, and heavy hams had to be sliced or sold in halves, plus the heavier the market hog weight, the more fat or lard yield and the higher the cost of gain for the producer. The packers again held the upper hand in this deal because they started really penalizing the lighter weight hogs and producers yielded to their demands. There had been a new trend in the retail sale of pork to go to more boneless cuts and the consumer was beginning to accept portioned muscle segments of the ham that were defatted and formed into a very trim attractive cured product. Also more loins were boned and defatted at the packing plant before shipment thereby reducing shipping weight costs. This made the use of heavier cuts from the heavier market hogs very acceptable to the consumer. It was also an indication that considerable reduction in fat per animal had been achieved. However it put a mad rush on seed stock pork producers to select, breed and produce animals that would grow to heavier weights, with no more fat cover than when they were marketed at 200 lbs. It appears that now, 12 or 15 years later, they have done a pretty good job of getting it done. Another change in presentation of pork products at this point was vacuum packaging of pork cuts; chops, steaks, ham slices, etc., and also offering frozen pork packaged in this manner. We had watched the research on this move for a couple of years and now it was being shown in the Annual Meeting of the Supermarket Institute. It has been a hard job selling some housewives on the fact that frozen packaged meat IS NOT OLD

MEAT. Dated packaging and other means have been used to try to overcome their objections, but it is still not the most popular system. However the research has helped to develop a vacuum-plastic wrap-frozen process for packing fresh pork for export. As export barriers come down there is a good chance we can increase exports of quality pork. For some years the pork and beef industry has been throttled back somewhat by the very efficient efforts of the U. S. Feed Grain Council with full cooperation and backing of the USDA. With the feed grain reserves having been built up and held by the USDA, they wanted to reduce some of the political pressures by increasing grain exports. The U. S. Feed Grain Council was born and thrived quickly with the funding made available thru USDA efforts. It has always bothered me that our government has fostered programs to increase grain production and price, then helped develop exports of grain to decrease storage pressures, and that exported grain was fed to animals in other countries that produced meat exported back into the U. S. Would it not have made better sense to feed those grains to livestock in this country, carry out the slaughter and processing of meat in this country, then underwrite or give strong assistance to the building of greater exports of meat around the world? When you stop to consider the number of jobs that this system would have produced, and the taxable income it would have generated it is no wonder the U. S. is having balance of payment problems. The Germans and Japanese have not been exporting ordinary steel to us. They buy our scrap metal and then send it back in the form of consumable products, cars, TVs and electronic equipment, but keeping their labor force fully employed and a solid tax base. On the second Monday after October Porkfest kicked off we received over 5,000 requests for pork recipes and information, and they continued to pour in for weeks afterward. The NPPC Porkfest program was now strong in 30 major cities that accounted for 45% of the food store sales in the United States. By this time we had programs for about every season of the year. This helped build working relationships with the retail chains, the processing industry and other tie-in products. The quality of our pork promotion materials attracted the consumer and the content of our information was factual and could be easily applied in the home. We utilized five major consumer magazines and the ABC, NBC and CBS TV networks in addition to the newspaper ads for this years Porkfest. Cooperating meat packers, processors and retailers helped distribute and place 78,000 kits of in-store pork promotion materials.

With the growth of our advertising and promotion we were able to work a multi-dollar saving re-design of the fees being paid to our advertising agency. I felt that every time we could bargain to save a thousand dollars it was the same as increasing the number of hogs checked off by 10,000. Wm. Buller, S. Dakota, an Ex. Board member was appointed by Pres. Rosendale to chair the new Nat. Feeder Pig Committee. This group of feeder pig representatives from major producing states in their first meeting decided that an up-to-date government feeder pig grading system across the nation was number 1 priority. They also expressed the need for research on handling methods before, during and after shipment of these young animals to find how to reduce weight loss, maintain health and reduce stress loss. Subcommittees were named to pursue these goals and this committee got off to a running start. Since 1971 the National Pork Producers Council staff and the Meat Board staff had been directed to cooperate under a memorandum of agreement adopted at that time. It was a rather broad termed blanket outline that contained few specifics. The major problem of the agreement was the fact that the two affected organizations were not equal in structure, funding, nor design at the start of the agreement and as the NPPC made rapid growth and increased its funding they became even less equal. The real fly in the ointment of discontent was MONEY. One organization had enjoyed the dignity of older structure and here was an upstart group, a member of theirs, that had become an energetic, strong, fast growing organization, DIRECTLY responsible to individual pork producers across the nation, whose funds supported both organizations. There were also some board members of the Meat Board that resented the start of the NPPC and even more the growth and stature that had occurred. Even tho the NPPC funding program that pork producers had worked hard to build, without assistance from the Meat Board, increased the funds to the Meat Board, they were not happy. Repeated attempts to cooperate in planning and funding of pork projects resulted in the Meat Board taking over the planning, taking the credit and identification for the project and the NPPC ending up with NO identification in the project even tho they had furnished half or more of the project budget and by agreement were supposed to have been a part of the planning and a share in the credit. We had staff members with equal or better qualifications to work the project, because two of them were former staff members of the Meat Board. Attempts to belittle or put down our staff only irritated the situation. President Rosendale, in an attempt to correct the situation, requested a meeting of the Executive Boards of the Meat Board and Pork Council. At that meeting, with Stroud and Garner the executive officers, out of the room, the two boards reviewed the old Memorandum, decided to retire it, agreed to meet at least once a year, and to have the Pres. and Vice Pres. of both groups sit down with Dave Stroud and I and instruct us to work out our problems and to cooperate in every way possible. I think I made every effort to comply with the request, but when you are responsible to as dedicated a group as the pork producers who were investing their own money in a program, you are expected to direct a staff and program to accomplish the best results that will benefit those pork producers. And that I continued to do. It is rather ironic but more than ten years after Stroud and I have both left our positions, the two organizations still have their problems, because why? MONEY, one has it and the other wants it.

REGULATORY PRESSURES HEAT UP

In December 1976 the NPPC sponsored a "Swine Health Symposium" in St. Louis, Mo. It attracted several hundred pork producers, swine veterinarians, and regulatory people. The APHIS (Animal Plant Health Inspection Service) of the USDA had stepped up their sampling of pork tissue in packing plants around the nation and the number of violations were up. With many pork production units now large enough to be marketing hogs every week of the year, it really stacked up big problems when a producer was notified he could not market any animals until he had brought in five animals for slaughter that would all pass the tissue test. This caused markets, packers and producers delays, excessive costs and lack of income, much less the loss from feeding hogs to excessive weights while a clean test was being sought. It was pretty evident that the National Pork Producers Council had become recognized in many quarters because we started getting heated phone calls from all segments of the pork industry that were affected by violations. When you are funded by a voluntary system you start reacting post haste. This was good because it kept us in touch with the problem areas so that we could follow up and determine why some areas were more affected than others. We had been battling this problem for some time, but the heat was on now and it was felt we needed more health information in hog management that reduced or excluded the need for feed additives. If we could not achieve a drastic reduction in the violations, then it was pretty evident that threats by the FDA to outlaw the use of feed additives would be forthcoming. Some producers that turned up with violative sulfa levels in their hog shipment often had to wait four to six weeks before the five animal carcass check results would get back to them. The APHIS division doubled their sampling efforts hoping to get enough violators that they could put additional pressure on the FDA to withdraw the use of sulfa containing feed additives. They took this action before they even knew the capacity of their testing lab in Peoria, Illinois. After we put on some heat for them to speed up their testing speed, they directed the pork industry to start using private labs to get their five hog samples tested. WARF, a private testing lab in Wisconsin, was about the only facility that APHIS would recognize and it was soon crowded, even tho there was a $600 fee that the pork producer was having to pay, plus often loosing the value of the carcasses from five hogs that the packing plants had to condemn and tank, if the test took longer than a couple of days. To further torment this serious situation, we started getting an increased number of heated calls from pork producers that said THEY WERE NOT USING ANY ANTIBIOTICS OR SULFA IN THEIR PROGRAMS and therefore demanded to know why their animals turned up with violative tissue levels. For some time we had suspected false positive tests were occurring, so we started looking for qualified scientists to help us find the problem. We finally located a laboratory scientist, well recognized by his peers, right in the USDA research system that would put in writing that if tissue samples taken from hog carcasses at slaughter time were not quickly refrigerated and correctly packaged for shipment to a lab that they could deteriorate to a point that they would give a positive test up to 1 part per million level, while the violative level considered positive by APHIS was 1/10 part per million, or ten times what was needed to give a violative level. Finally, we had something with which to fight the system and bring some common sense into the problem. Even the father of our National Pork Queen had turned up with violative tissue levels in his hogs. He certainly would not have intentionally put his daughter, who was trying to improve the image of the pork industry, in such an embarrassing position. He actually was using NO SULFA CONTAINING feed additives in his operation. It was rather ironic that in his first five animal test lot effort to get a clean test so he could resume marketing, two of the animals were lost in the packing plant, and the plant requested another test lot of five animals. This is a perfect example of why I had opposed blanket swine identification if there was no indemnification to compensate the pork producer for losses incurred. It is senseless to expect an individual pork producer to absorb losses incurred within a packing plant, after title has changed, without due recourse, and when human error is possible. My good friend Clayton Kingston, recent President of Hormel Co., and I had quite a number of discussions on this subject, but tho our debates were heated we still continued to be close friends and his company an excellent cooperator with the NPPC. By now we had a new administration in Washington; Carter in the White House; Bob Bergland had replaced Butz; Carol Foreman, the famous red head consumer activist, had been appointed Assistant Sec. of Agriculture; Angilotti had been named head of APHIS and all of them were eager to qualify their position and authority. We were invited in to get acquainted with Sec. Bergland by his right hand assistant Cliff Ouse, a former Hereford cattle producer from upper Minnesota. For a while after his appointment and approval it appeared that this cattleman assistant was the only person within the department the secretary could trust. Cliff Ouse always wore his cattleman boots to all functions, probably expecting to need them to wade thru all he might encounter. The administration carved up a farm program for Bergland to present to Congress that even his own party members jumped on. I'm sure appointing Carol Foreman as one of his Assistant Administrators was not of his own personal choosing; nor was Bobby Smith, another Asst. Sec. from Georgia, quite likely a close associate of Pres. Carter. With all of the adverse things that happened to Bergland in the early months of his administration, he kept within himself and I think gained respect and stature, at least a lot more than he had at first. I always could get access to him on important matters, the same as I had with Butz. About 18 months later, just days before my resignation, Sec. Bergland met with our entire NPPC Board in Washington, D.C., during which meeting he complimented me on my efforts for the pork industry and the respect that he and his staff had for me and our organization. I couldn't even buy a cup of coffee with his comments, but they sure sounded good to me at that point. The new administration also appointed Donald Kennedy, Commissioner of the Food and Drug Administration, and he hit the ground running. He had been part of a research team in a California University and within just weeks of his appointment approval he announced his intent to ignore the recommendations of an FDA Feed

Additive Task Force and move to outlaw the use of several popular antibiotics considered necessary in healthy pork production. At that point we considered Foreman and Kennedy to be on the same team and they were not wearing pork producer colors. Once we had proof that false positive tests on pork tissue could be causing false feed additive problems in the pork industry we asked for a meeting with Asst. Sec. Foreman to discuss the problem. She in turn asked me to meet first with her new appointee, Dr. Angilotti, the Administrator of APHIS. I had heard reports of this gentleman's past and that he had been pushed out of the FDA earlier, so I was partially prepared for him. His assistant received me, asked me to take a seat on a low level divan in the office, leaving a higher seated desk chair for Mr. Angilotti. Mr. Angilotti came charging in, nodded as we were introduced and burst out immediately with a challenging statement that he had been informed that we thought his department was doing a blankity, blank blank job of monitoring food inspection. He used terms that would have been out of place even in an army barracks, a bar room or a Rosanne presentation. Expecting something of this nature, but not quite that heavy, I replied; "YOU'RE DAMN NEAR RIGHT DOCTOR," and then we got down into some straight talk. After he found out that I didn't have any hay seed in my hair nor straw behind my ears, but was armed with some factual information, he retrenched back into a decent conversation and as I left, agreed to look into the problem and be back in touch. To that day nor since have I ever heard a person utter such words, even in anger, when opening a meeting with anyone, man or dog, for the first time. You would have to have a long shovel and dig several days to get down to the level of respect that I have held for that man ever since that meeting. A year later I couldn't help but smile as I rode down an elevator in the Senate Office building with he, Carol Foreman and others, where I had just watched him being hauled over the coals by a Congressional committee. Even tho she was under heat from the committee also, Foreman surprised me in not backing him up and asked for his resignation soon after. Dr. John Mare, a member of the NPPC Swine Health Committee prepared a fact sheet for the pork industry on what steps to take in controlling the spread of Pseudorabies, and how to improve herd management to avoid the disease. A St. Louis meeting of producer representatives, state vets, and APHIS staff structured a control program for APHIS to enter into the FEDERAL Register. This became a bureaucratic football that Mulhern of

APHIS didn't want to hold, so he punted to his assistants. A short time later at the '77 American Pork Congress, the delegate body voted approval of an eight step control program and instructed NPPC staff to present it to Sec. Bergland. It was presented, but pigeon holed again. We continued to seek funds to implement the program, but for some reason there was little support from the administration. Over 15,000 checked in for the '77 American Pork Congress in Des Moines Vets Auditorium, making it the largest one yet. Both floors of the auditorium, all major hotels and motels as well as those in neighboring towns were filled. The pork industry had many problems during this period including: feed additive residue, pseudorabies, nitrate use in pork products, turkey labeled ham, out-dated pork nutrition information, and other consumer challenges. Despite all of the negatives we had a pretty positive annual meeting. We had invited Sec. of Agriculture Bob Bergland to speak at our 1977 American Pork Congress, but he declined; due mostly to the problems he was having in getting his assistants appointments approved by Congress. Special program people this year included Will Rogers Jr., Ara Paraseghian, Notre Dame coach, and Doug Kiker, an NBC newscaster on the Washington scene. DEBBIE BRAND, Hopkins, Missouri was chosen Nat. Pork Queen and 34 more Pork All Americans were honored. Debbie Brand became the most traveled of all Pork Queens with promotional appearances from coast to coast and Texas to Minnesota. Pork Queen appearances had grown with the growth of our pork promotion efforts and recognition of the ability of these girls to spread the word about "New Pork." Shortly after the Annual Meeting the full board of the NPPC met in Washington, checked over program outlines prepared from committees, had dinner with invited congressional people from their states, and then visited the offices of those congressional leaders important to pork industry programs the next day. The Ex. Board had been making this trip in previous years but with the increasing involvement of regulatory programs in the profitable production of pork, they decided the full team would be more effective, each going to their own congressmen. This elected body of pork producers, representing their states and fellow pork producers, quickly gained the respect and attention of their Congressmen. We had prepared presentation packets that told a uniform story to every Representative and Senator that they visited. Everyone had been briefed and were in agreement on all points and was able to discuss them when questioned. NO BODY CAN SPEAK FOR PORK PRODUCERS BETTER THAN PORK PRODUCERS THEMSELVES and they continued to prove it. The following day Pres. Rosendale, Director Saunders, Missouri, and myself appeared before the House and Senate Ag. Appropriation Comm. requesting funds for Pseudorabies program and research. Director Saunders joined us in this effort on this particular occasion because Senator Eagleton from Missouri was chairing the committee that day. Something worked, because the next day the Agriculture Research Service was granted $60,000 to initiate pseudo research. Later legislation approved $300,000 for additional research and a tentative one million dollars to start a pseudorabies eradication program. Just when we got that part of the Washington scene tuned up, APHIS appointed a Pork Advisory committee that included two garbage feeders, no one from the feeder pig industry and no one from two of the states having the heaviest pseudorabies losses. Somebody was standing behind the door when the smarts were passed out on this one. The 1st National Pork Cookout promotion kicked off June 1, 1977 with 35 member states cooperating. During this three month pork promotion 85 million consumers were exposed to six different newspaper ads in 60 major cities covering 45% of the U. S. food store sales. Half page ads appeared in Woman's Day, American Home, Southern Living, Weight Watchers and Sunset magazines. For many years we had been holding the Nat. Pork Cookout contest in the midst of the American Pork Congress, actually showing the potential of pork to pork producers, when it was the urban consumer we needed to attract. On June 10-11 the 1st Pork Cookout Contest outside the APC was held at the Northwest Plaza Shopping Center, the largest in St. Louis, Mo. It was a beautiful outdoor setting around the fountain pool where we had two umbrella tables for each contestant plus a grill for each. A band played during each day while the contestants prepared their entry. Nat. Pork Queen Debbie Brand and her mother moved among the spectators and handed out pork recipes, plus doing interviews with TV and radio people. They also made public appearances in the larger Supermarkets. All during both days and the evening awards banquet, we had a movie crew shooting footage that was made into a 14 minute color movie for use by member states, PBS TV stations, and general pork promotion. Seventeen states were represented and the winner was Larry Foster, Indiana who received an expense paid trip for two to Hawaii. Pork producers and Porkettes from Missouri and Illinois formed teams to pass out pork promotion materials and

120

recipes in the major supermarkets of St. Louis. Thousands of people watched the contest, sampled the results, and took home copies of the various preparations used in the contest. The meat market managers of the supermarkets reported drastic increases in the sale of pork following this event. These were two very warm days, but with the tremendous input from Debbie, her mother, the seventeen contestants, pork producers, wives and Harold Minderman, the MC, it was our greatest live promotion yet. It was a very colorful and attractive affair that brought forth many good consumer comments. During this intensive pork promotion effort we were still juggling many important emotional problems that plagued the pork industry. At the center of many of our problems was the former consumer activist, but now Asst. Sec. of Agric. Carol Foreman. In one of her early interviews she said, "We (consumer activists) know an awful lot about how government operates and how to work within it. When it's screwing you all the time, you learn." She also added in that interview, "It's terrible . . . where your enemies are afraid of you." It took but a few months for her to learn that others knew how to work within the government too, and that damn few people were afraid of her, even tho we respected her intelligence. In July '77 the USDA entered their tentative Pseudorabies control program in the Federal Register, some two or more years late. The money that the NPPC had successfully forced into their hands put them in a position of answering to Congress as well. Foreman came out with another blast at the use of NITRATE in the curing of meat products and announced deadlines that the meat processing industry had to come up with research data proving their ability to use nitrate safely, even at reduced levels. The NPPC joined the American Meat Institute in gaining the ear of a number of congressional leaders to dull the sharp knife of the "red head." We found Senator Lehey and Lugar receptive to our information and they helped to slow the time table that had been laid down by Mrs. Foreman. It was kind of comical when Asst. Sec. Foreman named a vegetarian Jacobson, a fuzzy haired, bearded, Jewish lad and fellow consumer activist (a Nader disciple) to be on the expert committee working with the nitrate problem and its taste in the pork products. He refused to sample any of the products with the rest of the committee but had full vote on nitrate use. What a choice to represent consumers! At this same time Foreman took off on the use of MECHANICALLY DEBONED MEAT in the processed meat industry. She and her cohorts had com-

plained for some time about the amount of bone that ended up in the products when this method of separating meat from bones was used. She brought suit against the use of these machines causing machines worth over $20 million dollars, to stand idle while she lobbied to limit this type of product. Foreman's regulation referred to the deboned meat as "tissue from ground bones." This was not only a degrading term but one that would certainly not have any consumer appeal. It is ironic, but the presence of additional minute bone particles, high in calcium content, could be ideal nutritional help to reduce osteoporosis problems. This was mainly a meat packers problem, but it was damaging to the pork industry as well. Former Asst. Sec. of Agric. Richard Lyng and now President of the American Meat Institute spent many miserable hours fighting the actions of the woman that had taken his place. Asst. Sec. Foreman's assistants continued to blaze a hard fast fight on the sulfa residue problem. We had asked them to run 400 pork tissue samples thru their laboratory to give creditability to the data on a research project the NPPC had funded to check on how sulfa residues were caused. It would have saved us over $9,000. They refused, saying their labs were over worked and they had no funds. Almost within days they announced that they were going to go from 200 check samples to 1600 check samples in their monitoring of sulfa residue in pork. That was typical of the cooperation extended by the APHIS bunch. It was about this time that Myron Damen, a pork producer in Minnesota was sent notice that he had sold hogs with a violative sulfa level. Myron had been close to a PHD Degree in Chemistry before he left college to return to the farm. He was able to talk the laboratory language, and had not fed any sulpha since the pigs were weaned. After due study Damen raised question about the quantitative analysis using the 1968 Tishler adaption of the 1939 Bratton Marshall test upon which the government testing procedure was based. He said that this system measured only the diazonium salt of the sulfonamide molecule and many primary aromatic amines could form these salts, including other compounds in feed stuffs. Myron became a very involved party in our wrestle with the sulfa problem and his knowledge proved to be equal to and often better than that of those causing us so much problem. The APHIS folks set up regions for pork producers to send their tissue check samples to after being identified with sulfa residue animals. To show their elite ability to organize, the Iowa and Nebraska samples were to go to a Government approved lab in Kansas City, Mo., but offending Missouri pork producers were to send their samples to a Gov't. approved lab in Dallas, Texas. Out of all of this confusion we did get a promise out of FDA Administrator Kennedy that he would not take any further action until a statistically proven sampling test was assured. The real problem was that the Bureau of Foods in the FDA approved the products and standards for industry use, but the USDA's Food Inspection Service monitored the program. Neither of them appreciated having the other challenge their authority, and much less have pork producers challenge both. Sec. Forman had other challenges for pork in mind and in late summer she opened up a weak spot in her fight on nitrates. She contacted the FDA (Kennedy) to check on why they were approving the use of nitrates in poultry products while she was attempting to stop the use of nitrates in pork processing when both were consumed by the public. Kennedy pitched the hot potato back to her pointing out the limits of his responsibility and she came out with a statement that put her in opposite position to her own appointed Nitrite Expert Committee. Ellen Zaul, the consumer activist that had taken Foreman's former job was also one of her appointees to this famous committee. She was said to be at outs with the "boss" for her statement. The mix-up among the experts did help to get an 18 month delay on any further regulatory action until additional research was completed and Kennedy could have time to go out in the industry and hold meetings with the actual people involved in the problem. Another agitation on the Washington scene was the action of a SELECT NUTRITION COMMITTEE, chaired by Sen. McGovern of South Dakota. This poorly selected and mostly unqualified group came up with some nutritional goals for this nation's people that not only kicked red meat in the teeth, it was using quarter century old USDA data to do it. The work of this committee probably attracted the most meat industry heat in history and accomplished about as little of its objective as any committee ever appointed in Washington. It attracted self-appointed experts whom were looking for a horse to ride and finance their future with the emotion that surrounded the subject. One of whom was a young Chicago lawyer that attached himself to a few well meaning Illinois pork producers. He professed to have been a factor in the writing of the dietary guidelines of this McGovern Committee and posed himself as a force in the Washington scene to those he was seeking financial backing from. Little did he know that I was in the restaurant of the Washington Hotel in Washington on the morning he sought out Bill McMillan,

Vice President of the Nat. Cattlemen's Assoc. and Washington representative for them, to seek his assistance in helping him get a look at the McGovern Comm. report weeks AFTER IT HAD BEEN COMPLETED. It still grits in my craw that this jerk caused me to lose the friendship of a couple of people and helped cause a verbal lambasting of NPPC President Rosendale and myself that Virgil didn't deserve. I always believed that as a paid staff person I was legal game for any pork producer that invested in the program to take pot shots at, but not elected pork producer leaders such as Virgil. During this year we had an increasing number of pork producers report problems with the IRS pertaining to Investment Credit allowed on their tax returns. Following these complaints we started making the proper contacts in Washington to get pork producers the same treatment as allowed in other business IRS reports. We eventually accomplished our task in getting relief for the pork producers, all to find out that some opposed because it appeared to them to only benefit the larger producer. From my standpoint it was the devil if you do and the devil if you don't. I met one of those most unforgettable persons you ever meet when I was invited to moderate a panel discussion at the Annual Meeting of Livestock Marketing Assn., an organization of marketing people, many of whom cooperated in our voluntary funding program. Although I had heard him speak and watched him on TV I had never met Ralph Nader, the renown activist. He was on a panel including the Presidents of the Nat. Cattlemen's Assn., President of the Canadian Cattlemen, and John Huston, Vice President of the Nat. Livestock and Meat Board. The cattle fellows were fairly blunt in their comments and questions of Nader and he was likewise with them. Huston took Nader on with some charges pertaining to lack of accuracy in his claims and statements pertaining to the meat industry. Nader replied in his usual vague but negative manner. In all my days I've never been around a person that enjoyed so much being the lonely negative in a meeting of people. He appeared in a rumpled suit showing much airplane mileage, his shoes unshined, his hair patted down by hand and I found it dumbfounding as to how this man had attracted enough creditability to be so well known. I closed the panel discussion with that old story that "any jackass can kick down a structure, but it takes a good carpenter to build one." What a power this person could be if only he was a positive carpenter in life. As I mentioned earlier, Sec. Foreman had a bunch of holdovers from her activist days. In December of 1977 she came out with a challenge that packaged meat products such as bacon did not consistantly contain the poundage so marked. Her complaint was very attractive to the consumer and another headache to the packers that ended up being another burden to the pork producer and to the consumer also. During storage and shipping most packaged food products shrink some. For years the packers had put in extra for what was normal shrink. Foreman's demands got enough consumer noise started that most packers started putting in 17 ounces in a package marked one pound. This meant that 375,000 pounds of bacon would go out as one ounce additions to each pound of bacon rather than as that tonnage of saleable pounds of bacon. Guess who paid for the extra in the end. It sure wasn't Foreman, and this effort of hers was the fore runner of the 12 ounce package of bacon and hot dogs that prevail in many markets today. TENDER LOVIN' FARE was the theme for '77 October Porkfest. Each year this promotion had grown til now we put out 50,000 in-store promotion kits across the nation, with many packers, retail chains and retail IGA Co-ops helping with the job. Newspaper, radio and TV ads in our Image Cities plus over sixty-five other major cities, plus shopper newspapers in the bedroom areas surrounding major cities brought forth many favorable comments on increased tonnage of pork moved during this period when hog marketing numbers increase each year. It was the largest promotion ever conducted by a voluntary funded commodity group. With a 12% increase in hog numbers, hog prices during the fall had been forecast to go down to $35 or lower, but they dipped to only $40, so demand was created from some effort, and many gave the NPPC the credit. Kickoff of Chicago, Cleveland and Akron as additions to our year around Image City promotion was keyed to the opening of Porkfest. State and local pork producer organizations also used these highly visible times to promote in their home areas to help build more membership that was passing the 80,000 member mark. The Dime checkoff had been in effect for several months and participation was not entirely uniform, especially the states that had their own legislative checkoff. On December 7, 1977 the NPPC Board of Directors approved new additions to the Bylaws setting down standard participation by all states that desired to continue all rights and privileges as now extended them, such as Pork All Americans, Nat. Pork Queen entries, Nat. Pork Cookout Contest and delegates that were assigned by number of animals checked off from that state. A probation section was included, but in the months following we found a vast improvement in equal funding and participation. "Efficiencies of Pork Production" was a very successful and valuable symposium held in Omaha, Neb. Attended by more than 300 pork producers, there was a wide variety of valuable inputs by active producers, veterinarians, researchers and industry leaders. It was a good feeling to have such a positive activity to end up a year that had been filled with so many negative challenges. All information presented was put into a bound book form and made available to all pork producers.

CHAPTER V

'78 WAS A GREAT YEAR!

We had a small but great NPPC staff that were working their tails off doing a job for an organization that they had pride in. I'll have to confess that I was somewhat nervous when additional staff had to be hired. Back in the very early days of the NPPC when it was trying to get cooperation and a foothold to start, I heard a major farm organization head challenge our efforts by saying—"it'll be just like the old beef council, hire a big staff and Ad Agency and be broke shortly."—I had made a pledge to myself that I would prove that dude wrong, and I think we did. We had carried out programs approved by the Board that had helped producers build the largest membership, national promotion program, government recognition and a positive image for the pork industry in the nation, all on voluntary funds and with a smaller staff than most thought possible. And we had built up some reserve funds while working at it. I had some critics, most of whom never invested a nickel or dime, or even had hogs, that criticized the building of a reserve fund. Their vision barely reached the end of their nose. By this time we had member states with a payroll larger than the NPPC budget when I started. All of their funds came thru the NPPC voluntary funding program. Who would have funded these state staffs if there had been a major disease, government shut-down of slaughter, or massive packing house labor strikes? Without a reserve, we could be back to square one in short order. That reserve had been created by conservative management of the American Pork Congress, not from nickels or dimes, and was later available to build the present national office building. Why was our staff proud of the NPPC and those who supported it? The following letter in early January '78 sent into a state office is reason enough. Dear Doyce: Enclosed is a check for $119.40 which represents the butchers I sold in 1977 that didn't get checked off. Please see that it gets to the right place. 1977 was a better year than I expected with an av. of $43.25 cwt. I'm thoroughly convinced that the promotion being done by the SDPPC and NPPC is really helping. Keep up the good work. Sincerely V. J. M. This was not an isolated letter. We generally got quite a number of them just before Jan. 1 and April 15; but how many other groups would have business people that would voluntarily share their income like this fellow did? That was reason enough for we staff people to be proud and to make an extra effort to continue to deserve that trust. A long struggle for the pork industry came to a close in the spring of 1978 when the USDA officially declared the United States "CHOLERA FREE" at a special ceremony in Washington with Sec. Bergland and Congressional leaders attending. NPPC President Rosendale and Pork Queen Debbie Brand headed our NPPC pork group attending. This was a joyous occasion but it set off one big scramble for a major share of the annual 12 million dollars that had been a part of the USDA budget for many many years. We were sure that it would be best invested in the pseudorabies research and control program that the industry had recommended earlier. It later turned into quite a battle because some legislators with different commodity interests in their states wanted a piece of the pie also. To take the edge off of our happiness with Cholera being stamped out the USDA announced that Mike Jacobsen had been engaged as a consultant to the USDA and would be a part of a delegation going to Rome to discuss uniform standards for meat and food in international trade. A Nader-Foreman cohort of past reputation, this was the man that served on the Nitrate Expert Panel, that refused to eat meat and was the prime mover in the "Food Day, Meatless Dinner" program. The NPPC joined the American Meat Institute and National Cattlemen in filing complaints with that type of person being hired to advise any part of the USDA. I mentioned earlier that Sec. Butz had appointed Pres. Gerald Beattie and I to two committees of ATAC and Sec. Bergland extended those appointments. Agriculture Technical Advisory Committee on Livestock and Livestock Products was my assignment. Perhaps due to the total domination of the committee by its Chairman Marble, I feel my time spent on this effort was a total waste, even tho the government was paying all expenses for us to come in for the meetings. Marble was a devout cattleman, once referring to hogs as "the only good hogs are dead ones." He also deferred on the committees recommendation that pork be a major export push to Japan because we were already selling $135 million in pork compared to $45 million in beef and they ate more pork than beef. His reason? He had beef up in the number one priority, pork was down in the 4th or 5th spot and he didn't want the priorities disturbed at this point. Those are direct quotes from the minutes. Other members of the committee had like problems, so I wasn't lonesome. Our basic struggle in the export area for pork products was to keep agriculture and industrial products locked together in the trade negotiations with the Common Market people of Europe. They had been manipulating for our feed grains to be sold to them on a world market base price, then they added on tariffs and variable levees so their people were paying twice the U. S. price for the grain. They then turned around and used those profit funds to subsidize the export of their country's pork back to the U. S. and to Japan where we were attempting to build an export market. It is still a problem today. In May of this year I was invited by the USDA to join three swine research men on a trip to the Soviet Union and my board approved. After a few days in Moscow we went to Kiev where we served as advisors to a group of young translators who were part of a United States sponsored Agriculture Exhibit touring the Soviet Union. These young people were sharp minded and could speak the native language, but had very little depth of knowledge about agriculture. They had been selected from Eastern Colleges and Universities because of their ability to speak Russian. We worked with them at the exhibit, giving them some background information on the various segments of U. S. Agriculture shown in the exhibit. The Ukrainians came by the bus loads as thousands stood in line in the rain, paid about $1.75 each to come into this exhibit and see anything they could about the United States. They were a friendly people, starved for information, and eager to learn about the bountiful production of food and goods in the United States. It was a large dome like, low air pressure inflated exhibit hall that was extremely well designed to show many parts of our agriculture. KGB and plain clothes police constantly shoved and moved the people along as they stopped to listen to these young interpreters. This exhibit would stay in one location for one month, then take a month to move it to another region of the Soviet Union. It made six moves in the year. Shortly after we were there, three of these young exhibit speakers were seized and instructed to leave the Soviet Union because they had been making remarks considered to be detrimental to that country. It was thought to be just a way of discrediting the United States, more than anything these young people said. In addition to working with the exhibit, we had several meetings with swine researchers, large hog farm managers and government people pertaining to mutual problems in swine production and how we were attempting to solve them in the U. S. All presentations, questions and comments had to go thru an interpreter, who we later found to be a KGB agent, assigned to monitor us and our actions. It was an interesting trip; Moscow a bit foreboding, but Kiev was friendly people, colorfully dressed and appeared to be democratically bent tho their level of living was quite depressing. A few weeks earlier Asst. Sec. Carole Foreman had answered our earlier request when she invited the NPPC to take part in a meeting she was calling to discuss the sulfa residue problem with all parties affected including the FDA, Feed companies, Vets. and producers. She had included in her letter that she would like for us to come by her office before the meeting for a short visit and she would then accompany us to the meeting. Nat. Pork Queen Debbie Brand, Pres. Rosendale and I went to Foreman's office on the morning of Jan. 16, 1978 where we had a very casual and pleasant visit, during which we extended her an invitation to attend and speak at the '78 American Pork Congress. We told her that we wanted her to meet and see our pork producers in action during their annual meeting. She accepted on the spot. Dr. Robert Angilotti was summoned and we left immediately for the meeting. Foreman opened the meeting with reserved and cautious comments of concern and interest in the residue problem facing the pork industry. From that point on the next nine presentations were by government officials of FDA, USDA, research scientists and one USDA invited human medicine authority. Most of their comments were straight-line pursuit of already established policy of their particular phase of the sulfa situation. Some questions raised on those statements by the audience brought forth only continued tenacious clinging to earlier policy and current procedure. It was only after I made a few short statements and then introduced the Nat. Pork Queen's parents Richard and Lois Brand, Myron Dammen and Sam Kennedy,

each of whom gave their detailed experience of being accused of sulfa use violations, that we got down to the nuts and bolts of the sulfa dilemma. From a hard rock position of exactness in their earlier statements, we found a number of regulatory folks backing off into the protection of averages, theory or hedging positions due to unknowns that they had to admit. We asked that that group be directed to sit down around a table, face up to facts, evaluate the known dimensions of the problem and then develop a program that would be within the dictates of law and human health that would protect the individual pork producer businessman as well. Happily this session brought forth what the pork producers had asked for plus an independent survey of the reported violations that proved feed companies, sampling and testing systems, plus some unknowns were just as involved in the cause of the problem as the pork producers. Foreman was evidently convinced because she immediately instructed her people to get research and investigations under way with an educational program for the industry that would help relieve the problem for all. I've often thought of Jan. 16, 1978 being a major occasion for the pork industry because actual pork producers speaking for themselves with truth and fact, brought immediate action from the USDA. Nobody can better represent pork producers than themselves. Amidst all of the hubub that we were having with the USDA, APHIS and FDA there began to leak out some of the real problems going on behind the scene. It seems that some individuals in HEW (Health, Education & Welfare) which also includes FDA, had wanted to take over meat and food inspection and USDA was resisting like mad. It is a powerful and heavily budgeted part of their department. As I have mentioned FDA sets the standards and gives approval and the USDA checks to see if the FDA standards have been violated. Each felt their part was the most important. I firmly believe that the most powerful lobby force in this country is the government and there is no greater friction than when its segments start bucking each other. To illustrate the size of government, back at that time there were some 6500 staff members serving just 100 Senators, or an average of 65 each. That did not include the staff people serving on the House staff & committee work. Mix that many people up with the regulatory people and it is no wonder we had regulation diarrhea, and probably still do. Back in February I was more than a little surprised to receive a letter from FDA Administrator Donald Kennedy asking for recommendations to fill the position, Director, Bureau of Veterinary

Medicine. I was even more surprised when one of the applicants asked me for a letter of recommendation and later was appointed to that position. We began to think this Kennedy fellow might not be so bad as first suspected, and he wasn't. One of the things you liked about FDA Kennedy was that he had an open ear and mind, something we hadn't experienced before on the regulatory scene. March 23, 1978 Kennedy came out into the livestock country to hold hearings on the actions that his department had filed in the federal registry pertaining to feed additives and plans to restrict use of or withdrawal from the market. The NPPC and some 50 or 60 more organizations presented statements to Kennedy at his Ames, Iowa meeting. We had also attracted the cooperation of Congressman Berkley Bedell, representing a very heavy livestock production area of Iowa. He and his assistant requested that Administrator Kennedy have lunch in Ames with two well known toxicologists, Dr. Stowe of U. of Minn. and Dr. Lloyd of Iowa State, Dr. Leland West, myself and I invited John Soorholtz, who had recently become NPPC President at the '78 Pork Congress, to sit in too. Drs. Stowe and Lloyd presented some challenging and excellent information pertaining to some of the inequities of the present tissue sulfa testing program. In the meeting Mr. Kennedy asked for some human pathology information on the subject for him to further consider. A short time later Congressman Bedell arranged for a meeting in Washington bringing together Kennedy, Foreman, their staff people, Drs. Lloyd and Stowe, and the NPPC, represented by Steve Beckley, Pres. Soorholtz and myself. In all of the contacts and hearings that I ever attended in Washington, D.C. I have never seen a Congressman prepare and background himself in the details of a subject as well as Berkley Bedell did for this meeting. He asked pointed questions for specific answers that Foreman and Kennedy both passed to their research assistants to answer. We had supplied specific pork producer problems to Bedell and he interwove these into his hearing questions in such a manner that you knew he had spent several hours preparing for the meeting. I had never seen Asst. Sec. Foreman remain so quiet and she quickly turned over the governments position for Adm. Kennedy to answer. This meeting was held in the Capitol so that Mr. Bedell could go back to the floor in case a vote was called. The results of this meeting were: Bedell helped the industry buy time for research and convinced Kennedy and Foreman that there was an honest effort being made by the entire industry to work within the regulations yet survive in profitable livestock production. I also believe that several people gained a lot of respect for Bedell and Kennedy and they for each other. I know I did. A few weeks after this meeting in Washington, Bedell invited Kennedy to tour his Congressional district and visit individual hog and cattle farms to question individual producers on their use and knowledge of feed additives and antibiotics. He toured cattle feeding farms in the morning and at noon, Pres. Soorholtz and I joined them at a pork producers home for a bountiful country dinner, pork of course, cherry pie and the works. Kennedy seemed to really appreciate the genuine sincerity and conversation that followed as he toured the various parts of the hog farms. He questioned the grade and high school sons as to their knowledge of feed mixing on the farm and the awareness they had for correct feed additive use. He saw specific use of certain antibiotics to treat and protect the health of animals. There is no doubt that these meetings with Kennedy were effective and a bushel of the credit for the slow down on taking feed additives off the market should go to BERKLEY BEDELL, Congressman from the Le Mars, Iowa area. We could use more with his dedication on the Washington, D.C. scene. Lots of snow, bitter temperatures and rough winter weather in January had taken its toll in the pork business and Congress had not helped any by reducing research funds cutting back on the pseudorabies problem. As a result of this action, we set up a meeting in Washington for all member states to invite up to six state officers and members to attend. Over 100 attended with the first day divided into sessions on each of the most critical problems facing the pork industry at that point. These included Sulfa Residue, Antibiotic use, Nitrite use, Nutritional research and pseudorabies. That evening each state had invited Senators and/or Representatives from their state to join them for dinner and made appointments to visit them in their offices the next morning. This was our second event of this type that included more than just the NPPC Board of Directors. This was a real booster for the entire NPPC organization and I believe had much effect on the success that came later. Our requests for research funds came less than a month later and the final USDA budget showed the pork producers efforts. The producers were pleased with their efforts and reported back to their states on the reception they had with their state's elected officials. For the 1978 American Pork Congress in Kansas City, Mo. we opened up with recent Sec. of Agric. Earl Butz and more recently Sec. of Agric. Richard

Lyng, who at that time was President of the American Meat Institute. We got things in tune the first evening with the Oak Ridge Boys who were just beginning to hit the charts with "Elvira." The next day we had Asst. Sec. Carole Foreman speaking to 1400 people at lunch. Another USDA Asst. Sec. Bobby Smith attended the lunch and helped present awards. That evening everyone enjoyed Congressman Jerry Litton who was making quite a name for himself at that time and later that fall died in a plane crash with his family on the day he was elected U. S. Senator for Missouri. Many believed he would have become quite a factor in the United States political scene and a friend of agriculture, from where he had originated. After our program was all set, Bobby Smith who had just been recently approved as Asst. Sec. of Agriculture, and a home state friend of Pres. Carter called and asked if he might attend our American Pork Congress to get better acquainted with our organization and people. Naturally we were quite pleased to have him and grateful for his interest. It was ironic that just a few years earlier the NPPC was happy to attract USDA Department Heads and now we had this All-star lineup. What was more unusual and surprising to me, Mrs. Foreman and Mr. Smith were not bosom buddies, even tho both were fairly new appointees in the same department of a new administration. Even tho they arrived by plane within a few minutes of each other they wanted separate transportation to our convention hotel. Finding that there was friction I was careful to get them seated apart at the luncheon head table and also for a breakfast with the Board of Directors of the NPPC the next morning. Butz was out of the government at that point and he freewheeled in his comments, even to a greater extent than ever. He joked about having first chance at the audience before his favorite Redhead (Mrs. Foreman). In visiting with Mrs. Foreman just before the luncheon, I found her to be somewhat nervous and apprehensive of how she would be received by this agriculture based audience because quite a lot of her past work as an activist had attracted her quite a bit of negative reaction from people in agriculture. She positioned herself well, opening with the fact she was a native of Arkansas, had farm relatives, went to school in Fulton, Missouri, and her home state's favorite animal was a razor back. She stressed that in her actions with the USDA she was only following the laws of Congress and she chose her words carefully, leaving few handles for grasping an argument with her. Sec. Foreman announced she had formed a new program that had included the NPPC with the

FDA and USDA in the planning the previous week and that this was the task force requested earlier by the NPPC to deal with the sulpha residue problem. Reaction after her talk was very mild compared to what some had expressed earlier. I really believe she was impressed with the courteous manner that she was received and treated, knowing well that we were quite likely a negative audience, at least towards her past work. This is a sharp lady that dots her "i's" and crosses her "t's." She left shortly after the lunch to catch her plane. We had reserved her room at the hotel and fully expected to pay for it. However a couple of days later I got a letter from her with a check for her hotel room, asking to be excused for her hurried exit and expressing her appreciation for being invited to talk to, and the courtesy extended by, the pork people. A couple of weeks later I dropped by her office and left a pig-skin leather paper pouch, a token of our appreciation that we presented to speakers, judges and others sharing their time with us. About a week later I got it back in the mail with a letter saying thanks, but that she could not accept it. She pointed out that her department's meat inspectors were prohibited from accepting anything of value from interested parties and that she and her staff should abide with the same rules. A small and well intended gift on our part, but this lady leaves few if any snags that might embarrass her later. Tammy Moerer, Johnson, Neb. was elected Nat. Pork Queen, and 33 more pork All Americans were honored with their wives. Virgil Rosendale retired as President after an outstanding two years in helping build the NPPC program and gain recognition for the pork industry. John Soorholtz, Iowa and Bill Buller, S. Dakota were elected President and Vice President. Attendance was in the 15,000 range with over 2800 attending the annual banquet that honored the NPPC Board of Directors, the Pork Queen was crowned, the Pork All Americans honored and entertainer Orsen Bean, of TV and Carson's Nightshow program spoke. When affairs of this size are held, there are many chances for slip-ups and mishaps, and this '78 affair had its share. First the Oak Ridge Boys were prevented from selling any of their records or tapes because of local union restrictions who insisted on getting 40% of the proceeds if records were sold. Next the auditorium insisted on charging seventy-five cents for each hat or coat checked in their massive checkroom during the banquet. I knew that would go over like a lead balloon with pork producers so I threatened to invite in the Boy Scouts and Girl Scouts of Kansas City to run the checkroom for tips. This backed them off, but those in charge of the checkroom that night were not too attentive and some egg-head grabbed about eight coats and took off down through the acres of exhibits. He was caught by guards, the coats returned, and the involved parties very considerate of the incident. However the most embarrassing of all was the serving of 250 cold pork chop dinners. All of the food was prepared in the Hotel Muehlbach kitchens, put on plates, inserted into aluminum hot boxes and hauled by truck to the auditorium where the electric hot boxes were plugged in when unloaded. Unbeknown to anyone a circuit breaker popped and hot ovens with 250 meals were not hot when served. Tho late, during the program, those folks were served, but an offer to return their meal fees was made. Few requested refund. For this large event, with this many people involved, we had few problems. However our pork producers were most considerate and courteous people who accepted the mishaps with great patience. Every auditorium and hotel we used for the American Pork Congress wrote us letters praising the conduct of our people and their appreciation for the lack of wear, tear and damage occurring during the American Pork Congress. Thats a nice compliment and well deserved by pork producers and their families. I couldn't be more proud of my staff and the state staff that blended to make this annual event run smoothly and efficiently to make it the largest of any commodity affair in the nation. We had our pressure times but the results helped pork people enjoy themselves, plan and look forward to next year's event. During the final APC luncheon we honored a fellow who not only rendered yeoman service by taking charge of the seminars and educational sessions for several years, but had been a bright star in the swine industry from the "30's" when he was an outstanding Voc. Ag. Teacher in my home area of Missouri, an NPPC Director on the Ex. Com. representing the purebred portion of the swine industry, and many years Sec. of the National Hampshire Swine Registry. Harold Boucher was that fellow and at this writing has retired in the West Plains, Mo. area. I would be negligent if I didn't express appreciation and recognition to a handful of special duty people that went beyond the call of duty in helping make the American Pork Congress a success each of the years that I was responsible. They are Leon Olsen, Vice Pres. of Hawkeye Steel who guided and helped us format and design the layouts for the exhibit area each year; Mark Duffy, Show Manager for the Greyhound company that handled all arrangements of the exhibits and any other stage or meeting structures

we needed; Don Paulsen, Sec. of the Minnesota Pork Producers, who took charge of meeting the planes, escorting, registering in and seeing to the comforts of all of our featured speakers and entertainment; Doyce Freidow, Sec. of S. Dakota, Terry Schrick, Sec. of Nebraska Pork Producers and Rex Whitmore, Sec. of Wis. Pork Producers who assisted W. E. Smith in operation of a registration system for thousands. And a special pat for Steve Beckley, Dan Hoffman and Warren Pitcher, my key staff people who shared the many pressures, complaints and thanks during my latter Pork Congress events. They and the above mentioned individuals were a dedicated team that pulled together for a pork producer pleasing event. Later, in June, Kansas City was also the site for our largest Leader Training Meeting with over 150 producer leaders from the member states in attendance. A full Board of Directors meeting was held just previous and most of them stayed for the full training program. In this meeting we presented in-depth reports on the activities of the NPPC in the previous months, outlined the work program for the coming months, and previewed the promotional materials and programs for the summer and fall. We also had motivational speakers and media representatives giving tips on how to obtain the most exposure for the money in local level programs to increase membership, ways to get free publicity and how to take part in media interviews. It was a hard working group of pork producer leaders that attended these events and they appreciated all tips and assistance that would help their efforts. The NPPC Pork Promotion program had now grown into a year long event with special features during all seasons of the year. Houston, Philadelphia and Denver were added to the Image City program; the Summer Pork Cookout program ran from Memorial Day thru Labor Day complimented with six ads in 70 newspapers, 1,000 radio spots in 15 major markets, and 50,000 promotion kits in supermarkets across the nation. The National Pork Cookout Contest was held in Seattle, Washington at the site of the 1966 Worlds Fair. Over 10,000 watched seventeen contestants present their wares of special pork presentations prepared on outdoor grills. Wayne Jorgensen, Dover, Ak. was the winner. The owner of one the most famous restaurants in Seattle was one of our contest judges. In this effort we had excellent cooperation from the supermarket people and the packing companies supplying this area. Taking this event out to the public was a big plus over showing it to ourselves in the Pork Congress. A sixteen page insert, titled "Hogwash" in Forecast magazine went to 70,000

Home Economics people across the nation, an all new "Pork Microwave Cooking" was offered in ads in the Woman's Day and Seventeen magazines, and the Nat. Pork Queen had a heavy schedule of appearances. October Porkfest was expanded again with full page four color ads with a variety of pork featured and recipe offers included in five of the most popular housewife magazines. In-store materials, spots on 75 TV game show programs and radio spots gave national awareness to the "new" pork. This promotion had grown each year until now meat market managers, meat packers and processors were willing participants and the results were quite evident at the hog market. During the past nine years we had constantly tested, evaluated and carried out consumer surveys on the effectiveness of our pork promotion program. In addition we had carried out surveys on the changes that were occurring in consumer demands and directing changes to fit those demands. Our programs had won national awards in advertising competition and ranked high in evaluation comparison with other ads in major publications. We had grown into a respected commodity promotion program, using voluntarily invested funds of pork producers. In the April 24, 1978 Ex. Board Meeting I had reported that our office space lease would be up at the end of the year and I needed direction on which way to go since it was getting small for our office needs. After due discussion, the board approved the President appointing a Building Committee to pursue office space availability and possible sites for a building. John Sims was Chairman, Ron Liittjohann, Virgil Rosendale, Soorholtz and myself made up the committee. After checking a number of office spaces I found them much higher than what we had and it appeared that building might be advisable. After requesting the Iowa Development Commission to have a man check out the possible sites around the Des Moines area and not identify who might be in the market for them, he came back with about 21 sites. I toured the sites with the IDC fellow. When I first saw this 3.9 acre wooded site located on two Federal Interstate Highways, I felt it would fit our needs even tho it was accessed at that time from a gravel road. We checked on where the nearest water line was located and found that a city sewer was already in front of the site. The price of $90,000 was low in comparison to other sites and even tho it appeared a little rough and was on a gravel road, I was afraid someone might find out there was interest and the price would go up. I gave a personal check to tie the offer to purchase down, provided that the Building Committee and Board of Directors approved. The Committee, after meeting in Des Moines and visiting some of the sites I had seen and comparing, approved the site that I had put a hold on and extended that hold until the Full Board approved. They also instructed me to check on architects and their fees. I was amused when one of the firms wondered if pork producers might have the funds for a building, but not so amused when another didn't feel the job was large enough for them. The firm of Savage and VerPlogue not only was interested but they had a young pork producer on their staff that was interested in helping with the design. It was all go on a new headquarters building for the National Pork Producers Council. A tentative design with in-set slanted windows, meeting rooms, office space, and space for future growth was included. It was something that pork producers could point to with pride. More planning was to come later.

ARRWAD KICKS OFF

Despite membership growth to over 80,000 pork producers, checkoff investment now exceeding 52% of the potential, very evident success in obtaining increased federal funds for expanded pork production research, and a commodity promotion program that was the envy of many, we still had room to grow in our membership and voluntary funding of the NPPC. Over 100 pork producer leaders from member states met on August 18, 1978 to receive materials and instructions to kick off the largest, most organized and in-depth campaign to increase NPPC membership and voluntary funding that we had ever held. Having had a real battering time with government regulations for the past eighteen months, having successfully increased the voluntary checkoff from 5 cents to 10 cents per market animal, and also wanting to increase our pork producer membership base, I wrestled with a title for this drive that would tie all facets together. While doodling on a plane flight back from Washington one evening, I thought of a theme for this drive. ARE REASONABLE REGULATIONS WORTH A DIME? The title fit, but was too long, so we used the first initial of each word and it came out—ARRWAD—and it caught on. From our national meeting the states were to each have a meeting that divided up into state districts and from these were to be selected producer contact committees that would set up meetings with all Congressional and Senate candidates from their districts that were campaigning for office that fall. In these meetings they were to ask questions of each candidate and then express the wishes of the pork producers to those candidates. There was no political party affiliation nor promise of any funds, just that they were voters in that area and these were their feelings. Each county organization was given sign-up sheets for pork producers to sign, once they had read what the Pork Producers expected in government regulations. Copies of these sign-up sheets were taken to hog buying points and markets asking those marketing people to help get signatures, because they too were being affected by these irresponsible regulations coming down from Washington. From the Aug. 18 date, states were to hold their meeting by September 1, hold district meetings by Sept. 15, have the Candidate meetings in each district by Oct. 1 and report back to the state and national offices by Oct. 6. Remember, this was in the midst of Fall Harvest Time. Did it work? And how it worked. I even got calls in Des Moines from incumbent candidates because their name was not listed first in the meeting announcements that the pork producers had put in their local papers inviting the public to the meetings. We had a continuous flow of status reports to the state and district leaders informing them of new Washington and industry happenings that would pertain to ARRWAD efforts. The Nitrate problem had flared up again during this drive because the government was backing up on their time schedule to totally ban the use of nitrate in the curing of meat, and the activists were real noisy. States reported that people were calling in to find where they could sign the ARRWAD sheets. One packing company reported their union workers wanted to sign them too. Congressional aides were calling the NPPC office to get the latest information on problems in the pork industry so they could be prepared to meet with the pork producers in their home districts. Also in the midst of this drive I had been asked to make a presentation to the Leahy committee on nitrate use and Senator Lugar of Indiana was chairing the committee that day, thereby giving me a chance to nudge him for Indiana producers. Right in the midst of ARRWAD a report came out of Washington that the outbreak of AFRICAN SWINE FEVER in the Dominican Republic had grown to where they were seeking financial and staff help from the United States to eradicate the disease. The NPPC Swine Health Committee and Ex. Board quickly endorsed the request and fired off a letter to President Carter asking that he take action to carry out the request. We also restated the NPPC position on feeding of garbage to hogs and asked all member states to contact their state authorities and request the banning of all garbage feeding of hogs, which was believed to have been the method of spread in Africa and Europe. Early state ARRWAD reports had one state gaining 1,000 members after one week and signatures were running over 5,000 and up in some states. The design of this ARRWAD program could be compared to a freshly opened Pepsi. If the leadership had taken a swig with the National meeting and then set it back, it would have lost its fizz, the emotion would be gone. But if they went back and set their States and districts in action the fizz was still there. The fizz was the petition signing and meetings with the congressmen, but the real body and guts of the program was getting members signed up and hog markets to help increase the dime checkoff. The fizz stayed with this program for six weeks. Of all the programs and activities that I had helped originate and put in motion during the past nine years since July 1, 1969, this I believe was one of the best. And in the midst of this successful program, I TENDERED MY RESIGNATION. This came as a shock to many and I was truly surprised with the mass of calls and letters I received when the word went out. One of which was from FDA Administrator Don Kennedy in Washington; in which he stated, "You've been fair, decent and a good person to know. I hope our paths cross again often." These words I appreciated because our early contacts had been challenging, to say the least. Since 1956 when my Dad and others formed the Missouri Pork Producers and he became its first President, I had been a member and part of the growth of the Nat. Pork Producers Council. During those 23 years I had been Vice Pres. of the Missouri Assn., Ex. Board member of the NPPC, and the last nine plus as Ex. Vice President of the NPPC. Few, if anyone, had put in more hours helping to build the NPPC, its programs and its credibility than I had. No one could be any more proud of those results than I. Some years back, with Ex. Board approval, I had fired a close friend of my present President. When he attained office I expected abnormal pressure and wasn't surprised. One director had a family member that disliked me, another had a rebel faction in his state that opposed me and another director was afraid if he supported me he might not move up in office in the organization. In the six months previous to my resignation a motion requesting my resignation had been entered in two Ex. Board Meetings. One was defeated 6 to 3 and the other 7 to 4. For a few months I was able to do my job and withhold this extra pressure from my wife who had some health problems. Later, even tho I had a winning vote on my Ex. Board and Full

Board, I tendered my resignation because my president was threatening to call a delegate body session over the vote of the Ex. Board and seek my dismissal thru that means. That effort would have failed too, I believe, but I had spent too many hours, weeks, months, and years of my life helping build the National Pork Producers Council, of which I was extremely proud, and I did not want to see the achievements of thousands of pork producers be torn asunder from within. When I accepted this position there were fewer than 20,000 identified members in less than twenty full member states and our monthly income averaged less than $30,000. At this point we had over 85,000 identified members in 35 full member states (producing over 95% of the nations hogs), an annual budget of over 4.6 million voluntarily invested dollars and a reserve from Pork Congress to build the newly planned headquarters. I was extremely proud of the achievements of the NPPC and equally proud of having been a part of attaining them. My only dismay was leaving that majority of Directors that supported me, and with one exception, my staff that had helped and supported me too. It was an honor to have been a member of the team that built the largest membership and voluntarily funded organization of its kind in the nation. These final lines of an old poem seemed to fit:

"Life is sweet because of the friends we've made. And for the things in common we share We want to live on not because of ourselves But because of the people who care. It's living and doing for somebody else On THAT life's splendor depends And the joys of living when you've summed them all up Is found in the making of friends." And in closing my final NPPC radio tape, that I had made each week for over seven years and had grown to be carried by over 500 radio stations across rural U. S. A., I quoted a favorite of mine, Will Rogers and I repeat: "Common sense is not an issue in politics or business, its an affliction." And in using mine, I close, and so be it.

Plans for the new NPPC headquarters building were begun in 1978.

J. Marvin Garner, Secretary of Agriculture Bob Bergland, Virgil Rosendale and Debbie Brand at the USA Hog Cholera Free announcement, January 31, 1978.

J. Marvin Garner talking with Senator Lugar following a Senate Committee hearing in Washington, D.C.

Japan trip, 1976. From left to right, Mr. Horiuchi, Secretary of Agriculture for Japan, Sigman Meat Co. representative, J. Marvin Garner.

American Pork Congress Banquet, 1972. From left to right, Jimmy Dean, Euel Liner, Secretary of Agriculture Earl Butz, Roy Keppy.

Section IV

By Orville K. Sweet
NPPC Executive Vice President 1979-1989.

Part 1

FROM BEEF TO PORK

It was a Friday morning in early December, 1978 at the American Polled Hereford Association. There was no reason to expect anything other than the usual round of staff meetings, prepare an editorial for the Polled Hereford World Magazine and make plans for the usual weekend travel. The caller was Roy Sharp, a member of the Executive Committee of NPPC. Little did I know that this call would lead to events that would change my life and the lives of my family for the next decade.

Mr. Sharp explained he was a member of a search team looking for a new CEO for the National Pork Producers Council and wondered if I had considered applying. With little hesitation I informed him I wasn't aware of the opening and appreciated his call but I really wasn't interested.

On Monday morning Mr. Sharp called again and asked if I had given the idea any further thought and I explained I had no reason to be casting about or even considering another job.

He asked if I would forward a resume even if I wasn't interested. I hesitated, then consented if it would be kept confidential because I didn't want rumors to get started.

Mr. Sharp indicated to me a rather unusual style and tenacity not common to many livestock producers. Were there more like Mr. Sharp in positions of leadership in the pork industry? I wondered what it would be like to work for a group like Mr. Sharp.

A date for an interview was set. I met with the Search Committee of about a dozen pork producers and a professional consultant (head hunter). When I appeared for the interview I learned that there were about 30 applicants that had been screened down to about 7 who were interviewed and 5 were given a battery of written examinations.

The Search Committee was chaired by Bill Buller, a pork producer from South Dakota, a mountain of a man whose leadership ability was expressed in a number of ways. His manner and approach to his task of weeding out candidates he thought were light weights would have gained the respect of a CEO of a Fortune 500 corporation.

I have not met a man more dedicated to a cause than Bill was to the future success of pork producers.

I will never know if I was selected or simply happened to be the one that was remaining. Although I had serious reservations about leaving the many friends in the cattle business I never regretted making the career change.

I secretly felt I could be of mutual benefit to both segments of the livestock industry. Always a strong believer in competition I felt if I was successful in helping develop a strong competitor to challenge the beef industry that it may be shaken from its lethargy and reach heights it would not otherwise be challenged to achieve.

I served on committees for the beef industry through two efforts to pass a producer checkoff referendum. Each failed simply because of lack of unity in the beef industry.

The beef industry had endured the worst decade of beef prices and declining consumer demand in history, while the pork industry was introducing new technology and expanding at a rapid rate.

Another experience that impressed me with the pork industry was the 1978 American Pork Congress held in Kansas City at the Bartle Hall Convention Center. The producers meetings overflowed the Muehlbach Hotel and crowded our usual Thursday noon Rotary Club luncheon into other quarters.

About 12,000 pork producers registered and a headline program featuring top government officials impressed me. A year later the beef industry held their annual convention in the same facility and 1200 cattlemen registered. In fairness one must recognize the difference in the weather between January and March that definitely had an effect on the cattlemen's attendance.

I carefully considered the human resources and the attitudes characterizing pork producers. I also was aware of the nutritional attributes of the new pork and was confident that properly presented to the consumer it would find favor.

The limiting factor in the pork industry was funding. To plan and implement programs, hire adequate professional staff and funds to properly promote pork in the media would require dollars. The three and a half million available to NPPC was inadequate to mount much of an offensive. Human resources were abundant but money was scarce.

Pork producers had established an admirable record during the 13 years of NPPC activities. The momentum created an air of excitement and a confidence level that was convincing pork producers they could achieve anything they set their minds to. And this was literally true.

I accepted the offer by the Executive Committee to become the Executive Vice President effective March 1, 1979.

My first responsibility was to attend the American Pork Congress the first week of March in Indianapolis, Indiana. More than 15,000 pork producers registered. This was a record number that we never attained again until we initiated the World Pork Exposition in Des Moines in 1988.

My personal feeling was that we had a perfect match. I needed a new challenge after more than 16 years with the Polled Hereford Association. The pork producers offered that challenge.

I learned quickly to respect my two predecessors, Mr. Paul and Mr. Garner, for the good foundation they had prepared. I gained a high regard for the producer leaders, for their wisdom and selfless dedication.

I soon understood and appreciated the organizational structure that provided the maximum opportunity for producer input and involvement. This representative process was the basis of strength that provided for motivation and involvement resulting in strong organization and ultimate success. It was democratically oriented but like our U.S. Congress was in truth representative because elected representatives carried out the wishes of the majority to the best of their ability.

Part 2

A STUDY OF NPPC's STRENGTHS AND WEAKNESSES

When accepting the position with NPPC in 1979 it was with the understanding that we would conduct a professional study of the organization. The study would focus on the NPPC structure, strengths and weaknesses, staffing, funding and facilities.

Although there were a number of burning issues resulting from the delegate session in March to be dealt with, a high priority was given to the study. The American Society of Association Executives was engaged to do the study. A three man team conducted the study. They were Charles (Chuck) Mortensen, ASAE; Charles Ball, CAE, Executive Vice President, Texas Cattle Feeders Association; and Marvin Vinsand, CAE, Executive Vice President, National Feed Ingredients Association.

Their routine consisted of interviews with each member of the Executive Committee and staff. A study of the bylaws, programs, funding mechanism and committee structure. From the study they made 56 specific recommendations for change or additions to the existing organization.

The Executive Committee carefully considered each recommendation and as a result instructed staff to set about to implement 48 of the 56 recommendations.

The study team returned in 1982 to evaluate our progress. They were highly complimentary with the changes that had taken place. The study was featured in a special article in the "Association Management" magazine as a model approach to association evaluation.

Strengths recognized by the study were highlighted by: Unusual people resources (110,000), a high quality product with great potential, a young growing association buoyed by recent successes, a strong women's auxiliary with 17,000 members, strong voluntary leadership and a democratic policy structure.

Weaknesses were cited as: lack of funding, organizational stress, both internal and external, poor facilities, lack of adequate staff, outdated organizational structure, weak program of work, absence of long range strategy, weak public policy mechanism, and burdened with a historic image problem.

Most of the weaknesses could be attributed to a young fast growing organization. It was likened to an army that had advanced so rapidly its supply lines were stretched and were not functioning effectively.

The organizational stress referred to the relationship with the National Livestock and Meat Board

(NLMB) and the appearance of duplication of programs and costs.

The NLMB issue ran deep into the organization structure of NPPC, infiltrating NPPC's state affiliates, creating dissension and disunity.

The major issue with the NLMB traced to the origin of NPPC. Pork producers had attempted to develop a national checkoff program for several years. Leadership of the NLMB spearheaded by John Schuman, President of the American Farm Bureau provided the political clout that impeded the movement. At risk was a one cent per market hog checkoff that was initiated by the NLMB a number of years earlier. The effectiveness of the checkoff was limited to a few central markets and generated only a few thousand dollars.

NPPC agreed to compensate the NLMB for their original one cent checkoff by assigning one cent from each nickel per head collected to NLMB. The increase in the number of markets checking off quickly convinced the NLMB of the wisdom of this decision.

There was also a serious organizational flaw in the loose relationship NPPC had with its state affiliates. State associations were autonomous and independent even though states funds came from NPPC and the salaries of the state executives were subsidized by NPPC.

And thirdly, there was a lack of communications between the Porkettes (later changed to National Pork Council Women, NPCW) and the NPPC administrative staff as well as the executive committee.

These problems were deep seated in the organization's structure and needed to be addressed in a direct manner. It was some time before satisfactory solutions were found for all issues.

Poor office facilities were soon replaced by the new one million dollar headquarters building that had been approved in the 1979 Delegate Annual Meeting.

In my first executive committee meeting in March of 1979 authorization was granted to establish a Washington presence for pork producers. This had been an issue in suspension for several years because of lack of agreement on philosophy. Some contended that pork producers should make all of the contacts in Washington. While this view continued it became obvious that a daily presence was imperative to deal with issues that affected the best interest of pork producers.

Dr. Don Van Houweling was engaged and within a few months the pork industry had a functioning office in the nation's capitol.

Dr. Van Houweling had an impressive career in government. He served as Chief of the Bureau of Veterinary Medicine and held the post of the top livestock person with the Food and Drug Administration. He was uniquely qualified to assist the pork industry in addressing the problem being confronted in the regulatory area at this critical stage.

The decade of the 70's was stage one. Stage two was destined to be the challenging decade of the 80's.

A still new organization barely in its teens, the NPPC literally burst from its launching pad during its first few years. The council was ready to switch on its after burners and continue its journey into the excitement of a new decade.

NPPC had become the largest dues paying commodity organization in the world in only 13 years. Checkoff had climbed from $0 to $4 million. A renewed pride based on a spacious new organizational headquarters and a growing professional staff and eager leadership assured everyone that here was a movement to be reckoned with.

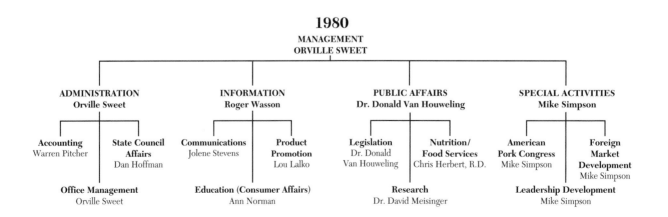

1980
MANAGEMENT
ORVILLE SWEET

ADMINISTRATION Orville Sweet	INFORMATION Roger Wasson	PUBLIC AFFAIRS Dr. Donald Van Houweling	SPECIAL ACTIVITIES Mike Simpson
Accounting Warren Pitcher / State Council Affairs Dan Hoffman	Communications Jolene Stevens / Product Promotion Lou Lalko	Legislation Dr. Donald Van Houweling / Nutrition/ Food Services Chris Herbert, R.D.	American Pork Congress Mike Simpson / Foreign Market Development Mike Simpson
Office Management Orville Sweet	Education (Consumer Affairs) Ann Norman	Research Dr. David Meisinger	Leadership Development Mike Simpson

TREASURER'S REPORT

NATIONAL PORK PRODUCERS COUNCIL

CONSOLIDATED STATEMENT OF CASH RECEIPTS AND DISBURSEMENTS
YEAR ENDED DECEMBER 31, 1979

	National Pork Producers Council	American Pork Congress	Total
Balance on hand, January 1, 1979			
Cash in bank	$ 15,932.31	$ 6,266.01	$ 22,198.32
Certificates of deposit and savings accounts —			
Current operating fund	750,655.78	9,992.26	760,648.04
Reserve fund	575,546.38	175,000.00	750,546.38
Total on hand, January 1, 1979	$1,342,134.47	$191,258.27	$1,533,392.74
Receipts	$4,569,627.60	566,618.25	5,136,245.85
Beginning balance and receipts	$5,911,762.07	$757,876.52	$6,669,638.59
Disbursements			
Returned to states	1,295,859.43	——	1,295,859.43
National Live Stock and Meat Board	391,766.45 [1]	——	391,766.45
Pork promotion and advertising	2,167,705.57	——	2,167,705.57
Research and development	236,454.19	——	236,454.19
Communications and publicity	213,600.40	——	213,600.40
Consumer relations	203,341.65	——	203,341.65
Organization and revenue development	130,407.75	——	130,407.75
Administration	474,426.57	——	474,426.57
Automobile	8,857.64	——	8,857.64
Building and equipment	991,835.16	——	991,835.16
American Pork Congress	——	226,163.95	226,163.95
Total disbursements	$6,114,254.81	$226,163.95	$6,340,418.76
Balance on hand, December 31, 1979	$ (202,492.74) [2]	$531,712.57	$ 329,219.83
Balance accounted for as follows:			
Cash in bank	$ (101,292.37) [3]	$112,118.40	$ 10,826.03
Certificates of deposit and savings accounts —			
Current operating fund	3,758.05	213,729.04	217,487.09
Reserve fund	906.71	100,000.00	100,906.71
	$ (96,627.61)	$425,847.44	$ 329,219.83

Part 3

PORK INDUSTRY DYNAMICS

Harnessing the potential of 110,000 pork producers and developing the organization to utilize their collective resources was a huge challenge.

The pork industry was a virtual dynamo with the capability to become reactive or proactive with vigor. There were decades of pent up energy. Pork producers represented a force ready to be unleashed.

The threat of regulatory control by government agencies in the mid-1970's emotionally charged producers and allied industry and forged them into a cohesive force. New production technology was bringing about rapid changes on hog farms. When a new practice sent shock waves through the productive system adjustments and new practices in other areas were necessary.

The introduction and use of confinement facilities increased the need for tighter disease control and increased use of antibiotics. New and more effective antibiotics required sophisticated testing procedures to assure safe use for consumers.

THE DELANEY CLAUSE

There have been hearings to consider amendment of the Delaney Clause but they have been little more than an exercise to placate industry. Congressman Delaney, whose wife died with cancer, attached an insignificant amendment to another piece of legislation. To this day Congress hasn't the courage to amend the Delaney Clause although it has been outdated since its passage.

The "Delaney Clause" became the nemesis to all producers of food and fiber. The Delaney Clause simply made it unlawful to use any substance as a feed additive or treatment if it was determined to be carcinogenic at any level of dosage. It simply legislated a zero tolerance level. Today it is impossible to adhere to a zero tolerance because of the development of super sensitive assaying instruments that will detect parts per billion, far less than is considered cancer causing. At the time of passage of the Delaney Clause such instruments were not available. In spite of attempts to amend the Delaney Clause it still stands as an impediment to rational application of government regulations related to carcinogens.

The Delaney Clause was an important factor in rallying pork producers to respond to the threat of government regulations.

By 1979 pork producers had swelled their ranks until they were the largest commodity organization in the world.

Probably no issue has done more to convince pork producers of the need for a strong national organization than the consumer activist movement in the 1970's and the dramatic influence these groups have had on public policy in Washington, D.C. and in state legislators.

The 1978 annual report to the members summarized the issues and the response by pork producers under the caption of "Getting Involved."

National Pork Producer Council members responded quickly to the need to "get involved" in Washington in '78 as the challenges kept growing. They came forth in numbers and with enthusiasm and determination.

AFRICAN SWINE FEVER

African Swine Fever, the world's most deadly hog disease, invaded Brazil and the Dominican Republic in 1978. Letters were sent to both the White House and the Secretary of Agriculture asking that all efforts necessary be taken to guard against spread of the disease to the United States. It was also requested that Brazil and the Dominican Republic be given aid to control the disease in their countries.

Another major issue during 1978 was the use of nitrites. NPPC's work to counter this problem continued into 1979 with constant monitoring of communications on Capitol Hill and with consumers. NPPC has coordinated its efforts through the Nitrite Safety Council, which NPPC helped to organize and fund.

NITRITE COUNCIL

The possible banning of nitrite by the USDA and FDA was of utmost concern to NPPC. Once again, involved pork producers contacted their elected representatives, urging them to make sure all facts are known before unnecessary action is taken by governmental agencies. The Council continued to work hand in hand with members of the Nitrite Safety Council to make sure nitrite remained in its rightful place.

In 1978 the Pork People again joined in cooperative projects with others in the meat industry, such as the U.S. Meat Export Federation and the National Livestock and Meat Board.

Another project in 1978 included the start of a new cooperative project with the National Livestock and Meat Board and USDA in the area of nutrition. This project came about as pork producers urged Congress to appropriate $200,000 to the USDA's Beltsville Research Station to study the nutritional composition of pork. A strong lobbying effort resulted in $740,000 being made available to update the nutritional information made available to the nation's dietitians.

WASHINGTON SEMINARS

Pork producers also made themselves heard in Washington by traveling to the Capitol City. Over 100 industry leaders, producers and state staff personnel reviewed those issues which were to be in the forefront of the coming months. They listened to the information presented by government representatives and met individually with members of their Congressional delegations.

1979 included a meeting of Past President Rosendale with President Carter and NPPC representation at hearings on many of the issues discussed earlier. Council representatives met with USDA and FDA veterinarians in Iowa and in Washington on the sulfa residue testing program and coordinated visits with producers.

Administrator of FDA, Dr. Donald Kennedy, made several personal visits throughout the year on the subject of sulfa tolerance in pork tissue. Kennedy toured several Iowa farms for a first-hand look at producers use of antibiotics.

The willingness of Pork People to get involved in their industry is a key to their accomplishments.

Part 4

PORK BECOMES PRO-ACTIVE

BUILDING FOR THE FUTURE

It was a proud moment and a beautiful spring day, May 31, 1980, when more than 500 pork producers from the 50 states gathered in Des Moines to dedicate the new national headquarters building for the pork industry.

Iowa Governor Robert Ray, and U.S. Senators Roger Jepsen and John Culver, along with other national and state dignitaries were present to mark the strides of progress made by pork producers symbolic in the impressive new structure.

The new 20,000 square foot, one million dollar building, clear and paid for represented the futuristic hopes and dreams of hog farmers.

The new national headquarters nestled among the giant shade trees on the west side of Des Moines, outfitted with new furniture including a board room with 60 pigskin executive chairs. Pork had a home for the first time and the dedication of that home was a milestone marking the hard work of the past and a commitment to the future.

Pork producers for generations mired in the mud with their hogs were desperate for a new image and self-esteem.

The rich glistening copper roof of the new building reflecting in the sun to be seen by a hundred thousand motorists a day traveling Interstates 35 and 80 went a long way toward satisfying that yearning.

The new national headquarters building dedicated in 1980 gave image to pork producers and stability to the NPPC.

A study of the details of the plans reveals a building of 12,000 square feet of office space and 6500 square feet of warehouse space and printing facilities. Total cost was $1,026,000, including $850,000 for the building and $91,000 for 3.4 acres of land, architect fees of $48,000 and $37,000 for legal fees, permits and inspection fees.

It was a happy day December 18, 1979 when we tacked a sign on the closed door at 4715 Grand Avenue, "NPPC has moved."

With the new national headquarters coincidentally came an element of self-confidence and renewed aggressiveness on the part of pork producers. It seemed as if no challenge was too great. There was an attitude of pride and a feeling of power sweeping through pork leaders all over America. They were ready to challenge traditional dogmas and industry barriers. The list of accomplishments in 1980 reads like a list of championship accomplishments.

The 1980 annual report reflects just some of the long list of achievements following the completion of the national headquarters building.

Turbulence best describes the year 1980 from the pork producer's perspective. It was a year when the pork producer and his national and state organizations had an opportunity to display that old "bounce-back" ability known as resiliency.

A MARKET CRISIS HITS

Never before had the economic soothsayers been so far off track. Never before had the market price of hogs been so erratic. Never before had weights and numbers varied so drastically.

On the positive side, never before had pork producers been so assertive; taken control of their destiny and turned the psychology of their industry around in so short a time.

Through strong leadership by the Executive Committee and dedicated support by the National Board of Directors, a bold plan to turn what could have been a market wreck into an orderly reduction in numbers was successfully implemented.

Dr. Van Houweling, our Washington Affairs Director, arranged an appointment with Secretary of Agriculture, Robert Bergland.

On Tuesday, April 1, 1980, NPPC President Bill Buller and I met with the Secretary and presented him with a 7 point plan designed to assist the pork industry through the hog crisis. We proposed to the

Secretary that we as an industry would address 5 of the points if he would address the other 2. He listened attentively as we explained our 7 point plan. The 7 points were:

1) To reduce the amount of pork being sold by encouraging producers to market at lighter weights; 2) To reduce the number of hogs by selling breeding sows; 3) To encourage super markets to reduce prices on pork to make pork more competitive at the meat counter; 4) Step up the promotional program to consumers with a coop advertising program with packers and super markets; 5) Establish an aggressive campaign to increase volume of pork being sold in fast food and regular restaurants; 6) Encourage a step up in government purchases of pork for school lunches, hospitals and welfare programs; and, 7) Encourage the Federal Reserve Board to allow small country banks to participate at the discount window to provide loans at lower rates for farmers.

Secretary Bergland followed through with his promise as did the pork industry. Within a week the USDA asked for bids on large quantities of pork for the school lunch program. And the Secretary also arranged for a meeting for all livestock groups to meet with Federal Reserve Chairman Paul Volker and arranged for banks servicing livestock loans to gain access to the discount rate which was reflected in the interest rate being charged farmers.

All these activities were designed to encourage producers to avoid panic selling and stay with their marketing plan. It worked.

It worked because of the total cooperation of state councils and confidence on the part of producers in their leadership. This was the key to the success of avoiding panic selling.

When producers were on the verge of panic selling, they adhered to the voice of strong leadership and avoided the tragic losses that would have accrued.

Although numbers had not been reduced to the optimum, they were trending in the right direction.

The problem was confused and compounded by glowing predictions from USDA of much higher prices in December of 1980 and January and February of 1981. These reports encouraged producers to hold hogs longer and let them get heavier before marketing. In fact, by mid-December 1980, the average weight of hogs going to market exceeded 247 pounds. This was only the second time in 30 years market hogs exceeded the 247 pound average.

Weights are a continuous problem with pork producers. If average weights were optimum today it would result in a reduction in the volume of pork going to the market equivalent to a 10 percent reduction in numbers of hogs. Pork producers in their producer polls since 1970 have indicated a need for the Pork Council to take a closer look at and study our marketing system as it relates to numbers, quality and prices received by producers.

The Pork Value Conference scheduled in August 1981 was the first step in that direction.

CONFRONTING THE ISSUES OF THE 80's

The report for 1980 presents an interesting scenario of highs and lows, positives and negatives, high hopes, and disappointments.

On the positive side, we could report great progress in the organizational efforts for pork producers.

For the first time, we were presenting an integrated annual report for the pork industry. The accomplishments of both the Pork Industry Group of the National Livestock and Meat Board and the National Pork Producers Council are combined into one report.

It was not only indicative of a serious effort to eliminate duplication of activities, but to squeeze more promotional value from the producers' dimes.

This great step forward led the way for other efficient moves.

As you read these pages you will find the results of the dedicated efforts of the volunteer leaders, elected directors and officers. You will also recognize the fine contributions being made by professional staff who were totally dedicated to the promotion of pork and profitability for the producers.

Pork producers and the industry felt the domination of government agencies as many important issues surfaced in 1980.

The challenges of nitrites, food safety, dietary goals and African Swine Fever forced the pork industry's attention on Washington, D.C. and unified the industry to fight back.

Following the announcement of the results of the infamous Newberne study by USDA/FDA officials, a group of university pathologists did not support the findings of the study. USDA/FDA then contracted with the National Academy of Sciences to conduct a complete review of the nitrite issues. This action ended a two year campaign in which NPPC was the leading organization in recommending Congress and FDA undertake such a review.

FOOD SAFETY

The readily apparent mishandling of the Newberne study only served to point out inadequacies in the food safety laws. NPPC began and continues a campaign for changes in these laws that will implement a risk/benefit evaluation of substances that are thought to be hazardous. A review process, which would be binding on the agencies involved, and an economic impact statement are the other modifications being sought.

AFRICAN SWINE FEVER

Perhaps the most potentially damaging issue which faced the pork industry in 1980 was African Swine Fever (ASF). NPPC saw the prevention of ASF's entry into the U.S. as a three part program:

1. Enact a federal garbage feeding law.
2. Secure funds for completion of the Plum Island Foreign Animal Disease Center.
3. Eradicate ASF from Haiti, a close island neighbor to the south.

Through the relentless efforts of pork producers and NPPC's Washington office these three objectives were met.

In an unprecedented flurry of activity, Congress passed the Swine Health Protection Act in the closing minutes of its preelection session, October 1, 1980.

The bill now required that all garbage fed to hogs be cooked to kill disease organisms.

This legislation is the result of a 23 year effort by pork producers to protect their industry from not only ASF but other communicable diseases that would enter the country via food products transported by tourists and immigrants. Excellent support from our North Carolina affiliate organization and Senator Jessie Helms was the key to success in this effort.

Good news came a second time as Congress finished work on the 1981 budget which included $10.1 million for completion of the Plum Island Foreign Animal Disease Center. This action resulted, in part, from NPPC's work with the USDA and the Senate Subcommittee on Appropriations.

The final challenge was met as the new administration was about to take office. In early January, the acting agriculture secretary signed an Animal Disease Emergency Declaration based on the presence of ASF in Haiti.

This emergency declaration made several million dollars available to contribute to a Haitian eradication program.

DIETARY GUIDELINES

Dietary guidelines established by USDA in recent years came under fire as industry representatives questioned the scientific accuracy and objectivity of these published recommendations.

Pork producers stated their opposition to USDA dietary guidelines and subsequent menu suggestions, which unnecessarily criticized the value of pork and pork products, in hearings, the media, and in written statements.

NPPC called for conclusive scientific evidence, and the freedom of choice among foods for American families.

In addition, NPPC voiced opposition to USDA's revised child feeding program menus based on the misrepresentation or lack of animal products in the buying guides.

NUTRITION LABELING

Pork producers supported voluntary nutrition labeling where government and industry are free to develop label formats which are beneficial and useful to consumers.

Industry representatives testified before the Senate Subcommittee on Nutrition, voicing strong opposition to mandatory labeling and called for a two year moratorium on labeling changes to allow time to study the consumers wants and the costs involved.

Opposition to mandatory labeling was based on the lack of up-to-date nutritional information available on fresh meats.

SUMMARY

The year 1980 was symbolic in that it was living proof of what pork producers can achieve if they remain united and totally objective. Great years had preceded and others followed but 1980 was a year of transition and a year of image building and self-assurance. It was a year when the pork producers of the present stood on the shoulders of those in the past, glanced back then focused resolutely on the future, determined to march ahead toward the 1990's and the time when pork would be the meat of choice and the center of fine dining.

Most significant about the year 1980 was the realization by pork producers that the real battlefield was not on the farms and in the hog pens but in Washington, D.C. That after 200 years of progress in livestock production and with the rush of new technology we could lose it all with the stroke of a pen in Washington.

Part 5

THE NITRITE FIASCO

A TWO BILLION DOLLAR BLUNDER

The nitrite debacle created by the bureaucracy cost the pork industry two billion dollars in value of pork bellies and bacon sales.

Nitrites had been used to preserve meats for more than 2000 years. In the rush of consumer activism the safety of this time-honored preservative was being challenged. Seventy percent of the pork consumed in the United States was preserved in some manner and most of it was treated with sodium nitrite. If nitrites were banned it would create havoc in the pork market, possible plunging it into a depression. It would require years to find an adequate sub-

stitute, if in fact one was discovered. Pork producers were ready to fight.

The issue stemmed from a study by Dr. Paul Newberne, of Massachusetts Institute of Technology (MIT), that prompted conclusions by federal agencies that nitrites must be banned. Dr. Newberne was discreetly quiet while the USDA set about to ban nitrites. Much later, however, he reported to the media that in viewing the history of nitrite usage and its value as the only available additive that will prevent botulism in cured meats, that government officials had gone much further than he believed his results warranted in their indictment of nitrites as a cause of cancer. "I don't have the answer to what action regulatory agencies should take (with regard to nitrites). The study raised interesting questions, and further studies may give us the answer on whether we are really in danger from nitrites."

The NPPC petitioned the National Academy of Science to review the Newberne study. The result of that review indicated the Newberne study had been seriously flawed and that the conclusions drawn from the Newberne study were presumptive.

Two personalities were highly influential in the development of the nitrite issue and its final resolution.

Carol Foreman, Assistant Secretary of Agriculture, pork producers "favorite redhead," was a tough adversary.

Mrs. Carol Tucker Foreman, Assistant Secretary of Agriculture and head of the Marketing and Food Safety Quality Service entered her job with a fervor and the religious zeal of a crusader. Having been the president of Consumer Federation of America she carried the consumer banner into the new position with enthusiasm of a zealot. She soon acquired the image of anti-agriculture and pro-consumer which was anathema to farmers. She was described as the "Dragon Lady" in agricultural circles.

Dr. Don Van Houweling took early retirement in 1979 and accepted the position as NPPC's first full-time Washington representative. Dr. Van Houweling was well experienced in the ways of Washington.

He had served as the chief of USDA Bureau of Veterinary Medicine, the chief livestock person in the Food and Drug Administration and was instrumental in the development of the National Animal Disease Laboratory at Ames, Iowa.

Dr. Van Houweling was an observer and participant in the previous years of creeping regulation by government bureaus and regulatory agencies. He was an obvious authority to determine when bureau-

crats had over-stepped their bounds. He was likewise knowledgeable of the procedures that must be followed to insure the validity of scientific research.

He was aware that the Newberne study had not had an adequate peer review before Assistant Secretary Foreman issued instructions to initiate the process to ban nitrites. He also understood the implications of the labeling proposal for nitrite free meat products. More important than the economic implications he was concerned for the immediate safety of consumers who would assume that all processed meats were preserved as in the past and they would treat them as traditional product with a long shelf life.

Dr. Van Houweling called me and said we had an excellent chance to get an injunction to prevent the USDA from going forward with the proposed labeling of nitrite free meat products because of the potential hazards to consumers.

A conference call to our Executive Committee authorized the expenditure of up to $100,000 to press legal action to prevent the introduction of nitrite free labeling for meat products.

The nitrite issue made ideal target practice for pork producers on the war path. Their patience had worn thin after several years of being on the defensive from government regulatory action and they were ready to go the offensive.

Producers reacted enthusiastically to their Executive Committees decision to fight back.

PORK CHALLENGES BIG BROTHER

The court hearing was held in Des Moines, Iowa before Judge W. C. Stewart.

The nitrite issue became a landmark case not only for pork producers but for the USDA. It marked the end of an era when government regulators ran rough shod over producers unchallenged. It ended a period of apathy for farmers and reassured them that government can be made accountable to those it is elected to serve. Even more important it gave renewed confidence to pork producers that while others were intimidated by the power of big government by uniting their resources and expressing the courage to challenge they could make a difference.

The purpose of the challenge was to get a court injunction to prevent the USDA from implementing a rule approving the labeling of no-nitrite products. The no-nitrite products would look and taste similar to traditional nitrite preserved products. The question was whether or not consumers would be at risk and if the USDA was in effect promoting a private label product in its program of advertising the availability of the nitrite free products.

In the National Hog Farmer magazine account of the hearings and subsequent ruling of Judge Stewart it stated:

A VICTORY FOR PORK

Pork producers won the first round in their court action to prevent marketing of products that look like traditional cured pork products and bear the traditional names, but have no protection against botulism.

NPPC President Bill Buller addresses the nitrite controversy.

Federal Judge W. C. Stuart granted an injunction preventing USDA approval of labels for no-nitrite products. The injunction will be in force until the judge makes a final ruling on the case and either grants a permanent injunction against the products or approves the USDA regulation. That decision was not expected for several weeks.

The suit was filed by the National Pork Producers Council and three congressmen, Charles Grassley of Iowa, Tom Hagerdorn of Minnesota and Steven Symms of Idaho. They were joined in opposing the USDA rule by the National Independent Meat Packers Association.

After a day-long presentation of evidence and wit-

nesses, followed later by closing arguments, the judge ruled "the plaintiffs have shown they will probably by successful on the merits on one or more of the propositions (challenges to the USDA rule) advanced. In any event, sufficiently serious questions have been raised to make the issues fair grounds for litigation."

The evidence presented at the hearing involved these issues:
- The legality of the rule.
- The purpose of the rule, why USDA was making such products with this labeling available.
- The potential hazard from such products.
- The sufficiency of the required label to make consumers aware that these products did not contain protection against botulism.

USDA lawyers argued at the hearing that the court could consider only the administrative record on which the rule was issued and could not consider testimony presented by producer witnesses. The judge took that objection under advisement and permitted testimony, subject to a later ruling in his final decision.

On the first issue, the judge, in his ruling, noted that the plaintiffs claim the regulation is unlawful because the similarity requirement—the requirement that the no-nitrite products look and taste like the traditional products—is a radical departure from previously promulgated standards of identity and bears no rational relationship to the purpose of standards of identity. They claim, the judge said, that previous standards have involved ingredients and set parameters for permissible percentages. "Here a committee of three persons in the USDA will make a subjective judgment on the similarity of the non-nitrite product to the taste, appearance and feel of the nitrite product. Plaintiff's claim that such subjective standard is beyond the department's authority.

"The difficulty or impossibility of inspection to monitor compliance is obvious. The approval of the label woul.d amount to an endorsement by the USDA of the similarity of the product."

The judge also noted the charge that the regulation is contrary to law because it requires unpreserved products to imitate familiar, preserved products, but fails to require the uncured products to bear the label "imitation," as required by law.

The second issue, the purpose of the rule, involves a statement in the final impact statement issued by USDA in conjunction with the regulation for the products. That statement pointed out that 34 establishments have been marketing 168 different no-nitrite meat products, primarily sausage-type products, under past regulations which require that they must be labeled "uncured cooked sausage" and cannot contain the traditional names, such as frankfurter. USDA said:

"Since these products cannot be marketed under traditional product names, consumers are, in many cases, unaware of their current name with the traditional cured product. This information issue has slowed development of the market. This regulation will facilitate consumer choice by establishing the existence and availability of non-nitrite alternatives to traditionally cured meat products."

Donald P. Colleton, attorney for NPPC, argued that USDA exceeds its authority when it uses the labeling regulations to promote a product.

The USDA lawyer, Theodore C. Hirt of the Department of Justice, said the rule was issued "not further some private interest, but to make it possible for consumers to consume products not containing nitrites."

Testimony at the hearing brought out that USDA has printed 1.2 million copies of a pamphlet on no-nitrite meats, has hired a private enterprise to distribute a million of them through supermarkets, has distributed the rest through USDA offices and anticipates a second printing. The USDA representatives had difficulty explaining how the pamphlets did not represent promotion of a product, but rather were designed to protect the consumer from a hazard which they claimed would not exist.

Neal Black, long time editor for the National Hog Farmer followed the nitrite issue over a period of years and had strong feelings about USDA and some consumer advocates obsession to deny the food industry of its use.

His reaction to the pork producers legal challenge to USDA and the judge's ruling is interesting. Pork producers can celebrate a victory in the first round of their court battle over the elimination of nitrites from their products, but this isn't a one round fight.

A SUBTLE PLOT

There are those both within and outside of government who are determined to eliminate nitrites from our food supply, whatever the cost, either in human health or dollars. They've demonstrated that they'll use any means to accomplish that end.

They distorted the results of a research project, failed to request scientific review of the results until forced to by the industry and hid that failure from the public. A story in this issue presents the final data from that project. It was interesting to hear Dr. Newberne discuss his study. He's not anti-nitrite. He

thinks the study must be confirmed before any regulatory action is taken. He's not at all the ogre that he seemed to be. It was the government reaction to his study that made it necessary to discredit it, to prevent precipitous regulatory action.

The testimony in the NPPC suit against no-nitrite franks provided further evidence of the lengths the anti-nitriters will go to achieve their goal. They put government scientists and regulators in the position of defending indefensible positions under oath.

It would have been funny, if it hadn't been so ominous, hearing USDA officials explaining, on the witness stand, that no-nitrite products would not be hazardous, in the face of previous statements by their superiors to the contrary. They had to attempt to justify distribution of more than a million copies of a pamphlet outlining the hazards of the products they were testifying weren't hazardous. They were put in the position of defending labeling requirements as sufficient to warn consumers, when their only basis for that conclusion was one letter from a consumer commenting on the proposed rule.

This trial doesn't concern the major issue of whether or not nitrites are safe to use, but it does have a bearing on that issue. It's perceived by many to be an attempt by USDA to do an end-around on the issue. In the unlikely event that these no-nitrite products didn't cause any botulism outbreaks, the USDA could say, after a couple of years: "See nitrite isn't needed, let's ban it." It's revealing that they're willing to take a chance with the lives of consumers they're charged with protecting, to prove a point.

As was expected the USDA appealed Judge Stewart's ruling to the Federal District Court that met in Minneapolis in August of 1981. The appeal was upheld by the District Court. A little known but interesting fact was that in June 1981 the National Academy of Science (NAS) completed its peer review of the Newberne study. The report confirmed the flaws that others suspected in the Newberne research. While USDA had control of the report in June it refused to release the report until after the court hearing nearly 60 days later. The Newberne study was the basis of the aggressive action by USDA to promote the use of nitrite free products. Obviously with the NAS study pointing out the flaws in the research and the errors in procedures committed by USDA and the Food and Drug Administration it amounted to a great victorious pork council and an embarrassed government regulatory group.

It is another costly example of how an industry can be victimized when the media and government agencies respond to perception rather than fact.

Part 6

PUBLIC POLICY AND PORK

Public Policy, better known as Political Decision Making, impacts every aspect of our lives.

Public policy influences what we eat, what we wear and where we sleep. It determines the cost of food and clothing, houses, cars, gasoline, the quality of education, entertainment and our whole standard of living. It has a great deal to do with where our children go to school and with whom. In fact, it determines whether a baby has a right to life or will be destroyed before birth.

For some to say they aren't interested in politics is to abdicate the responsibility for their future and that of their children to leave it up to the judgment of others in many instances less capable of making wise decisions.

The question is not whether pork producers should be involved but how should they be involved and to what extent.

In the early days in the formation of NPPC there were some members who felt NPPC should be involved only in the promotion of pork products.

Washington seminar soon became an annual event for pork producers.

PORK GOES TO WASHINGTON

It became obvious that political issues would have to be addressed in order to give birth to NPPC. Funding through a voluntary checkoff program required an amendment to the Packers and Stockyards Act.

The pork industry was blessed by the presence of a strong leader in Jim Nance of Tennessee. He knew how to play hard ball politics. Through his political savvy and good relations with congressional leaders the Packers and Stock Yards (P&S) Act was amended to legalize a voluntary checkoff at the point of

sale. The National Livestock and Meat Board (NLMB) under the able leadership of Farm Bureau President John Schuman resisted the action by pork producers because of their desire to protect a meager NLMB one cent checkoff in a few markets. A few thousand dollars was at stake. However, when Jim Nance revealed that the NLMB checkoff was illegal, according to the current P&S rules, the Meat Board leadership shifted their support in favor of the amendment. There was an agreement that the NLMB would continue to receive one cent of each nickel NPPC collected.

The Farm Bureau never ceased their vigorous opposition to checkoff programs and open resistance to commodity organization activity in Washington. One must conclude that much of Farm Bureau's opposition comes from their reluctance to share Washington turf with producer groups. The giant general farm organization would obviously like to be the only kid on the block when farm policy controversy arises.

Checkoff didn't become a reality while Jim Nance was in the leader role but Nance led the fight to change the law. He set the stage for the modern day checkoff program that yields $31 million per year to promote pork.

The first tough battle for existence was fought by pork leaders on the capitol turf. Every major issue since the beginning of organization has either found its roots in public policy at the Washington level and chances are the solutions were found there.

The issues of the 90's may be expected to intensify at the federal level. Consumer activists have their national headquarters in Washington, D.C. along with all of the special interest groups who impact the public policy process. General farm organizations and national commodity groups either have their home office in WDC or maintain a satellite office with professional lobbyists.

The controversy concerning the feasibility of establishing a permanent Washington office with hired professionals to represent pork producers on a daily basis raged within NPPC for many years. Many felt that voluntary producer contacts were more effective because they were constituents who vote in the congressman's home district.

There is no question that the home district voter had better access to congressmen's ears. But lobbying has attained a high level of professionalism and issues are an around the clock occurrence. Volunteers were not available for a spur of the moment call. Obviously the alert systems and communication must be more efficient of producers were to make timely responses to public policy formation.

The most serious threat to developing honest public policy in the past two decades is the growth of Political Action Committees (PAC). The PAC system allows for the accumulation of vast sums of money from association members to buy good will from congressmen. Congressmen repeatedly state "their vote cannot be bought" but their voting records tell a different story. Many congressmen admit that when they shuffle their mail and pending phone call those received from PAC contributors lands on top. Some PAC's have a policy of only contributing to the campaign of incumbents. Consequently incumbents are returned to office for several terms. Some even spend a lifetime as congressmen and become captive of powerful special interest groups serving a rather narrow scope of interests. Currently 98% of all incumbents are reelected, consequently little culling takes place on the basis of poor performance.

NPPC established its Washington office in the home of Dr. Don Van Houweling in June of 1979.

A WASHINGTON OFFICE?

In March of 1979 the question of professional representation in WDC was a controversial issue that divided producers. The Executive Committee was hesitant to make the decision to establish a visible Washington office. I had informed them of my limitations in this area and that I must spend my time building the organization. I also emphasized the need to hire a specialist well oriented in the Washington environment and whether he was located in Des Moines or Washington was secondary. I asked for their approval to hire such a person and for permission to decide where he should be located to be the most effective. This suggested plan met no opposition.

An issue that had divided the ranks of the leadership for a decade had been resolved on a low key level and the movement toward establishing a pork producer awareness and presence in Washington was gaining momentum.

Few people are aware of the important role Dr. Don Van Houweling played in gaining recognition and prestige for pork producers in Washington and among peer group professionals.

His years of experience in federal agencies and the key role he played in carrying out public policy for regulatory enforcement uniquely qualified him to represent NPPC.

It was at his suggestion that NPPC filed for a legal

Dr. C. Don Van Houweling directed the establishment of the Washington office.

injunction to prevent the USDA from implementing a "nitrite free label" that had threatening implications. This highly visible and gutsy move by the fledgling NPPC generated an image of progressiveness and created a reputation for action.

Dr. Van Houweling began immediately to train a successor realizing he did not plan a long tenure. Several directors of the Washington office followed, Mike Mishoe, Doyle Talkington, and now Rick Pasco have succeeded him as Director of the Washington activities. Each left a legacy of high performance and dealing forthrightly with critical issues.

The responsibilities of the Washington office have compounded over the years and require a number of professionals to serve producers. Maintaining contact with regulatory agencies is critical due to their direct impact on the production sector. Regulatory control of feed ingredients, animal health and marketing procedures are high priority that directly impact producer profit. A special role is filled by staff to advise and consult with government specialists concerning the feasibility and predicted impact of regulatory change.

A number of government programs designed to enhance the domestic and foreign markets are available. Staff is key to evaluation and implementation of these key programs in order for producers to benefit.

THE CANADIAN ISSUE

The Canadian import issue was managed by the Washington staff. As Canadian importations of heavily subsidized pork continued to escalate and US markets began to decline US producers demanded that action be taken.

In 1983 NPPC launched legal action to establish countervailing duties on pork imported from Canada. The process involving both the legal systems and the bureaucracy results in a long laborious and costly procedure. After a cost of more than $200,000 and approximately 8 months of hearings and meetings on July 25, 1984 the International Trade Commission on a 2 to 1 vote with 2 abstaining ruled a split decision. The decision was to place countervailing duty on live hogs but to deny the duty be placed on pork products. The decision was based on the lack of understanding of the pork industry by ITC members. Their contention was that pork products were not the concern of pork producers and questioned the right of producers to become involved in the issue of pork products.

In the ensuing months when live hog imports declined while pork products soared the truth regarding the impact of a continuous line of product became evident.

NPPC never to be counted down and out continued its determined effort to gain legislation that would force the ITC to consider the question of "continuous line of product" when considering countervailing imported products because of unfair trade practices. Canadian hogs were subsidized at times by as much as $40 per hog. This gave a competitive advantage that devastated US hog producers who never solicited or accepted government subsidies.

NPPC's Washington staff and producer leaders were successful in achieving legislation that required the ITC's consideration not only of primary product in question but the impact of unfair trade practices on secondary products.

The legislation initiated by NPPC was responsible for a revision of the original ITC ruling and countervailing duties were imposed on all pork products imported from Canada.

The 1988 Omnibus Trade Bill was the vehicle for introducing the special provision. The bill required a more intelligent consideration by the International Trade Commission and the Court of International Trade of the continuous line of products affected.

Although the cost of legal and administrative services was burdensome to NPPC it is conservatively estimated to have improved live hog prices by $1.50 per cwt which totals more that $400 million per year.

The Canadian countervailing duty project is an example of the pork organization at work to protect the interest of pork producers. The Canadians have repeatedly attempted to change the ruling that increases their costs of marketing hogs in the US by about $5 to $9 per head. The ruling still stands today as an excellent example of what can be accomplished by US pork producers through organization.

VICTORIES IN WASHINGTON

The list of achievements in public policy by pork producers grows longer each year. In addition to winning the battle to save nitrites in 1979 and imposing countervailing duties on Canadian pork in 1984 the NPPC Washington staff can fly the victory banner celebrating achievements in many other issues. African Swine Fever (ASF) in 1980 was avoided by seeking aid to eradicate ASF in Haiti and drafting legislation to ban the feeding of raw garbage to hogs.

In 1983 NPPC requested the USDA provide funds for a pilot project to determine if the costly disease, Pseudorabies (PRV) could be controlled or eradicated. NPPC offered $100,000 and asked USDA to match it with $400,000. Thus began the long awaited ASF program.

In 1987 NPPC requested and received a Congressional appropriation to fund a 10 year program to eradicate PRV. The cost will total about $20 million.

The Pork Act was made into law in 1985. This Act alone increased revenue available for pork promotion from about $10 million in 1985 to $31 million in 1990.

NPPC was instrumental in development of a hog identification program in 1988.

These and many other programs and issues have been addressed and victories won on the Washington scene. All have been the result of a strong outpouring of support that rank and file producers all over the nation gave during critical periods.

There is adequate proof that the strength of the pork producer organization stems from the grass roots. There is equal evidence that their efforts must be based on factual communications and coordinated through organizational channels. This is where the Washington staff and informed producer leaders are vital to success.

PAST PRESIDENTS SPEAK

Here is what NPPC presidents who were involved in the development of the prevailing public policy philosophy had to say about our strong Washington effort:

Bill Buller, President 1979-80, said, "The number of issues impacting pork producers in the Washington arena were becoming so numerous we couldn't stay on top of them. We knew the jobs would build. The issues were so complex and the system so vast we needed an insider to help us cope."

John Saunders, President 1981-82, said, "The interaction and intermeshing of professional staff into an effective problem solving machine has catapulted NPPC into a position of prestige in American agriculture. In no area of activity does this apply more than on the Washington scene and in public policy development."

Wayne Walter, President 1983-84, said, "Pork producers are willing to take their lumps in the market place brought about by their own action. We are even willing to understand when grain producers are in trouble and in need of changes in government programs."

"But," Walter continued, "the addition of just one more government program threatening an already troubled hog market is where we draw the line. Strong action is required to get the government's attention and we are now in a position to take that action."

Ron Kahle, President 1985-86, said, "To think we could continue to operate effectively without a permanent Washington presence was a dream. It required both strong dedicated producers in the Congressional Districts and a well informed communicative Washington staff. The dynamics of WDC are too intense and must be addressed on a day to day basis with a professional staff."

The reactions of these four past presidents are cited because their terms coincided with the initial efforts to develop an effective Washington presence. Their terms spanned the time from establishing the Washington office and through the development of the Pork Act. Each led in a meritorious fashion to meet the challenges of the day and typified the unusual dedication by each producer president of NPPC during his day.

Part 7

RIDING THE CYCLE

THE MIRACLE OF 1984

A "boot strap" program is the best description of the way NPPC leadership responded to the 1983 hog market disaster.

It seems ironic that live hog prices hit an all time high of $67 in August of 1982. Ten months later hog prices declined by 33%. What went wrong? Two major happenings.

First, the retail price spread hanging over from the high hog prices ten months previous was still in effect. Second, a series of packing plant strikes and closings reduced the competitive bidding for hogs.

After the June hogs and pigs report it looked like the depressed hog prices would continue through the fourth quarter of 1984, according to Glenn Grimes, NPPC market consultant. He predicted hog prices to be in the low $30's.

With that bleak outlook the NPPC Board of Directors organized a task force.

The task force was charged with the job of designing a strategy to stabilize market prices and reduce the impact disastrous low prices would have on hog producers.

After a two day meeting in June of 1984 the task force reported a strategy comprised of 4 major emphasis points. It became known as "The Pork 4 Program."

The points were:

MARKETING: Reduce breeding numbers by 10% and market hogs 10% lighter.

DEMAND: Concentrate on narrowing the retain spread by providing retailers with a greater incentive to promote pork.

FINANCIAL MANAGEMENT: Develop a plan to help cost efficient producers survive periods of economic stress and encourage more professional financial management.

PROMOTION: Evaluate all promotional programs with additional emphasis placed on programs that have a direct impact on producer profit.

Each major point was strengthened with careful detailed strategies. Nine months later the "Point 4" program was declared a success.

Market analysts were quoted as saying "Pork 4" had contributed to the turn around in the hog market and that all points were successful.

First, there was a tremendous sow sell-off to reduce anticipated numbers of hogs in the future.

"Pork 4" was credited with increasing producer awareness and in addition to a reduction of numbers hogs were marketed at lighter weights by about 3 to 11 pounds.

As successful as the herd reduction program was

the increased promotion of pork by producers at the local level reinforced by NPPC's stepped up national promotion had a dramatic effect.

Some states' pork associations had their Governors sign pork proclamations while others held area meetings to increase the level of awareness and response by producers. As a result of the pork industry's response to all the factors pressuring the market hog prices stayed above $50 for the remainder of 1984 and well into 1985. Top market hogs have maintained a value of $40 or more since 1984.

The success of the "Pork 4" program had a dramatic effect on the attitude of producers. It reinforced their self-confidence. It was convincing proof that self-help programs will work if the strategy is right and well communicated.

It also provided an excellent demonstration of the value of organization. Individually each producer has little impact but collectively they pack a powerful wallop.

The few dimes each contributed to the checkoff seemed insignificant but collectively the sum can send a powerful message to the consumer.

The "Pork 4" program gave credibility to the value of the checkoff program.

A producer who markets 1000 hogs per year contributes two dimes per hog, or $200 to the checkoff. An increase of $10 per cwt in the market price will return $24 per hog. This reflects a total profit of $24,000, an 800% profit.

One can question the direct response to checkoff dollars but a reasonable thinking person must admit the value of cooperative effort that is the result of organization.

Part 8

THE TICKING TIME BOMB

1985 was the year of decision for the NPPC.

THE FLAW IN THE ORGANIZATION

In my first annual report and state of the council address at the American Pork Congress in St. Louis in March 1980, I stated, "There is a serious flaw in our organization. NPPC may be the largest commodity organization in the world but it will never be a great organization until we address the issue that threatens our unity. We must come to grips with the loose state/national relationship." At this time some states were operating in flagrant violation of funding formulas mandated by the delegate body. Iowa had been the glue that held the state coalition together because of its pragmatic and unselfish role and big brother support of the funding formula.

NPPC was like a gangling adolescent. Having gone through a period of rapid growth. It had developed the muscle and the capability to strongly express itself. It was still, however, awkward as an organization. Like the 17 year old with pimples it was anxious to improve its self-image and establish an identity of respectability.

The crucial question resurfaced at every delegate session. Was NPPC a federation of state associations, gathered for the purpose of raising funds to be used on national initiatives or was it a loose confederation of independent states whose autonomy must be maintained at the expense of national goals?

THE TEST OF NATIONAL UNITY

The history of every nation or organization is marked by a period of confusion and frustration. The question is who are we as an organization? What is our purpose? What do we as individuals have to gain by giving up our individuality?

America experienced its time of the ticking time bomb during the Civil War. Great sacrifice was made to maintain the Union. The whole was reaffirmed to be more important than the parts to the future of mankind. The integrity of the Union has been questioned but never tested since that war.

The tragedy of the conflict of 1985 stirred the whole organization. The council reacted as a family when the conduct of one of the siblings threatened their unity. NPPC was the nail that held the parts together.

It was a crucial time when the character of the organization and the moral fiber of the leadership was tested.

The inner conflict which arose setting the Iowa Association against the other state affiliates was destined to make or break the shaky national unity which had been in question since the beginning of the council's existence.

Iowa, the big brother and leader of the states, represented 25% of the membership. It provided 25% of the funding for national programs. Iowa producers long contended they were being slighted in the delegate body. There was a continuous search by

Iowa delegates for ways to strengthen Iowa's influence on the delegate floor and to gain a greater voice in the resolution process.

The delegate body determined the formula for the allocation of funds. With the graduated scale giving larger hog states a smaller percentage of the funds, Iowa was receiving only about 12% of the funds collected on Iowa hogs while other states with smaller numbers received as much as 50%. The balance of the funds were held in the national treasury to fund industry programs.

The Iowa association to its credit was assuming a more aggressive role on the state level and serving many more producers. The need for more funds was obvious.

THE ROLE OF STATES DEFINED

The philosophy established in the early days of NPPC was that the state associations were charged with the primary responsibility of generating checkoff funds and building membership while the national association would be responsible for promotion.

This was obviously an outdated philosophy. As the national role was changing so was the role of states. The issues on both the national and state levels were becoming more numerous and complex. State associations wanted to become more involved in promotion. Environmental issues were first incurred on the state level and must be dealt with at that level. Communications with an ever increasing number of producers was becoming more critical as industry issues arose. There was clearly a need for more funds at the state level.

In addition to the conflict between the Iowa association and the other state affiliates there was a growing independence on the part of most larger states. When state executives were hired the states became more ambitious. Staffing at the state level increased. A clamor for states rights began to place more stress on the ties that bound national and states together.

In January 1985 the NPPC Executive Committee met in a retreat environment in Phoenix, Arizona and discussed a number of issues, one of which was long range funding of the council.

LEGISLATIVE FUNDING
PHILOSOPHY IS BORN

It was recognized that the voluntary system had peaked with about 57% of the producers participating and in the past 3 years had declined to below 55%. It was obvious that some producers were tired of carrying the load of funding the national promo-

tional programs while others were getting a free ride. It was at this meeting that the council leaders first discussed the possibility of a national legislative checkoff. It was generally conceded that a uniform checkoff rate with total compliance by the states would never be achieved on a voluntary basis.

There was general agreement among the Executive Committee members that a national uniform funding system must be developed. There was some apprehension, however, concerning the timing. There was a question if producers were ready for a legislative mandatory approach.

It was decided to present the concept of a legislative checkoff to the delegate body in March, two months hence, to determine their willingness to support such a program.

Among the many other issues addressed during the 1985 delegate session the possibility of legislation leading to a mandatory checkoff and 100% participation was debated and approved for further study.

Coincidentally, speakers for the Pork Congress were Senator Helms, North Carolina, Chairman of the Senate Agriculture Committee and Senator Grassley, Iowa. While at the Pork Congress both were asked their advice regarding the introduction of enabling legislation. Both recommended that the legislation be a part of the 1985 Farm Bill that was currently being developed.

The Executive Committee instructed the staff to begin drafting language that could be shaped into a Pork Act as soon as possible.

IOWA'S ACTION

After returning home from the Pork Congress I asked three key staff members to assist me to study and discuss the crucial elements in drafting a proposed Pork Act. Within a week the basic provisions of a proposed act were completed and ready for consideration by the Executive Committee.

The series of events that followed the drafting of the proposed Pork Act happened swiftly and precipitously. Within a week of our internal staff discussions in preparation of the National Pork Act a bill was introduced in the Iowa Legislature providing for a state mandatory checkoff in Iowa. The bill provided for a special council made up of Iowa pork producers to determine use of the funds to be collected in Iowa beginning July 1, 1985.

This action took the pork industry by complete surprise. It placed Iowa in the same category with other states that had never conformed to the national delegate body's formula on funding. The unfortunate aspect of the Iowa action was two fold: First, that it happened in the middle of the budget year after NPPC had entered contracts that were irrevocable. The contracts were entered into based on an assumption the funds from Iowa were forthcoming as they had been for the past 17 years; Second, it changed the formula for collecting from .3 percent to .25 percent which was in conflict with the surrounding states. The interstate shipment of hogs into and out of Iowa created an accounting nightmare for the marketing agencies collecting the checkoff.

It certainly didn't contribute to harmony and unity as the NPPC made plans to encourage enabling legislation for a national pork checkoff program.

From the Iowa pork producers perspective, however, it appeared a perfectly rational thing to do. Iowa leaders had discussed on earlier occasions the possibility of a mandatory state controlled checkoff. It was felt to be a way to assure greater voice for Iowa pork producers over the expenditure of their checkoff funds.

A second factor entered into Iowa producer rationale. The Iowa delegation had vigorously opposed an increase in the voluntary checkoff rate from 2 dimes per hog to 3/10 of a percent (.30) of value to become effective July 1, 1985. Thus Iowa's legislation provided for .25% to apply in their new state checkoff plan.

Iowa's action was considered an attempt to set the rate of checkoff at less than the national rate and more consistent with their own desires as expressed in the delegate debates.

DEALING WITH DISSENT

Within a few days of the successful passage of the Iowa state legislation creating a separate state checkoff, a petition was circulated by 10 of Iowa's sister states calling for Iowa's expulsion from NPPC.

The grounds for this action were basically that the conduct of Iowa as a member of the corporation "violated the fundamental objectives and rules of the corporation and brought the corporation to disrepute."

The petition for expulsion followed the guidelines prescribed by the bylaws of NPPC. The usual required notices and time requirements were followed. A 3 man commission consisting of pork producers was appointed. The hearing was chaired by NPPC Past President Wayne Walter. Other members were Jim Dailey, South Dakota and Ray Hankes, Illinois.

The plaintiff states and the defendant state members were represented by legal counsel.

It required most of two days for each of the 10

states to present their case and for concluding comments to be presented.

The commission had 5 options after weighing the evidence: They could recommend that the Executive Committee reprimand, censure, place on probation, suspend, or terminate Iowa's membership.

THE COMMISSION REPORT

The commission recommended:
1) Provide for the appointment of an independent blue ribbon panel to review this report.
   a. The panel would be comprised of three members. One member should be appointed by the IPPA. One member would be appointed with the concurrence of the first two members.
   b. No member of this panel should be a pork producer, a member of or associated with the pork industry, or have been involved in the politics or policy-making of the pork industry. The members should be individuals such as current or retired presidents of colleges and universities, judges and distinguished attorneys.
   c. The panel should be asked to review this report and determine whether:
      1. the NPPC bylaws have been followed;
      2. the findings and conclusions are accurate; and
      3. the recommendations are fair.

   If the panel believes this report was inadequate in any regard, it would make alternative recommendations to the NPPC Executive Committee.
2) That the NPPC Executive Committee suspend the membership of the IPPA in the NPPC for a period of 1 year beginning March 1, 1986.
3) That this suspension shall not become effective if prior to March 1, 1986, the IPPA submits to the NPPC Executive Committee a written pledge that it will abide by:
   a. The decisions of the NPPC delegate body including but not limited to compliance with the transition formula and the NPPC funding plan; and
   b. That it will conduct itself in future NPPC activities in a manner consistent with the procedures established pursuant to the NPPC Articles of Incorporation and Bylaws.

   As a matter of good faith, we believe each member state association should sign the same or similar pledge. The pledge represents the basic commitment each member state association should have to the NPPC.

4) That if the IPPA leaders or delegates shall intentionally violate the terms of the aforementioned written pledge, as determined by the NPPC Executive Committee, the suspension of membership privileges for the IPPA shall become immediately effective for a period of 2 years.

5) That the Executive Committee investigate the concerns raised by the IPPA about under representation in the NPPC and inadequate funding. If substantiated, these concerns should be addressed by the NPPC delegates.

THE COMMISSION CONTINUES ITS REPORT BY SAYING:

The Complainants may believe that this recommendation represents restrained action on the part of the Hearing Commission. We believe the recommendation is restrained. We have been asked to confront the situation of a dissident member that has disregarded the rules and programs of its national organization. This recommendation simply requires that the IPPA adhere to those rules and programs - *the same commitment they made when they joined the NPPC.*

We cannot ignore the Iowa decision to violate the bylaws of the NPPC. But it is also not our desire to punish the Iowa pork producers. We believe our recommendation is a means to deal with the problems that have arisen while providing for continued membership in the NPPC.

That membership, however, can only be retained if there is a commitment to a course of conduct that is expected and required of all other states.

We realize these are difficult times for agriculture generally, and that Iowa is the focal point of economic trauma on the farm.

It will require an abundance of understanding and tolerance on the part of those in and out of agriculture to survive one of the most severe agricultural recessions in history. Unity is the key to survival.

The Commission appeals to the Complainants to accept this rational approach to restoring trust and understanding in the greatest commodity organization in the world. We extend a special appeal to Iowa to examine its conduct of the last few months and demonstrate a special kind of leadership as we set about healing the wounds of the most serious internal conflict in our organization's history. (End of report)

The commission's recommendation was delivered to the Executive Committee in July 1985. The recommendation was held in deliberate suspension for several months because the Executive Committee and the entire membership, including Iowa, was preoccupied with passage of the National Pork Act which was a part of the 1985 Farm Bill.

PORK ACT PROVIDES SOLUTIONS

The Farm Bill passed Congress in the closing days of December with the Pork Act safely folded in its main provisions.

The Pork Act was omnibus in nature solving many critical issues for the Pork Council. *First,* it brought all of the member states together in a unified funding system. *Second,* it resolved the problem of transfer of checkoff funds across state lines. *Third,* it mandated the cooperation of all markets to collect the checkoff funds and to send funds to one central collection point. *Fourth,* it spread the burden of funding industry activities over the total pork production sector and gave relief to the few who had been cooperative on the voluntary system. *Fifth,* it relieved the tension between the Iowa Pork Producers Association and the other state affiliates. The Federal Pork Act superseded all state legislative programs.

The February 1986 Pork Report headlined an article "NPPC Unity Reaffirmed." "The NPPC Executive Committee and the Iowa Pork Producers Association (IPPA) have resolved the circumstances surrounding IPPA's violation of NPPC's Bylaws in attaining their state legislative checkoff. The 10 states which filed the original charges have recommended that NPPC's Executive Committee not bring any disciplinary action against IPPA. In return, IPPA agrees to join NPPC's other member states in reaffirmation of their support for NPPC.

"In the interest of national unity, the NPPC Executive Committee accepts the suggestion of the 10 states, with the concurrence of Iowa," says NPPC President Ron Kahle.

The original action against IPPA began last summer, when 10 NPPC members states: Illinois, Missouri, Kansas, Nebraska, South Dakota, North Dakota, Wisconsin, Minnesota, Arkansas, and Ohio charged IPPA with violating NPPC Bylaws. A formal commission hearing and report followed, which presented NPPC's Executive Committee with several courses of action. After much deliberation, the industry forces came together to reach an amicable solution.

As part of the resolve, the NPPC Executive Committee agreed to establish a special committee with IPPA, to restore better future dialogue between NPPC and IPPA. This "dialogue committee" will also review and monitor future organizational relationships."

The major flaw in the organization, referred to earlier, that had been a hindrance to all attempts to bring about national unity appeared to be vanishing. The traumatic experience of challenging Iowa's membership eligibility served as a valid test of the character of the organization. Much credit is due pork leaders in Iowa as well as the national organization for keeping cool heads and charting a sensible course during this heated period of the most serious controversy in the council's history.

It is a mark of leadership when strong leaders have the courage to step forward and confront difficult issues head on rather than side step them because they may become unpopular.

Iowa's challenge to the national organization and the ten states' insistence on accountability on the part of their majority sister state represents a milestone in the history of associations. The pork industry is stronger from having had the experience.

Honest men, cool heads and reasonable minds so typical of pork producer leaders prevailed and another crisis was averted. And so pork continues to improve in image and find favor with consumers.

The ticking time bomb had been diffused and a benchmark established in how associations should resolve problems with differing members.

Part 9

LEADERS THAT MADE A DIFFERENCE

"The genius of a good leader is to leave behind him a situation which common sense, without grace of genius can deal with successfully."
(Roosevelt Has Gone) 4/14/45

Until recently very few associations had annual revenues of $5 million. Even today, with more than 5,000 associations reporting, only about 3,000 have more than $5 million in revenue. Most of these associations have been in existence for 50 years or more.

The National Pork Producers Council has grown from a fledgling association to one with $31 million in revenue in only 23 years. By 1992 the revenue will exceed $40 million.

Growth in its ability to influence public policy and communicate effectively with consumers and allied industry has paralleled the growth in revenue.

While the number of issues has expanded greatly from its original program NPPC's mission has never changed. Its mission has always been to enhance the profitability of pork producers.

Playing a key role in the growth and success of NPPC has been the volunteer leadership epitomized in producer presidents.

By the time a president reaches the top position he will have had several years of experience in working his way through the state leader positions and gained the respect of his peers.

A volunteer leader for non profit associations requires a great deal of time and sacrifice. Most pork producers are not wealthy people who own sophisticated organizations, at least not in the earlier years. Consequently they must leave jobs undone at home to attend meetings and represent their constituency. At times this has proven to be more of an economic sacrifice than they could endure.

It is safe to assume without the dedication and self-sacrifice of the producer presidents the pork industry's future would not be so bright.

The final test of a leader is that he leaves behind him in other men the conviction and the will to carry on. Without exception each president of NPPC has met this test.

Wilbur Plager
NPPC President 1954-1956

Wilbur Plager will be enshrined in the memories of pork producers as one of the most dedicated of all men to the swine industry.

His leadership and contributions to his coveted friends of the pork industry spans his lifetime.

His contributions have been many and varied. As breed executive, consultant, arbiter and industry leader he has had a profound impact on the history of pork.

His service as the pork industry's first President will be lasting and he will be ever remembered as a pioneer president.

The pork industry is proud to induct Wilbur Plager into its historical section where he will be remembered as its first President.

American Pork Congress
March 7, 1980

James B. Nance
NPPC President 1957-1960

Jim Nance is leadership personified. As an articulate spokesman he is said to have "legitimized the pork industry" through his determined assistance in attaining federal approval of the "checkoff" for the pork industry.

His unique ability, insight and business acumen provided the Council with a special kind of leadership and set standards for the selection of future leaders as he served as its second President.

It is with pride and privilege that pork producers include James B. Nance in the historical section of their National Headquarters.

American Pork Congress
March 7, 1980

Laverne "Dutch" Johnson
NPPC President 1961-1963

Known and respected by his peers as a "grassroots" leader, "Dutch" Johnson led the pork industry when it was first introduced to the problems of federal regulatory agency assertions. Feed additives and meat preservatives were first highlighted as problems during his tenure.

Quiet, meditative but discreetly forceful, Dutch Johnson laid the groundwork and established guidelines for the Council's handling of problems which became more complex and numerous in years to come.

It is with admiration and appreciation that the National Pork Producers Council places his record in the Historical Place for perpetuation.

American Pork Congress
March 7, 1980

James Peterson
NPPC President 1964-1965

Described as a leader ahead of his time, James Peterson united the pork industry. Through his leadership, the infant organization known as the National Swine Growers Council began to show signs of maturity.

It was in St. Louis, Missouri in 1964 that the name was changed to "National Pork Producers Council" and the voluntary funding concept began to be accepted.

James Peterson with his close ties to county leadership, his impeccable reputation and strong leadership quality provided the Council with self-confidence and an image of pride and determination.

It is with gratitude for his devotion of time and talent that pork producers place him in the Historical Place provided for its great leaders.

American Pork Congress
March 7, 1980

William R. Rothenberger
NPPC President 1966-1967

Bill Rothenberger was a forceful, dynamic leader, excellent thinker with a natural love for people.

It was during his tenure as President of the National Pork Producers Council that the now successful voluntary checkoff program was tested.

The American Pork Congress was also a result of his leadership when the National Pork Industry Conference and the National Pork Producers Council's annual meeting combined.

The pork industry is indebted to Bill Rothenberger for his unique talent and tireless effort in its behalf and proudly presents his portrait and record for permanent keeping in the Historical Section.

American Pork Congress
March 7, 1980

Albert Gehlbach
NPPC President 1968-1969

It was during the genesis of today's National Pork Producers Council, that a new day dawned for hog men. It was the beginning of new and exciting things to come.

Much of this new creative activity is credited to the imaginative thinking, progressive attitude and leadership ability of Albert Gehlbach.

The Council's checkoff program began, the first staff was employed and the first promotional projects initiated.

The pork producers of the nation, in recognition of his outstanding contribution to the industry during lean years and in appreciation for his dedicated efforts enthusiastically endorses Albert Gehlbach for induction into the Historical Section of the National Pork Producers Council.

American Pork Congress
March 7, 1980

Roy Keppy
NPPC President 1970-1971

Few men enjoy the respect and admiration of their peers as does Roy Keppy.

He enhanced the image of the pork industry and brought respectability to the National Pork Producers Council as its 7th President.

His unquestioned integrity and solid reliability as a leader provided the fledgling organization with direction and stability while it endured pains of rapid growth.

It is with deep appreciation for his devotion and dedication to the ideals of pork producers and his contribution to the advancement of their organization that the National Pork Producers Council provides a special place in its annals of history for Roy Keppy.

American Pork Congress
March 7, 1980

T. Euel Liner
NPPC President 1972-1973

T. Euel Liner served the National Pork Producers Council as its eighth president, 1972-1973.

With unparalleled devotion and tireless effort he expressed the pork producer's concerns and views throughout the land.

It was only through the unusual contributions by unusual men like T. Euel Liner that pork producers have attained the level of image and respect they now enjoy.

The National Pork Producers Council hereby reserves a place in its coveted Hall of History in recognition of his contribution to the pork industry.

American Pork Congress
March 7, 1980

Gerald Beattie
NPPC President 1974-1975

Quiet, reflective and soft-spoken Gerald Beattie provided National Pork Producers Council with unusual kind of leadership as its ninth President. His seasoned personality, meditative thoughtfulness and high credibility marked him as the right man at the right time.

His sterling character and unique leadership enhanced the image of pork producers at a time when it was most appreciated.

The National Pork Producers Council and its 97,000 members are most happy to provide Gerald Beattie a lasting place in its coveted Historical Room in recognition of his contribution to progress of the industry.

American Pork Congress
March 7, 1980

Virgil Rosendale
NPPC President 1976-1977

In recognition of his unusual leadership and tireless effort while serving as an articulate spokesman for the nation's pork producers.

While serving as the Council's tenth president, the industry was experiencing rapid growth and extreme pressure from regulator agencies. His steady guiding hand and exercise of wise and astute judgment laid the foundation for the Council's procedure for coping with difficult problems.

The National Pork Producers Council and pork producers of the nation extend to Virgil Rosendale their sincere appreciation for his unselfish devotion and use of unusual talent in motivating progress for the pork industry.

American Pork Congress
March 7, 1980

John Soorholtz
NPPC President 1978-1979

His life-long contribution to the development of seed stock and his devotion to pork people has resulted in a lasting impression on the livestock industry.

He provided progressive leadership to the National Pork Producers Council during his 5 years as a National Director and while serving as its 11th President. The 97,000 member organization was undergoing rapid growth, stress and change during his tenure as its leader. His devotion and staunch determination were the marks of leadership that characterized his success.

The National Pork Producers Council on this 7th day of March 1980 presents this scroll in appreciation for his devotion, dedication and selfless contribution which has benefited all mankind.

William "Bill" C. Buller
NPPC President 1979-1980

William "Bill" Buller served as President during a time of rapid change. His unique ability, drive and determination marked him as one with strong leader qualities and persuasive character.

In the years 1979 and 1980, Bylaws were revised; producer investment was doubled; a Washington, D.C. office activated and a new national headquarters constructed.

His sincerity and devotion to the pork industry instilled confidence in his judgment and enhanced not only the credibility of the Council but built a progressive image of the pork industry.

Pork producers of America will long reap the benefit of his dedicated efforts and untiring leadership for years to come.

His reputation for progressiveness will endure in the minds of his peers as will this tribute displayed and preserved in the historical section of the National Pork Producers Council.

American Pork Congress
March 7, 1980

John Saunders
NPPC President 1981-1982

His personal concern, empathy for others and dedication to the pork industry have made John Saunders an impressive national leader. At 39 years of age he was the 13th and youngest man to be President of the 110,000-member organization.

His ability to communicate the Pork Council's position on national issues affecting the industry distinguishes him as a recognized leader by the entire livestock industry.

His leadership ability was best demonstrated in the notable achievements during his administration. The NPPC Long-Range Strategic Plan, which established a new plateau in the development of NPPC, was implemented as a result of his insight and guidances.

The National Pork Producers Council and pork producers nationwide extend sincere appreciation to him and his family in recognition for his accomplishments in the pork industry.

American Pork Congress
March 10, 1983

Wayne Walter
NPPC President 1983-1984

Special recognition and appreciation is extended to Wayne Walter who served as president of the National Pork Producers Council for a two year period.

His excellence in leadership was displayed throughout his tenure in articulating the problems of the pork industry at all levels of government and in the private sector.

During his presidency he sought solutions to unique and unusual problems which required a special kind of talent, determination and character possessed by few leaders.

His strength of leadership, special dedication and resolve, coupled with his talent to communicate, have resulted in his making a lasting contribution to the enhancement of the image of pork and profitability for pork producers.

American Pork Congress
March 7, 1985

Ron Kahle
NPPC President 1985-1986

The years 1985 and 1986 were truly two of the most challenging and pivotal in the history of the National Pork Producer's Council.

Ron Kahle's timely ascension to the leader position was truly fortunate for pork producers.

Fate thrust him into the role with little time to prepare. The substance of his leadership was tested within days of his presidency.

Patience, fairness, understanding, and compassion stand out among his many leadership qualities that led the Council through perilous times.

His unquestionable honesty and high credibility influenced decisions and attitudes that greatly enhanced the industry in overcoming adversity.

His dedication and enthusiasm in representing pork producers before national leaders and the media has brought a positive and progressive image to the pork industry.

Pork producers will always owe Ron Kahle a debt of gratitude.

American Pork Congress
March 5, 1987

Tom Miller
NPPC President 1987-1988

Tom Miller was the 16th president of the National Pork Producers Council. His was the first full administration during the crucial period after the passage of the Pork Act and the development of the National Pork Board.

His diplomacy and patient understanding has contributed to the positive atmosphere that resulted in a smooth transition and a clear definition of the roles of the Pork Board and NPPC.

Highlighting his administration was the development of crucial farm credit legislation, a statement of principles for long-term cooperative action between the Pork Board and NPPC, and the introduction of "Pork The Other White Meat" and "America's Cut."

The contribution to the industry of Tom and his wife, Jana, will long be remembered and appreciated by the nation's pork producers.

National Pork Industry Forum
March 5, 1988

Ray Hankes
NPPC President 1988-1989

Ray Hankes assumed the role of President of NPPC with strong qualifications, great energy, and progressive goals for the pork industry. There followed a period of adaptation and adjustment for the Pork Board and NPPC which required his kind of leadership with keen insight, understanding, and the ability to develop consensus.

World Pork Expo had its debut, and pork's place in the *Guinness Book of World Records* for the biggest barbecue ever was established. The historic referendum, to assure future funding, was passed. Ray Hankes chaired the committee which initiated the highly successful "Pork, The Other White Meat" program.

His dynamic leadership, drive, and enthusiasm for the pork industry made 1988 one of the pork industry's most successful years.

The National Pork Producers Council is proud to recognize Ray Hankes as one of its outstanding leaders.

National Pork Industry Forum
March 3, 1989

Don Gingerich
NPPC President 1989-1990

Don Gingerich, during his term as president, helped bring an expanded role for the National Pork Producers Council as a key player on the national and world stage.
Don brought to the NPPC presidency a determination to strengthen the influence of pork producers in the public policy arena. In pursuit of that goal, he worked to enhance the effectiveness and credibility of NPPC's Washington, D.C. programs.
On the production and marketing side, Don Gingerich's term of office was perhaps best symbolized by the pork industry's renewed commitment to improve product quality through introduction of the Pork Quality Assurance Program and establishment of a long-range industry goal of establishing pork as the meat of choice in the United States by the year 2000.
The statesmanlike leadership of Don Gingerich throughout his term as president has brought great credit to the National Pork Producers Council and to America's pork producers.

National Pork Industry Forum
March 10, 1990

Part 10

PORK INDUSTRY HALL OF FAME

Wilbur Plager
Hall of Fame

Association Executive – Motivator – Industry Leader

The pork industry had been fortunate in having outstanding leaders. Pork leaders were responsible for the rapid progress enjoyed by the industry over the past three decades.

The past presidents in their first annual meeting in 1979 discussed the Hall of Fame concept but decided to forego any recommendations. Their decision was consistent with the modest nature of pork producers who were characteristically low key and not inclined to seek recognition.

The Executive Committee, however, discussed the merits of giving special recognition to outstanding leaders who gave generously of their time and talent. There also was a feeling that good leaders were good role models and should be made visible for young aspiring leaders to observe.

In 1983 the Executive Committee created the Hall of Fame, set standards for candidates and designated the past presidents as a special Hall of Fame Committee. The role of the Hall of Fame Committee is to screen candidates and recommend individuals they deemed worthy of the honor.

The standards established were generally simple but assuredly high to exclude novices. To be inducted in the Hall of Fame one must have made an outstanding long and continuous contribution to the pork industry as a producer and leader. Candidates may be recommended by state affiliates or the Hall of Fame Committee. The Hall of Fame Committee must consider all candidates and make the final recommendation to the NPPC Executive Committee. Induction takes place at the annual meeting of members of the Pork Industry Forum.

The Executive Committee has maintained the highest standards and all those who have been so honored thus far have received the highest respect from the pork industry.

Wilbur Plager inducted as a charter member of the Pork Industry's Hall of Fame for his lifetime of untiring efforts which resulted in pork industry improvement.

His influence as field secretary of the Iowa Swine Producers Association established him as a friend of the pork producer. He was influential in the development of the Iowa Swine Test Station, the Iowa Master Swine Producers Program and the Meat Hog Certification Program.

He was the first president of the National Swine Growers Council, forerunner of the National Pork Producers Council.

He was instrumental in the development of *National Hog Farmer*, the first publication totally devoted to the pork industry's problems, plans and progress.

He was widely recognized as a swine judge, serving in that role at events in 36 states and three foreign countries, and served as chairman of the National Barrow Show's Prestigious Judges of Champions Committee.

As executive secretary of the American Yorkshire Club for 15 years, his relentless efforts were largely responsible for the dramatic improvement and widespread use of the Yorkshire breed in swine herds throughout the nation and the world.

The pork industry is proud to honor Wilbur Plager as a charter member of the Pork Industry's Hall of Fame.

Presented by the National Pork Producers Council
March 8, 1984

Russell Plager
Hall of Fame

Youth Leader – Judge – Packer – Banker

Russell Plager inducted as a charter member of the Pork Industry's Hall of Fame following a lifetime of dedication to the improvement of the pork industry.

He was a member of the Iowa State Champion Livestock Judging Team. He achieved a record point total as the top collegiate judge at the International Livestock Show.

He served as president of his senior class at Iowa State University.

He shared his talents with countless 4-H and FFA youngsters at judging clinics and as a judge of numerous junior livestock shows.

As an employee of the National Live Stock and Meat Board, Swift & Company, John Morrell & Company, and FS Services, Inc., he educated pork producers in a practical way of the value of producing a lean, meat hog.

He also shared his knowledge of meat animal evaluation with the pork industry with his input into the Meat Hog Certification Program.

He served as chairman of the National Barrow Show Judges of Champions Committee.

His distinguished career includes serving as vice president of the Central National Bank & Trust Company, where he continued to advise his favorite audiences, farm youth and pork producers.

The pork industry is proud to honor Russell Plager as a charter member of the Pork Industry's Hall of Fame.

Presented by the National Pork Producers Council
March 8, 1984

Carroll Plager
Hall of Fame

Leader – Judge – Innovator

Carroll Plager inducted as a charter member of the Pork Industry Hall of Fame following a lifetime of dedication to the improvement of the pork industry.

As a teenager he was the top livestock judge at the Iowa State Fair.

He was elected the first president of the Iowa Boys 4-H.

As a hog buyer for Geo. A. Hormel & Company, he pioneered grade and yield hog marketing systems.

His involvement led to the formation of the industry's Meat Hog Certification Program.

He was the first superintendent of the National Barrow Show. He implemented innovative programs to improve the meat quality of hogs. His service as superintendent spanned a 25 year period.

He judged national swine shows during his 40 year employment by Geo. A. Hormel & Company.

He influenced Hormel in becoming the first pork packing company to implement the implied consent checkoff plan on January 1, 1968, to support the research and promotional efforts of the infant National Pork Producers Council.

He edited the *Hormel Farmer* for 25 years. He instilled pride in pork producers and influenced profit in the entire pork industry.

As a leader, judge and innovator, his word was gospel in the pork industry.

It is with pride that pork producers recognize Carroll Plager as a charter member of the Pork Industry's Hall of Fame.

Presented by the National Pork Producers Council
March 8, 1984

Dr. James Hillier
Hall of Fame

Scientist – Educator – Administrator – Leader

Dr. James Hillier inducted as a charter member of the Pork Industry's Hall of Fame following a lifetime of dedication to the pork industry.

As a university educator, department head and administrator at Oklahoma State University, he trained and influenced numerous livestock and meat industry leaders.

His development of the ruler backfat probe revolutionized the pork industry and has had a lasting influence on the value of the hog by elimination of fat through measurable, predictable genetic matings.

He personally contributed to the development of a more desirable pork product by serving in a leadership role and as architect of the industry's Meat Hog Certification Program.

His leadership with the Oklahoma State University's swine herd resulted in the breeding of two of the Hampshire breed's first five certified meat sires.

He developed the "Model" line of Yorkshires that influenced the meat lines of the breed.

He was in great demand as a breeding and market hog judge. Highlighting his judging career was his chairmanship of the National Barrow Show Judges of Champions in both 1958 and 1959.

He greatly influenced the development of the Oklahoma Swine Test Station.

The pork industry is proud to honor Dr. James Hillier as a charter member of the Pork Industry's Hall of Fame.

Presented by the National Pork Producers Council
March 8, 1984

Bernard Collins
Hall of Fame

Producer – Motivator – Leader

The late Bernard Collins of Iowa was a prime mover in several progressive steps by pork producers. He helped establish Iowa's first swine test station and served as its first board chairman. He was an early director of the Marketing Board, Iowa Department of Agriculture. He moved through leadership chairs in both his county and the Iowa Swine Producers Association. He helped put together the first October Pork Month.

An efficient and large-scale commercial producer, Bernard Collins played a key role in establishing the NPPC as a national promotion association, funded by a voluntary market deduction on hogs. He initiated a "get ready" fund to launch the new NPPC. He personally invited delegations from Midwest states to the "Moline Meeting" where 90 leaders vowed to make this proposed organization fly.

Bernard Collins was widely recognized for his leadership skills and his creative approach to improving the pork industry. He was a Master Swine Producer; won the Skelly Agricultural Achievement Award for livestock leadership; spoke at swine institutes, conferences and conventions; testified at many government hearings (some of which resulted in the hog cholera eradication program).

A man of creative ideas and sound judgment, Bernard Collins richly deserves a prominent place in the Pork Industry Hall of Fame.

Presented by the National Pork Producers Council
March 7, 1985

Rolland 'Pig' Paul
Hall of Fame

Producer – Executive – Motivator

Rolland "Pig" Paul came along when the pork industry had to organize itself, solve its own problems, or die. Plans were made to build membership organizations in hog states, to convince farmers to fund their own promotions and research, and to convince the markets to collect a producer checkoff.

At that time, the project needed a motivator ... and Pig was just that.

Pig has an uncanny ability to activate volunteers ... to convince people that problems can be solved, that their industry can be made healthy again.

The record testifies for his skill. In three years as the National Pork Producers Council executive vice president, he convinced dozens ... then hundreds ... of busy producers to call meetings, enroll members, explain "nickels of profit," convince markets to "make the deductions for pork."

In those three years membership was built to 46,000 ... and checkoff went from none to 28% of the nation's hogs.

With 24 states organized, with funding and membership established, with some promotion and consumer research underway, Pig went back to raising purebred hogs. Managers and planners and accountants and marketers and personnel directors could carry on. Pig had earned his niche in the Pork Industry Hall of Fame.

Laverne "Dutch" Johnson
Hall of Fame

Producer – Organizer – Leader

Laverne "Dutch" Johnson of Illinois is an excellent example of a successful pork producer whose major contributions to the industry were often made very quietly at the local level.

To Dutch, the major challenge was to encourage swine improvements on the individual farm ... and he believed that all segments of the industry should work together to achieve progress.

Dutch helped organize a Swine Improvement Association on a sub-county level in 1945 and six years later helped to consolidate several tiny associations into the DeKalb County Association. In 1947, he worked with a committee to establish a statewide Illinois Swine Improvement Association, and later served it as an officer. In 1954, he represented the National Swine Growers Council on the Live Stock and Meat Board. Later, he served as the third president of the National Swine Growers Council.

In subsequent years, Dutch Johnson "talked quality" in many meetings, judged county 4-H and FFA swine shows, and in the mid-1950s was active in his county livestock marketing association.

As a busy community leader, Dutch was involved in 4-H leadership, the Farm Bureau, Extension Council, and county fair board. After 40 years of pork industry involvement, he continues to support his county, state and national pork industry programs. Dutch Johnson will feel comfortable in the Pork Industry's Hall of Fame.

Presented by the National Pork Producers Council
March 7, 1985

Presented by the National Pork Producers Council
March 7, 1985

James Nance
Hall of Fame

Advisor – Lobbyist – Leader

Jim Nance earned his place in the Pork Industry Hall of Fame by giving the early pork producer organization a vital input: political savvy.

Jim served three terms as president of the National Swine Growers Council, which later became today's National Pork Producers Council. In the mid-1960s, while Jim was chairman of the National Live Stock and Meat Board, proposals to fund the NPPC via a checkoff were in jeopardy because wording of the Packers and Stockyards Act appeared to outlaw such a producer checkoff. Using his lobbying skills, Jim got the legality of voluntary checkoff funding clarified … and the Pork Council was free to function and grow.

Jim remained active in producer circles as an advisor and confidante to NPPC presidents for nearly 20 years.

Jim served on President Kennedy's Agricultural Advisory Committee, held leadership roles with the Meat Board, the International Livestock Exposition in Chicago, the Tennessee Live Stock Association and other agriculture organizations. He was named "Man of the Year" in *Southern Agriculture* and was awarded the *National Hog Farmer's* Prestigious Service Award in 1984. His persistent efforts in many areas of the industry make him a worthy Pork Industry Hall of Fame member.

Presented by the National Pork Producers Council
March 7, 1985

William R. Rothenberger
Hall of Fame

Producer – Innovator – Leader

The late William R. Rothenberger of Indiana had an unusual combination of personal assets. He was an innovative and highly efficient hog producer. He used his considerable leadership skills during a critical period in the early life of the National Pork Producers Council. And … Bill Rothenberger made friends of everyone he met in a relatively short but exemplary life.

Rothenberger was president of the struggling NPPC in 1966-67, when attempts were being made to establish producer organizations in several hog states; to undertake year round nationwide pork promotion under a self-help program; and to fund the program with market deductions collected by "first buyers" of hogs.

Bill gave the new program solid support during a period when much of the industry predicted its failure. He was also instrumental in early efforts to establish understanding between the new NPPC and the Meat Board. Bill later served as the Pork Council's representative on the Meat Board.

Bill was active in Top Farmers of America, was president of the Indiana Farm Management Association, was a director of his local bank, and was deeply involved in agricultural activities at Purdue University.

For his efforts to build a strong pork organization, Bill is a deserving Pork Industry Hall of Fame honoree.

Presented by the National Pork Producers Council
March 7, 1985

T. Euel Liner
Hall of Fame

Producer – Innovator – Leader

T. Euel Liner inducted into NPPC's Industry Hall of Fame following a lifetime of dedication to the pork industry.

A true hog man, he has earned this recognition based on years of experience as a highly successful and innovative producer, and as an aggressive leader and pork promoter in Texas and throughout the nation.

He pioneered many modern production practices on the farm, and was nationally recognized for his ability to select meaty, highly productive animals. This was evidenced by his prominence as a show judge and as a highly successful exhibitor at top shows across the nation.

He served his fellow producers in many other capacities. He was president of the Texas Swine Breeders Association in the early '50s and was the first recipient of the Texas Master Pork Producer Award. In 1968 he was elected to the NPPC Executive Committee, and went on to serve as its president in 1972.

He was also appointed by U.S. Agriculture Secretary John Block to serve as a member of the Advisory Committee on Swine Health Protection. His many state and national honors are testimony to his years of service.

T. Euel Liner has earned the respect of fellow producers across the country for his many accomplishments, his integrity, and his devotion to the industry. He is a truly deserving inductee into the Pork Industry Hall of Fame.

Albert Gehlbach
Hall of Fame

Producer – Organizer – Leader

Albert Gehlbach inducted into NPPC's Pork Industry Hall of Fame for his decades of organizational service.

In 1947 he helped organize his local organization at a time when almost no producer organizations existed in the hog business. He has taken a leadership role ever since.

He went on to become the second president of the Illinois Pork Producers Association. For five years he represented Illinois on the Executive Committee of the NPPC, and served as national vice president for two years. Upon assuming the presidency in 1968, he directed implementation of the first National Pork Checkoff Program.

He was an innovator on the farm as well. He pioneered many new developments in pork production facilities design, and worked with the University of Illinois to help make these ideas available to more farms. The Gehlbach family hosted thousands of visitors who observed the farm's pork production facilities.

His achievement was recognized by his selection for the Ford Farm Efficiency Award, the Prairie Farmer Master Farmer Award, and the highest award offered by the Illinois Society of Professional Farm Managers and Rural Appraisers.

The pork industry owes a debt of gratitude to Albert Gehlbach. He has earned his place in the Pork Industry's Hall of Fame.

Presented by the National Pork Producers Council
March 13, 1986

Presented by the National Pork Producers Council
March 13, 1986

Robert Parkison
Hall of Fame

Organizer – Leader – Innovator

The late Robert Parkison inducted into the NPPC Hall of Fame for his important role in the birth of the National Swine Growers Council (forerunner of the NPPC).

Bob was a man of great personal courage and a dedicated leader who recognized the need to organize pork producers for the betterment of the industry in the 1950s.

Although an auto accident in 1937 confined him to a wheelchair, his handicap failed to deter Bob. In the state of Indiana, he helped initiate the Hoosier Barrow Show and the Produce Swine Evaluation Station. He served as president of the Indiana Swine Breeders Association. His other major activities include work with the *Hoosier Hog Farm* magazine, *National Hog Farmer* magazine, and The Indiana Swine Health Certification Program.

On the national level Bob drove thousands of miles promoting, organizing, selling and nurturing the young National Swine Growers Council. Bob served ten years as secretary of the Executive Committee of the National Chester White Breeders Association.

Bob was a devoted family man, a person with great character and vision, and an accomplished purebred swine breeder. Few have contributed so freely while carrying such a heavy personal burden.

Bob was one of the giants of the pork industry. His death in 1959 ended over 22 years of industry service. Because by all measures he is one of the finest and most dedicated leaders the pork industry has ever known, he truly belongs in the NPPC Hall of Fame.

Presented by the National Pork Producers Council
March 5, 1987

Bernard W. Ebbing
Hall of Fame

Educator – Promoter – Packer

Bernard Ebbing earned his place in the Pork Industry Hall of Fame by dedicating more than 30 years of service to improving the quality and consumer image of pork.

As livestock service director for the Rath Packing Company, Bernard set out to improve swine quality through a variety of educational efforts in cooperation with the Extension Service. He was a driving force in the development of swine testing stations at Iowa State University and New Hampton, and was a pioneer in the utilization of cross-section views of pork carcasses to evaluate quality.

He was nationally recognized as a swine judge, having participated in the national conferences of all eight major breeds, and every major barrow show in the United States. Having helped set standards for all major swine breed certification programs, he worked diligently to implement the systems through a variety of demonstration projects.

In addition, Bernard was always an enthusiastic supporter of youth projects, including FFA, 4-H, and Block and Bridle. He served as superintendent of the National Collegiate Livestock Judging Contest for many years.

Bernard's industry honors include "Honorary Master Pork Producer" from the Iowa Pork Producers, outstanding service recognition by *National Hog Farmer* magazine, and recognition by the Iowa Vocational Agriculture Instructors for his service to agriculture.

Pork producers across the nation have profited from his efforts to improve the hog. It is easy to see why he is a member of the Pork Industry Hall of Fame.

Presented by the National Pork Producers Council
March 5, 1987

Paul McNutt
Hall of Fame

Producer – Leader – Organizer

Paul McNutt earned a place in the Pork Industry Hall of Fame for visionary leadership and untiring dedication spanning more than 30 years.

Paul led the Iowa delegation at the "Moline 90" meeting, which resulted in the start-up of the national checkoff program.

He served as a board member of the National Swine Growers Council in the 1960s, a time when crucial decisions were made in organizing the future National Pork Producers Council. Paul was also on the board of the National Live Stock and Meat Board from 1968-1981.

On the state and local level Paul organized his county pork producers group at a time when few local associations existed. He went on to serve as a director and president of the Iowa Pork Producers Association.

His awards have been many, including the *National Hog Farmer's* Distinguished Service Award, membership in the Iowa State University Animal Science Hall of Fame, and the Iowa Master Pork Producer Award. He has served his community well as a district governor of Rotary International, trustee of the Hoover Library and Foundation, and president of the advisory board for Iowa City's Mercy Hospital, to name a few.

But most important is his total commitment to service above self. He serves as a worthy example for all pork producers to follow. Paul was always ready and willing to get involved for the betterment of his industry and his fellow man.

He has truly earned his place in the Pork Industry Hall of Fame.

Presented by the National Pork Producers Council
March 3, 1989

Roy Keppy
Hall of Fame

Leader – Judge – Master Breeder

A member of the "Moline 90," Roy Keppy was a key leader in the origin and development of the National Pork Producers Council. His personal influence was a motivating factor in gaining the recognition of others for the need of cooperation and an appreciation for strong organization as a solution to many of the pork industry's problems.

His dedication and giving of himself, his time and talent in service of the pork industry, is exemplary and has inspired others in the role of voluntary leadership.

He served 14 years as a member of the National Live Stock and Meat Board and as its president in 1985.

His personality and character are woven into the fabric of the National Pork Producers Council from its inception. He served as the Council's seventh president.

Pork producers will ever be indebted to Roy Keppy and his wife, Myrtle, for their unparalleled contribution to the advancement of the pork industry.

Presented by the National Pork Producers Council
March 4, 1988

George Brauer
Hall of Fame

Producer – Innovator – Leader

George Brauer earned a place in the Pork Industry Hall of Fame by improving production technology on the farm, perhaps more than any other man.

He pioneered the modern day concept of confinement pork production including innovative building designs. A creative perfectionist, he constantly tested new ideas and unselfishly shared his experiences with others for the betterment of the entire industry.

George also understood the importance of industry organizations in moving pork production forward. He helped organize his local and state pork associations, and served as their president. He was chairman of disease research committees in Illinois and on a national level, and helped to secure funds to conduct the early research on TGE. As a true progressive, he spearheaded a private group called "SEMINAR" to encourage early action and contributions to deal with the nitrite issue of the 1970s. Although NPPC took over the challenge later, George helped motivate industry leaders to build a strong organization that could deal with similar public policy issues in the future.

George Brauer's time tested talent for quietly achieving unmatched success exemplifies the highest standard of excellence in pork production. He has clearly earned a prominent place in the Pork Industry Hall of Fame.

Presented by the National Pork Producers Council
March 3, 1989

Virgil Rosendale
Hall of Fame

Producer – Industry Leader – Spokesman

Virgil Rosendale earned an honored place in the Pork Industry Hall of Fame as a result of his extraordinary years of dedicated service as a producer leader in several industry organizations.

As the first president of the National Pork Board, Virgil's calm but resolute leadership helped guide the industry smoothly through the transition to the new legislative checkoff.

In his numerous industry roles through the years, as president of the National Pork Producers Council (1976-77), as chairman of the National Live Stock and Meat Board (1981-82), as an early leader in development of the U.S. Meat Export Federation, and as president of the National Pork Board (1986-89), Virgil Rosendale has been an unexcelled leader and articulate, effective spokesman for America's pork producers.

During his tenure as NPPC president, hog cholera was eradicated in the United States, a voluntary checkoff for market hogs was increased, and a nickel voluntary checkoff on feeder pigs was initiated.

Later, in his leadership position at the Meat Board, Virgil helped to forge a more coordinated relationship between that organization and NPPC to ensure that there was no duplication of effort in the work of the two groups on behalf of pork producers.

Through the years, Virgil Rosendale has unselfishly brought his personal credibility and superb leadership talents to the service of his fellow producers through the organizations that serve them.

Presented by the National Pork Producers Council
March 10, 1990

ROLLAND "PIG" PAUL
NPPC Executive Vice President
1966-1969

J. MARVIN GARNER
NPPC Executive Vice President
1969-1978

ORVILLE K. SWEET
NPPC Executive Vice President
1979-1989

Part 11

WOMEN–A PART OF THE ACTION

PART 1.
PORKETTES 1961-1985

PART 2.
NATIONAL PORK COUNCIL WOMEN 1985

AN HISTORICAL COMMENTARY ON THE
NATIONAL PORKETTES

compiled by Kathryn Louden, Iowa – 1981

When looking for ways to describe the Porkettes' road of progresss from that day in December, 1961, several words immediately come to mind: determination, change, progress, flexibility, growth, awareness are just a few.

Little did those 26 women gathered in Springfield on Dec. 9, 1963, realize the potential or see into the future to visualize an organization encompassing 34 states and over 16,000 individuals as the Porkette organization now does. What they saw was the need to be part of the action—part of their pork-producing team! The National Swine Growers' Council wanted to start a promotional program and it was felt that the addition of a women's auxiliary could aid in many ways. The main promoter and instigator of this idea was W. E. (Gene) Smith who was at that time the executive secretary of the National Swine Growers' Council. After consulting with their executive board, he approached the women who were attending that December meeting and helped them with the formation of a Pork-Ette organization.

Although each woman present returned to her home state with enthusiasm and plans, only two states organized in the year of 1964: Iowa and Illinois. Struggling and slow growth characterized the first few years of the organization. The officers were the ones to do the planning, write the by-laws, and work for more states to organize. And they had very few membership dollars to work with. By 1967 there were six organized states with around 300 members. Membership continued to have spasmodic growth until the middle 70's when it seemed to grow by leaps and bounds. Membership continues to be a challenge as the potential for a much larger organization is there waiting to be tapped.

The structure of the Pork-Ettes has developed as the organization has grown. The first few years the officers were the guiding force, then in 1968 a board of directors was formed consisting of a member from each organized state. They met twice a year and the national officers were elected from this board. In 1972 an Executive Committee of nine was established with those members being voted into office yearly by the members present at the annual meeting and the officers elected from this body.

The board of directors was still retained with one member from each organized state. Then in 1974, three-year staggered terms were introduced in order to give continuity to the executive committee and provide a systematic rotation for all states on the board of directors. It was at this time that the delegate system was initiated giving the states representation in accordance with their respective membership numbers. Today the Porkette Program is effectively identified and developed by Porkettes involved in committee or board representation locally or nationally.

Due to the fact that a meat processor was using the name Pork-Ettes as the trademark name for one of his products, it was necessary in 1970 to change the spelling to its present form—Porkettes. Over the years questions have been raised concerning the suitability of the name Porkettes. Some of our urban friends even snicker at the name, not understanding its meaning or its connection with Pork. In 1979 the Board of Governors voted to retain the name and to proceed with registering it so that it cannot be used by anyone outside the organization. This was completed in 1980.

One of the first projects assigned to the Pork-Ettes was the Queen contest. That has, over the years, developed into quite a sophisticated affair. To

Queen Kristi Nash and her Court, 1986.

Ann Norman, NPPC staff, coordinator for the Pork-ettes during their early development.

many, the annual crowning of the National Pork Queen is the highlight of the American Pork Congress.

In 1967 the Pork-Ettes had as a major project to conduct a meat survey for the National Pork Producers Council. Consumers in five metropolitan cities were questioned about their meat-buying habits. Survey results verified that pork still had difficulty with its image among consumers. "Old wives tales" tend to make a lasting impression that continually plague the pork industry. Educational efforts are continual, to help the consumer understand the "truth about pork".

Distribution of video tapes featuring outdoor cookery was a 1968 project. These starred the National Pork Queen, Mary Ann Ebbing. In 1970, in cooperation with the National Live Stock and Meat Board, the Porkettes assisted in a campaign proclaiming that "Happiness is a Better Breakfast!" This included dispensing radio tapes, buttons and bumper stickers. Also in 1970 the first attempt was made to get correct and current pork information into the high school home economics departments. Several states had led the way in this project which helped national to develop good guidelines. This was called "Pork Goes to School". It was revised and improved for several years and reached many young consumers.

The hiring of Ann Norman by the NPPC, and giving her the responsibility of working with the Porkettes was really a much needed shot in the arm! The time was 1972, there were 19 organized Porkette states with the total membership a little over 2,000. Her enthusiasm and expertise were welcomed to strengthen the organization. Under her direction new projects were developed, memberships increased and new states were added to the organization.

Major project work included distribution to the states of the model pig, Jasper. He was the prototype of a national carcass contest winner and has done much to promote the new image of pork. Jasper made his way to many hog buying stations, vocational agricultural departments and personal pig collections. The manufacturer would deal with only one outlet and the Porkettes served as the clearinghouse for thousands of Jaspers on their way to state Porkette organizations.

Forty-two thousand messages were sent in 1973 and '74 to general practitioner doctors in states where Porkettes were willing to handle the mailings. Each contained a golf tee or a ball marker as an attention-getter, with a factual message about pork!

A National Pigskin Kit was developed in 1976. Three were completed and made available on a loan basis. Included were instructions for the handling and sewing of pigskin, cutting information, samples of construction detail and helpful hints. At this time a brochure *Winning Ways with Pigskin* was printed. In the succeeding years both the brochure and the kit have been updated. Porkettes have always been interested in using pigskin for crafts and in garment construction. Style shows have been in demand for many occasions. As the pigskin supply and quality have improved, so has the interest in its promotion heightened. The current chairman of the pigskin committee now represents the NPPC and the Porkettes on the National Pigskin Council. This council includes representatives from any facet of industry that has a vested interest in pigskin.

"Teaching about Today's Pork" is the current home economics student education packet. It contains up-to-the minute lesson plans and teaching aids. Two new spirit masters were added to the kit in 1981. It has been very well received with thousands being distributed nationally.

One of the major responsibilities of the National Porkettes has been to provide member states with organizational and project helps. The Director of Consumer Affairs and officers have traveled to many states to assist in forming a state Porkette group, to help with a project or attend a special event. As a guide to organization, the *Porkette Handbook* was printed, first in 1975 and updated since then. Some of the other printed helps for states include *Pork Queen Rules and Guidelines, October Porkfest Ideas,* and *Promoting Pork.* To replace the *Porkette Handbook* and consolidate other Porkette materials, the *Porkette Reference Manual* was begun in 1981. This was first distributed at the Nashville Porkette Information Conference.

Queen Eunice Schroeder with Secretary of Agriculture Earl Butz and Euel Liner at the 1972 Pork Fest.

The American Pork Congress has provided a platform for the sharing of ideas among states. Attractively arranged in the Porkette Room are the Record Books from the individual state organizations. Each, packed with project information, comes alive with activity. The mini-displays are chosen activities visually presented in a small space. These, along with the women's programs that are available, are designed to enrich the individual, share knowledge, help solve problems and provide inspiration.

Through the year 1970, annual meeting time contained oral reports from each of the attending states. Then as membership grew and activities became more numerous, a written report was furnished. These had no specific format to follow. Some were four pages in length and some only one or two paragraphs. Therefore, in 1973 a questionnaire was developed, and from these reports the *Porkette Annual Report* is now compiled into a concise, attractive booklet.

During the Annual Porkette Breakfast, March 1979, a 15th Anniversary program was given celebrating the progress of the Porkettes. All of the past presidents were in attendance to highlight events that occurred during their time in office. Within that year we were saddened by the death of our sixth president, Maxine Nash. She was a credit to the Porkettes and her absence is felt.

Reflecting the wishes of the states for a leadership session just for Porkettes, the board of directors has planned for and held three Porkette Information Conferences in the fall of 1977, 1979 and 1981. The locations have been Louisville, KY, Amana, IA and Nashville, TN.

Legal council recommended in 1979 that the National Porkettes incorporate. The membership numbers and the amounts of money that were handled far exceeded the amounts that would be normal for an auxiliary, also it was necessary to have status as a tax-exempt organization. Other sound reasoning was put forth and after approval of the voting delegates, the incorporation was finalized in 1980. A Memorandum of Understanding between the NPPC and the Porkettes was completed at this time, also. With an NPPC bylaw provision, the Porkette president is now serving as an ex officio member of the NPPC Executive Committee. Porkettes are also represented on NPPC Program Planning Conference Committees such as Legislation, Consumer Affairs, Communications and Promotion Advisory. These committee appointments are made annually by the NPPC President. The Porkette Program of Work is developed from Porkette committees. This program of work is then communicated to NPPC committees to define staff or Porkette completion of the jobs and funding responsibilities.

This acceptance of Porkettes as a viable part of the NPPC emphasizes that our goals are one and the same. Together we work as a team to reach those goals and meet the challenges that are presented to the pork industry. The last few years have seen Porkette officers in Washington, D.C. talking to influential congressmen or testifying before committees, addressing legislative issues pertinent to the good of the pork industry. The NPPC program reflects a cooperative interest of producers and Porkettes.

In November, 1981, the NPPC placed on staff a full-time Director for the National Porkettes, Marjorie Ocheltree. This NPPC staff person will serve as staff coordinator for all aspects of the National Porkette Program. The position is a new one and was designed to provide better service to the auxiliary and better communication and program planning between NPPC and the Porkettes. Establishment of this position by the NPPC Executive Committee is a commitment to the purpose of the Porkette organization.

As in 1963, Porkettes are still working on promotional efforts for pork and pork products. However, horizons are broader and responsibilities are greater. The individual involvement that was paramount at the onset is still of prime importance in making Porkettes the organization it is today and the organization it can become.

NATIONAL PORKETTE DATES STATES WERE ORGANIZED

1964	Iowa, Illinois
1965	Oklahoma, Kansas
1966	Nebraska, Minnesota
1967	Mississippi
1968	Montana, Colorado, Ohio, Texas
1969	South Dakota, Indiana
1970	Arkansas, Missouri (Colorado dropped)
1971	Louisiana, North Carolina, North Dakota, Wisconsin, Michigan

1972	Pennsylvania
1973	South Carolina, Idaho, Kentucky, Wyoming
1974	Colorado, New York, Virginia
1975	Oregon
1976	California
1977	Delaware (Texas dropped)
1978	Arizona, Washington, Georgia
1979	—
1980	Maryland, Tennessee

Part 11 – Part 2

HISTORY OF THE NATIONAL PORK COUNCIL WOMEN

1980-1981

The National Porkettes were under the leadership of Millie Jordan, Virginia, during 1980-1981. Programs focused on leadership development through the Information Conference held in November 1981 in Nashville, TN; school foodservice through the development of Today's Pork Goes to School; membership development; the queen program; pigskin development; and farrowing house schools.

1980 also brought the following activities:

- finalizing the incorporation of the National Porkettes.
- registration of the National Porkettes and Porkettes name for copyright purposes.
- establishing a National Porkettes Fellowship in the amount of $5,000 to be awarded to a student working towards their doctoral degree in an area related to pork as a food.
- developing a pigskin sewing construction slide set and a pigskin style show slide set.
- organizing two new Porkette associations—Tennessee and Missouri—for a total of 34 state associations.

- attaining a nonvoting, ex officio seat on the NPPC Executive Committee and Board of Directors.

In 1981 the NPPC hired a full time staff person to direct and coordinate the program of the National Porkettes. As the women's auxiliary became more active, it was necessary to have a staff member responsible for working with the leadership of the organization.

1982-1983

During the term of President Charlene Wilken, Illinois, the National Porkettes focused on communications. The development of the National Speaker Corps took place at this time. The program consisted of a speaker's manual, two slide/tape presentations on pork production and consumer information, and a 16mm film on the American farmer. The Porkettes were very active at American Pork Congress with a hospitality room, pigskin demonstration room, and seminars focusing on national and state programs.

The Information Conference was held in the

western region of the country in Colorado Springs, Colorado where 206 attendees learned about education programs, promotion activities, computerized record keeping and much more.

1984-1985

During the mid-'80s, the role of women in agriculture was changing. Because of the farm crisis, many farm women either went to work off the farm or took on a new job on the farm. Women in all facets of life were taking on jobs away from home, and they had fewer hours to spend volunteering. This had an effect on the National Porkettes in several ways. First, the organization became more focused on its programs and activities. Work was finalized in the pork industry's first story book, The Case of the Purloined Pork and the companion educational kit. The National Porkettes expanded their work in the education area by developing a classroom public demonstration booklet and the Speaker Corps training. 1985 was the first year for the Speaker Corps training session where the attendees were taught how to work with the media and how to do platform speaking. The purpose of the training is to establish a corps of people to speak out for the pork industry and organization.

1985 was a landmark year for President Carmen Jorgensen, Arkansas, as she was the only president to serve the National Porkettes and the National Pork Council Women. The delegates to the annual meeting voted in March of 1985 to change their name from National Porkettes to the National Pork Council Women. This was a very professional, progressive move for the women's organization.

1986-1987

Karen McCreedy, Iowa, took over as President of the National Pork Council Women in 1986. During her term the women continued distribution of the educational materials. They received a grant from Transmisol to distribute the story book in the New York City schools. The women began a membership recognition program called the Early Bird contest. They continued the state activities books which outlined successful programs for the states to carry out. The NPCW also developed a national pork industry coloring book for distribution at the local level. The women became more active in the legislative area and public policy as well during these years.

1988-1989

Joan Keever, Illinois, became president of the National Pork Council Women in 1988. A new program area of diet/health was established to work in the

Annual Porkettes meeting.

consumer and medical profession areas. The Speaker Corps program was enhanced and expanded to cover all issues of the pork industry.

1988 was the final for the National Pork Industry Queen program. Christi Bentley, Ohio, served as the last queen. The program was replaced with an all youth program (Pork Leadership Institute) that involved young women and men in learning more about the pork industry.

During 1988-89 the National Pork Council Women worked with NPPC and AIF in developing a computer software educational program on animal agriculture. The program was designed for the 4th-6th grade levels and was the first effort by commodity groups to get animal welfare information into the classroom.

1989 was the first year for the NPCW Newsletter which was sent to all 15,000 members in 28 states. 1989 was also the year the NPCW Fellowship Fund became self-sustaining.

Over the years, the NPCW has played a vital role in the development of programs and activities in the areas of education, promotion, communications, and leadership development. The pork industry would not be where it is today without the involvement of the women.

NATIONAL PORKETTE/NPCW OFFICERS
FROM 1963-1990

Year	Office	Name	State
1963	President	Dorothy Collins	Iowa
	Vice President	Martha Beatty	Illinois
	Secy-Treasurer	Norma Coddington	Illinois
1964	President	Dorothy Collins	Iowa
	Vice President	Martha Beatty	Illinois
	Secy-Treasurer	Lula Bell Wolf	Kansas
1965	President	Dorothy Collins	Iowa
	Vice President	Martha Beatty	Illinois
	Secy-Treasurer	Lula Bell Wolf	Kansas
1966	President	Mary Jeckel	Illinois
	Vice President	Thelma Boe	Nebraska
	Secy-Treasurer	Beverly Thurston	Minnesota
1967	President	Mary Jeckel	Illinois
	Vice President	Thelma Boe	Nebraska
	Secy-Treasurer	Beverly Thurston	Minnesota
1968	President	Mary Jeckel	Illinois
	Vice President	Thelma Boe	Nebraska
	Secy-Treasurer	Beverly Thurston	Minnesota
1969	President	Thelma Boe	Nebraska
	Vice President	Ruth King	Kansas
	Secy-Treasurer	Myrtle Keppy	Iowa
1970	President	Thelma Boe	Nebraska
	Vice President	Eulila Harris	Ohio
	Secy-Treasurer	Myrtle Keppy	Iowa
1971	President	Julie Heberer	Illinois
	Vice President	Eulila Harris	Ohio
	Secy-Treasurer	Delores Kiehne	Minnesota
1972	President	Julie Heberer	Illinois
	Vice President	Eulila Harris	Ohio
	Secy-Treasurer	Delores Kiehne	Minnesota
1973	President	Julie Heberer	Illinois
	Vice President	Maxine Nash	Indiana
	Secy-Treasurer	Delores Kiehne	Minnesota
1974	President	Maxine Nash	Indiana
	Vice President	Bonnie Erickson	South Dakota
	Secy-Treasurer	Delores Kiehne	Minnesota
1975	President	Maxine Nash	Indiana
	Vice President	Bonnie Erickson	South Dakota
	Secy-Treasurer	Delores Kiehne	Minnesota
1976	President	Bonnie Erickson	South Dakota
	Vice President	Helen Nichols	Nebraska
	Secy-Treasurer	Delores Kiehne	Minnesota
1977	President	Bonnie Erickson	South Dakota
	Vice President	Helen Nichols	Nebraska
	Secy-Treasurer	Delores Kiehne	Minnesota
1978	President	Helen Nichols	Nebraska
	Vice President	Mildred Jordan	Virginia
	Secy-Treasurer	Delores Kiehne	Minnesota
1979	President	Helen Nichols	Nebraska
	Vice President	Mildred Jordan	Virginia
	Secy-Treasurer	Delores Kiehne	Minnesota
1980	President	Mildred Jordan	Virginia
	Vice President	Carlene Wilken	Illinois
	Secy-Treasurer	Delores Kiehne	Minnesota
1981	President	Mildred Jordan	Virginia
	Vice President	Carlene Wilken	Illinois
	Secretary	Rita Brown	South Carolina
	Treasurer	Delores Kiehne	Minnesota
1982	President	Carlene Wilken	Illinois
	Vice President	Carmen Jorgensen	Arkansas
	Secretary	Rita Brown	South Carolina
	Treasurer	Karen McCreedy	Iowa
1983	President	Carlene Wilken	Illinois
	Vice President	Carmen Jorgensen	Arkansas
	Secretary	Rita Brown	South Carolina
	Treasurer	Karen McCreedy	Iowa
1984	President	Carmen Jorgensen	Arkansas
	Vice President	Karen McCreedy	Iowa
	Secretary	Norma Aukerman	Ohio
	Treasurer	Kay Anderson	Minnesota
1985	President	Carmen Jorgensen	Arkansas
	Vice President	Karen McCreedy	Iowa
	Secretary	Norma Aukerman	Ohio
	Treasurer	Kay Anderson	Minnesota
1986	President	Karen McCreedy	Iowa
	Vice President	Joan Keever	Illinois
	Secretary	Jan Williams	Indiana
	Treasurer	Lorraine Harness	Missouri
1987	President	Karen McCreedy	Iowa
	Vice President	Joan Keever	Illinois
	Secretary	Jan Williams	Indiana
	Treasurer	Lorraine Harness	Missouri
1988	President	Joan Keever	Illinois
	Vice President	Lorraine Harness	Missouri
	Secretary	Margie Holt	Kentucky
	Treasurer	Sandy Schmitt	Montana
1989	President	Joan Keever	Illinois
	Vice President	Lorraine Harness	Missouri
	Secretary	Margie Holt	Kentucky
	Treasurer	Sandy Schmitt	Montana
1990	President	Lorraine Harness	Missouri
	Vice President	Jody Hauge	North Dakota
	Secretary	Ginny Roesler	Minnesota
	Treasurer	Martha Glissendorf	South Dakota

Orville K. Sweet

Part 12

THE LEAN THEME

A number of surveys in the 1970's and 80's continued to reveal consumers traditional negative perception of pork. Old wives tales and oft repeated cliches portrayed pork as a fat laden product that clogged arteries and caused heart attacks. In addition to the circulatory problem the newest health concern created by activists was that consumption of red meat was a cause of cancer.

Consequently about one third of the population admitted to avoiding pork in the diet because of images many consumers continued to harbor were outdated.

Although by 1980 the fat content of a hog carcass had been reduced by 50% this fact had not changed the unhealthy perception most consumers still held.

A number of think-tank sessions held by NPPC staff and consulting marketing specialists were devoted to exploring ways to dispel the myths about pork that inhibited its use by many consumers.

In 1982 a survey of 85 executives heading the nations leading meat industry firms indicated their greatest concern was the diet-health issue.

LAUNCHING THE LEAN PROGRAM

Fat was the main culprit in the diet-health controversy. Fat and pork had become synonymous terms. It was critical that the pork industry address the issue and tell the consumer the story about the new pork.

A two pronged strategy was designed in 1982 to change the image of pork. First, the "Pork Value Program" was designed to develop new incentives to encourage pork producers to produce leaner hogs. The Pork Value Program captured the attention of the pork industry and resulted in the appointment of a special Pork Value Task Force.

The problem seemed fairly simple. Pork produced at that time was still too fat to meet consumer desires in spite of the progress in producing a leaner hog. The problem loomed unanswered at least until producers took it upon themselves to find solutions.

The Task Force made headlines during 1982 when they released their revolutionary plan providing incentives to producers with lean hogs. Along with the plan was a drawing of the ideal hog appropriately named "Symbol." Pork producers, packers, marketers and seed stock producers provided a consensus for the final drawing of Symbol.

The incentives to produce leaner hogs still was in the packers hands. There remained a reluctance on the part of packers to reduce the weight of hogs they paid top prices for. In order to increase the lean content of carcasses many felt it necessary to limit weights for top prices to about 220 pounds.

The Pork Value Program provided the main incentive and substance for the lean program and laid the foundation for the promotional campaign.

The second phase was to address the consumer misconception problem. Armed with a positive image and an aggressive all-out campaign it was felt pork could be America's favorite meat. The message needed to be positive. We needed to find a need within America's lifestyle and fill it. Having already found America's number one trend, physical fitness, and having pork leaner than ever it was a matter of choosing the proper words for a clear concise message to the consumer.

THE PORK CHALLENGE

If we could convince America that pork is as lean as it truly is, pork could easily become the "meat of the '80's."

Clearly, it was time to reposition pork and take the offensive. It was time to turn pork's negative image into a positive one. An all-out promotional and educational campaign was needed. Its goals:
- To improve consumer attitudes and demand about pork.
- To involve producers and increase the opportunity for profitable pork production.

But it must be more than just an advertising campaign. It must reach out in every American community and say, "Pork is lean ... Pork is healthy."

So, with "lean" as the buzz work, the NPPC set out to develop the most far-reaching, profit-oriented promotional campaign in the history of the pork industry. It's called appropriately, The Pork Challenge.

First, a definite rallying cry centering around the word "lean" was needed. The theme was to be simple, memorable, honest. Out of the 70 themes discussed, 20 were selected for testing.

After surveying pork producers and testing the themes in shopping malls, one theme emerged and consistently stood out from all the rest: "America Leans on Pork."

Three variations of the theme were then selected and carefully scrutinized: "America is Leaning on Pork," "American Leans on Pork," and "America You're Leaning On Pork."

Even though the three variations say essentially the same thing, there's a big psychological difference between them.

The Council finally chose "America You're Leaning on Pork" because it personalizes the message, bringing it home to each individual who hears or sees it.

SYMBOL IS BORN—
THE PIG AND THE PRODUCT

With "America, You're Leaning on Pork" as the rallying cry, creative energies were focused on another challenge: developing a symbol, one illustration virtually communicating pork's lean message.

Much brainstorming and several drawings later, one simple symbol emerged: a pork chop (the most familiar cut of pork - cinched up with a measuring tape (an item often associated with tailors and waistlines). Graphically, this little symbol says it all — pork is lean.

The next step was getting photographs of the symbol using an actual chop.

It's funny. Each chop began to take on a character all its own after a while. Some were too tall, some were too thick, some were too fat. After working with them all day long, we had a pretty good idea which chop was the best one.

Besides choosing the perfect chop, we had other problems to solve. Like, should the chop be cooked? Where should it be cinched up? How should it be standing? What size should the tape measure be? All in all, it was a fascinating experience. We could have easily spent two more days doing it.

So, around five short words and a simple symbol, the largest promotion/education campaign in pork history was launched.

Television and radio commercials were a big part of that campaign. Effective TV and radio ads need a jingle, something catchy and uplifting that people can sing along with, so music was needed.

The lean campaign began to have significant impact on consumers and ultimately the pocketbooks of producers.

The Lean On Pork Campaign was featured in 1983 and 1984 while NPPC continued to attack the myths and misunderstandings about pork and presented the positive nutrition story.

Research proved the campaign was successful in reducing the number of non-users. In just 2 years the number of non-users changed from 40% to 36%, an increase of nine million new pork eaters.

SYMBOL is a 240 lb. market barrow from a litter of 10 pigs marketed. He demonstrates a feed conversion efficiency of 2.5 from birth to a market age of 150 days. At slaughter, his last rib fat depth measurement is .7 of an inch and his loin muscle area is 5.8 sq. inches. The average of his three backfat measurements is 1.0 inch. His 180 lb., 32-inch-long carcass yields 105 lbs. of lean pork. He demonstrates a lean gain of 3/4 lb. per day of age.

Part 12A

SYMBOL
THE PICTURE THAT'S WORTH MORE THAN A THOUSAND WORDS

If a picture is worth a thousand words, then Symbol must be worth more than a thousand because he is the result of thoughts and opinions from a hundred thousand pork producers.

Webster's Dictionary says a "symbol" is a "visible sign of something invisible." No name could be more appropriate for the picture that is the symbol of 100,000 pork producers' thoughts.

When one considers how Symbol came into being, then one must agree that he is more than just a picture. He is symbolic of the mainstream of thought from an industry.

From the artist's first sketches, as the group of seedstock and commercial producers described the highly functional, high-performing pig to artist Tom Phillips, to the final touches spurred from thousands of producers' suggestions, Symbol actually became the symbol of the thinking of an industry.

The fact that the concept of Symbol was first born in the minds of men as they thought of standards of performance gives him credibility. But he symbolizes more than just a concept of a perfect functioning pig.

To truly appreciate Symbol, one must realize he

symbolizes the sincere intent, efforts and dedication of an industry to improve its product.

He symbolizes the result of a plan which began with consumer surveys at the meat case, and continued as pork producers, packers and market people took a hard look at what the consumer was really trying to tell them.

He symbolizes the activity that the Pork Value Task Force experienced in a series of meetings with men who rarely agree. They went through the thought process of getting comfortable with each other's motives. They began to realize each could benefit.

Now the performance purists will say, "We don't need a picture to tell us what he should look like. He can come in any shape or form." The purists forget, however, that we communicate through signs and symbols. Nature has through evolution designed all species with certain characteristics of shape to enable them to survive and perform efficiently in a given environment.

The National Pork Producers Council is in the information and communication business. Symbol will serve as the picture that is worth a thousand words of explanation.

In a few months, the term "symbol" will immediately mean to the animal husbandry world a high-yielding pig with the substance and stamina to endure the stress of controlled environment and to perform efficiently in feed conversion and reproduction.

He is not the result of show ring pressure from a group of faddists, but the result of a concept—the consensus of an industry transferred to an artist's brush.

He symbolizes the result of volunteer leaders of all segments of an industry which gave the best of their thoughts and time, without regard to personal benefit or gain.

He is the symbol of a progressive industry that realizes its future depends on how well it serves the needs of a health-conscious consumer.

He symbolizes that segment of pork producers who are profit conscious and realize that their future depends on efficiency in their own production units.

He symbolizes the epitome of an organization that must be cost effective as it strives to serve a progressive industry in the most efficient way. He is a visible sign of a great deal which is invisible.

Each retiring president of NPPC is awarded a 50 pound bronze engraving of Symbol to mark his years of dedicated service and ascendancy to the highest position in the National Pork Producers Council.

Part 13

PORK THE OTHER WHITE MEAT

"The Dumb Idea Is Changing Minds" was the caption for an article in the December 1988 issue of the National Hog Farmer Magazine. This was the reaction of some experts in the food industry and many of the not too expert.

The NPPC took a major gamble when it launched the Pork The Other White Meat (PTOWM) campaign. There were enough skeptics who had predicted total rejection by the consumer before it was ever introduced.

The program had been well researched, however, and the pork industry was ready to risk it all for a chance to make giant strides with the consumer. It was like Allen Sheppard's first step on the moon. One small step by the Pork Council was a giant step for the pork industry. It was a gutsy decision that paid off.

A number of advertising agencies had presented proposals to the staff of NPPC. They were screened down to 4 firms. Each was given 2 hours to make their proposal.

Each agency presented proposals that had merit but the last proposal presented by Bozell Jacobs was unique and challenging.

The BJ staff had researched pork so thoroughly that facts were revealed that were yet undiscovered by NPPC. The presentation began by showing 3 campaigns that research had revealed to be of questionable effect. the fourth campaign, however, was revolutionary in its approach. It carried with it an element of shock by presenting pork as a "white meat." The "white meat" concept had a special appeal because of the high interest of the consumer in the diet health issue and the common belief that white meat was leaner and lower in fat and calories.

At the end of the presentation the lights came on and found some of us in a state of shock. It was difficult to respond to the presentation. The lingering question was how pork producers would react to a slogan identifying pork with chicken when for many years they had spent their checkoff dollars selling

Peggy Fleming, spokesperson for "Pork The Other White Meat."

pork as a red meat.

There were other elements to the proposal that had strong appeal. Peggy Fleming, popular olympic skating champion was suggested as our spokesperson, a strong message for the health professional community, and because of our limited dollars to spend on TV, print, media, and radio would dominate the communications. The critical question was whether or not producers who provided the funds were ready for a revolutionary approach to promoting pork. As the grapevine began to circulate the reports about our considering a block buster approach for an ad campaign the negative resistance began to build.

A week later Russ Sanders accompanied me to Omaha where we asked the agency to repeat their presentation. The new presentation revealed that 35% of the consumers already believed pork was a white meat. I responded at that time the documentation to justify use of the term "white meat" was not strong enough. It wasn't enough to get pork producers to accept it. We must have more evidence to reinforce our philosophy.

I asked that a call be placed to Dr. Richard Wilham, Professor of Animal Science, Iowa State University, whom I considered the animal research community's foremost historian. I asked him about the historical background or the definition between white and red meat. He answered, "I've never been asked that question before but give me an hour." On his return call he said he had searched his Greek mythology and animal science history books and found no reference to red or white meat.

However, in the 1934 unabridged edition of Webster Dictionary it defined red meat as the flesh from cattle, calves, sheep and some wild animals and white meat as the flesh of chicken, fish, and swine.

We felt on the basis of the Webster definition we could pursue the possibility of using the PTOWM slogan.

Not until we received documentation from Texas A & M University, however, were we comfortable with the position we had taken declaring pork as a white meat. In this data we learned that myoglobin is the oxygen carrying substance in the flesh that determines its redness of color. Red meat has a much higher level of myoglobin while pork has the approximate same level of myoglobin as fish and chicken.

Further study of the origin of the use of red and white meat terms traces to the late 1940's and early 1950's. Chicken began to make its move as a competitive product to beef and pork and with the diet-health concerns becoming more prevalent chicken began to identify itself as a white meat. This provoked a reaction by the National Livestock and Meat Board to vigorously respond with the red meat campaign.

The PTOWM campaign has succeeded beyond our wildest dreams. It was the right message at the right time for pork and the consumer. It provided the pork industry with right messages to dramatically break through all the promotional clutter and do so without the repetition usually required to successfully promote a product.

The PTOWM slogan reinforced with strong follow-up in personnel and written material has boosted pork demand in measurable amounts.

One West Coast retailer stated, "The white meat campaign increased sales 37% more than any other promotion campaign we've ever run in our meat departments." Other large chains have credited PTOWM program for big upswings in pork demand. In a 1989 survey 58% of the restaurants featured pork as a white meat. By 1990 70% were listing pork as a white meat.

It's interesting to note that while packers and retailers gave a reluctant yes to the campaign producers were enthusiastically saying "Go for it." It was a radical program that worked mainly because it was an idea whose time had come.

The National Hog Farmer Magazine carried an article assessing the success of the PTOWM campaign. They quoted Barry Pfouts, Vice President of NPPC's Consumer Product Marketing.

Americans are starting to buy the idea that pork is a white meat. Pfouts notes before the advertising campaign began, surveys found 12% of the folks answering to the survey in the target cities thought of pork as a white meat. Only 10 weeks later, in the cities where NPPC used heavy television advertising, 72% said pork was a white meat.

In cities with less TV advertising the figures jumped to 56%. And in test cities where folks didn't see any TV ads, only those in consumer magazines, the 12% had grown to 35%.

Pfouts puts that in perspective. He recalls working on a salad dressing campaign where "after three years and $36 million spent on advertising, and we finally hit 40% awareness. The salad dressing folks were ecstatic. They felt if they ever got to 60% it would be a miracle. Yet, Pork - The Other White Meat went to 72% in just 10 weeks in those cities with heavy TV advertising!"

But does that make folks more likely to eat pork? Pfouts says, "We've got strong evidence that the positive selling points of other white meats are rubbing off on pork."

He continues, "Our surveys show a steady drop in the 'negatives' that come to mind when most folks talk about pork." Negatives like:

• Calories. Before the White Meat effort, pork chalked up an index score of minus 40 for being high in calories. A year later, that index figure was down to minus 25.

• Cholesterol. Before White Meat, the index stood at minus 42 for being high in cholesterol. A year later, that was down to minus 25.

On the positive side, folks who said pork was versatile went from 18 points to 35 points. Both taste and appeal and ease of preparation scored about the same kind of advances.

"People not only believe pork is a white meat, but the 'positive freight' that white meat carries is now being carried over to pork."

Probably one other survey question sums up all those opinions. Each individual was asked if he generally preferred red meat or white meat. Before the White Meat campaign, 42% voted for white meat and 28% for red meat.

A year later, asked the same question, 44% voted for white meat—not a big increase. But NPPC professionals were shocked to see the vote for red meat had dropped to 19%.

That vote means a lot of folks moved from being red meat fans to a neutral position. And Pfouts says those neutrals obviously will consider having pork for dinner.

Part 14

A GIANT LEAP FOR PORK

THE TRANSITION FROM VOLUNTARY TO LEGISLATIVE CHECKOFF

Since the earliest days of the old National Swine Growers Association in the 1950's the dream of hog men had been to have a national organization supported by all pork producers and to have the funds necessary to carry the pork message to consumers.

On July 25, 1985 pork producers wrote a new chapter in the pork history book.

In a nine hour special session of the delegates they decided to change from a voluntary checkoff system that had become sacred. The consideration was of a mandatory system that carried with it government enforcement to insure that all pork producers contribute to the checkoff. The arguments for the change were based on the assumption of 100%

participation and tripling the funds available to promote pork.

Opponents of the proposed change maintained that there was danger of big brother government becoming dictatorial and interfering with the producers prerogatives to spend his checkoff funds as he chooses.

The supporters of the change felt it was worth tolerating some government monitoring to gain the support of the total pork industry.

The trends in producer response to the voluntary checkoff were not encouraging.

Response to the voluntary checkoff had grown steadily to 1981 when participation peaked. Fifty-seven percent of all hogs marketed were checked off in 1981. The number had declined to 54% by 1984.

There was expressed concerns that a trend in producer participation in the checkoff would continue to decline because many producers were tired of carrying the full load of funding pork programs while others were getting a free ride.

The fact that Iowa pork producers had at this same time instituted a state legislative checkoff program led many to believe that other states would also break ranks, adopting their own programs.

Debate was eager and persuasive. Arguments were offered pro and con in typical pork delegate fashion.

Observers are always impressed by the skill and intensity of the pork delegates representing their states as they staunchly defend their positions. There is no better example of democracy at work than in the National Pork Producers Council's delegate sessions.

After hours of debate and the final vote was taken the majority supported the proposed change.

Each state had a representative sign a giant copy of the resolution. Copies of the historical document were made and distributed to each state to display in their home office vowing their support.

The next five months were occupied with the grueling process of drafting legislation, negotiating changes and getting the draft into the 1985 Farm Bill.

Negotiations with some state affiliates that had implemented their own legislative programs were the most difficult. North Carolina, South Carolina, Virginia, Alabama, Iowa, Montana, and Texas had established programs mandated by legislation. Most were at a lower rate than that proposed by the Pork Act.

The final form of the Pork Act was the result of the art of negotiations.

Some would call it agreement arrived at through horse trading American style. Most legislation in Congress goes through the same process.

It is said that the legislative process is like making sausage. It is not appetizing to watch but in the end is a delightful product.

In the final analysis the Act achieved what pork producers had hoped for with the beginning of the "Nickel for Profit" campaign in 1967. In that year producers gathered to discuss their blueprint for progress and map a course for the future of the industry. The result was a historic change for the entire pork industry.

The legislative checkoff began November 1, 1986. The Pork Act provided for a national producer referendum to be conducted within 24 months after checkoff implementation. September 7, 8 and 9, 1988 the referendum was passed with nearly 79% of the producers voting casting a "yes" vote.

The final version of the Pork Act contained most of what producer delegates had requested. A high priority by producers was placed on producer control. Although general farm organizations lobbied hard for representation on the delegate body and the Pork Board the pork producer wishes prevailed. Producers agreed to allow for representation by pork importers. This seemed reasonable because of the significant funding contributed by importers of pork.

In drafting and lobbying the Pork Act from dream to fruition the pork industry reached its finest hour. It sharpened its political tools and achieved its greatest victory thus far on Washington turf. There was a ground swell of support by producers all over the nation.

NPPC President Ron Kahle in a December 1985 Pork Report editorial said:

"NPPC producer delegates drew up the bill's initial components at a Special Session last July. On pork producers' behalf, Congressman Tim Penny (D-MN) and Senator Edward Zorinsky (D-NE) sponsored the bill in the House and Senate for inclusion into the 1985 Farm Bill. Opposition from a few general agricultural organizations created some uncertain moments for pork producers. But after a determined effort, producer time and energy paid off as all sides came together to reach a workable compromise.

"I can't say enough about the solid support we have received from our state organizations, the National Pork Council Women and individual producers all over this nation," says Kahle. "They have, by the thousands, let members of Congress know by phone, by letter and in person just how they wanted them to vote on the Pork Act."

With passage of the Pork Act revolutionary changes were anticipated. The way the Pork Council functioned would change drastically. Now a whole new dimension was to be added to the pork organization. The Pork Act called for a new pork delegate body and a Pork Board of 15 producers. This new body would be quasi-government and be accountable to the Secretary of Agriculture.

The Pork Board would have total responsibility and control of all checkoff funds. Clearly the NPPC as an organization would be required to make dramatic adjustments in its budgeting and program development. All programs receiving checkoff funds would be subject to the close scrutiny and approval of the new Pork Board.

In anticipation of these new challenges NPPC leaders and staff had taken several steps to assure a smooth transition. It was foreseen that competition and turf guarding must be avoided at all costs.

Prior to the passage of the Pork Act a transition task force was appointed.

Special care was exercised to see that seasoned and experienced pork leaders were appointed to the Task Force.

The Task Force was responsible for the development of strategies to make a smooth transition from the voluntary to the legislative checkoff. The strategy included structuring the Pork Board into working committees. A crucial work of the transition team was to establish the relationship between the two delegate bodies and the NPPC Executive Committee that establishes policy for the Pork Council and the Pork Board that is bound by the provisions of the Pork Act.

The transition team studied and made recommendations on staffing and site selection for the Pork Board's permanent home.

These were all decisions that must ultimately be made by the Pork Board. Research and study by the transition team in advance of the Pork Board election was a great advantage to the Pork Board whose responsibility was assumed immediately after election in October 1986.

The successful leap from the traditional voluntary program to the mandatory checkoff can be credited to a carefully laid strategy by pork leaders. The diligent efforts of the transition team was key to maintaining the basic philosophy that had been sacred to pork producers since they organized in the early 1950's.

The plans were so well strategized that the pork philosophy had permeated every corner of the country before the Pork Board was appointed. Most candidates for the Pork Board were committing themselves to the principles voiced by pork producers before their appointment.

The consensus for an operating policy was:

The Pork Board should be held accountable for efficient use of checkoff money.

The Pork Board should only collect and disburse funds.

Promotion programs should be contracted with existing organizations. Most Pork Board members agree that the industry cannot afford duplication of effort between the Pork Board and other groups, such as NPPC and the National Live Stock and Meat Board (NLSMB).

In the statements made at the time they were nominated, several appointees shared the view that even administrative needs of the Pork Board should be "farmed out" to existing groups.

The Pork Board must be "bottom line" oriented. Most of the new members say producer profits should be the best measure of how well checkoff dollars are being put to work.

The successful transition from the voluntary checkoff to the mandatory system and the leap from $10 million annual funding to $26 million in one year can be credited to carefully planned strategy by pork producers.

It may have appeared to have happened by chance, however, that assumption is far from the truth.

In the first long range strategic plan developed in 1983 projected a need for a doubling of funds by 1986. The issues to be addressed and the services demanded by pork producers in their annual delegate meetings foreshadowed the demand for more funds.

The handwriting was on the wall. It was clear that the soft-sell voluntary funding methods of the past were inadequate for the future.

To be competitive in the decade of the nineties pork producers would have to play hard ball. Poultry had two decades of success surpassing pork in per capita consumption and was rapidly overtaking beef.

Beef had already attempted and failed in two referendum attempts to get producer approval.

When pork announced its intent to pass a Pork Act in May 1985 beef producers were motivated to make a third attempt. We learned a great deal as we observed others in the commodity checkoff activities.

Important to success was having legislation that allowed a trial period before the producer referendum.

Some have questioned the strategy of allowing the funds to slip from NPPC control. Granted legislative checkoff funds have greater restrictions and it requires that NPPC seek funds from other sources to address public policy issues.

Taken in its full scope the funding level today is more than 3 times greater than before the Pork Act. Checkoff funds have made it possible to increase consumer demand by 5% to 10% and promises to be even more effective in the future.

There is an obvious need for funds to address public policy issues.

The success of the checkoff funded programs and the benefits derived by pork producers should motivate greater voluntary efforts by state associations and producers.

The dream is very much alive. Those living today who experienced the early modest results from great sacrifice and effort of pork leaders can appreciate more than anyone else the pride and prestige the pork industry enjoys in the decade of the nineties.

Truly pork is on its way to being the meat of choice by the year 2000.

NPPC President Ron Kahle and President Ronald Reagan at the White House.

Part 14A

WORLD PORK EXPO (WPX)

From the beginning WPX was recognized as a colossal event. The record attendance of 60,000 and the uplink satellite to communicate it around the world assured its success as a media event. The record barbecue, where 20,000 pounds of pork was cooked and 35,000 people served, earned it a place in the Guinness Book of Records.

This miraculous media event piggybacked to the success of the American Pork Congress 1970-88 (Section III-Garner) and to the Pork Industry Conference in 1958-69 (Section II-Paul).

I attended my first American Pork Congress in March 1979 and where I was introduced as the new Executive Vice President of the National Pork Producers Council. Attendance was the largest ever this year. It exceeded more than 15,000.

The spacious convention center in Indianapolis was filled to capacity with industry displays and jammed with pork producers. From a viewing window high above it was an awesome sight to see the thousands of pork producers edging their way through the crowded isles to get a glimpse of the trade show booths. The long lines waiting to be registered, halls filled to capacity, seminar rooms with standing room only and meal events sold out. This was overwhelming for a cowboy who was accustomed to conventions of two to three thousand.

I began to realize that the pork industry was an aroused sleeping giant flexing his muscles, ready to challenge all competitors hoping to become the meat of choice.

I marveled at the tremendous resources in the form of technology and human expertise brought together at this event.

I observed something about the pork industry that I hadn't seen before in the livestock industry. There was enthusiasm and a youthful alertness that was willing to break with tradition if necessary to produce a quality product.

Even during the 8 years of farm crisis in the 1980's APC continued to thrive as a media event. However, these deflationary years took their toll with numbers of pork producers shrinking by about 50%. Serious producers dwindled from about 400,000 to about 200,000 while numbers of hogs marketed remained rather constant at about 85 million head.

APC had its beginning in the Midwest and was easily accessible to pork producers. Cities such as Omaha, Nebraska, Des Moines and Davenport,

1970 American Pork Congress, Des Moines, Iowa.

Iowa all were limited in convention facilities. It wasn't difficult to handle trade shows of 200 display booths. When the industry requests exceeded 300 it became difficult to accommodate them. Hotel facilities were strained when attendance reached about 4,000 and space for educational seminars was inadequate.

In looking at the dwindling numbers it was obvious that APC had reached a critical point. Dramatic innovations were needed.

The loss of producers and the weak farm economy impacted attendance at APC dramatically with attendance dropping to an average of about 7,000.

It was early in 1987 at a meeting of senior staff members that we discussed the international Olympic Games in Los Angeles. Peter Uberoth achieved the status of genius when he managed this prestigious event by adapting mostly existing facilities when most sponsoring countries virtually created new cities to host the event. Why couldn't we return APC to the center of pork production and use existing facilities?

From these discussions we decided to ask the Executive Committee to appoint a task force of producers to plan a new innovative pork industry event to replace APC.

In staff discussions we concluded it was time to rethink APC and develop a new event with new approaches for educational seminars and promotional activities.

We realized we needed someone to manage the event that was not bound by past experiences of

APC but also was not a novice to the pork industry.

We found such a person in Ernie Barnes. Ernie had an excellent background as a breed executive and had served on the NPPC Executive Committee. His strongest attribute was his enthusiasm, creativeness and ability to get along with people. Coupled with a competitive determination to win we felt he was the perfect selection. He didn't disappoint us.

The job of planning the pork industry largest event had begun and the foundation was being laid. It was the beginning of the quest to make pork the meat of choice by the year 2000.

As I review the activities that led to the success of this event a key factor came to mind. Its success could be credited to an ingenious NPPC staff.

Their creativity, and ability to improvise and innovate was responsible for turning a rough, drab fairground facility into an attractive, inviting and comfortable open air trade show.

Their ability to organize, program and coordinate in a professional manner made it possible to conduct numbers of successful events concurrently. Several staff worked 24 to 36 hours without sleep while preparing for this event.

Each of four major areas of the Expo required creative planning and expert execution. The trade show section managed by Marilyn Rockwell was the largest ever with more than 700 booth spaces.

The breed show managed by the breed executive directors was a major success with record crowds, volume of consignments and prices. The consumer information and BarbeQlossal informed and fed over 35,000 people. Robin Kline, Director of Consumer Affairs, and Joe Leathers, Director of Marketing, worked tirelessly to create this event.

The Producer Education Seminars coordinated by Dr. David Meeker posted new numbers of produc-ers and involved a greater dimension of activities to better inform producers of new technologies.

World Pork Expo was plowing new ground. It was definitely creating a new paradigm in the pork industry. We were asking allied industry for huge commitments. We didn't really know how much to promise in return.

In a later staff meeting we asked each to give their estimate of the number to expect. The highest estimate was 20,000. I recall I estimated 35,000 but in all honesty I was being optimistic to bolster the confidence of the staff.

It was difficult to envision the potential of a new event because we were a captive of the Pork Congress paradigm.

World Pork Expo is designed to be the modern approach to displaying new technology, information and equipment. It will open new, creative and interesting approaches to exposing innovations to the industry. World Pork Expo is the visionary agriculture show that will lead the industry into the 21st century.

World Pork Expo is to agricultural events what Walt Disney's Epcot Center in Orlando, Florida, is to the amusement parks of the past century. They are both a giant leap in the evolutionary process—educational, innovative and extraordinary. Pork producers and their families now feel they owe it to themselves to spend a couple of days at World Pork Expo each year.

The success of WPX with its record number of 60,000 attendance created a positive atmosphere throughout the pork industry. A new wave of pride and optimism began to pervade the industry and provide the impetus to pass the checkoff referendum in September 1988 and served as a kickoff for the new campaign to make pork the meat of choice.

World Pork Expo BarbeQlossal made the Guinness Book of World Records as the World's largest barbecue.

1989 World Pork Expo.

Part 15

THE DREAM IS STILL ALIVE

For pork producers new technology will offer opportunity for a breakthrough in production advances and product enhancement through new processing and marketing techniques.

The dream of pork producers for decades has been to position pork as the centerpiece of fine dining. That dream is still alive and is near reality. With the new technology that is available and increased funding made possible by the checkoff program pork is in a strong position to become number one in consumer preference, even before the year 2000.

The determining factor in the march toward success for pork producers to improve their product and market it effectively continues to be strategic planning.

The success enjoyed in the past 50 years of the pork organization has resulted from planning. Progress was painfully slow the first few years because planning was so difficult. The dream was shared by only a few but was never abandoned.

With each passing year more producers became interested in the organization and began to share the dream. As time passed there were more who believed in the cliche that what the mind can conceive man can achieve.

Most of the changes were taking place on the farm in production of leaner hogs. Rapid generation turnover is about 1 year because of the inherent nature of the hogs genetic makeup. This made it possible to change type and conformation rapidly, a decided advantage over beef where the generation turnover is about 3 years.

Even with the short generation interval changes on the farm and within the organization were slow and required careful research and deliberate planning. In those early days resources were limited. Dreams were abundant, however, in those early years of organization development.

In their first efforts to develop a pork organization in 1940 there were no funds. Producers paid their own expenses to meetings and the main purpose was to exchange ideas and information and establish common goals for genetic progress. Hog shows became the main rallying points.

Their dream consisted mainly of a time when consumers would see pork products as tasty, nutritious and desirable without the slightest clue as to how this would come about. They were confident they could produce the product but were not sure how

they could communicate the pork message to the consumer. The latter was an important part of their dream.

Never in their wildest dreams did they envision a national checkoff program that would generate $30 million.

Pork producers were happy with their dreams and were ready to pay the price to make them come true.

A dreamer is defined as one whose conduct is guided more by ideals than practicalities.

Dreams enter the realm of practicality when faith is so strong that it motivates one to start the planning process followed by determined action.

The pork industry in the decades of the 1940's, 50's and 60's remained a segmented industry with packers, seed stock producers and commercial pork producers not inclined to interact or to combine their efforts. On rare occasions when government intrusions affected the whole industry some cooperative efforts would be observed.

Pork producers began a planning process in mid to late 1960's called the "blueprint for progress" that led to the development of NPPC and the voluntary checkoff. Most planning then was designed to generate funds for the purpose of developing an organization with full time staff. There was the hope that eventually enough funds would be generated to allow for some consumer advertising.

The earliest budget in 1970 was illustrated with a chart that showed 90% of the funds to support the administrative staff with 10% being used for consumer advertising. The 10 year projection was to reverse the spending formula to 10% administrative and 90% advertising.

The earliest goal in the pork producers' planning process was to reduce the fat content of hogs. The trend toward leanness spread across hog country and was a dominant factor in hog shows throughout the nation.

Hormel Packing Company became the sponsor of the National Barrow Show in 1947. It was in the showring at Austin, Minnesota at the National Barrow Show that the trend toward leaner hogs had its greatest impetus.

Not enough credit can be given to Carroll Plager, head buyer for Hormel, for the contribution he made. Through his influence on hog buyers, judges, and breed associations officials fat became a dirty word. No one was in a better position than Carroll Plager and Hormel Company to focus on the value differences between lean and fat hogs although there were many others who early adopted the leaner hog concept.

Pork producers have done their job on the farm by producing leaner hogs resulting in higher quality, more desirable pork products. The animal health industry has supported production by providing new antibiotics and health sustaining materials. The feed industry has provided new improved feed formulas. Equipment manufacturers have given us innovative handling facilities. Packers and processors have done their job by creating new pork cuts and enhancing promotional efforts.

The amazing record of success achieved by the pork industry in the decade of the 80's can be attributed to sound strategic planning and programs designed to carry out the strategies.

My decision to leave the security of a long time position and change careers was influenced mainly by the agreement of the NPPC Executive Committee to consider a sound, strategic planning process. To my knowledge no other commodity group had planned and implemented a long range strategic plan although some had plans on paper collecting dust.

Restructuring of NPPC and its first formal program of work on record began in 1979 with comprehensive evaluation of the Council conducted by a 5 man team provided by the American Society of Association Executives. In the final summary the team made 56 recommendations, 48 of which had been implemented within two years. Some recommendations were premature and seemed radical to be adopted immediately. One of those was a change in the name of the women's auxiliary from "Porkettes" to some other name of their choosing. The mere suggestion raised the hackles of thousands of Porkettes who regarded the name as sacred. The name was finally changed in 1985. Another recommendation was to discontinue the National Pork Queen Contest and institute a youth program. This was done in 1988.

Beginning in 1979 with Bill Buller as president, a three year plan was drafted and approved by the Executive Committee. At that time NPPC was reacting more like a fire station responding to emergency calls. Most issues were being generated by the federal bureaucracy. Such issues as the nitrite debacle, trichinosis, the dairy buy out issue and African Swine Fever in Haiti were draining much of our staff resources. We also were confronted with a market cri-

sis in 1980 that caused the loss of thousands of pork producers.

Our first serious effort to construct a professional long range strategic plan was in 1981 and was implemented in 1982 under the presidency of John Saunders. Bill Van Dusan, a former staff person from the American Management Association, was our facilitator.

Our strategy was built around the following mission statement: "Our mission is to influence and affect, when possible, the internal and external factors relating to pork production on the farm, marketing the live hog, processing the product and merchandising the product to the consumer in ethical ways in order to enhance the producer's opportunity for profit."

One of the key goals of the plan was to increase funding available to NPPC from $5 million to $17 million in five years.

When we progressed 3 years into the plan it became obvious that we could not achieve this goal via the voluntary checkoff.

Eight of the 36 state affiliates were operating with a state legislated checkoff and other major states were considering abandoning the volunteer method of checkoff and drafting legislative programs. Under state legislated programs NPPC stood to lose much of its existing funding.

In 1985, during the term of Ron Kahle as president delegate support was given to study the possibility of a national legislative checkoff program. The effort began. In retrospect the summer and fall of 1985 is remembered as a continuous round of negotiations.

In short, the Pork Act was enacted into law in the closing hours of Congress in December of 1985. The law provided for the mandatory checkoff to begin on November 1, 1986 with a referendum to be held in September 1988 to determine if the checkoff would continue. The referendum, held September 7 and 8, 1988, passed with approximately 79% in favor.

The Pork Act increased funds available to the pork industry from $10 million to $27 million in one year. By 1990 checkoff had risen to $31 million.

Passage of the Pork Act dramatically affected the way NPPC was to function. The pork industry would never be the same.

Attendant with the Pork Act was the requirement that a new quasi government structure be created to act as the fiduciary agency for the USDA and be responsible to the Secretary of Agriculture. It was first envisioned by the pork industry that the NPPC would serve as this body but adversarial groups within NPPC and on the legislative level objected strenuously.

Consequently there is a new Pork Act body that parallels NPPC in structure. It consists of a 15 person board and a delegate body of about 150 pork producers. The Pork Board's responsibility is to collect the funds, disburse them and account to the Secretary of Agriculture.

The NPPC has become the primary contractor to provide the programs and as a result receives considerable funds from the Pork Board.

These funds are restricted to use for promotion, research and education. NPPC finds it necessary to seek funds elsewhere to carry on its activities in government affairs and organizational development.

The area of government affairs and public policy has become one of the highest priorities to insure continued profitability of pork producers.

The creation and integration of the Pork Act and the Pork Board into the national pork structure is one of the admirable achievements of the pork industry's planning process.

The drafting of the Pork Act and the research and development of the transition plan from voluntary to legislative checkoff stands today as a model for all commodity groups. No other group has achieved this task with the professional ease and smoothness as did pork producers. Much credit is given to the leadership of Virgil Rosendale, President of the Pork Board and Ron Kahle, President of NPPC at the time.

The compatibility of the two groups has helped to bond them together into a unified cooperative coalition that gets the job done for pork producers efficiently and effectively.

A key factor has been the strategic planning process in which both organizations were actively engaged.

The second long range strategic plan was drafted in 1986-87. The facilitator was Dr. Frank Edwards of Louis Allen and Associates of Palo Alto, California. The mission statement was amended to the following: "To instill a true commitment to quality throughout the pork industry, establishing pork as the consumers meat of choice by the 21st Century and enhancing the pork producers opportunity for profit and ability to remain autonomous regardless of size."

Early agreement on the mission, issues, key goals and strategies has drawn pork leaders together while maintaining the autonomy and identity of both NPPC and the Pork Board each with different responsibilities.

A strong consensus by all members of the Pork Board and NPPC's Executive Committee has been to get the most value for pork producers from the checkoff dollars. Close monitoring and accounting studies leads one to believe this goal is being achieved.

Much has been said and written about the success of pork producers and the elevated prestige pork enjoys but claims of success are hollow without positive proof.

Major victories for pork in the decade of the 80's were chalked up on the farm, in super markets, in the halls of Congress, in foreign trade, and in the market place.

As we usher in a new era for pork in the 1990's we see a new profile of the producer. He is an agripreneur with a proud self-image. He takes pride in the fact that he has acquired a new set of skills. The pork producer of the 90's has a combination of business, financial and technical skills never before brought together in agriculture.

He is business oriented, financially astute, globally aware, politically active, technically adept, and skillfully articulate.

Fifty years ago pork producers had a dream.

They dreamed of a time when hogs would no longer be associated with mud and when pork for the first time since Adam and Eve would no longer conjure up images of trichinae.

They dreamed of a time when producing pork would no longer conjure perceptions of feeding garbage but would be seen as a profession with a glorious history.

They dreamed of a time when consumers would no longer assume pork to be a fatty product that clogged arteries but would be seen as a delectable, nutritious protein that exceeds all other sources in safety and wholesomeness.

They dreamed of a time when they could hold their heads high and pridefully claim their identity with the profession they love.

Today they are elitists, visionaries, that have achieved their earlier dreams and have set new ambitious goals to be reached by the end of the century. The dream is still alive.

Part 16

EPILOGUE: MAKING PORK THE MEAT OF CHOICE

BY RUSS SANDERS

This book has captured the challenges and excitement of the first fifty years of U.S. pork organization history. Producers got together to accomplish things collectively that they couldn't get done on an individual basis. They succeeded. Through the dedication of literally thousands of producers, a solid foundation has been built for the *next* fifty years of pork industry evolution.

But, where do we go from here? The years ahead will be filled with a number of critical choices regarding industry direction.

Winston Churchill once said, "Take change by the hand, before it takes you by the throat." Above all else, change will be the key element in our future. Few of the "constants" that characterized the *hog* business of years past will be true for the *protein* business of the '90s and beyond.

Several of the megatrends affecting society in general will have a direct impact on pork producers. Environmentalism, concern about food safety, and animal rights are only three of perhaps dozens of legislative and regulatory issues that must be successfully managed. And, in addition to facing challenges at the federal government level, the role of state legislatures in shaping public policy will become even more crucial. More than ever, pork producers who now represent less than one tenth of one percent of our U.S. population will need to be much more politically active and articulate spokespersons on behalf of the industry.

The use of new technology, including biotechnology, offers great potential benefit. But, unlike in years past when consumers cared little about how food was produced, we now must provide assurance to our customers that the food they consume is produced safely and humanely.

The structure of our industry will also present new dynamics. Thirty years ago we had a fairly homogeneous production sector. Today and tomorrow, diversity in size of production units and the different philosophies of producers within the industry will make it more difficult to please all producers all of the time. Fewer, larger production units have clearly been the sustained trend for many years, and it shows little sign of changing. In 1935, there were one million pork producers. In 1990, there are fewer than 200,000. This phenomenon impacts the development of industry services and the number of people-intensive industry programs that are possible.

At the same time, the level of business professionalism and technology acceptance by producers is trending in a positive direction. This presents exciting opportunities for dramatically improving industry efficiencies that will help us better compete in the domestic and global food market place.

As we look ahead to the year 2000 the opportunities for pork are vast. The unprecedented success achieved by pork producers to date, whether it be in the area of product improvement, pork promotion or effectiveness in the public policy arena, has truly set the stage to make pork the meat of choice.

But, as was true in the first fifty years of our organization's history, the quality of our leadership is the most important element. Producers always have, and always will have, the most to say about controlling their own destiny.

There are, I think, four key leadership characteristics that are vital to achieving our long term goals:

1. Creative, non traditional thinking and a willingness to take risks.
2. An ability to anticipate and to manage change by continuing to focus on the big picture.
3. The realization that we're in the food business, not the hog business.
4. A customer service orientation that helps us remain close to the producer, while at the same time responding to the changing needs of our consumer customers.

The potential for pork is unlimited. We have an animal that can adapt and change to produce high quality protein in an extremely efficient way, perhaps even more so that poultry. New product development and versatility opportunities are just beginning to be tapped. Pork continues to be the world's most preferred meat, far exceeding global production of both chicken and beef. The U.S. has the most efficient pork production capability of any nation on the face of the earth.

However, the most critical element is our producer. Pork producers have never been afraid of change. Back in 1960, who would have thought it possible to reduce the fat content of our product by over 60% in just thirty years?

We are entering a time of challenge, possibilities and questions. Although it is a time of uncertainty, it is filled with opportunity. What an exciting time to be in this industry.

Part 17

MILESTONES OF THE PORK INDUSTRY

1493 • Christopher Columbus brought the first swine to the Western Hemisphere.

1600's • Pork production develops into major economic activity in Atlantic Colonies.

1640 • The first meat packer in the U.S., William Pynchan, Springfield.

1810 • Cincinnati, Ohio becomes "Porkopolis", leading pork processing market in the country.

1812 • Pork is responsible for "Uncle Sam" being a a national symbol. A barrel of pork stamped U.S. for the American Army was marked by an observant Quarter Master for his "Uncle Sam."

1820 • Pork packing became a prominent enterprise.

1848 • First stockyards in Chicago.

1850 • Hogs preceded cattle in the great trail drives of the 1870's. Trails left behind later became routes for railroads.

• Hog population equaled one for each two people.

• Development of American breeds.

1861 • Civil War, 1861-1865, hog production shifts to Midwest.

1863 • Chicago, Ill. replaces Cincinnati, Ohio as pork packing capital.

1865 • Founding of Union Stock Yards, Chicago, Ill.

1879 • Invention of refrigerated rail car enables fresh pork to be shipped considerable distances without spoilage for the first time in history.

1882 • USDA established in 1882, achieves Cabinet status in 1889.

1890 • First federal meat inspection law passed.

• High market demand for animal fat met by the lard-type hog.

• Concentration on production of extreme lard type.

1925 • Market for lard begins to decline. Pork industry begins development of meat-type hog.

• New trend toward lean-type.

1927 • National Swine Show, National Barrow Show established to develop industry standards for meat-type hogs.

1934 • USDA imports Danish Landrace hog.

1943 • Pork goes to war in World War II in "C" and "K" rations in the field, Spam in the mess halls.

1950 • S.P.F. (Specific Pathogen Free) swine are produced.

1951 • Crossbreeds first shown in production test barrow contest.

1954 • National Swine Growers organize to improve pork quality. Emphasis on meat type hog.

• National Swine Growers Association established.

1960 • Cross breeding systems are introduced as standard production practices.

• Breeding companies are formed.

1965 • National Pork Producers Council is formed.

1975 • National Swine Improvement Federation formed to set standards of performance.

1977 • National Pork Producers Council becomes largest commodity organization in the world. (110,000 members)

1979 • Pork producers file law suit against USDA to prevent unreasonable regulations.

1982 • Pork slogan - AMERICA YOUR LEANING ON PORK.

1986 • Pork's most successful campaign - "Pork the Other White Meat."

Part 18

NPPC HISTORICAL LANDMARKS

- **1940** First National Pork Association of record. (American Pork Producers Association.)

- **1954** National Swine Growers Association organized.
    Keith Myers, Executive Secretary
    Bob Parkinson, Secretary Treasurer

- **1958** First National Swine Industry Conference

- **1962** First checkoff funding concept introduced in the swine industry. Iowa Test Station.

- **1963** Amendment to Packers and Stockyards Act to legalize market checkoff.

- **1965** Meeting at Moline, IL and approval of "Blue Print for Pork" a master strategy to organize pork producers into a pro-active organization.

- **1965** Roland (Pig) Paul named Executive Vice President of the national organization.

- **1965** The National Pork Producers Council (NPPC) is formed from the National Swine Growers Association.
    James Peterson, President
    Roland (Pig) Paul, Executive Vice President

- **1966** Producer poll favored a national checkoff.

- **1966** 800 pork producers met in Springfield, Illinois and issued a mandate for a market checkoff to fund a national promotional campaign to promote pork.
    (5 cents for market hogs, 3 cents for feeder pigs)

- **1967** First checkoff funds collected in 6 pilot counties in Illinois - Knox, Henry and Whiteside counties. In Iowa - Scott, Muscatine and Clinton counties.

- **1969** J. Marvin Garner appointed Executive Vice President.

- **1969** The first Pork All American recognition program sponsored by Shell Chemical Company.

- **1970** The first American Pork Congress. This resulted from combining the NPPC annual meeting and the National Swine Industry Conference.

- **1973** The first Pork Producers Legislative Seminar, WDC.

- **1977** The NPPC membership reaches 100,000 as the result of the ARRWAD Program, (Are Reasonable Regulations Worth a Dime), a program designed to resist unreasonable federal regulations.

- **1979** Orville K. Sweet appointed Executive Vice President.

- **1979** NPPC resorts to court action and is successful in preventing the USDA from banning nitrites as a time honored safe preservative for pork.

- **1980** NPPC dedicates new national headquarters building.

- **1983** Campaign introduced - "America's Leaning on Pork".

- **1985** NPPC drafts a legislative initiative to provide for mandatory checkoff which increases funding from $10 million to $26 million.

- **1986** Campaign - "Pork the Other White Meat".

- **1987** Introduced America's Cut.

- **1988** The first World Pork Exposition is held in Des Moines, Iowa. Attendance of 60,000 was a new record for a commodity organization. The world's largest barbecue was a part of the festivities and was listed in the Guinness Book of Records.

- **1989** Russ Sanders appointed Executive Vice President.

- **1990** NPPC dedicates second building program.

PORK INDUSTRY HALL OF FAME

A TRIBUTE TO BILL BULLER

Producer – Dedicated Industry Leader

Bill Buller has earned an honored place in the Pork Industry Hall of Fame as a result of his long record of service to the industry, beginning as a founder of the South Dakota Pork

Russ Sanders, NPPC Executive Vice President, July 1989 –

Bill Buller
Pork Industry Hall of Fame

Producers Association, through his presidency of the National Pork Producers Council (1979-81), and more recently as a member of the National Pork Board.

Buller served as NPPC president at a time when pork producers were under great stress from a combination of devastatingly low hog prices and a government attempt to ban nitrites as a pork preservative. He led a one-man crusade in the halls of Congress to make the plight of America's pork producers known.

Largely due to his leadership efforts, NPPC was successful in its legal challenge of the government nitrite issue, an action that saved the pork industry in excess of one billion dollars.

His persistence also resulted in the government purchase of $100 million worth of pork for use in its various feeding programs, an action that bolstered producer hog prices at a critical time.

During Buller's term as NPPC president, producers' checkoff investment doubled, and NPPC organization was restructured, and a Washington, D.C. office was established so that producer legislative and regulatory interests could be represented on a daily year-round basis.

A new NPPC headquarters building was completed in suburban Des Moines, Iowa, providing America's pork producers a national home of their own for the first time. During the dedication ceremony, Buller proclaimed, "This organization intends to lead, not to follow."

As a result of his years of enthusiastic dedication to the needs of America's pork producers, Bill Buller deservedly takes his place in the Pork Industry Hall of Fame.

Presented by
National Pork Producers Council
March 9, 1991

Mike Wehler
NPPC President, 1990

John Hardin
NPPC President, 1991

Tim Rose
NPPC President-Elect, 1991

Orville K. Sweet

197